WHEN PITTSBURGH WAS A FIGHT TOWN

BY

ROY MCHUGH

COPY EDITOR: DOUGLAS CAVANAUGH
INTERIOR DESIGN: DAVID FINOLI
COVER DESIGN: LIZZIE SCHINKEL

COVER PHOTOS:
<u>LEFT TO RIGHT TOP-</u> TOMMY YAROSZ (LEFT) & BUNNY BUNTAG (RIGHT), LEE SALA,
HARRY BOBO.
<u>LEFT TO RIGHT BOTTOM-</u> CHARLEY BURLEY, AL QUAILL, BOB BAKER

TABLE OF CONTENTS

PART FOUR

Miscellany

PART FIVE

Exotica

INTRODUCTION

When I was first approached by boxing writer and historian Douglas Cavanaugh about helping him in his pursuit of getting his mentor's manuscript on the history of boxing in Pittsburgh published I was very much honored and intrigued. After all his mentor was iconic sportswriter Roy McHugh, who recently passed away at 103-years of age. Roy was a hero of mine growing up, and the manuscript gave incredible insight into a sport I loved. As I began to read it, I not only was in awe but it was apparent my knowledge of the history of boxing in western Pennsylvania only scratched the surface of what McHugh had seen firsthand. The manuscript was truly a masterpiece.

I am thrilled to have had a small hand in the production of the publication of this book by designing the interior as was our talented cover designer Lizzie Schinkel.

Below is the firsthand account of how Douglas met Roy and helped keep his dream alive of publishing what I consider to be one of the greatest pieces of boxing journalism that I have ever read.

                                                        ---David Finoli

Being a longtime boxing history writer and nerd, I am constantly immersed in studying old films, reading old magazines and perusing online newspaper archives and microfilm. Many years ago, I noticed that several of the old-time fighters I admired happened to be from Pittsburgh. I had loved the Steelers since I was a kid growing up in the 70s (No slam on the Rams, but Bradshaw, Harris and Lambert were infinitely more exciting to me than Ferragamo, McCutcheon and Elmendorf. Shoot me), so I was intrigued as to why the city that spawned my favorite football team also spawned my favorite boxers.

Not long afterward a *Pittsburgh Press* emeritus named Roy McHugh published an article in *The Ring* listing the greatest fighters his city ever turned out: Harry Greb, Billy Conn, Charley Burley, Fritzie Zivic, Sammy Angott, etc. It fascinated me and I ate up every word, all the while wondering how this outstanding boxing tradition had not been recorded in book form. It was especially strange considering Pittsburgh is a town known for appreciating and celebrating its sports icons.

Little did I know, but somebody had already done it. It just hadn't been published at that time, and unfortunately would not be published in its brilliant writer's lifetime.

Roy McHugh was my friend. As a boxing fan I knew who he was long before I cold-called him about 15 years ago (I was amazed and delighted to find that he was listed!). I don't even recall what pretext I called him under, but I knew that I wanted to talk boxing with the man, and he seemed happy to chat about it as well. In fact, we talked much longer than I would have expected, his enthusiasm for the history of the sport and what he himself experienced in all his years as a boxing beat writer making for wonderful conversation. Tim Conn took me to meet Roy in person at his apartment in Pittsburgh a few years later and the three of us spent a memorable afternoon there in Roy's study.

The first thing that impressed me was the man's appearance. If one was even remotely familiar with the old-time sportswriters like Grantland Rice, Damon Runyon, Ring Lardner or Shirley Povich—how they dressed, how they carried themselves, etc. -- then you knew what Mr. McHugh was the moment he answered the door. He hadn't an ounce of pretense to him, but with his starched long-sleeve shirt, nice tie, pressed slacks and his shining penny loafers he was unmistakable. This was a "sportswriter" in the purest sense of the word and 20th Century archetype; a professional from head to toe.

I almost felt like an eavesdropper as I watched Tim and Roy discussing their shared history, the stories of the different people and events they knew and experienced. They spoke of Tim's father, former Light-Heavyweight Champion Billy Conn and all he did during his career and after. It was like a shot of a powerful drug to a boxing history junkie like me. Then Roy pulled out these ancient scrapbooks of boxing clippings that he'd put together as a kid and laid them on my lap. Many of the yellowing photos within were fairly common images today (a quick Google search would bring up about 80% of them), but in the 1920s a kid would have to search far and wide for a long time to find these, hours of work only a true fan would log in. Roy was a true fan, then and now, and that fact became more and more apparent as he narrated each page that I turned to.

It was something that became the hallmark of our friendship; that love for the history of the sport. We talked about it often, and with the enthusiasm of two teenagers swapping their favorite baseball cards.

Internet research fascinated him and he was amazed at some of the things that could be exhumed from the online archives. He once asked me to see if I could find any of his old high school football stats from 82 years previous. Apparently his friends didn't believe that he played due to his slight build (even in his youthful prime Roy couldn't have weighed more than 130 lbs) and were dismissive of his attempts to try and convince them otherwise.

Luckily I was able to find a few articles with his name and deeds in them and I mailed them off to him. When we next spoke, he was obviously very happy to finally have the evidence he had needed for so long to silence his friendly doubters.

Not so welcome were the writings I sent him from his days as a young writer at Coe College in Iowa. I thought he would be thrilled to see these articles, almost all of which he hadn't seen or read since the 1930s. On the contrary, it was akin to showing a painter his grade school doodling's or an actor a film of his Jr. High attempts at Shakespeare. He was mortified.

Though he enjoyed how they brought back to mind various events, people and places of his youth, he couldn't get past his style. "Ugh! I was awful..." he said.

Several years ago Roy sent me a few chapters of the book you now hold in your hands. He did it for my enjoyment and also to ask what I thought overall. I, of course, loved it. But I felt compelled to point out a few historical errors within the pages. I cringed as I mailed my corrections off to him (regular mail only; Roy didn't do email), hoping his writer's ego wouldn't feel braced by this upstart young Los Angeles writer who dared presume he knew more about Pittsburgh boxing than the man who actually *lived* it.

His response a week or so later underscored exactly how ego-free of a writer he was. On the contrary, he seemed thrilled at the prospect of fine-tuning his work, while at the same time mortified at having made the various errors pointed out. For instance, he had the great Henry Armstrong, who fought his early career in Pittsburgh under the name "Melody Jackson, listed as "Honey Mellody", another welterweight champion from an earlier era. An understandable mistake, but Roy was distressed over it all the same.

He asked me if I wouldn't mind if he hired me to proofread and edit the manuscript. I gladly accepted and the collaboration was one of the happiest assignments of my entire life. His professional perfection was breathtaking to me as I combed through each page of what I consider to be his magnum opus as a writer. After we were done I tried hard for a long time to find a publisher, but nobody seemed to want to take a chance with what they considered a "niche" subject.

Roy eventually lost hope of his manuscript ever seeing the light of day, so he asked me to take it and do as I saw fit. I never gave up the hope of finding a publisher, but after Roy passed earlier this year at age 103, I felt it would be unjust to wait any longer for a reluctant industry to put out his work. And so here it is, *When Pittsburgh was a Fight Town.*

Looking at this book as well as his writings over the decades, one can't help but be struck by Roy's consistency in taking himself almost completely out of the picture when he wrote. The person or thing he was writing about was ALWAYS to be the star in a Roy McHugh article, not himself. In a field where writers have historically often used their columns to elevate themselves to the level of their subject (indeed even beyond at times) and create a cult of personality, it is refreshing to know that there was a man like Roy out there doing the exact opposite. He never wanted to be the "star" of his work and remained a humble scribe from the beginning of his career until the end of his life.

The one event where you'd think he couldn't escape being the star would have been at his own funeral. But Roy was obviously prepared for that and his request that there be "no services" upon his passing came as no surprise to those who knew him. It was/is classic Roy.

So, I look at this introduction as something of a farewell to my friend and mentor. I guess now he can stop kicking himself about having never asked Cuddy DeMarco more about Harry Greb when he had the chance (he gets to ask Harry himself now). I shall miss his letters, our talks, our visits and the classic "Table Full O' Micks" meetings at Atria's (CONN! ROONEY! CAVANAUGH! McHUGH!).

Knowing Roy McHugh was a high point of my life, something I will always treasure. Much love, with a touch of Irish melancholy....

---Douglas Cavanaugh

PREFACE

Folklore and fact often differ. Time was, an enduring myth has it, when five of the eight world boxing champions were from Pittsburgh. Not quite. Between July 13, 1939, and November 18, 1941, Billy Conn, Sammy Angott, Fritzie Zivic, Billy Soose, and Jackie Wilson, in that order, won championships, but they were not all champions concurrently. Sometimes two of them were, and once, for a while, three, but never all five.

In the second place, only Conn, Zivic, and Angott had their championships all to themselves. Multiple sanctioning bodies – and disagreements among them – are nothing new. When the New York State Athletic Commission recognized Soose as middleweight champion, the National Boxing Association recognized Tony Zale. When the NBA recognized Wilson as featherweight champion, the New York commission recognized Chalky Wright and then Willie Pep. There was never any argument about Conn's light heavyweight or Zivic's welterweight title, but Angott, recognized by the NBA, had to beat Lew Jenkins, recognized by New York, for absolute ownership of the lightweight championship.

Strictly speaking, Angott was not a Pittsburgh fighter. He lived in Washington – Washington, Pennsylvania. And Soose's hometown – the first one, anyway – was Farrell. Call them Western Pennsylvania fighters. It's sufficiently astounding that so limited a geographical area could produce so many champions at a rate unmatched by any other section of the country before or since.

Hardly less to be wondered at, this was when championships meant something. Back then, the New York commission and the NBA were the only real sanctioning organizations. Today there are almost too many to keep track of, each with its own set of champions, separate and indistinct. Back then, there were still only eight generally recognized weight classes. Today there are something like seventeen. Do the math and you end up with 102 champions all told. Hyperbole failed the late Jim Murray when he wrote," They come in triplicate, quadruplicate, quintuplicate. There's one for every three letters of the alphabet." As boxing associations proliferate, giving birth to in-between weight classes – the super this, the junior that – titles are devalued to the point of worthlessness. The magazine Inside Sport, now defunct, had a columnist called The Good Doctor. "Settle a bet, Doc – who's the heavyweight champion?" somebody wrote in to ask. The Good Doctor replied, "No one knows."

By the 1930s, which in Pittsburgh, anyway, was boxing's Augustan Age, Western Pennsylvania had become a breeding ground for champions. Frank Klaus and George Chip, middleweight champions before World War I, were the forerunners. Then along came Harry Greb, the legendary Pittsburgh Windmill, a cult figure now, and after Greb there was Teddy Yarosz. Here were four world middleweight champions in a little over two decades, all from within a fifty-mile radius of the Golden Triangle, and while the last of the four, Yarosz, was still active, Billy Soose became the fifth. Except for the flyweight division, Western Pennsylvania has had a champion in each of the eight traditional weight classes, and Willie Davies, from Charleroi, would have been the flyweight champion if Frankie Genaro had been willing to fight him again after losing big to Davies in a non-title bout. Unrecognized by the NBA and the New York commission, Tony Marino of Duquesne was a bantamweight champion in the Ring Record Book by edict of its magisterial editor, Nat Fleischer, a sanctioning organization all by himself.

Was there something in the environment to account for all this, for how Western Pennsylvania produced so many boxing champions? Without much doubt, the reason was primarily cultural. Why did Western Pennsylvania turn out legions of good football players during roughly the same time span? Because of qualities in the native stock. From the late nineteenth century until World War I put a stop to the flow, millions of immigrants crossed the Atlantic Ocean to work in the steel mills and coal mines of the area. They were Poles, Hungarians, Serbs, Croatians, Slovaks, Lithuanians, Italians. The Germans and the Irish – the potato-famine Irish – had preceded them; American blacks from the Cotton Belt were to follow. Life was a test of fortitude. Only the strong could survive. To their descendants they handed down a legacy of toughness and grit. Even prizefighting and the risk of brain damage looked attractive when the alternative was long hours, low pay, exhausting labor under intolerable conditions in the mills and the mines, and the likelihood of not making it to an impoverished old age.

Prizefighters came from the mean streets – from the steel towns, the mining towns, the rowhouse neighborhoods of Lawrenceville and Garfield and Pittsburgh's North Side. Pittsburgh in the 1930s was a fight town even more than a football town. Somewhere or other there were fight cards six nights a week. There were fights on Christmas day, an idea that to subsequent generations seemed outlandish. Bunny Buntag, a boxing man of the old school with a courtly way of speaking, never could understand why. "It was always a very popular thing, a Christmas-day fight show," he said. "Oh, my. Oh, my. People came dressed up. A lot of *women* went to fights on Christmas day."

Christmas was different back then. Nobody called the Christmas season "the holidays." Pittsburgh was different, too. Black smoke hung in the air, obliterating the sky. On sunless days in the wintertime, the streetlights burned at high noon. Dirt, soot, and grime were the city's integument. It was folly to wear a white shirt. The very atmosphere affected behavior. With no cause to take pride in their surroundings, people littered the sidewalks and streets (some things never change). Rubbish piled up in vacant lots. Thirty feet overhead, utility wires crisscrossed the intersections downtown. Clanging streetcars jostled for space with an ever-increasing number of automobiles and trucks. The rivers were open sewers, bringing annual floods. On St. Patrick's Day 1936, flood waters submerged the Golden Triangle. When at last they receded, there were forty-seven dead and sixty-seven thousand homeless. Where the building boom called the Renaissance created Point State Park in the 1950s lay thirty-six acres of warehouses, flophouses, shanties, tenements, and railroad tracks. Students of urban pathology quoted H. L. Mencken, who wrote after passing through Pittsburgh on a train that he didn't object to the filth so much as to "the unbroken and agonizing ugliness, the sheer revolting monstrousness of the place." Mencken was a puncher, not a boxer.

There were those who liked Pittsburgh exactly the way it was. They liked the lurid red glow of the steel mills at night. They liked the smoke, because smoke meant jobs, and the 1930s were Depression years. Working in the mills was better than standing in breadlines. It was better than selling apples on the street. Father James Cox, a Catholic priest from the beaten-down Strip district, led an army of the unemployed in a hunger march on Washington, D.C. Working in the mills was better than not working at all, and, for anyone with money to spend, the 1930s weren't bad.

Pittsburgh downtown was more alive in the 1930s, undeniably so from dusk to dawn. Downtown, before its trumpeted rebirth in the 1950s, had a night-time vibrancy that no longer exists. In the 1930s and 1940s there were many more popular eating places – Kramer's, Klein's, Dimling's, the Union Grill, the Hofbrau, the Cork and Bottle, the Law and Finance Building Restaurant, Gammon's, Childs, Alex Tambellini's Wood Street restaurant, Stouffer's on Wood Street, Stouffer's on Smithfield Street, Stouffer's on Penn Avenue, all in the heart of the Golden Triangle. There were restaurants that never closed – Childs, Gammon's, the Naples, Thompson's Cafeteria, the Purple Cow in the Roosevelt Hotel, the Webster Hall dining room out in Oakland, the Harvey's in Penn Station. Fast food wasn't called fast food, and when you wanted it you went to a White Tower.

The population was larger – 670,000 the year it peaked, more than double the current number. There were night clubs downtown, and jazz clubs, and dance halls that booked the big bands. There were movie palaces, a burlesque house, a newsreel theater. Broadway hits came to the Nixon. The key clubs opened after midnight, membership cards on sale at the door. Jim Rooney, whose brother Art owned the Pittsburgh Steelers, gave fifty-dollar tips to hatcheck girls, even though, unfashionably, Jim Rooney did not wear a hat. On the hottest days of summer, men wore hats, dark, woolen suits, and neckties. To appear downtown in a T-shirt and shorts was unthinkable. Hairy male legs were not for public display.

At 4 o'clock one morning in an after-hours club, the sports editor of the Pittsburgh Post-Gazette, Harvey Boyle, made a telephone call to his friend Stanley Woodward, sports editor of the New York Herald Tribune. It was cold – almost zero. From Ohio to New England, a heavy layer of snow covered the ground. Woodward, in a voice that resembled the croak of a frog, answered Boyle's call on the ninth or tenth ring. "Stanley!" Boyle shouted. "Did I wake you up?" "No," Woodward said. "I was outside watering the lawn."

Everybody talked about the baseball team, the Pirates; a privileged few watched them play. At Forbes Field in Oakland, a park of heavy iron girders and ivy-covered red brick walls, a park in an urban pastoral setting, daylight games started at 3:15. In the smallest crowd there'd be several hundred racket guys. They stood behind the seats on the third-base side of the field, waving money at one another and making bets. Paul Waner, after a night on the town, would show up for batting practice glassy-eyed. "Three for four today," he would promise the ushers, and then, as they liked to remember, that's what he'd get – three hits in four times at bat. In the newspapers -- the dailies -- Paul Waner was Big Poison and Lloyd Waner was Little Poison. Only the Courier, the African-American weekly, paid attention to the Homestead Grays and the Pittsburgh Crawfords, as good at the game as they were.

Football fever was less virulent in the 1930s. Pitt, Duquesne, and even Carnegie Tech recruited hard-bitten players from the mill towns, players who could take them to a New Year's Day bowl, but there were no civic orgies when they won. The Pitt coach, Jock Sutherland, was a raw-boned immigrant Scot, 6 feet 3 inches tall. His pre-season training camp in the mountains near Johnstown made Devil's Island look like Club Med. Out of Sutherland's work ethic, so similar to that of Andrew Carnegie and Henry Clay Frick – Sutherland supplied the ethic, his players did the work -- came the renowned Dream Backfield of Marshall Goldberg, John Chickerneo, Curly Stebbins, and Dick Cassiano.

In 1938 the inconceivable happened. Dream Backfield and all, Pitt lost to Tech. Another year, Pitt lost to Duquesne. But Pitt drew big crowds, Tech and Duquesne smaller ones. Pitt had its own stadium, seating 58,000. Tech and Duquesne, like the Steelers, of necessity played at Forbes Field. Art Rooney, a big-time horse player and small-time politician, had been a college and sandlot football star, a minor-league batting and base-running marvel, and an amateur boxer of no mean ability. Art Rooney scraped up $2,500 in 1933 to buy a franchise in the National Football League, and he filled the thousands of empty seats at every home game, or tried to, by handing out complimentary tickets to Catholic priests, to friends and acquaintances, to politicians and newspapermen, to incredulous total strangers.

Originally, if that is the right word, the Steelers were called the Pirates. By any name, Pittsburgh considered them a sandlot team. There were hockey fans, but not many. Basketball was almost an underground sport. No real Pittsburgher gave a hoot about hoops. Reflecting the general indifference, Pitt's home court was a dungeon in the depths of the football stadium and Duquesne had a gym about two sizes larger than a broom closet. The Pirates and Pitt football were what sports was about. Nothing else mattered – unless a big fight was coming up.

And there were big fights the year round – title fights involving Yarosz and Conn; their three fights with each other; Conn's fights as a teen-ager with leading contenders in the welterweight and middleweight divisions, including Zivic; Zivic's three fights with Charley Burley, the best Pittsburgh boxer who never won a title; Zivic's fights with Angott and Jenkins; fights between neighborhood rivals like Buck McTiernan and Jimmy Belmont. When Conn and Yarosz met for the third time, Billy Soose boxed Al Quaill and Sammy Angott boxed Leo Rodak of Chicago on the undercard, giving the patrons that night a look at one former champion (Yarosz) and four future champions (everybody else except Quaill). If they were Willie Davies, Mose Butch, or Jackie Wilson, even flyweights and bantamweights could draw. On mornings after, fight fans lined up at the newsstands downtown to buy the first edition of the Pittsburgh Press and see what Regis Welsh, the paper's boxing critic, had to say.

Many of these shows were outdoors, at Forbes Field. (On the night in 1941 that Conn came close to beating Joe Louis in New York, a crowd of 24,738 was in the stands at Forbes Field for a Pirate game. Minutes before the start of the fight, the umpires called time. Both teams retired to their dugouts, and for the next sixty minutes, while Conn won and lost the heavyweight championship – he was leading on points when Louis knocked him out in the thirteenth round -- everyone sat and listened to the amplified radio broadcast.) On a somewhat smaller scale, there were outdoor promotions at Meyers Bowl in Braddock and Hickey Park in Millvale. Meyers Bowl had an exterior of sheet metal. It could hold five thousand people, and every seat was a good one. The great Henry Armstrong, whose ring name at the time was Melody Jackson, boxed at Meyers Bowl in 1931. A Pittsburgher, Al Iovino, knocked him out in the third round. During the indoor season, from September to April, Motor Square Garden operated on Mondays, Duquesne Gardens on Wednesdays, and Moose Temple on Fridays. In the neighborhoods, there were boxing clubs and gyms. Managers and promoters could still make a living at their trade.

World War II broke the continuum. World War II brought an economic boom that rolled on into the 1950s, constricting a source of supply. Who needed to box when the pay was so good and working conditions so much improved in the mills? After World War II, nothing was ever the same. The champions of the thirties were finished. Charley Burley was still around but dying on the vine. Opponents of the requisite stature avoided Charley Burley like poison ivy. And television, by accustoming people to free fights they could watch at home or in the neighborhood bar, doomed the small-time entrepreneurs. With no place in town for talent to develop, there came a time when none did. Ever so briefly, it looked as though Bob Baker might be the next Joe Louis and Lee Sala the next great Western Pennsylvania middleweight, but their achievements were never a match for the expectations of their fans.

In 1951 there was one last Roman-candle burst, the heavyweight championship fight at Forbes Field in which Jersey Joe Walcott took the title from Ezzard Charles, knocking him out with a single left hook. Over the next two years, the promoters of that fight – Art Rooney, Barney McGinley, and McGinley's son Jack, the triumvirate's key man – put on ball-park shows of lesser importance, but the writing even then was on the wall. David L. Lawrence and Richard King Mellon, mayor and financier respectively, were giving Pittsburgh a bright new look. Little by little, political power and economic leverage cleaned up the rivers and eliminated the smoke. In a civic makeover dubbed the Renaissance, worn-out buildings, including the ramshackle Duquesne Gardens, fell to the wrecking ball. And, like the slum dwellers evicted by eminent domain, boxing was out on the pavement. Hickey Park was gone. Heidelberg Arena came down, leaving Pittsburgh without an outdoor site except for Forbes Field.   Fringe promoters found makeshift locations – a dance hall here, a movie theater there -- but Jack McGinley, doing well as a beer distributor, padlocked the Rooney-McGinley Club. At the dawn of the 1960s, Pittsburgh had no arena, no promoter of any consequence, no full-time managers, precious few trainers, even fewer places to train, and a dwindling cadre of fighters.

Promoter-manager Don Elbaum, the boxing-crazed son of a hearing-aid retailer from Erie, carried on for a while at the Palisades (a dance hall in McKeesport) and, on special occasions, at the Civic Arena. Opened in 1961, the Civic Arena was a dome-shaped Renaissance structure in the Lower Hill suitable only for major attractions. Other than Johnny Morris, a middleweight with good fundamentals, there were no Pittsburgh fighters of main-bout caliber, and Morris was lacking in box-office appeal.

Periodically in the 1960s, Archie Litman, like McGinley a successful beer distributor, brought big-name fighters from out of town to the Arena. Muhammad Ali and Sugar Ray Robinson boxed there -- Ali when he was still Cassius Clay. He knocked out a rehabilitated ex-football player, Charley

Powell. Robinson's fight with New York middleweight Joey Archer on November 10, 1965, drew well. At the age of 45, Robinson still looked perfect. In bursts of a few brave seconds he could give the illusion of being all that he ever had been, and the crowd of nine thousand was on its feet at the final bell, cheering for Sugar Ray, cheering for the fight itself. The much younger Archer, working carefully from behind his left jab and then mixing it up at times, had won every round, but the announcement of the decision cast a pall over the building. In the silence, promoter Litman took stock. "I looked around," he said the next day, "and everybody was crying. Damnedest thing I ever saw."

This was not the way fight fans behave, and he knew what to make of it. They had come, these sentimentalists, for one last glimpse of Sugar Ray, pound for pound the most skillful practitioner of his art, and they wouldn't be back. They had come for a piece of history, sensing that after twenty-five years and 201 fights, Sugar Ray was ready to call it quits. Thirty days later, at a big farewell party in New York, he officially retired. Litman retired too, without fanfare. There was no farewell party, no formal good-bye. He simply stopped putting on fights.

Ben Anolik, who had ties with the Pittsburgh Post-Gazette's Dapper Dan Club, promoted a fight on a barge -- in the Allegheny River near the shores of Point State Park. A crowd of 1,365 paid $3,700 at the box office, making it a one-time success. But then in 1968, at Presbyterian-University Hospital, Anolik became the thirty-seventh person to undergo heart-transplant surgery. He was 46. Fifteen months later, by that time well known as the longest surviving transplant recipient, he died, leaving no one to fill the promotional void -- no one with roots in Pittsburgh.

Don King, the flamboyant internationalist, touched down briefly at the Civic Arena to promote a heavyweight title fight in 1981 between Larry Holmes, the champion, and a nondescript challenger named Renaldo Snipes. Holmes got up from a knockdown to put Snipes away. After that, for maybe five or six years, the Arena was just a venue for closed-circuit telecasts of big-money fights from Las Vegas, telecasts made obsolete by the coming of the pay-per-view networks.

There have been two champions from Western Pennsylvania since the dawn of the alphabet-soup age -- Michael Moorer and Paul Spadafora.

Moorer grew up in Monessen, a Monongahela River steel town, but boxed there only once. Wherever he boxed, he always won. Eventually one of the newer sanctioning bodies, the World Boxing Organization, recognized him as light-heavyweight champion. He made a title defense in Pittsburgh on December 15, 1990, disposing of a challenger named Danny Stonewalker by an eighth-round technical knockout at the Civic Arena. Moving on, he won and lost two versions of the heavyweight title.

To start with, he unified the World Boxing Union and International Boxing Federation championships by taking a close decision from the capable Evander Holyfield, a linear successor to all the preceding legitimate champions. Moorer was now undefeated in thirty-six fights, but later that same year -- 1994 -- he lost both titles to George Foreman, who knocked him out with one punch, a right to the jaw.

Moorer had been the first lefthanded heavyweight champion; whether he knew his left from his right, though, is uncertain. After nine rounds, he was comfortably ahead of Foreman. Teddy Atlas, his trainer, had been telling him, "Move to your right" -- away from Foreman's right -- at one point grabbing his fighter's right arm and explaining, "This is your right." Moorer never got the idea. He kept moving to his left, or not moving at all, and in the tenth round Foreman nailed him. Foreman, at the time, was halfway through his forties, a ponderous, dawdling fat man with a big punch. It had been twenty years since the Rumble in the Jungle, when he entered the ring in Zaire as the one and only heavyweight champion and lost his title to the aging ex-champion, Muhammad Ali.

Moorer, pushed by Atlas, made a comeback of sorts, regaining the IBF piece of the title in 1996 by winning from a German, Axel Schulz, on German soil. Fight fans regarded this as no big deal. Back in Las Vegas, the site of his previous important fights, he polished off Francois Botha, an unbeaten former IBF champion stripped of the title after testing positive for steroids, and the insignificant Vaughn Bean.

Halfway through the fight with Botha, Atlas called the referee to Moorer's corner and said to his fighter, "I swear to God I will have this man stop the fight if you don't wanna fight. Do you hear me?" Moorer heard. He floored Botha twice in the eleventh round; in the twelfth and last round, the referee did stop the fight, declaring Moorer the winner. Atlas walked out on Moorer after his fight with Bean. Moorer then lost a rematch -- and his title -- to Holyfield.

Spadafora, who came from McKees Rocks, a few miles down the Ohio River, had somehow inherited Billy Conn's nickname, "The Pittsburgh Kid." Around the turn of the new century he was one of a half-dozen or so lightweight champions.

Although he fought in places like the David L. Lawrence Convention Center and the I. C. Light Amphitheater in Station Square, Spadafora did his training in Las Vegas and sometimes in Erie, his manager's hometown. He was long and lithe and decorated with tattoos. His punches didn't hurt -- they exasperated. But he punched fast and often and from every possible angle. His opponents, fighters a bit below the top echelon, had trouble connecting with Spadafora, whose head was never still. He dodged and twisted and slithered out of reach. Body punchers couldn't get to him, headhunters found a moving target. Boxing lefthanded, he peppered them with small-arms fire.

He had not lost a fight when drugs, booze, guns, a quick temper, and who knows what else combined to short-circuit his career. With a round from a pistol, he scored a direct hit on his pregnant girlfriend one night. She had driven his sport utility vehicle over a concrete highway divider, an unforgivable provocation. The girlfriend lived to avoid giving testimony at his trial for attempted murder. She was still in love, but it made no difference to the judge. Spadafora went to prison anyway, and later to a state-run boot camp, serving, in all, thirteen months before his parole.

He returned to a pugilistic graveyard, and at the age of 38 was attempting a comeback. At the Casino Racetrack and Resort in West Virginia, he made a bid to win something called the interim World Boxing Association light welterweight title and experienced defeat for the first time in 50 fights, a total that included one draw. In the Pittsburgh Kid's hometown, it was not big news.

In Pittsburgh, except for sporadic, short-lived resuscitations, an industry that flourished when open-hearth furnaces were blazing night and day is just as surely a thing of the past -- gone with the smoke and the steel mills and gone with a lost way of life.

PART ONE

The Early Years

Ossie "Bulldog" Harris was a tough and popular journeyman middleweight. He engaged in a series of entertaining fights with Jake LaMotta and Fritzie Zivic, Zivic humorously recalling in later years "Ossie had such a huge head that you couldn't miss it with a punch!" (photo courtesy of Douglas Cavanaugh)

In 1886, heavyweight champion John L. Sullivan's appearance in Allegheny City for a fight at the Casino Rink was about as welcome to the civic and clerical authorities as a smallpox epidemic. Witnessed by a small crowd, the match took place over the strident objections of Allegheny City's mayor and a committee of churchmen. Before the second round was over, police climbed into the ring and in defense of the common good, not to mention the physical welfare of Sullivan's opponent, halted the shameful spectacle There was no public outcry. Forty years later, when the charismatic middleweight Harry Greb died, a line of mourners filed past his casket all through the night before the funeral. Shortly after daybreak it was five blocks long. An American Legion Guard of Honor accompanied the hearse to St. Philomena's Church on the East Side of Pittsburgh for the services, a police escort leading the way. For better or for worse, times had changed.

CHAPTER 1

"A STAIN ON THE COMMUNITYS FAIR NAME"

Frank Klaus was Pittsburgh's first world champion. Many top challengers claimed the vacant title after the murder of middleweight champion Stanley Ketchel in 1910. Klaus earned universal recognition after slowly but systematically beating almost all of them. (Photo courtesy of Douglas Cavanaugh)

In and around Pittsburgh it went back a long way, the taboo against fun and games. By the well-bred it was rigidly observed, by the common folk quietly resented. The founders of the Commonwealth -- English Quakers and Scotch-Irish Presbyterians -- were by nature inclined to be spoilsports. Under the Great Law of 1682 the slightest display of interest in any form of amusement whatever could result in a five-shilling fine plus five days on the rock pile. Later the rules were more lenient, and west of the Alleghenies there were no rules at all.

West of the Alleghenies the pioneers hunted and fished, but they hunted and fished for a living. It was all in the day's work. Only at weddings, house raisings, and Fourth of July celebrations did they let themselves go. They ran races, they broad-jumped, they shot at targets; bands played, corn licker flowed, the mountainsides rang with their shouts. And nearly always the main event was a fight -- a bare-knuckle fight with elements of wrestling and mayhem.

But then as a primitive town grew up where the Allegheny River met the Monongahela to form the Ohio, the audience for such diversions became increasingly restricted. Sports were the occupation of the lower orders -- "river boatmen, traders, loafers, sharpers, workmen, young dandies," an early historian sniffed. They would gather in taprooms and inn yards, mostly on Sundays and holidays, for bull baiting, bear baiting, and cockfighting. Of team sports, there were none except lacrosse, a homicidal game invented and played by the Indians.

All of that ended with the dawn of the Victorian Age.

By the 1880s, sports of the rowdier kind were illegal. On Sundays you went to church. On weekdays, only baseball games, bicycle racing, boat racing, and horse racing were tolerated. Prize fights were clandestine affairs, staged in defiance of the law. Dominick McCaffrey, the first Pittsburgh fighter of any real consequence, boxed only once in his hometown. And when McCaffrey challenged heavyweight champion John L. Sullivan in 1885 there was trouble with the police in the state's largest metropolis, Philadelphia.

To prevent the fight from being held there, the police arrested both principals. The scene then shifted to Cincinnati, where the police arrested Sullivan, but not, for some reason, McCaffrey. The charge was intent to break the law by engaging in a prize fight. At a court hearing, Sullivan's lawyer argued successfully that Ohio law permitted "sparring matches" with three-ounce gloves So, late on the afternoon of August 29, 1885, with a wink from an acquiescent judge, Cincinnati was treated to a fight mislabeled as a sparring match -- a fight for the heavyweight championship.

The venue was Chester Park, a half-mile racecourse beyond the city limits. Excursion trains from New York, Pittsburgh, Chicago, New Orleans, and Atlanta brought six thousand out-of-towners to Cincinnati. The total attendance of fifteen thousand included three thousand gate-crashers and twenty hack loads of "doxies," as a newspaper called them, "perched on their carriages to get a better view."

John L. Sullivan was an early American idol, although from the vantage point of the twenty-first century it is hard to understand why. As portrayed by his fellow Bostonian, the upper-crust novelist John P. Marquand, he was dull, boastful, and "quarrelsome when drunk,"-- his usual condition. And yet, in spite of these shortcomings, newspaper reporters "hung on his words." Completely without acting skills, he could pack any theater in the land. On the stage and in the ring, he earned at least a million dollars and spent almost every cent of it. Boys and grown men tagged along behind him on his daily rounds. Everybody everywhere hungered to shake his hand.

Only one explanation suggested itself to Marquand: "Mr. Sullivan said frequently and profanely, drunk or sober, that he could lick any so-and-so in the world. Others before and since have made the same remark, but Mr. Sullivan was different from most of the others. He was always ready to try it, and usually he could do it, and on the rare occasions when he couldn't he did not come to the reporters with an alibi." (Delicately, Marquand avoids using the earthier expression Sullivan would have substituted for "so-and-so.")

Inside the ring, Marquand wrote, there was nothing fancy about Sullivan. He didn't dance, he didn't dodge, he didn't duck. "He was out there firmly on his feet to smash down an opponent's guard with clean, straight blows." That was the idea, but smashing down McCaffrey's guard with clean, straight blows would entail a foot race.

McCaffrey, you see, was no fool. He knew a lot better than to slug with his opponent. A 21-year-old failed seminarian who claimed to be "ten times the boxer" Sullivan was, he stood only 5 feet 9 and weighed, at the most, 165 pounds. The champion's advantage in height was less than two inches, but in strength and sheer bulk there was no comparison between the two men. And so, judiciously, in the interest of self-preservation, McCaffrey elected to fight on the run.

The tactic had worked for him, he announced to the press, in a sparring session with Sullivan only one year before. Sullivan, to be sure, was half drunk at the time. The sparring took place in Boston, where a couple of nights later McCaffrey boxed a friend of Sullivan's, Peter McCoy, at the Windsor Theatre. In the second round of that fight McCoy used an illegal wrestling hold, and a riot broke out. McCaffrey's Pittsburgh fans -- fellow iron workers -- stormed the ring, whereupon Sullivan, who'd been acting as a second for McCoy, "decked half a dozen of them," according to a Boston newspaper report. The bad blood this engendered would come to a boil in Cincinnati.

McCaffrey and McCoy boxed one more round after the riot subsided, and the bout went into the record books as a draw. Between 1881 and 1893 McCaffrey had thirty fights, winning fifteen and losing six, with two draws. There were seven "no-contests," which may have been bare-knuckle affairs interrupted by the police. In 1906, after thirteen years on the shelf, he returned to the ring at the age of 43 and was knocked out in two rounds by someone named Reddy Moore in Philadelphia. Altogether, McCaffrey boxed ten times in Philadelphia. His one appearance in Pittsburgh, where prize fights had the status of dog fights, was on April 26, 1884. It resulted in a four-round draw with the Englishman William Sheriff, whose credentials were equal, or almost equal, to McCaffrey's.

They wore gloves, the likelihood is. Bare-knuckle fights, in which anything went, and which sometimes lasted for hours, were beginning to seem barbaric even then. Under the rules of the London Prize Ring, a round only ended with a knockdown, and a fight only ended when one man established total dominance or when both men were totally exhausted. At this kind of mauling, if he had bothered to train, Sullivan usually excelled. But Marquess of Queensberry rules, which called for gloves, three-minute rounds, and ten seconds to recover from a knockdown, cramped his style, and for the first time in a heavyweight title fight Queensberry rules applied in his match with McCaffrey.

Ponderous and slow at 232 pounds, he chased his elusive quarry around the ring. In the August heat, it was difficult work. When he was able to overtake McCaffrey, he pounded or pushed him to the floor. After seven rounds, one more than the agreed-upon distance, Sullivan and even McCaffrey were ready to call it quits. Not so their handlers.

McCaffrey's chief second was his brother Jimmy. In photographs, Dominick McCaffrey, with his plain, open countenance, looks guileless if not quite angelic. This was a lad who had studied for the priesthood, after all. His brother Jimmy appears to have been the combustible type. However, that may be, as the principals and their attendants waited for Billy Tait, the referee, to announce his decision, one of Sullivan's handlers, a well-known English bareknuckle fighter named Arthur Chambers, said something offensive to Jimmy McCaffrey. The Pittsburgh Commercial Gazette did not have a reporter on the scene, but Tait, in an interview published several days later by the newspaper, was kind enough to describe what happened next.

"The greatest commotion ensued," he began. Jimmy McCaffrey "launched himself" at Chambers and closed his left eye with "a solid right-hander." Partisans of both fighters made a rush for the ring. Confronted by Sullivan, Jimmy drew from his belt "a tremendous cowboy revolver." Sullivan's boast that he could lick any so-and-so in the world excluded so-and-so's packing cowboy revolvers, and he judiciously backed off. The entire Pittsburgh contingent -- again, mostly iron workers -- had come to Cincinnati with an arsenal, and "one big fella," Tait confided, "stood right up against me, jamming a pistol into my ribs." Tait easily guessed what the message was -- that if he valued his personal well-being he would not declare Sullivan the winner. "But Sullivan had won, and that was the way I decided it," Tait said. That was the way he decided it, but not until forty-eight hours after the fight, having meanwhile put distance between himself and the gun-toting McCaffrey gang.

Forever after, McCaffrey's supporters maintained that Dominick had deserved at least a draw. There was no demand for a return match. In 1888, McCaffrey lost a ten-round decision to the highly esteemed middleweight champion, Jack Dempsey the Nonpareil, at the Pavonia Rink in Jersey City, and in 1890, at the Fifth Avenue Casino in Brooklyn, he lost a four-round decision to James J. Corbett, who would win the heavyweight championship from Sullivan eventually.

Sullivan, after his not very glorious win over McCaffrey, devoted the next thirteen months to uninterrupted dissipation. Then on September 18, 1886, he unpredictably turned up in Allegheny City, across the Allegheny River from downtown Pittsburgh, to fight the woefully unaccomplished Frank Herald, a Philadelphia pug so obscure that the Commercial Gazette spelled his name "Hearld."

Absorbed by the North Side, a place called Allegheny City no longer exists, but in 1886 it was still an independent municipality. Just as Cincinnati had been a fallback location for Sullivan and McCaffrey, Allegheny City was a fallback location for Sullivan and Herald. Out of concern for the sensibilities of the public, Union City, New Jersey, their original choice as a site, had declined the honor.

Allegheny City was scarcely more receptive. A committee of "respectable citizens," composed for the most part of Protestant clergymen, told the Commercial Gazette that to allow such an exhibition would be "a stain on the community's fair name." The mayor, a man referred to by the newspaper simply as Wyman, echoed the committee's sentiments, but the fight went on as scheduled at the hastily rented Casino Rink. In a partial concession to the fears of the respectable citizens, the promoters -- not identified in the Commercial Gazette by name -- charged two dollars apiece for tickets "to keep out the rougher element."

Although "hardened sportsmen," as the Commercial Gazette put it, made the journey from Boston, New York, and Philadelphia to be at ringside, the attendance fell short of one thousand. The fight itself was "a miserable disappointment." Herald, according to the Commercial Gazette, "had as much chance of victory as a terrier would have against a lion. Sullivan could have killed him in the very first round," the author of the paper's unsigned critique wrote scornfully. As it was, Sullivan restrained himself until the second round and then knocked Herald down with "a tremendous blow to the mouth," a blow he helpfully described as "a left-handed cross counter, one of the most difficult punches to land." Still alive, and back on his feet, Herald fell into a clinch. At that point, "under pressure" from the authorities, the police stepped in and put a halt to the mismatch.

In its post-fight coverage, the Commercial Gazette monitored Sullivan's behavior. "During his short stay in the city, he was comparatively temperate," the paper noted. "He indulged somewhat in beer, wine, etc., but his friends, with tremendous effort, kept him within bounds."

A proposal to bring Herald back for a fight with somebody less ferocious than Sullivan met with no encouragement. "It is not likely," the Commercial Gazette editorialized, "that any fight will be held here for some time to come."

None was -- certainly no fight of any importance. Sullivan's next big fight was with Charley Mitchell, the wiry little English champion, on the country estate of Baron Alphonse Rothschild in France, near Chantilly, on March 10, 1888. Mitchell, like McCaffrey, was never much more than an oversized middleweight When they boxed in New York's Madison Square Garden in 1885, wearing gloves, McCaffrey had won a four-round decision. Mitchell and Sullivan fought with bare knuckles. After thirty-nine "dragging and ineffectual" rounds, the verdict agreed upon was a draw. The adjectives "dragging" and "ineffectual" are those of Arthur Brisbane, who covered the fight for the Hearst papers. A "drenching rain" had turned the battle site --

the turf behind the baron's stable -- into slippery mud, Brisbane wrote, and Sullivan, his "once astonishing power" a thing of the past, was "seized with chills."

Sixteen months later, bulldozed into condition by the noted trainer William Muldoon, Sullivan outlasted Jake Kilrain in the fight that put an end to the bare-knuckle stone age of boxing. On the grounds of a lumber camp in the Mississippi woods, a crowd of three thousand "sportsmen" watched the battering and bleeding for two hours, sixteen minutes, and twenty-five seconds. Mississippi in midsummer can be hot, which meant that, as one account has it, the ring was "a scorched inferno." Spectators "keeled over like nine pins" and the backs of the fighters were "blistered by the sun." Before the start of the seventy-sixth round, a doctor from the New York Athletic Club sought out Kilrain's manager and said with urgency in his voice, "Your fighter will die if you keep sending him out there." The manager prudently "threw in the sponge."

It was the last fight Sullivan ever won. On September 7, 1892, at the Olympic Club in New Orleans, he lost his heavyweight championship to Corbett by a knockout in the twenty-first round.

Here in Pittsburgh, there was never much ring activity until the last few years of the century.. On New Year's Day, 1897, a fighter of some renown who would later teach boxing at the Pittsburgh Athletic Association -- Joe Choynski -- made an appearance at the World's Theater, but his match there with someone named John Gallagher degenerated into slapstick. According to the Commercial Gazette, Gallagher's "very appearance" was comical. "He had absolutely no science whatever and would not have been able to land on Choynski in a year." He'd been trying for nine minutes -- the time it took to complete three rounds -- when a police captain dragged him off the stage. "It was well that he did," editorialized the Commercial Gazette, "or some of the spectators would have died from excessive laughter."

In the Pittsburgh of the Gay Nineties, entertainment was where you found it. At an outdoor band concert in the Lower Hill on that first day of 1897, a cigar-smoking two-year-old child diverted an audience gathered on the sidewalk in front of a mission house. As reported on page one of the Commercial Gazette, the "little tot" -- dressed in a checkered coat and blue velvet cap and holding his mother's hand -- "complacently puffed away, unabashed by the stares of the crowd." The father, meanwhile, "beamed proudly at his offspring, as much as to say, 'Ain't he a dandy?'"

Competing attractions notwithstanding, "a very large crowd" had turned out to see Choynski. A fraction of an inch short of 5 feet 11, Choynski never weighed more than 170 pounds but boxed all the nineteenth-century heavyweight champions -- Sullivan, Corbett, Bob Fitzsimmons, and Jim Jeffries -- plus Philadelphia Jack O'Brien, a light-heavyweight champion. On the lower end of the scale, he boxed a couple of welterweight champions, Kid McCoy and Joe Walcott (the original Joe Walcott from the Caribbean island of Barbados). Choynski beat none of them, but a long time after his twenty-round draw with Jeffries, the old grizzly-bear heavyweight said to a sportswriter, "Know who hit me the hardest? That skinny Jew, Choynski. He nearly took my head off with a left hook."

Preparing for his doomed attempt to win back the title from Jack Johnson in 1910, Jeffries used Choynski as a sparring partner. The thinking was that Choynski knew the secret of beating Johnson, having knocked him out nine years earlier in the black fighter's hometown of Galveston, Texas. Whatever tips he may have provided were not at all helpful to Jeffries, who never had a chance against Johnson.

According to Finis Farr, the author of a Johnson biography, the punch that laid him low in the third round of his fight with Choynski was "without a doubt the hardest he ever took. When he came to," continues Farr, "he found himself looking up into the face of Captain Luke Travis," a Texas Ranger. "You boys are going to the crossbar hotel," Travis said, including Choynski in his offer of hospitality. Mixed-race fights, it seems, violated Texas state law.

So Johnson and Choynski spent three weeks in jail, where they were treated like guests of the management. Each day for the enjoyment of the warden and the guards, they sparred in the prison courtyard.

The Choynski-Johnson fight took place on February 25, 1901. Six weeks earlier, on January 14, Johnson had boxed a white man from Pittsburgh in Galveston, and their "disregard for the rules," as the anonymous reporter from the Galveston Daily News put it, may have reminded the civic authorities that there indeed was a reason for the law prohibiting inter-racial encounters.

Like Choynski, the Pittsburgh fighter, Jim Scanlan, weighed in the neighborhood of 170 pounds. He had boxed in Galveston on no fewer than six previous occasions without losing, and he took an impressive record -- 26-4-4 with 24 knockouts -- into his fight with Johnson, who was 22 years old at the time and not yet the polished craftsman he would become.

One of Scanlan's earlier fights in Galveston, which he won by a knockout as usual, was with Tim Hurley of Chicago on May 31, 1900. In its coverage the next day, the Daily News reported that "a certain negro [sic] pugilist" had challenged the winner. This, of course, would have been Johnson, but Scanlan announced after polishing off Hurley in six rounds that he "never had made it a practice to fight a Negro and would hold himself to this vow." By the following January, having meanwhile won four fights in Memphis and another in Pittsburgh from white opponents, Scanlan reconsidered. He agreed to a 20-rounder with Johnson at the Galveston Athletic Club.

"IT WAS NO CONTEST," exclaimed the Daily News headline on January 15th. Because of "repeated fouling," the referee stopped the fight in the seventh round. The nature of the fouls, and the referee's name, were undisclosed in the newspaper story and are therefore lost to posterity. Before the referee's intervention, the paper asserted, "Johnson had the better of the contest. Had he been the stiff puncher Scanlan is, matters would have come to an end early in the action. He is quicker, cleverer, and equally as good in ring generalship, but lacked the driving power of his white antagonist."

In declaring the fight "no contest," the customary verdict when there's a double disqualification, the Daily News headline was at odds with the referee, who elected, after leaving the ring, to call it a draw.

A preliminary bout preceded the main event. In it, the Daily News informed its readers, "two negroes, each minus one leg, furnished entertainment." Such was the cultural atmosphere from which Jack Johnson struggled to break free on his path to the heavyweight championship.

Jim Scanlan grew up in Lawrenceville. He boxed from 1897 until 1906. almost always in far-away places after his first twelve months as a pro. As nearly as we know, he had eighteen fights in Australia, one in Honolulu, two on the Pacific Coast, six in Hot Springs, Arkansas, and three in Denver. Records for a fighter of Scanlan's vintage tend to be unreliable, but Douglas Cavanaugh, who does some remarkable spadework for the International Boxing Research Organization, has been able to determine that Scanlan had

62 fights, winning 42. with 35 knockouts and losing 11. There were nine draws, including the one with Johnson. After retiring from the ring, Scanlan walked a downtown police beat in Pittsburgh for many years.

Getting back to Joe Choynski, he called it quits as a fighter in 1904 to become the boxing instructor at the Pittsburgh Athletic Association, or a forerunner of the PAA, which wasn't officially chartered until 1911, two years after the completion of its Venetian Renaissance building in Oakland. Choynski coached there until 1919, when a business opportunity in his native San Francisco made him realize where his heart belonged. The fact that the ritzy PAA had a boxing instructor meant that barriers to the sport were coming down. Only in isolated cases now was there any kind of resistance from the guardians of public morality.

Thus, on March 9, 1903, Pittsburgh opened its arms to a reigning welterweight champion and a future light-heavyweight champion. The welterweight -- Joe Walcott -- won a ten-round decision from Mike Donovan of Rochester, New York, at Masonic Hall in Allegheny City; that same night, in nearby Spring Garden, light-heavyweight Philadelphia Jack O'Brien was prevailing over Jim Jeffords of California, also in ten rounds, at the Pittsburgh Athletic Club (not to be confused with the PAA).

It bears mentioning that the inter-racial Walcott-Donovan fight aroused not a ripple of protest. Neither the clergy nor any secular committee spoke up. As reported by the Pittsburgh Gazette, successor to the Commercial Gazette, a "good-natured crowd" was on hand. These affable and, up to a point, broad-minded onlookers "literally packed Masonic Hall from dome to ceiling," a feat that is not easy to visualize. The crowd's sympathies, of course, were with Donovan, "the white fighter." Considering the outcome, sympathy for Donovan may not have been out of place. Walcott was the clear winner, and nobody seemed to feel that Allegheny City's fair name had been stained.

By contrast, the mere announcement that O'Brien and Jeffords were to box incensed the burgess of Spring Garden, Ernest Orth, "and some fifty citizens" he had sworn in as vigilantes. The fight, Orth suggested, would attract "an undesirable class of people." In full agreement, the Pittsburgh Gazette reminded its readers that promoter James "Red" Mason had orchestrated fight shows in Millvale "which were followed by arrests and lawsuits."

Burgess Orth solemnly vowed that he would keep Spring Garden undesecrated. The fight would positively not take place.

Before 1,500 spectators who "filled the Pittsburgh Athletic Club to overflowing," the fight took place. Constable James Glenn held up the proceedings only long enough to mollify the burgess by arresting Mason, O'Brien, and Jeffords. He did not pretend that it was anything other than a pro-forma gesture. When O'Brien and Jeffords entered the ring, Burgess Orth climbed onto his chair and announced in what the Pittsburgh Gazette called "a deep German accent" that the minute he observed any "rough stuff" he would stop the fight. The crowd interpreted this as low comedy, "cheering and hissing." Partway through the fourth round, Orth jumped up and shouted, "Gentlemen, I stop this fight now." The referee and the boxers ignored him. At the end of his wits, Orth called for help from a platoon of county detectives. They advised him to sit down and keep his mouth shut.

The fight was as rough as Orth had thought it would be. At the finish, O'Brien held out his hand, but Jeffords brushed it aside and made "a highly uncomplimentary remark." O'Brien responded by giving Jeffords a shove. Jeffords shoved back. In a moment, they were down on the canvas, Jeffords using his superior weight to advantage. With no assistance from Constable Glenn or the county detectives, friends of the two fighters untangled them.

Slowly, as time went by, opposition to the Sweet Science crumbled. In an atmosphere of cigarette and cigar smoke, there were fights all over town -- at Turner Hall on Forbes Street in Oakland, at Kenyon Hall on the North Side, at the Millvale Opera House, at the South Side Market House, at the old City Hall in Diamond Square, now Market Square, and in almost any public building with room for a few hundred spectators.

One locale, the most desirable of all, was off-limits. In 1900 an amusement-park owner named Andrew McSwigan had bought the Pittsburgh Traction Company's car barn on Craig Street in Oakland, directly opposite St. Paul's Cathedral, for $200,000, and later that year he spent an even larger sum converting it into a pleasure dome. Built in 1890 to shelter horse cars and their teams, the barn became an anachronism when the horse cars gave way to trolley cars powered by electricity. Still, "there was nothing cheap or sleazy about it," wrote the fine-arts critic Jamie Van Trump in a 1956 retrospective for Pittsburgh magazine. The two-story building was brick, with sandstone trimming, and spacious by the standards of the day. Potted palm trees surrounding an ornate fountain in the lobby, with crystal chandeliers hanging above it, gave McSwigan the inspiration for the barn's new name -- Duquesne Garden, later pluralized.

In 1901 McSwigan put in an ice-skating rink, and from then on there were hockey games at the Gardens. Ed Magee, the traction company's president, had insisted as part of the sales agreement that the new sports palace must be "a nice place where nice people go to see nice things in a nice way." Accordingly, it was not until late in the decade, when the time seemed to be ripe, that McSwigan opened the Gardens to prize fights. Jack Blackburn and Mike Donovan headlined the first card there on November 23, 1908, Blackburn winning a six-round newspaper decision. Years later, he trained and taught the great heavyweight champion Joe Louis. On June 30, 1909, eight thousand nice people, behaving nicely enough to suit even Ed Magee, saw the six-round no-decision fight between heavyweight champion Jack Johnson and Tony Ross of New Castle.

Boxing's lowlife reputation would cling to it through the years, but its appeal had undeniably widened. A transformation was occurring in the attitude of the public and therefore in the attitude of politicians and police. Nor did it hurt that Pittsburgh fighters such as middleweight Frank Klaus were making names for themselves.

With the lowering of the bars at Duquesne Gardens and the climb to the top of Klaus, Pittsburgh as a fight town came into being.

CHAPTER 2

TWO OF A KIND

On the morning of October 14, 1910, the world lost its middleweight boxing champion when Stanley Ketchel, 24 years old, died before his time -- "fatally shot in the back," wrote John Lardner, "by the common-law husband of the lady who was cooking his breakfast." It happened in the kitchen of a Missouri health farm, where Ketchel had gone for rest and relaxation. Too much of his relaxing had been done with Goldie, the farm's hired girl.

Almost as soon as rigor mortis set in, every halfway reputable middleweight with an enterprising manager was claiming the vacant title. Frank Klaus, a leading contender from East Pittsburgh, had credentials inferior to no one's. He was undefeated in fifty-six fights, many of them, it is true, no-decision bouts. As it happened, the records of most fighters in Frank Klaus's day were sprinkled with the two-letter acronym for no decision -- ND. Countenanced in some states, prohibited in others, boxing was on the fringes of the law. States like New York and Pennsylvania tried to straddle the fence, allowing "exhibition matches" without a declared winner. If a fight didn't end in a knockout, leaving no room for argument, the sportswriters decided who won. Gamblers paid off accordingly, but it was not a good way to establish a pecking order. The W's and L's in a fighter's record -- the wins and losses -- are conclusive, whether merited or not. NDs only signify that a fighter was still viable, although not necessarily possessed of all his faculties, at the close of the final round. A no-decision fight in 1909 between Ketchel and the world light-heavyweight champion, Philadelphia Jack O'Brien, ended with O'Brien unconscious and flat on his back, but providentially saved by the bell.

Along with Klaus, the middleweight pretenders ambitious to succeed Ketchel were Billy Papke, Cyclone Johnny Thompson, Frank Mantell, Eddie McGoorty, Jimmy Clabby, Jack Dillon, Jeff Smith, and Mike Gibbons. Papke, the "Illinois Thunderbolt," had been champion in 1908 between his knockout of Ketchel and Ketchel's knockout of him. He now reclaimed the title, but on February 11, 1911, in Sydney, Australia, he lost a 20-round decision to Thompson, and Thompson claimed the title. By the following year, Thompson had outgrown the division -- the weight limit at the time was 158 pounds -- and once again Papke claimed the title. He immediately lost a 20-round decision to Mantell -- who of course claimed the title. As when Papke and Thompson were claiming it, nobody paid much attention.

Boxing commissions as we know them today did not then exist. Pennsylvania had no commission until 1923. Ordinarily, champions became champions by defeating the incumbent or by an informal -- and disorderly -- consensus arrangement, in which sportswriters' opinions carried a lot of weight. It was difficult to overlook Klaus. He had stopped Mantell and had more than held his own with Papke.

According to the Pittsburgh Press, the Klaus-Papke fight on November 11, 1909, at Duquesne Gardens "stirred up more interest" beforehand than "any other ring event in the pugilistic history of the city." Klaus's adherents, the paper disclosed, were "going clean daffy." Klaus himself, caught up in the excitement, told the anonymous Press reporter, "Just say for me that I'll be there to fight, fight, fight. When the bout is over, I will not be the defeated man."

Nor was he. In the judgment of the observer from the Press, Klaus took five of the six rounds. Papke, the Press writer said, "finished in hurricane fashion," but Klaus was far enough ahead to win the newspaper decision. A crowd of "between 3,000 and 4,000" -- the Press used extremely round numbers -- certified its daffiness by actually attending the fight.

The following year, on March 26th, the great Ketchel was in town to box Klaus. This time "hundreds" were present. A crowd of hundreds sounds smaller than "between 3,000 and 4,000," but the Press's new boxing critic, a medical doctor named Cratty who self-effacingly used the byline Jim Jab, said it was "possibly the largest that ever peeped at a local passage-at-arms."

Pulling no punches, Jim Jab made it clear that the hundreds had been disgracefully short-changed. "This throng," he wrote, "deserved fair treatment from the gladiators. Did they get it? No! Ketchel and Klaus pulled off a flagrant frameup. The men put in six rounds but had hard work to consume the time by clinching, fiddling, fussing and stalling." The unhappy spectators "roared in disgust." They shouted at the referee, demanding action, but "apparently," Jim Jab reported, "he was in on the deal himself." If the scoundrel had a name, Jim Jab did not reveal it.

He gave the edge in the "stallfest" to Klaus, who exerted himself a little more often than the champion did. But when "men of reputation meet for six-round matches under our no-decision gag," Jim Jab counseled his readers, it is wise not to expect an honest fight. In a situation where two good fighters have nothing to gain or lose, then what is to keep them from clinching, fiddling, fussing, and stalling?

It's "the boys in the prelims" who really try, Jim Jab declared, by implication praising Buck Crouse and George Chip, opponents that night on the undercard. Their fight was in the third round when Crouse "put the bug on Chip" -- Jim Jab's way of saying that he won by a knockout. Just a few years later, Chip would be the middleweight champion.

`` In the sorting-out process after Ketchel's death, Klaus lost decisions to Leo Houck, Jimmy Gardner, and Hugo Kelly, faces in the crowd, but later he won from Houck twice, from Gardner, from Jack Dillon twice, and from Cyclone Johnny Thompson. On balance, his record was still an impressive one. Klaus had no affectations as a person and he fought with the same lack of subtlety. "He was a stocky guy who could walk right into you and keep going to the body all the time," the old fight manager Bunny Buntag once told me.

Klaus always entered the ring with a cap on his head. If he was fighting outdoors, he dressed for warmth, wearing, besides the cap, a long, loose topcoat. Gorgeous silk robes with piping and gold lame adornments were not yet a part of even the most upscale pugilist's wardrobe. As late as the 1920s, a champion like Jack Dempsey would simply put on a sweater for the walk down the aisle or throw a bath towel over his shoulders, a practice revived among the moderns by Mike Tyson, who did not even bother to wear socks.

In keeping with his no-frills approach, Klaus was shocked to discover that Georges Carpentier, the dandified Frenchman who would one day fight Dempsey for the heavyweight title, used scent. The fact became evident to Klaus when he huddled with Carpentier for the referee's instructions before their 20-round bout on June 24, 1912, in the French seaport town of Dieppe, where thirty years later, during World War II, the Germans who occupied it wiped out an assault force of six thousand Canadians and British. Returning to his corner, Klaus informed his manager, George Engel, that Carpentier was "all perfumed up."

"Am I supposed to fight him or kiss him?" Klaus asked.

There was never much doubt as to which it would be. Carpentier, just 18 years old but already the best boxer in France, took a thorough drubbing. But for the solicitude of the referee, the fight would have ended in the sixth round, when Klaus, going to the body, hammered his aromatic opponent to the floor. Writhing in agony, Carpentier claimed a foul, and the referee gave him a ten-minute rest. Again, in the fourteenth round, Carpentier hit the deck, looking done for, but the timekeeper quickly rang the bell, and the mismatch continued. By round nineteen, Carpentier's manager, Francois Descamps, had seen enough. Under French boxing rules, a manager disqualified his fighter by jumping into the ring. This Descamps did, and Klaus was the winner on a foul. In the United States or anywhere else, the result would have been a technical knockout.

Routinely, Klaus declared himself middleweight champion. Also, routinely, his declaration fell on deaf ears. In the absence of a central authority, the various contenders went blithely on their way, fighting or ducking one another as they chose.

There was certainly no shortage of activity. Middleweights named Sullivan formed a virtual division of their own, and Klaus, over the years, licked four of them. On opposite coasts, he knocked out Montana Jack Sullivan and Montana Dan Sullivan, one in New York, the other in Oakland, California. Montana Jack and Montana Dan were brothers. Another pair of Sullivan's, Jack and Mike, from Boston, were twins. Both had been knocked out by Ketchel. Klaus took the measure of Jack, but never had a chance to box Mike. Consequently, he missed a grand slam, having knocked out a Massachusetts Sullivan named Tom.

Klaus was a fighter with an old-fashioned work ethic. In Philadelphia one night, he knocked out the middleweight champion of England, Harry Mansfield, in two rounds. As always, Klaus had gone to the body, and Mansfield's corner yelled foul so convincingly that the crowd, switching its allegiance to the foreigner, was on the verge of a riot. Klaus restored something like order by agreeing to box a second opponent, a New Yorker named Jim Smith. This one he knocked out in one round, and Smith joined Mansfield in the hospital, where they were treated for identical injuries -- broken ribs and broken noses.

In October of 1912, Billy Papke crossed the ocean to Paris and won from Carpentier the way Klaus had done four months earlier, with Descamps stopping the fight in the seventeenth round. In Paris the next year on March 5thPapke and Klaus got together again, with the winner to be recognized, finally and by acclamation, as middleweight champion.

Their no-decision fight had been competitive. This one was all Klaus. He won on a foul -- the usual ending to a one-sided fight in France -- when Papke, about to go down in the fifteenth round, deliberately butted him. "Practically every American in Paris was at ringside," one paper said, and they joined enthusiastically with the rest of the crowd in loudly deriding Papke. At odds of 2 to 1 in Papke's favor, Klaus had bet on himself "heavily," and he came back to Pittsburgh a little too well off, perhaps.

His stay at the top was at any rate a short one -- seven months and six days, to be precise. Eager to cash in on the championship, he quickly lined up a series of no-decision fights. He could lose his title, but only by a knockout, so it made no difference that sportswriters at ringside gave Jack Dillon the edge over Klaus in Dillon's hometown of Indianapolis because the fight went the distance, ten rounds. Also, according to the newspapers, Klaus won from Eddie McGoorty in Pittsburgh and boxed a draw with McGoorty in Milwaukee. In Boston, he knocked out Jimmy Gardner. Still ahead was a modest payday with George Chip, the former "prelim" fighter.

Dillon and McGoorty were leading contenders. Chip was what promoters called an "opponent" -- an experienced journeyman, fearless but not exactly fearsome. Born in Scranton of Lithuanian parents named Chipulonas, George and his brother Joe, who was also a boxer, had worked in the coal mines around New Castle. Like Klaus, George Chip habitually went to the body and almost never backed up. "He was an easy guy to fight," Bunny Buntag recalled. "He could punch, that's all, and he was tough."

The meeting between Chip and Klaus on October 11, 1913, was scheduled for six rounds at the old City Hall in Market Square, which had a second-floor auditorium. As in his fights with Dillon, McGoorty, and Gardner, Klaus could not lose his title except by a knockout -- and he had never been knocked out or knocked down. He went into the ring full of confidence, and so superior did he look through the first five rounds that midway during the sixth the fans started walking out.

There had been long, tedious stretches of infighting, since both men punched to the body. It was a punch to the jaw, however, that made an ex-champion of Klaus. They were banging away in the middle of the ring, wrote Jim Jab, when Chip landed it. The blow was an "up-from-the-floor right." With fine attention to detail, Jim Jab recounts its effect. "Over reeled the veteran" -- Klaus was 26, only one year older than Chip -- "hitting the floor with the back of his head. He got up with the most peculiar look on his face, and Chip went after him like a tiger. The referee stopped the fight with Klaus trying to protect himself on the ropes."

Because six-round no-decision title fights were so unusual, rumors inevitably spread. Had Chip agreed to go through the motions -- as Klaus had with Ketchel when Ketchel was champion -- and then pulled a double-cross? Whatever the truth may have been, Klaus at once demanded a return match. Like almost everybody else, he believed that Chip's victory had been a fluke. Klaus did get his return match, on Christmas Eve at Duquesne Gardens, and the only difference in the outcome was that Chip knocked him out in five rounds instead of six, again with a right to the jaw.

Knowing himself to be, as Jim Jab put it, "no longer the bearcat of old," Klaus retired. He could afford to, he said, having earned $56,000 during his years in the ring. The reign of Chip was even shorter than his predecessors had been. On April 6, 1914, to accommodate a promoter in Brooklyn, he substituted for his brother Joe against Al McCoy, a lightly regarded southpaw. McCoy's real name was Al Rudolph. His father, a poultry farmer from New Jersey, considered Chip a sure thing and bet one hundred of his chickens against a five-cent cigar that young Al would lose. McCoy's timidity during the pre-fight introductions reminded Jim Jab of a frightened rabbit, but apparently frightened rabbits can be dangerous. Early in the first round McCoy "planted himself," Jim Jab wrote, "and lashed out with a left hook as Chip moved in." Ten seconds later, the title had once more changed hands.

Chip went on fighting until 1921. His opponents were some of the best in the business -- Mike Gibbons, Tom Gibbons, Harry Greb -- all just a little too good for Chip. Against Greb, he kept coming back for more, losing to the future champion three times in four no-decision fights after winning the first. Chip had two no-decision fights with McCoy when McCoy was an ex-champion, six with Buck Crouse, the Pittsburgh middleweight who had once put the bug on him, and ten with Jack Dillon. All in all, Chip fought Dillon twelve times. Somewhere along the way, Dillon won a decision from Chip, and in 1915, when Dillon was light-heavyweight champion, they boxed to a ten-round draw.

In 1916, Chip traveled 10,500 miles to get himself knocked out by Les Darcy in Sydney. Twenty years old, Darcy was the newest boy wonder. He had knocked out Buck Crouse and Eddie McGoorty and twice he had beaten Jimmy Clabby. Darcy, his admirers believed, was the next middleweight champion. But after taking Chip apart, in nine rounds, he never fought again.

World War I had been raging in Europe for two years, Australia belonged to the British Commonwealth, and Darcy would be eligible for service on his twenty-first birthday. Instead of waiting to hear from the military, he slipped out of Sydney on an oil tanker and eventually turned up in New York City, minus a passport. Among the managers who welcomed him, offering a contract, was the opportunistic Jack Kearns. The newspapers in Australia were calling Darcy a slacker, which didn't bother Kearns, but when the governors of three states -- New York, Ohio, and Louisiana --announced that no illegal alien would be given a license to box, Kearns lost interest immediately.

He would do better in the years just ahead with Jack Dempsey. Darcy, confused and friendless, protested that his only purpose in coming over here was to earn enough money so that his parents and their nine other children, eight of them younger than he, could stay off the dole in case he did not return from the war. He explained to the governors that his father, the only wage earner in the family, had health problems. The governors were unsympathetic.

Needing cash, Darcy appeared in exhibition bouts with a sparring partner and went on tour with a vaudeville company. The tour fizzled, and on April 16, 1917, the day the United States entered the war, he was stranded in Memphis. Jumping at the chance to clear his name, he joined the soon-to-be-federalized Tennessee National Guard. Before his call-up he died of a sudden, mysterious illness, possibly typhoid fever. Romanticists claimed that the real cause of his death was a broken heart.

Those who considered Darcy the best-looking young fighter they ever had seen included Chip. Back in Pittsburgh, he buttonholed a sportswriter friend, Regis Welsh, to tell him how good Darcy was. Demonstrating the punch that had knocked him out, Chip reproduced its force with such exactitude that he knocked Welsh out, on Fifth Avenue downtown, to the astonishment of passers-by.

Frank Klaus came out of retirement in 1918 to take on Harry Greb, who was just then reaching his prime. Sports editors of the seven Pittsburgh newspapers, unaware that smoking is a cause of lung cancer, heart disease, and almost every other ailment imaginable, had decided to raise money for a shipment of cigarettes to the American troops in France. With their publishers' financial support, they promoted a benefit boxing show at Duquesne Gardens. Greb, who was waiting to be inducted into the Navy, offered his services. A difficulty arose when the sports editors could not find an opponent for him, so Klaus volunteered.

Although the match was billed as an exhibition, it would be his first ring appearance in five years, whereas the younger, better-conditioned Greb had been boxing frequently. "Don't worry, Frank," Greb told him, "we'll make it look good." They did. They made it look good enough to fool the most knowledgeable observers. "My God, they tried to kill one another," a mutual friend exclaimed, and Jim Jab wrote that there was little to choose between them after six fast rounds.

Klaus died at 60 of a heart attack, George Chip at 72 when he was struck by an automobile while crossing the street in New Castle. Except on the two occasions they boxed each other, Klaus was the better fighter. His reputation has not had much staying power, but Nat Fleischer, the venerable boxing historian, considered him the sixth best middleweight of all time. Fleischer's first five -- he tended to overrate the fighters of his own generation -- were Ketchel, Tommy Ryan (a nineteenth-century champion), Greb, Mickey Walker, and Ray Robinson.

In the 1920s Klaus became a manager. His most likely looking prospect was a middleweight named Al Tilicki. "You can't fight under that name," Klaus told him. "Who ever heard of a fighter named Tilicki?" Tilicki came from Braddock; a hotel in Braddock was called the Belmont. "From now on you're Jimmy Belmont," Klaus decreed. By whatever label, Tilicki/Belmont could fight. Before he was through, he had beaten some good opponents and lost to some better ones.

Klaus enjoyed teaching amateurs, and he kept his instructions simple. "Get him in a corner!" he shouted one night to a novice who was being out boxed. The fighter did as he was told. "Now let him have it!" Again, the fighter did as he was told -- and knocked the other guy stiff.

It was satisfying to coach amateurs, but at heart Klaus remained a professional, with professional standards. Driving the kid home, he said to him, "What did you get for that fight?"

"A stickpin."

"Let me see it."

The kid handed over a piece of cheap jewelry.

"Is that the best they can do?" Klaus said. Without another word, he rolled down the window and threw the stickpin out of the car.

He was making a point: Know what you're worth.

Klaus had uncomplicated beliefs, and he expected his fighters to think the way he did. "No matter how much a guy's hitting you," he would tell them, "you're hitting him, too." A tradeoff like that -- the other guy's best punch against his own -- was all that Klaus himself ever asked.

CHAPTER 3

WHITE HOPE

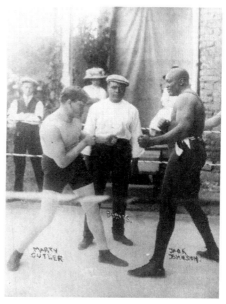

Shown here in a fight against Marty Cutler (left), heavyweight champion Jack Johnson (right) became the first African-American to hold the crown. Johnson said of Pittsburgh's Frank Moran "I never saw a man who could stand up to punishment the way Moran did. I hit him harder and oftener than I ever hit any other man, but I couldn't put him down. I wore myself out hitting him." (Picture Courtesy of the Library of Congress, LC-USZ6-1824)

Frank Moran's career as a substitute left tackle on the University of Pittsburgh football team ended prematurely in 1908, the year it began. No doubt this was all for the best. His athletic energies rechanneled into boxing, a sport that had gained him entrée into Theodore Roosevelt's White House, he proceeded to make something of a name for himself.

Twice he attempted to win the heavyweight championship of the world. Twice he was unsuccessful, but boxing enabled him to travel and spend money; it enabled him to consort with artists and writers, with actresses and

show girls, with a president enshrined on Mount Rushmore, and with one of
the more feckless Princes of Wales; it was his passport, finally, to Hollywood
and the movies.

Unremarkable in themselves, both of Moran's fights for the heavyweight
championship have a certain arcane historical interest.

One was with Jack Johnson in 1914 in Paris, with Moran in the role of
White Hope. What sets it apart is the fact that, for complicated reasons
involving, as we shall see, Moran's strained relations with the promoter of
the fight and Serbia's strained relations with Austria-Hungary, neither fighter
got paid. The box-office money -- all of it -- ended up in the Bank of France.
Two years later, the fight between Moran and Jess Willard, Johnson's
successor as champion, was the cause of, or, rather, pretext for, a New York
state law that made boxing a criminal offense.

Born in 1887, Francis Charles Moran was a native of Cleveland but spent
his formative years on Pittsburgh's North Side, one of nine brothers and
sisters. His father, a saloon keeper, died when Moran was 11. He appears to
have been a likable fellow -- witty, self-confident, popular with the girls.
Fully mature, he was 6 feet 2 inches tall and weighed more than 200 pounds,
impressive dimensions for the early 1900s. His freckled face and reddish-
brown hair gave him a reassuringly wholesome country-boy look.

He enlisted in the Navy out of Allegheny High School. Within a year and
a half, assigned as a quartermaster to the presidential yacht, the Mayflower,
he had caught the attention of Theodore Roosevelt. An enthusiastic boxer
who believed in testing himself, Roosevelt liked to spar with Moran, among
others, in the White House gym. Boxing cost Roosevelt the sight of his left
eye, but there was never any truth in the story, once prevalent, that a punch
from Moran did the damage. Roosevelt himself, in his autobiography, put
the onus on a young artillery captain's deadly right cross.

While still in the Navy, Moran began fighting for money. Back home, and
a freshman at Pitt, he continued to fight. When the academic authorities got
wind of it, they banished him summarily from the football team -- from the
scrub team, actually, for Moran never had played in a game. He shrugged off
his disappointment, gave some thought to enrolling in the Pitt dental school,
and kept fighting.

One of his early opponents was Johnson. Late in 1909 they boxed a four-
round exhibition at the Gayety Theater, downtown. No doubt Johnson, a

natural showman, bantered with the crowd; no doubt Moran was the accommodating straight man.

Dentistry forgotten, he worked at Pitt that year as the football team's trainer, meanwhile keeping busy in the ring. Of his first nine fights, he won five. There were two defeats, a no-decision, and a draw. His tenth fight, against a pretty good opponent named Kid Cotton at the Princess Skating Rink on the North Side, ended in the first round with Moran on the floor, claiming a foul. The referee, Eddie Kennedy, hadn't noticed any foul and counted him out. "Moran jumped to his feet," Kennedy recalled years later for the Pittsburgh Post, "and came at me with fists flying." According to himself, he was more than holding his own when the police climbed into the ring and pried the antagonists apart. They were placed under arrest, taken to the nearest station house, and ordered to put up bond for a hearing the next morning. At the station house Moran was bareheaded -- a sartorial impropriety back than -- and in shirtsleeves. Amid the confusion at the Princess Rink, someone had stolen his hat and coat.

Only Kennedy appeared at the hearing. A disgruntled Moran, feeling unappreciated in Pittsburgh, forfeited his bond and took off for New York. He was never to box in his hometown again until almost the end of his career.

In the New York-Brooklyn area, his base of operations for the next year or so, he started knocking guys out and soon was a main-event fighter. Then in September of 1911, having earned a reputation as a puncher, he crossed the Atlantic Ocean for the first of many times and knocked out a succession of Englishmen. Off and on into the 1920s, Moran was the scourge of British heavyweights, knocking them out as routinely as his friend and former sparring partner, Theodore Roosevelt, gunned down wild animals in Africa.

To judge from the way he looked against Johnson and Willard (films of those fights still exist), Moran's skills as a boxer were never more than rudimentary. His one simple purpose was to land a roundhouse right swing that he referred to with affection as "the old Mary Ann." Of the thirty-nine fights Moran won -- he lost twenty-two and had seven draws -- thirty-one ended in knockouts. So, Mary Ann was a *femme fatale* in her way, although she tended to be unpunctual.

At some point -- details are hard to come by -- Moran was a deck hand on J. P. Morgan's yacht, the Corsair. Either the job didn't last long or it made few demands on his time, for in 1912 and 1913, continually on the move, he boxed in London, Paris, New York, Cleveland, Juarez, San Francisco, New Orleans, and Philadelphia, winning White Hope status along with most of his fights.

The search for White Hopes had begun in 1908 after Jack Johnson's humiliation of game little Tommy Burns down in Sydney, Australia. When Johnson knocked out Burns in the fourteenth round, becoming the first black heavyweight champion, white supremacists like Jack London were beside themselves. "But one thing now remains," wrote the celebrated author of tough-guy novels. "Jim Jeffries must emerge from his alfalfa farm and remove the golden smile from Johnson's face. Jeff, it's up to you."

Jeff, as it happened, wasn't equal to the task. Coming out of retirement on July 4, 1910, six long years after his last appearance in a ring, he met the same fate as Burns. "Once again," London wrote from Reno, Nevada, the scene of Jeff's shellacking, "has Johnson sent down to defeat the chosen representative of the white race, and this time the greatest of them." Never before had Jeffries lost a fight. Johnson, after toying with him for fourteen rounds, knocked him out in the fifteenth. "Where now," London asked, "is the champion who will make Johnson extend himself, who will glaze those bright eyes, remove that smile, and silence that golden repartee?"

Waggishly, Johnson had been in the habit of dealing out punishment with a gold-toothed grin and with an answer to every taunt from his hapless opponent's corner. Between the fifth and sixth rounds of his fight with Jeffries, he leaned over and said to John L. Sullivan, who was sitting at ringside, "I thought this fellow could hit." For London and many others, it was simply too much. The jibes and the insolent grin had to go. But with Jeffries sent back to his alfalfa farm, beaten and disgraced, where indeed was the next White Hope?

Fireman Jim Flynn stepped forward, and though Jeffries' defeat had ignited race riots all over the country (there were eight deaths in New York and eleven in the South, mostly the result of what can only be called lynching's), America yawned. Fireman Jim was a burnt-out case, a pathetic foil for Johnson when they met in Las Vegas, New Mexico, a dusty copper-mining town. (Bugsy Siegel had not yet invented the better-known Las Vegas in Nevada.) Midway through the ninth round, an overweight sheriff with a gun in his belt rushed between the fighters and put an end to the mismatch. Hostility toward Johnson now took a different tack.

In Chicago, where he owned a saloon, the local police arrested him on a trumped-up federal charge -- violation of the Mann Act. The woman in the case, Belle Schreiber, was a prostitute based in Pittsburgh. According to the indictment, Johnson had illegally "transported" her to Chicago for purposes including "unlawful sexual intercourse" and "crimes against nature."

Tried, convicted, and sentenced to a year and a day in prison -- there was also a thousand-dollar fine -- but still at liberty pending an appeal, the unrepentant debaucher jumped bail. His third wife, Lucille, joined him in Montreal, and together they sailed for France. Like his second wife, who committed suicide, Lucille was a white woman -- one more inflammatory factor.

In Paris, Johnson met Dan McKetrick, an American entrepreneur, and agreed to defend his title against Moran, the newest White Hope, with McKetrick promoting. The date McKetrick chose -- June 27, 1914 -- was seven months distant, so meanwhile, for a French promoter, Johnson engaged in a tune-up fight with another black American boxer, Jim Johnson (no relation). The champion won a ten-round decision but broke a small bone in his left forearm.

McKetrick, an irascible sort, was annoyed, and Moran now irritated him further by taking on a "personal manager," Ike Dorgan. McKetrick had counted on managing the fighter himself. As Finis Farr tells it in "Black Champion: The Life and Times of Jack Johnson," McKetrick summoned Moran to a conference, at which the dialogue went like this:

McKetrick: "Let's you and I sign a contract, Frank."

Moran: "I don't need no contract."

McKetrick: "Well, I do!"

Moran: "I'm sorry, Dan, when I left the Navy I took an oath never to sign no papers."

McKetrick: "You took an oath? What if I take a punch at your head?"

Moran: "You've got more sense than that."

It was McKetrick's belief, Farr goes on, that Johnson, having neglected to train, would lose to Moran. McKetrick, as Moran's manager, would then own the heavyweight title. He left his meeting with Moran in high dudgeon.

Claiming that Moran owed him $1,500 for "expenses," he went to his lawyer, a Frenchman named Lucien Cerf, and arranged to have the box-office receipts impounded as soon as Moran's fight with Johnson was over. Moran would not get the $10,000 due him nor Johnson his purse of $14,000 until McKetrick gave the word.

A crowd of twenty thousand attended the contest at the Velodrome d'Hiver. Mistinguett, Maurice Chevalier, the Dolly sisters, a Rothschild or two, and assorted Vanderbilt's were present. Although the French seemed impervious to White Hope hysteria, they pulled for Moran to win, greeting his few sallies with tumultuous cheers.

The cheers were unavailing. Even an undertrained Johnson with a weakened left arm was still the best fighter in the world. Once when Mary Ann finally made contact, Johnson stepped back, smiled, and pounded his gloves together in mock applause. He then launched an uppercut that reddened Moran's nose.

At the end of the twentieth and final round, referee Georges Carpentier, who had not yet reached his twenty-first birthday, lifted Johnson's hand. In another part of the velodrome, the police, in obedience to Lucien Cerf's instructions, were scooping up the gate receipts for delivery to the Bank of France.

The very next day, a Serbian nationalist in Sarajevo assassinated the Archduke Franz Ferdinand of Austria-Hungary, starting World War I. France swiftly mobilized, and Cerf, a reservist, joined his regiment. Thrown into action against the German Army at once, he was killed. Inexplicably, he had not left McKetrick the papers to retrieve the box-office money. McKetrick appealed to the Bank of France, but the bank refused to give up the cash. Fighters and promoter went to their graves without ever collecting, as the history books always put it, a sou.

For 1914, Moran's ring earnings totaled zero. He did not have another fight until the following March. Back in London, he knocked out the easy-to-hit Bombardier Wells, an opponent Moran described as "all chin from the waist up." English chins of that size were made to order for Mary Ann. Jack Johnson's next fight, on April 5th, was the one in which he lost the heavyweight championship to Jess Willard by a 26th-round knockout under a blazing hot sun in Havana. In suspecting that Johnson was ripe for the plucking, McKetrick had not been wrong.

Bombardier Wells was the first step in a comeback for Moran. Lingering briefly in London, he knocked out Gordon Sims. On this side of the Atlantic again, he knocked out the Irishman Jim Coffey in New York and repeated the trick soon afterward. Promoter Tex Rickard now matched him with Willard.

It would be Willard's first title defense, in a manner of speaking. Moran could win the championship, but only by a knockout. Under New York boxing law there could not be a decision and the bout could not exceed ten rounds.

Moran was one of two logical contenders. Willard astutely chose him over Fred Fulton because of his demonstrated drawing power. Neither Rickard nor Willard had cause for regret. The crowd that turned out on March 25, 1916, filled Madison Square Garden to capacity. (This was Stanford White's three-million-dollar Moorish Renaissance Madison Square Garden, topped by a 340-foot tower supporting a giant bronze statue of the goddess Diana. It was there in 1906 that a rich and demented Pittsburgh playboy, Harry K. Thaw, jealous of White's attentions to Mrs. Thaw when she was Evelyn Nesbit, an artist's model from Tarentum, shot and killed the architect at his table in the roof-garden restaurant.)

The Willard-Moran gate receipts, $152,000, broke all records for an indoor sporting event. "Millionaires, governors, and society ladies are going to be at this fight," Rickard had boasted to the newspapers. Dress was informal, but the millionaires and governors came in black tie and the society ladies wore evening gowns.

As big as Moran was, he looked like a pygmy next to the 6-foot-6, 252-pound Willard. Kept at a safe distance by the champion's long left, he couldn't do much. Tad Dorgan, Ike Dorgan's brother, covered the fight for the New York Journal. He wrote that there was only one exciting round, the seventh, in which Willard and Moran staggered each other and Willard opened a cut over Moran's right eye. "Women were screaming, seconds were waving towels, old men with silk hats were throwing them into the air," Dorgan reported. The rest of the fight was rather humdrum. It ended with sportswriters in agreement that Willard had won.

Like Moran's fight with Johnson, this one had an unexpected sequel. Charles Samuels recapitulates the story in his biography of Rickard, "The Magnificent Rube." Moran and Willard got their money -- Moran's share was $22,500 -- but the unfavorable reaction of William Randolph Hearst brought about a New York Journal campaign that drove boxing underground in the Empire State. Although the Journal's own expert had dismissed the fight as boring, publisher Hearst took a contrary view. A front-page editorial decried the "ghastly spectacle." Here were "two big human animals trying to render one another unconscious with clenched fists."

John L. Sullivan, last of the bare-knuckle and first of the gloves-wearing heavyweight champions, was incredulous. "The only brutal thing about that fight was the prices they charged to see it," said the one-time Boston Strong Boy. He added, "If them two bums are champion and challenger, I'll take on both of them the same night."

Hearst, undissuaded, kept his editors and columnists on the case until the New York legislature acted. Boxing was officially abolished in the state. For the next three years, the only fights in New York were unsupervised "club" matches. Instead of tickets, the spectators bought "memberships." Then in 1920 the enactment of a new state law not only turned back the clock but authorized fifteen-round title bouts to a decision.

Losing to Willard was not the end for Moran. Until the ban went into effect, he continued to fight in New York, winning more often than he lost. A famished-looking kid from Colorado, Jack Dempsey, had arrived on the scene with a cardboard suitcase and big ambitions, but when his manager, John the Barber, informed him that he was fighting Moran, Dempsey balked. Moran, he protested, was "too tough." "Either fight this guy," said John the Barber, "or get the hell out of town." Embittered and discouraged, Dempsey went home, riding the rods. He'd be back.

With a new manager, Jack Kearns, Dempsey started doing things that revolutionized prizefighting. Where the heavyweights who preceded him stood up straight and waited each other out, Dempsey continually attacked, bobbing and weaving. A Frank Moran, who could hit with only one hand, wouldn't have had a chance against this well-conditioned, steak-fed Jack Dempsey. In 1918, the 6-foot 7-inch Fred Fulton knocked out Moran in three rounds. Dempsey knocked out Fulton in eighteen seconds. The qualitative difference between Dempsey and Willard's other challengers, or between Dempsey and Willard himself, was immense. Slumped in his corner, broken and bloodied after three horrific rounds with Dempsey (he was down seven times in the first three minutes), Willard handed over the title on the afternoon of July 4, 1919, in an open-air stadium outside Toledo.

In 1920, Johnson returned to America, gave himself up, and went to prison. Moran kept fighting until 1922. He still cut a figure in London, knocking out opponents as fast as the promoters could supply them and socializing with the likes of George Bernard Shaw, H. G. Wells, Augustus John, and the future King Edward VIII. Sculptor Derwent Wood made a bust of Moran, which he put on display at the Royal Academy, side by side with a bust of David Lloyd George. "Two great fighters," Wood said, explaining the juxtaposition of boxer and wartime political leader.

At the Chelsea Ball, a photographer posed Moran with Augustus John. "What do you want us to be doing?" asked the painter. Playfully, Moran suggested, "Hit me on the chin." Augustus John was as sturdy as an oak tree; the right hand he threw from Buckingham Palace landed with full force and it dazed Moran, knocking him back on his heels. "Hardest wallop I ever received," said the man who had taken Jack Johnson's hardest wallop.

In his pugilistic dotage, Moran eventually lost to an Englishman, Joe Beckett, showing, by one account, "the greatest pluck" in a seventh-round TKO defeat. He came back to Pittsburgh for one of his last fights, a ten-rounder at Duquesne Gardens with Denver Jack Geyer. A slight difficulty occurred when he was unable to find sparring partners. In the gym one day, his manager pro tem, Luke Carney, asked a middleweight journeyman named Gus Camp to work with Moran.

"He'll throw the right hand and kill me," Camp said. Carney said, "I'll tell him not to use the right." So, Camp agreed to spar and was having his own way with Moran. After the second round, the big man complained to Carney, "You're letting him show me up." Carney said, "O.K., then -- go ahead and use your right." Moran did, just once, and smelling salts were needed for Camp.

Carney, bending over him as he came to, was worried. "Are you all right, Gus? Shall I call a doctor?" he asked. "Hell, no," answered Camp. "Call a priest."

Moran's opponent at the Gardens, Jack Geyer, looked like a piece of cake, but not to the old lightweight champion, Battling Nelson. From his seat in the audience, Nelson dispatched an usher to Moran's corner at the end of each round with a note, telling him what to do. Moran put up with it for as long as he could, and then he sent back a reply. He said that if one more message came he would stop fighting Geyer, get down from the ring, and fight Nelson.   There was no further advice, and no need for any, from his well-meaning counselor.

In his book about Tex Rickard, Charles Samuels wrote that Moran liked women "wherever he found them" and found them wherever he went = "on Broadway, in Piccadilly, on the boulevards of Paris." Moran's "sweethearts," Samuels noted, included "the agile Pearl Buck, the great movie-serial queen." (At the end of an episode, she was likely to be hanging from a cliff). Another of his companions was Lillian Lorraine, "the most seductive beauty ever to grace the Ziegfeld Follies." Romantically, Moran ranged far and wide, and then he settled down with a girl-next-door type, Rebecca Herbst of New York City, whose parents were Austrian Jewish immigrants. They were married at St. Kevin's Catholic church in Dublin the year of Moran's retirement from the ring.   Among the guests were two of his cousins from County Mayo.

Matrimony domesticated Moran. He moved with Rebecca to Hollywood, where, according to the Los Angeles Times, his "clear blue eyes and fighter's face" landed him a job as a film actor. There were no more high jinks and no more bright lights. The Moran's had two children, both girls. "The thing I'm most proud of," he told a reporter when he was 59, "is the fact that I've recently become a grandfather for the second time."

Between 1928 and 1949, Moran was in thirty-three pictures. "He'd be the guy who played the cab driver," said an acquaintance from those days, the fight trainer Nate Liff. More often, he'd be a cop or a longshoreman or a boxer or a villain of some kind.   As the heavy, he'd lose a violent, prolonged fist fight with the leading man. He could make phantom punches look like the real thing, whether called upon to give or receive them. Taking a make-believe whack on the chin from 6-foot-2 Victor McLaglen, himself a former boxer who had been in the ring with Jack Johnson, or from 5-foot-5 Alan Ladd, Moran always hit the deck convincingly.

The pay was good in Hollywood -- one hundred dollars a day and up. On the side, Moran worked for the California Athletic Commission as chief inspector. "Unlike many fighters, Frank Moran never got punchy," reads a 1946 press release from RKO Studios. Moran's face, it is true, bore the scars of his old profession, and there was this: "Occasionally he accentuates a raspy-voiced remark with a short right jab" -- all that was left, perhaps, of Mary Ann.

At such times, the press release said, Moran would lapse into "the picturesque lingo of the ring." Maybe so. Finis Farr, in "Black Champion," puts stress on Moran's use of double negatives. Normally, though, the cosmopolitan ex-pug was well-spoken, and he thirsted for education as long as he lived. "Frank is a familiar figure at the Hollywood Public Library," the press release states. "He doesn't care for fiction, but goes in for history, even reveling in Plato, Aristotle and similar works." To show his cultural versatility, Moran reveled also in classical music and opera, subjects on which the RKO publicist had no hesitation in pronouncing him an authority.

Moran kept in touch with Theodore Roosevelt, and also with Mrs. Roosevelt after the irrepressible old Rough Rider's death. His friendship with the Roosevelts, the 1946 press release says, was "material for a story which is still told in ring circles." Exactly what that story may have been, the writer leaves us to speculate. Although the press release goes on for another page and a half, there is no further mention of it.

Frank Moran died at 80 -- "one of Hollywood's most substantial and respected citizens." He was "vastly different," RKO wanted the public to know, "from the popular conception of what a prizefighter of the old school would be like." Or from any other stereotype, it is easy to believe. As the guys who hung out at the Hollywood Public Library in the 1940s would say, he was *sui generis.*

CHAPTER 4

THE PITTSBURGH WINDMILL

1

Once upon a time in Pittsburgh every neighborhood saloon with a sports-minded clientele had a picture of Harry Greb on the wall, an unchanging presence behind the bar. The one in Frankie Gustine's restaurant on Forbes Avenue in Oakland, a blown-up, hand-painted photograph, belonged to Art Rooney. There was something oddly haunting about it. Almost absent-mindedly, Greb had assumed a fighter's stance, but with no hint of combat-readiness in his attitude. The lowered head, the preoccupied gaze were suggestive, rather, of peaceful contemplation. He appeared to be thinking sad, profound thoughts.

In life, Greb was hardly the meditative type. Middleweight champion from 1923 to 1926, the year of his death, he fought with unbridled fury, using every trick known to the trade, legal or illegal. Outside the ring, his reputation was that of a ladies' man, a roughneck, a dude.

Even for a middleweight he was short, barely 5 feet 8, with corded and powerful bandy legs. His eyes were dark and brooding; his nose had lost its shape and structure; his complexion was chalk-white. In the fashion of the 1920s he parted his dark hair near the middle and plastered it down with Pomade. His vanity seems to have been enormous. He carried with him on most occasions a pocket mirror, a comb, and -- "Marvel at it," Gene Tunney once said -- a powder puff.

The only fight Tunney ever lost was to Greb. Boxing historians wrote about it for years. "The bell rang," John Lardner's account reads, "and it suddenly became clear to the sellout crowd of 13,000 in Madison Square Garden" -- the New York landmark built by Stanford White -- "that Tunney was in the ring with an uprising of nature."

Greb never gave him a chance. In their first exchange he broke Tunney's nose in two places. "Blood began to pour from it like wine from a bottle." As the rounds went by, Tunney bled from his mouth and from cuts over both eyes, and he swallowed so much blood that he choked on it. Greb, unrelenting, fought as he always did, punching incessantly. For Tunney -- five inches taller and twelve pounds heavier than Greb -- "it was like trying to wait out a cloudburst," a cloudburst that never abated. In the last round, the fifteenth, Greb was stronger and faster than in the first. "He pummeled me from pillar to post," Tunney acknowledged.

The fight took place on May 23, 1922. Since August 29th of the previous year, Greb had been boxing with a probable detached retina, sustained by a thrust to his right eye from the busy left hand of Kid Norfolk. That is the accepted doctrine. Certainly, an injury of some kind occurred. But the gouging that finished what Norfolk had started may have been the work of a heavyweight who called himself Captain Bob Roper and sometimes entered the ring with a pet snake coiled around his neck.. He boxed Greb in Buffalo on November 10, 1922 and in Pittsburgh on New Year's Day 1923; both times, with the fight irretrievably lost,, Roper stopped trying to hit Greb and attacked with the laces of his gloves.

Afterward, during a week-long stay in Pittsburgh's West Penn Hospital, Greb wore patches over both eyes. Those who exonerate Roper attribute Greb's trouble at the time to an infection. So much of what we know, or think we know, about Greb is open to debate..

In any case, he boxed for a stretch of several years with no sight at all in the right eye. To fail a pre-fight medical examination in the 1920s, Greb might have needed a seeing-eye dog and a white cane.

Gouging in Greb's day was far from unusual. Greb himself was believed to have made a specialty of it. There's a story, in fact, that he intended to give Norfolk the treatment. "I hear this boy has one bad eye," he supposedly said to a friend, Hap Albacker, before the fight. "Maybe I'll work the other one over." What he supposedly said after the fight, also to Hap Albacker, was simply, "It looks like he beat me to it."

These second-hand quotes are to be found in a biography of Greb called "Give Him to the Angels" by James R. Fair, a Western Union telegraph operator who may have worked at ringside in some of Greb's fights. A discussion of Fair and his book's consequences will appear in this narrative later on. For now, it's enough to say that the fight game's fact checkers believe very little of what Fair ever wrote about Greb. They do not put much credence, as far as that is concerned, in what a great many others wrote or said about Greb. Sometimes it seems as if the truths about Greb are outnumbered by the half-truths, quasi-truths, and untruths.

One thing we can be certain of is that Greb would get into the ring with a good black fighter like Norfolk at a time when the best white fighters gave black fighters a wide berth. Greb feared nobody, least of all opponents who outweighed him -- Norfolk, Tunney, Billy Miske, Battling Levinsky, and Bill Brennan, to mention a few at the top of the list.

Norfolk, a broad-shouldered light-heavyweight no taller than Greb was, boxed at a time when black fighters got matches with white fighters by accepting limitations on how well they performed. The reports on how Norfolk performed against Greb are inconclusive.

He knocked Greb down in the third round. Jimmy Fair writes that Greb jumped right up and proceeded to hand Norfolk "the pasting of his life." Newspaper accounts describe a close fight, with Greb outlasting Norfolk in a down-to-the-wire finish. Regis Welsh, the Pittsburgh Post reporter, had Greb winning six of the ten rounds, and Yock Henninger, the referee, told someone afterward that his vote would have gone to Greb had it not been a no-decision fight.

Conversely, Jim Jab of the Pittsburgh Press implied that Norfolk took it easy with Greb after flooring him. Jim Jab's prose seems archaic now, but his meaning is clear. "The Kid contented himself with scant mauling," he wrote. "Greb clung to him. The Kid rarely if ever tried to set himself free and fight. Significant? You said it." Continuing, Jim Jab is reticent about picking a winner, which was not his style. "It's a tough job," he hedges. "If you count the little earnest fighting, the honors should go to the black boxer."

In the crowd at Forbes Field that night was a pretty good amateur boxer who in time would become the owner of Pittsburgh's team in the National Football League. Years later I asked Art Rooney if Jim Jab might have been on to something. "I hate to say it," Rooney answered, "but yes, I think he was."

Greb had 299 recorded fights, and he lost very few. It is difficult to put a number on either his defeats or his victories because so many of his fights were no-decision affairs Certainly Greb wasn't easy to knock off his feet. He was down for the count of ten only once -- in 1913, his first year in the ring.

At this stage of Greb's career, his manager, Red Mason, was careful not to overmatch him. Miscalculating for once, he accepted Joe Chip as an opponent. Chip could hit hard and he was more experienced than Greb He weighed 156 pounds; the 19-year-old Greb weighed 142. They met at the old

City Hall in Market Square, and Chip flattened Greb in the second round with a looping right hand. "I felt the effects of the punch for days afterward," Greb told the sportswriter Harry Keck.

Six years later, in Youngstown, Ohio, Greb and Joe Chip boxed a second time and Greb won handily, taking eleven of the twelve rounds and completing his mastery of the Chip brothers. He had beaten George, the older of the pair, three times after losing the first of their four fights. Greb beat thirteen world champions all told, starting with George Chip.

A punch thrown by Greb himself resulted in his only technical-knockout defeat. He was fighting Kid Graves, a claimant to the vacant welterweight championship, at the Penn Power House in December of 1915. A minute or two into the second round, Greb hit Graves on the head and felt something snap in his left forearm. He had broken the radial bone. When the bell rang for the third round, Greb remained in his corner, unable to continue. His arm healed imperfectly, leaving it somewhat crooked, and this deformity, Greb always said, gave his left jab the percussive effect of a hook, which was all to the good.

An opponent who knocked Greb off his feet more than once was Soldier Jones, a heavyweight from Canada who chose not to use his baptismal name -- Horace Beaudin.. Jones knew the secret of getting the jump on Greb. In the second of their three fights, he knocked Greb down in the first round. In their third fight, he knocked Greb down twice in the first round and had him in serious trouble. But Greb would bounce back up like a rubber ball or get to his feet slowly and, in the words of one spectator, "hit Jones a thousand times."

Greb hit them all a thousand times. He won two of his fights with Jones by knockouts and the third on a newspaper decision.

Rarely was he satisfied to beat a qualified opponent only once. He fought them again and again -- Fay Keiser nine times, Whitey Wenzel eight times, Chuck Wiggins seven times, Clay Turner seven times, other solid workmen six times, five times, four times.

His 1924 return match with Norfolk, held in Boston, was for blood. As one of the Boston sportswriters put it, both fighters wrestled, held and hit, hit low, butted, and used the laces of their gloves. At the end of the sixth round, Norfolk hit Greb after the bell, and Greb flew at him. He was punching non-stop when "a riot broke out." The referee, forced to take action, disqualified

Greb. Up to the time of the premature ending, Greb had been giving a little better than he got.

As vicious as Greb could be, never until that night had he lost on a foul. Never afterward would he lose on a foul. Perhaps in Greb's day anything went. Like the maladroit Mike Tyson, Greb used his teeth one night. Or did he? According to Jimmy Fair, he "bit a hunk" out of Chuck Wiggins's nose during their fight in Grand Rapids, Michigan, on November 15, 1923. Unlike Tyson, he got away with it -- if we can assume that Fair, who seemed bent on mythologizing Greb, was being factual. The Grand Rapids Herald's reporter merely noted that Greb's punches blackened one of Wiggins's eyes. No mention of any carnivorous activity.

"Boxing ain't a noble art," Fair quotes Greb as saying, "and I ain't its noblest artist." Curiously, his opponents seemed to understand that if Greb ignored the rules he meant nothing personal by it. Here is Gene Tunney in praise of Greb's "sportsmanship" [sic]: "Anything he did to you -- and he did all he could to dismember you -- you could do back to him and he wouldn't complain."

Which apparently made it all right. Greb was just a guy who liked to fight, and he fought them all -- the best in four divisions, from welterweight on up to heavyweight -- often, if need be, on short notice. He was simply too fast for the heavyweights he boxed. He won his three fights with Bob Roper by clear margins, He won his four fights with Bill Brennan, who was leading Jack Dempsey on points when Dempsey knocked him out in the twelfth round. He won his two fights with Willie Meehan, the California fat boy who took a four-round decision from Dempsey. He won two of his three fights with the underrated Billy Miske (their first fight was a draw). He won a newspaper decision from Gunboat Smith, who had beaten Sam Langford, Jess Willard, and Frank Moran, and knocked him out in two minutes with a whirlwind attack when Smith was at the end of the trail. "Greb would take those fellas and annihilate them," the old-time manager Bunny Buntag recalled.

Four different times in 1920 Greb sparred a few rounds with Dempsey himself and embarrassed the great champion in his own training camp. On two of these occasions, Greb swarmed all over Dempsey, "landing punches from all angles," as one of the newspaper accounts had it. Many times, Greb offered to fight Dempsey for real. The final answer, a succinct one, came from Dempsey's manager, Doc Kearns. He said, "The hell with that seven-year itch."

2

Born on June 6, 1894, Greb was from Garfield, a neighborhood contiguous with Bloomfield and Lawrenceville. Within walking distance of all three is East Liberty. It may be that in the first few decades of the twentieth century there were more fighters to the square foot in those four neighborhoods than anywhere else on Earth.

Greb's first teacher, if he can be said to have had a teacher, was not Red Mason. Possibly it was someone at the Garfield Boys' Club. Actually, neither Mason nor anyone else could have taught Greb his style, which was no style at all. No one who ever lived could have taught Greb to fight the way he did. "He was just a slapper, he just kept punching, punching, punching all the time, and he hit you with everything he threw," Bunny Buntag told me. That is the standard description of Greb: he just kept punching; he never let up.

If all Greb did was slap, it explains the relative paucity of knockouts on his resume, but perhaps he could do more than slap. "He'd beat the hell out of guys," said Jack Henry, who carried Greb's water bucket at the age of nine and went on to become a fight manager, sportswriter, and sportscaster. "When they'd start to fall," Henry recalled, "he'd grab them and hold them up." Beating the hell out of guys was fun, and Greb never wanted it to end. Besides, he could fight all night. He was tireless, a perpetual-motion machine, often leaving his feet to land punches. In the 1920s every fighter had to have a nickname, and some anonymous sportswriter crafted one for Greb -- the Pittsburgh Windmill.

Greb's father, Pius Greb, disapproved of boxing. He wanted his son to be a stonemason like himself, or, failing that, a baseball player. Greb had no aptitude for either calling. Pius Greb was an immigrant from Germany. His American-born wife, Anna Wilbert -- Greb's mother -- was of German origin too. The story that she was Irish is one of the many unquenchable fictions about Greb. To this day there are those who believe that he was Jewish, that his real name was Berg, and that he took it upon himself to reverse the spelling. The only name he ever changed was the double-barreled one he received at baptism, Edward Henry. For pugilistic purposes, he borrowed the first name of a younger brother who had died at the age of nine months.

When he was 14, Greb ran away from home and moved in with friends. There was always discord, for some reason, between Greb and his father. He returned to the house in Garfield after two years, stopped going to school, and took a job as an electrician's apprentice in the East Pittsburgh Westinghouse plant, earning twelve dollars a week. Before he was 19, he cut the ties with his family one last time and started boxing.

He won all five of his amateur fights. Success as a pro did not come instantly. On the night in 1913 that George Chip knocked out Frank Klaus to win the middleweight championship, Greb was on the undercard, and Jim Jab gave him his first favorable notice in the Pittsburgh Press. "Sent in to be slaughtered by the veteran Hooks Evans," Jim Jab wrote, the novice refused to cooperate. "Tiring under Greb's assaults, Evans deserved at best a draw."

This was Greb's fourth fight with Red Mason in his corner. He fought just as often as he could, mostly in Pittsburgh and nearby small towns. One of the myths about Greb is that he disliked to train. Greb trained when he felt the need. Normally, he boxed often enough to use each fight as preparation for the next. On successive nights in 1915 he knocked out George Hauser and won a newspaper decision from Fay Keiser. He had six fights in twenty-three days in November of 1916 and six fights in nineteen days in September of 1917.

Not even Greb's marriage on January 30, 1919, after a brief stint in the Navy toward the end of World War I, was allowed to interfere with his activity in the ring. Right up to the exchange of vows with 18-year-old Mildred Reilly, a good-looking brunette who had danced in the chorus at the Academy Theater, a downtown burlesque house, and later worked as a telephone operator, there was no slacking off. Greb boxed Leo Houck in Boston on January 14th, Young Fisher in Syracuse on January 20th, and Paul Sampson at the South Side Market House on January 23rd, winning all three fights. In "The Fearless Harry Greb: Biography of a Tragic Hero of Boxing," William B. Paxton writes that the original date of the wedding was January 27th. Greb postponed it to take a fight on the 27th with Soldier Bartfield in Columbus, Ohio. It was their fifth meeting in a little over a year. As usual, Greb won.

According to Paxton, Greb did some roadwork on the morning of the 30th and was half an hour late for the Catholic wedding ceremony at the Epiphany Church in the Lower Hill, directly across the street from the Pittsburgh

Lyceum, where he sometimes trained. Waiting at the altar was Mildred Reilly; waiting in and outside the church were one thousand others.

Afterward, for relatives and friends, there was a wedding breakfast, "with entertainment," at the Fort Pitt Hotel. It lasted four hours. Greb and his bride then took a train to Cleveland, where they spent the night and where Greb was boxing again on the following night, January 31st. At the Cleveland Athletic Association's auditorium, he won a ten-round decision from Tommy Robson. Returning to Pittsburgh, the honeymooners moved into a new house in the East End. Two days later, on February 3rd, Greb dispatched Len Rowlands at the South Side Market House in three rounds.

Nineteen nineteen was Greb's busiest year. He had forty-five fights and won almost all of them. For some time, his opponents had included top-notchers -- Mike and Tom Gibbons, Jeff Smith, George Chip, Eddie McGoorty, Mike McTigue, Bill Brennan, Battling Levinsky, Billy Miske. Greb beat two reigning middleweight champions, Al McCoy -- twice -- and Mike O'Dowd, but neglected to knock them out. Therefore, under the no-decision rule, the loser in each case hung onto his title. McCoy, derided in the newspapers as a "cheese champ," took full advantage of the no-decision rule to remain a cheese champ for three and a half years. Then O'Dowd knocked him out and defended the title sporadically until he lost it to a challenger he underestimated, Johnny Wilson, in 1920. :

By this time, Greb had no superiors in the middleweight division, but Jim Jab, never his most ardent supporter -- the belief is that there was animosity of some kind between them, mostly on the sportswriter's part -- was able to keep from overpraising him. His account of a fight at Forbes Field between Greb and Mike Gibbons on June 23, 1919, went like this:

"The fans howled with joy during Harry's spells of pernicious activity" -- the phrase is vintage Jim Jab -- "but they didn't appreciate the fact that he was out of control, off balance, and therefore handicapped in his timing." Gibbons, on the other hand, "gave a masterly display of the art that was pleasing to the eye and mind. Ick," continued Jim Jab, meaning Greb -- the origin of the moniker is unknown, but it somehow lacks the resonance of Pittsburgh Windmill -- "has a dandy gag of sticking a long left in a foe's face, covering his eyes with the mitt, and then measuring the victim with a slashing right." Gibbons would duck the right, Jim Jab wrote, and frustrate

Greb with his "swift and shifty tactics, superb coolness and eel-like maneuvering." Jim Jab's vote went to Gibbons.

Other reporters covering the fight -- a majority -- thought that Greb was an easy winner. Often it seemed as if no two people watching Greb fight ever saw the same thing. Paul Sullivan, in later life a sportswriter, lawyer, and Western Pennsylvania boxing commissioner, was in the crowd as a boy of 15. "Greb was throwing punches from left field, first base, and everywhere else," he remembered. "But Mike Gibbons was a hell of a good boxer and he wasn't going to get hit with any of that stuff." A minority vote, perhaps, for Gibbons and Jim Jab.

Two years before, in Philadelphia, Greb had not been ready for a fighter as accomplished as Gibbons and lost to him unmistakably; So, this was progress. Mike and Tom Gibbons were brothers from St. Paul. Tom, the younger and larger of the two, a full-grown light-heavyweight, also had beaten an immature version of Greb That fight was in St; Paul. They met again at Forbes Field in May of 1920, and on Jim Jab's scorecard Gibbons won every round. There were few dissenters. It was Greb's worst showing as a main-event fighter and probably, for Gibbons, his best.. By an astonishing margin, Gibbons outboxed and outfought Greb.

Preparing for a rematch, Greb polished off three opponents of no great distinction and sparred for the first time with Jack Dempsey at the heavyweight champion/s training quarters in the middle of New York City. Back in Forbes Field on the last day of July, Greb was more of a handful for Gibbons. True to form, Jim Jab gave the fight to Gibbons, but only by a shade. Another sportswriter called it a draw. The remaining four thought Greb won decisively, and so did Paul Sullivan. "But I know this," he appended. "Gibbons at no time was in danger of death."

He came a bit closer to that perilous situation in his next fight with Greb -- on March 13, 1922, in Madison Square Garden. Dating from his first encounter with Norfolk six months earlier, Greb had been having an eye problem. If it bothered him unduly, there was no way to tell, for he had not lost a fight in the meantime -- had not lost a fight since the first of his two with Tom Gibbons in Pittsburgh. Under a new manager, George Engel, he was fighting less frequently but going farther afield. Engel took him to Dallas, to New Orleans, to Montreal, to Toronto. For the first time, he boxed in Madison Square Garden for promoter Tex Rickard, winning a fifteen-round decision from one of the mid-level heavyweights, Charley Weinert.

Engel, like Red Mason, was a Pittsburgh guy -- he had managed middleweight champion Frank Klaus -- but with better connections in New York, where the money was. A fight there with Gibbons in the Garden would be an opportunity for Greb to show his true worth to the New York media. Gibbons, renowned for his skill as a boxer, had knocked out all but two of his twenty-two most recent opponents, indication enough that he could punch. One year later, out in Shelby, Montana, where an oil strike had created a boom town, he'd get a shot at the heavyweight title. In a fight that left the over-optimistic promoters deep in debt, put four banks out of business, and ended up with every cent of the gate receipts, about $280,000, going to Dempsey and his manager, Gibbons lasted fifteen rounds with the champion, which nobody else ever had done, and came close for a while to holding his own. Against Greb in New York he was overwhelmed.

Gibbons had told a friend of his, a Catholic priest from Pittsburgh named Griffin, "I'll let him go ten rounds and knock him out in the last five." The next time they met, Griffin asked, "What went wrong, Tom?" "Father," Gibbons answered, "I was going to start in the eleventh round, just like I said, but that was when *he* started." Summarizing his first official defeat in forty fights since the last time he had lost, Gibbons said to a sportswriter, "His punches seemed to come from everywhere -- from the gallery, from under my shoes, from behind my back."

Even Jim Jab, upholder of the proprieties in boxing, finally gave the devil his due -- in a lefthanded way, to be sure. "Gibbons never saw so many mitts," he declared. "Monkey mauling, you may style it if you will, but don't overlook the fact that it's a winner. Greb," Jim Jab concluded, "is the world's greatest freak fighter."

Back in Pittsburgh, he was much more than that. Overnight, it seemed, Greb had become a civic treasure. Like the Super Bowl-winning Steelers and Stanley Cup-winning Penguins of a much later period, he returned to a royal welcome. Paxton, in his book, restructures the scene:

At Union Station, when the train pulled in, a brass band was playing. Thousands of Greb's fellow citizens had gathered there on a weekday morning to whistle and cheer and toss their hats into the air. Thousands more lined the streets of Downtown to watch a mile-long victory parade. Riding with Greb were his wife and their two-year-old daughter. When they arrived at the City-County Building, admirers hoisted Greb onto their shoulders and carried him upstairs to the mayor's office. He gave a speech and then he moved on to the Gayety Theater for the launching of a two-month vaudeville tour.

In the Pittsburgh of the 1920s -- in the America of the 1920s -- prizefighters were more revered than football or hockey players. Never up to then in the city of Greb's birth had there been a reception like it for a sports figure.

3

Over a period of ten months, starting with the Gibbons fight, Greb won decisively from the three best light-heavyweights in the business -- Gibbons, Gene Tunney, and Tommy Loughran.

There were five fights all told between Tunney and Greb. Going into that first one, Tunney had sore hands, he later said. Whether or not this was so hardly matters. He was too busy defending himself to do any punching to speak of. While they were waiting for the decision to be announced, Tunney walked over to Greb's corner and said, "Congratulations, Harry. You were the better man -- tonight."

Irrationally, it seemed, Tunney was now convinced that he could beat Greb. A highly cerebral fighter, he had noticed certain telltale moves by the Pittsburgher -- the dropping of a shoulder, the shifting of a foot -- that preceded certain follow-up moves. "The next time I meet him I'll turn the tables with a vengeance," he said with great assurance to the boxing adjudicator Nat Fleischer. "I was puzzled by his erratic rushes and his mauling style and made the mistake of standing off and trying to box him. You can't box a buzzsaw. The only way to stop a buzzsaw is to throw a hunk of iron into it. That's what I'll do if I fight him again." Explaining this, he sounded like the British general Edward Braddock, who declared as he was dying of the wounds he received when a French and Indian army ambushed his troops on the banks of the Monongahela River, "We shall know better how to deal with them the next time."

It was hard to believe, and still is, that Tunney was not deluding himself. From everything we hear and read about Greb -- no usable film that shows him in the ring seems to exist -- his moves were not the predictable kind. He made them up as he went along. And yet by the fifth and last episode in their series, Tunney's hunks of iron had put the buzzsaw out of commission.

In 1976 the collector Jimmy Jacobs turned up a 35-millimeter nitrate film of that first Greb-Tunney fight, the equivalent, he told me, of coming across an undiscovered Rembrandt. Disappointingly, the nitrate was so shrunken that to put it through a projector would have destroyed it. "As soon as I can," Jacobs promised, "I will spend the enormous amount of money it would take to have a 35-millimeter optical negative made." He never did, or perhaps the attempt was a failure.

In pummeling Tunney from pillar to post, Greb won a meaningless championship, the American light-heavyweight title, concocted in 1920 by Tex Rickard after Georges Carpentier, a Frenchman, knocked out the faded world champion, Battling Levinsky, in a fight Rickard promoted at Boyle's Thirty Acres on the fringes of Jersey City. As risk-averse as McCoy and O'Dowd, Levinsky had lost five no-decision fights with Greb, most of them one-sided. Now that he was left without a title to protect, Rickard matched him with Tunney, proclaiming them to be the best of the American light-heavyweights, and Tunney won all twelve rounds.

One of Greb's first fights as the new titleholder was a no-decision eight-rounder with 19-year-old Tommy Loughran, a future world light-heavyweight champion, in Loughran's hometown, Philadelphia. Jimmy Fair describes Loughran as "religious, handsome, ambitious, courageous, the epitome of clean living, and one of the most polished boxers of all time. He couldn't knock your hat off," Fair then asserts, "but he was so defensively clever that you couldn't knock his hat off, either, unless your name was Greb." At least this time, Loughran's hat, if boxers wore hats, would have remained on his head. The New York Times gave the fight to Greb, whose speed, its writer said, was "bewildering" to Loughran, but the Philadelphia papers disagreed, and Greb himself reluctantly explained,, "I was caught off-guard."

They boxed a no-decision ten-rounder six months later in Pittsburgh for which Greb declared he'd be ready. Alerting Jim Jab, he said, "I'm rarin' to go. Just watch me." Jim Jab watched Loughran as well, perceiving "a nice left and fair right, prettily timed," but Greb had the better of the infighting and Jim Jab pronounced him the winner. He "speared, smeared, mauled and mussed" Loughran, a harbinger of things to come. Just two weeks after this fight, they were at it again in Madison Square Garden with the American light-heavyweight title at stake, and Greb won ten of the fifteen rounds in his best, or worst, roughhouse fashion.

Even Loughran, who considered himself invincible, dismissing any evidence to the contrary, knew he had been outgunned. Loughran didn't think much of Greb, or, for that matter, of Tunney. The reason he lost his only fight with Tunney, Loughran told me years later, when he was living in an Old Soldiers and Sailors Home in Hollidaysburg, Pennsylvania, was that he had taken him too lightly. "See, I was sort of contemptuous of Tunney," Loughran said. "I thought, gee, if he lost to Harry Greb . . . "

Loughran had just had his first fight with Greb, "and I beat him easily, yes," he said, "I beat him all the way." In his own mind, Loughran won five of their six fights. "I'd take the play away from him," he said. "I'd walk right into him, which nobody else ever did." That may well be. The record book, nonetheless, shows two wins for Greb, one for Loughran, two no-decisions, and one draw. The fight Loughran won was on an inexplicable off night for Greb in Boston. Greb had the edge in the two no-decisions, including the one in which he was caught off-guard, as he put it, and newspaper accounts of the draw make it clear that Greb's "butting tactics" cost him two rounds he otherwise would have won.

A month after beating Loughran in New York, Greb again beat Tunney, also in New York, but Tunney got the decision, a split one. To fair-minded observers, it seemed obvious that Greb had won. Afterward, he told reporters, "I was deliberately jobbed." And that was the way it looked. Rumors that the fix was in, that Tunney couldn't lose, had been rampant. Referee Patsy Haley cast the deciding vote against Greb after berating him from the first round to the last for holding and hitting. Jim Jab (who gave the fight to Greb) called Tunney "an improved mixer," but Tunney himself confessed, "No one was more surprised than I was when Joe Humphreys [the ring announcer] lifted my hand in token of victory." (Only Tunney would have added those last four words.)

Along with the decision, Greb lost the American light-heavyweight title. Six months later in the Polo Grounds, where the New York Giants played baseball, he won the far more significant world middleweight championship. Johnny Wilson, after outpointing O'Dowd in a return bout, had carefully avoided fights to a decision in the accepted fashion of the day. Neither

Wilson nor his manager, Marty Killelea, wanted anything to do with Greb. According to Jimmy Fair and others, Greb put their fears to rest by allowing himself to be seen in various New York bars with a whiskey glass always in his hand. Fair writes that the glass contained "colored water," whatever colored water may be. Naively, Wilson took the bait. How could he lose his title to a rummy? He agreed to fight Greb.

The real story, a rather more prosaic one, can be found in S. L. Compton's "Live Hard, Die Young, the Life and Times of Harry Greb," published in 2013 after eleven years of comprehensive research, Compton writes that the New York State Athletic Commission pressured Wilson and his new manager, a mob guy called Frank Marlowe, into giving Greb the chance he had earned. A southpaw with the instincts of an octopus, Wilson (born Giuseppi Panica) was not an easy man to fight, but Greb did a number on him for fifteen rounds ..

Although he took some time off before coming home, another brass band was at the station to greet him and officialdom had arranged another parade. In one way, however, it wasn't the same. Four months earlier, at the age of 22, Mildred Reilly Greb had died of tuberculosis.

Greb's nagging reputation as a Jazz Age carouser must now be addressed. By the testimony of those who were closest to him, he'd been a devoted and faithful husband. He admitted that for a time after the death of his wife there'd been "wild parties." Later, as a man about town in the Prohibition-era, he patronized a few speakeasies and got involved in a couple of essentially harmless early-morning scrapes that got into the papers. He kept late hours but drank very little, if at all.

Jimmy Fair, in "Give Him to the Angels," enthusiastically puts stress on the fighter's "sexual exploits." Even Fair, though, concedes that Greb did not "run around" during his marriage. For Greb's sister, Ida Edwards, it was not enough to balance the scales. After Fair's book appeared in 1946, she,threatened the publisher with legal action, and he promptly removed all the unsold copies from the market.

To say that "Give Him to the Angels" was not well received would be no exaggeration. Even the author's prose style took a hit. George Bernard Shaw, in a letter to his pal Gene Tunney, describes the book as "barbarously written." Yet until Paxton's book came out in 2009, Fair's was the only biography of Greb, and it therefore defined him. I first picked up this very thin volume with the yellow cover in the sports library at the Pittsburgh Press. On the flyleaf someone with an impressive vocabulary had written the word "Meretricious." And meretricious it was, but no matter. Its readers over the years included columnists and magazine writers interested in Greb, and so 'Give Him to the Angels" has gone a long way toward shaping his image.

Paxton, attempting to set the record straight, offers a pertinent quote from Harry Keck, the sportswriter closest to Greb. Keck told someone that if he ever got around to writing "the real Greb story" he wouldn't know what to do with it, because publishers, he had found, "preferred the myth."

4

After his first fight with Tunney, Greb's manager, once again, was Red Mason. Greb had replaced him with the more enterprising Engel in order to get bigger purses. He now fired Engel, in part, it is thought, because Engel had promised him a heavyweight title fight with Dempsey and failed to deliver.

Under the new Pennsylvania law permitting fights to a decision, Greb defended his middleweight title in Pittsburgh against Brian Downey, who had lost to Johnny Wilson while Wilson was champion on a foul seen by no one except the referee. Wilson was on the canvas, apparently unable to get up. So, the referee stopped counting and announced that Wilson had been hit while he was down. The referee then disqualified Downey. Greb won from Downey without any help. As Jim Jab was forced to acknowledge, "Downey took a beating he will not soon forget."

Next, in a bid to regain the American light-heavyweight title, Greb lost to Tunney again in Madison Square Garden. This time, although the pro-Tunney crowd turned against him and booed the decision,, the fight was so close it could have gone either way.. Jim Jab, in one of his last digs at Greb, noted that Tunney -- who in his estimation had won -- "still lacks a lot" and "couldn't be labeled a first-class fighter."

Greb had two weeks to prepare for still another meeting with Tommy Loughran. The fight was on Christmas day 1923 at Motor Square Garden in Pittsburgh's East Liberty section,, and Greb out finished Loughran, leaving him helpless at the final bell There was never any question as to whose hand would be raised. Back in Madison Square Garden for a rematch with Wilson,

Greb waited until the sixth round to assert himself and then controlled the last ten to win as he pleased..
. There was no rest for Greb over the next six months. He defended his title against an old Pittsburgh rival, Fay Keiser, in Baltimore, where Keiser was now a fan favorite. Their meeting was the ninth and last between them, and Greb battered Keiser into a twelfth-round TKO. After the untidy brawl with Norfolk in

Boston, he boxed the Englishman Ted Moore in the main event of an all-star production in Yankee Stadium for New York City's milk fund, with Gene Tunney and Tommy Loughran on the undercard. Greb beat Moore and would have taken him out if the fight had gone twelve rounds instead of ten. Tunney dispatched an Italian import, Ermino Spalla, in the eighth round, but Loughran lost the decision to a fast-rising heavyweight from Macon, Georgia, Young Stribling.

Greb boxed here, there, and everywhere. In Fremont, Ohio, a small town engulfed by neighboring big towns -- Cleveland, Toledo, Detroit -- he needed all of his skills to win a far from unanimous newspaper decision over Tiger Flowers, a black fighter from the South with just a regional reputation. Up in Buffalo, an exciting young stylist named Jimmy Slattery, like Loughran a future light-heavyweight champion, was ready for the big time. His admirers wondered how he would do against Greb. They were boxing six rounds, the maximum distance in New York state for fighters of Slattery's age, which was 20. Slattery put up a good fight but Greb won.

There remained little to choose between Greb and Tunney. Their fourth fight, ten months after the third fight, was in Cleveland on September 17, 1924. Between Pittsburgh and Cleveland lies Mingo Junction, Ohio, so Greb made a stopover there on September 15th and knocked out an overmatched Billy Hirsch in the eighth round. The Tunney fight was a no-decision affair, Cleveland having not yet taken the fetters off boxing, and Greb thought for sure he had won. Many sportswriters at ringside agreed. Among those who did not was Regis Welsh (a friend of Greb). The Pittsburgh Post ran Welsh's story with a picture of Tunney captioned "Too Much for Our Boy," and Greb never spoke to Regis again.

Our Boy was at last showing signs of erosion. By now Greb had reached the age of 30, with zero vision in one eye and increasing fogginess in the other. He was slipping, sportswriters said. And getting down to the middleweight limit of 160 pounds had become a bothersome chore. After the draw with Loughran ended their six-fight series where it had started, back in Philly, he continued to fight often and win, but not against elite competition.

On March 27, 1925, in St. Paul, the Greb-Tunney cycle came to a conclusion, and none too soon for Greb. Tunney won without question. He alleged in his memoirs that Greb whispered to him near the end of their ten-rounder, "Gene, don't knock me out." Tunney wrote this after Greb had died, and Greb's partisans refused to believe it. Such a request, they contended, would have been out of character for him. They were right. But it was equally out of character for Greb to announce, as he did before leaving St. Paul, "It's time for somebody else to fight that guy. He's getting too big and strong and he hits too hard. He'll whip Dempsey."

A year and a half later, when his chance came, Tunney did beat Dempsey. "Pick Tunney," Greb had been advising sportswriters he liked. Only Harry Keck, sports editor, then, of the Pittsburgh Gazette Times, acted on the tip. When Tunney unexpectedly won, it transformed Keck into an oracle. Greb, meanwhile, had changed his mind before the fight, telling an Associated Press sportswriter in Atlantic City that he now thought Dempsey would win.

Barely three months after his loss to Tunney in St. Paul, having dusted off Johnny Wilson a third time and half a dozen lesser lights for the first or second time, Greb found the resources for one last superlative effort. He defended his middleweight title against the swashbuckling welterweight champion, Mickey Walker. On the same card at the Polo Grounds were two other bouts so attractive that James P. Dawson, in the New York Times, pronounced it "the greatest fistic carnival ever seen in a local ring." Boy wonder Slattery was to box the veteran Dave Shade, after which Harry Wills, denied a title match with Dempsey because of a Jim Crow policy adhered to by promoters, managers, and boxing commissions, would be on display against Charley Weinert, one of the heavyweights Greb had defeated.

As Jimmy Fair tells it, Greb saved the show. It's a fanciful tale. Slattery, who'd been knocked out by Shade in the third round, came for solace to Greb's dressing room and was crying on his shoulder when Humbert Fugazy, the promoter, broke in on them, bringing news of a calamitous sit-down strike. It seems that Wills, at the last minute, had decided he should be in the main event. Otherwise, he would not go on. Fugazy, distraught, was asking Greb, "What can we do?"

Greb's answer came instantly, writes Fair. He raced to Wills' dressing room and confronted him, shouting, "Listen, you big tramp" -- Wills was 6 feet 3 and weighed 220 pounds -- "I'll fight you right now to settle this thing." Fugazy, who had followed Greb, pinioned his arms. Just then an emissary from the New York boxing commission arrived on the scene and read Wills the contract he had signed. It said unmistakably that he was to box in the semi-final. Wills stopped arguing and marched down the aisle to the ring.

There's some truth in that, but also a lot of embroidery. The facts are in S.; L. Compton's book. "During last-minute [contract] negotiations," Fugazy actually did agree to put Wills on top. Greb, responding angrily, said to Fugazy, "Toss Weinert off the bill and I'll fight Wills myself. Or I'll fight him in the gym to prove he doesn't belong ahead of two world champions." Fugazy gave in. So did Wills -- eventually and reluctantly.

Anyway, after Wills knocked out Weinert in two rounds, Greb and Walker took the stage. And the crowd of 65,000 saw two great fighters in top form. The early rounds seem to have been close. After the fifth, Greb was his old, fast, bruising self. He hounded and pounded Walker, closing his right eye. He snarled at the referee, Eddie Purdy, for pulling him away from Walker after they clinched. Twice Greb managed to trip Purdy and make it look accidental. Of the ten rounds after the fifth, Walker could win only one or two. The decision was hard-earned but undeniably Greb's.

The aftermath of the fight, as related by Walker a long time later, with Greb no longer around to confirm or deny it, has gone down in boxing lore. Walker said that along toward midnight he met up with Greb at Billy Lahiff's tavern, a hangout for the fight crowd. They had a drink or two with friends -- Greb ordering "colored water," presumably -- and then adjourned by themselves to a place called the Silver Slipper. On the sidewalk outside, as Walker told it, he remarked to Greb in a friendly way, "I just want you to know, Dutchman, that you wouldn't have licked me if you hadn't stuck your thumb in my eye." That did not sit well with Greb, Walker went on. "He said he would lick me again, right there, and started to take off his coat." While he was doing this, Walker "let him have it" (Walker claimed), knocking him down.

Published accounts differ as to what happened next. Grantland Rice, in his syndicated column, wrote that two police officers came on the run and hustled the combatants into two separate taxicabs. Quentin Reynolds' version in Collier's magazine was more colorful. He described a fight as exciting as the one in the Polo Grounds. Hardly anyone who knew Greb believed any of these stories, although Hap Albacker corroborated one detail. Greb and Walker met at the Silver Slipper, exchanged a few words, and squared off, he told Jimmy Fair, adding, "But somebody stepped between them and no blows were struck." Researchers who doubt Fair's accuracy also doubt Albacker's.

Whether there had been one fight or two -- and Walker had left the ring badly marked up -- Greb was back in action just two weeks later with another future light-heavyweight champion, Maxie Rosenbloom, in Cleveland. Greb always knew how to deal with these upstarts. "He stuck his two thumbs in my eyes and said, 'Now, be a good boy and quit trying to knock me out,'" Rosenbloom was to reminisce, adding that he took Greb's advice.

The Rosenbloom fight was on July 16th. For the rest of 1925 and on into 1926 Greb took on outclassed opponents all over the country. To prepare for a title defense against Tiger Flowers, he barnstormed by rail from Pittsburgh to the West Coast and back, with stops in Omaha, Los Angeles, San Francisco, and Phoenix.. He had some good nights and some not-so-good nights but never came close to losing.

Most spectators felt that Greb did not lose to Flowers on February 26th over the championship distance of fifteen rounds in the "new" Madison Square Garden at 49th Street and Eighth Avenue. Sharing their opinion was the referee, Gunboat Smith, the same Gunboat Smith knocked out by Greb in the first round of a fight back in 1920. The split decision, nevertheless, went to Flowers, making him the first black middleweight champion -- the first black champion in any division since Jack Johnson, whose refusal to accept his designated place in the social order had outraged so many white Americans.

Flowers was an Atlanta-based church deacon. Tigerish in name only, he fought the way Johnny Wilson did. Both were southpaws, both were tricky, both were spoilers. The niche Flowers occupies in boxing's pantheon is far below Greb's. After his no-decision fight with Greb in Fremont, the Deacon had boxed Jack Delaney, a hard-hitting French-Canadian from Bridgeport, Connecticut who would one day be the light-heavyweight champion. Delaney knocked him out in the second round with a single punch. Four weeks later, Delaney did it again, only this time in the fourth round. (Tommy Loughran told me that Delaney's handlers would slip a metal bolt into his glove if they had bet on him to win by a knockout. "It's a wonder he didn't kill somebody," Loughran said. Among those who escaped death at Delaney's hands was Loughran himself. In their only meeting, they boxed to a 10-round draw.)

Greb, unwilling to believe what was evident to many others -- that he had lost his dynamism -- trained doggedly for his guaranteed return match with Flowers. He set up camp in Hot Springs, in the Ozark hills, and there he parted company one last time with Red Mason. They had argued over money. On his own, Greb arranged for a couple of tune-up fights with respected journeyman middleweights, winning both. Flowers used six fights to get ready.

On August 19th, they were back in Madison Square Garden . One of the foxiest managers in the business, Jimmy Johnston, presided in Greb's corner, but the fight was a duplication of the one in February, rendered tedious by excessive clinching. As before, the referee -- Jimmy Crowley on this occasion -- voted for Greb and the two judges voted for Flowers. Spectators, protesting, threw bottles, hats, and everything else they could get their hands on into the ring. Crowley told Greb, "It was your fight." Gene Tunney said the decision was "unjust" -- that Greb had won "substantially." Regis Welsh concurred but wrote that both fighters were guilty of "mauling, tugging, wrestling, and fouling."

To Jim Jab, the question of who won and who lost was immaterial. "Harry Greb's lucky star has set," he wrote. "No longer does his spectacular splashing captivate ring jurists. Its charm is gone. Those plunging, plowing spurts that discouraged his foes are sporadic now. They flare and fail. Adversaries, sensing the decline in his speed and stamina, tear in fearlessly. Nature has finally taken its toll."

Greb was disconsolate. "Well, that was one fight I won if I ever won any," he said. According to Jimmy Fair, he predicted, tearfully, that Flowers would lose the title the first time he defended it against "anyone who could fight." Flowers did lose the title the first time he defended it -- to Mickey Walker, who could fight. Walker knocked him down a couple of times, but the decision, let it be said, like the two involving Flowers and Greb, was debatable.

5

Exactly how good was Harry Greb? In the absence of film documentation, it's hard to say. Film reveals all, or nearly all. The written word can mislead. Fighters thought to be marvels in their day, if their day was in the early 1900s, look like novices to us now, always allowing for exceptions. Jimmy Jacobs had a theory about that. "Boxing skills have improved dramatically," he said to me in the 1970s, "but the language we use to describe those skills is still the same. When we read about the old-timers, we come across phrases like 'superb footwork' and 'great finesse.' Well, those phrases don't mean what they mean today. The sportswriters were comparing what they saw to what they had seen and were telling the truth by the standards of their time."

I remember watching a film of Jack Johnson with a group that included a Pittsburgh champion of the 1940s, Fritzie Zivic. Johnson had no jab or hook -- he sort of slashed with his left -- and had no straight right, just an uppercut. "Joe Louis," I said, "would take Johnson out in one round." Reconsidering, I asked myself if I hadn't overstated it. But Zivic, meanwhile, was saying, "One *round*? One *punch*!"

What the old films clearly show is that skills were unrefined until the 1920s, when Harry Greb flourished, and then the dramatic improvement began. Boxers developed new techniques, just as painters had done in the first hundred years of the Renaissance. By the 1930s the fistic renaissance was complete. Undeniably, there were more good fighters in the 1930s than at any time before or since. Greb, in a sense, belongs to the 1930s as well as the 1920s because fighters he had beaten -- Walker, Loughran, Rosenbloom, Slattery -- remained active and successful into the '30s.

Ray Arcel, one of the fight game's most sought-after trainers for sixty years, gave the fighters of the 1920s and 1930s an edge over those who came later for several reasons. First, because of their number. In quantity there is quality. Second, there were more gyms, more promoters, more trainers, more teachers. Third, because they fought so often they learned their trade. Certainly, Harry Greb knew his trade. It is probable, if not provable, that there was no better middleweight until Sugar Ray Robinson came along, and boxing men who saw both in their prime were doubtful that Sugar Ray could have handled Greb.

A limited sampling of opinion:

Bunny Buntag: "Greb wouldn't give you a chance to move. The middleweight never lived who could beat Greb."

Whitey Bimstein, a New York trainer celebrated in A. J. Liebling's "The Sweet Science": "I don't put nobody over Greb."

Nate Liff, a bantamweight boxer before 1920 and a training-camp operator in the 1930s: "I had high regard for Ray Robinson, but I'd have to go for Greb. He kept you so busy blocking punches you didn't have time to hit back. Another thing: Greb fought heavyweights. If Ray Robinson hit Greb with a right hand, it would feel like a punch from a lightweight."

Paul Sullivan (who lived to be 98) did not quite commit himself. "Greb was unique," Sullivan said. "He'd be just as much of a problem for modern fighters as he was for the old ones. He would mix with them and be all over them. They'd have to adjust their style to his. Was he better than Robinson? It could only be decided in the ring."

Robinson, the conventional wisdom has it, was the greatest fighter, pound for pound, who ever lived. There is no way to confirm or refute a judgment like that. Certainly Robinson at his peak was a dazzling performer. But the greatest who ever lived? The greatest welterweight, yes. There can be no doubt whatever about that. As a middleweight, though -- as a five-time middleweight champion, -- Sugar Ray was no longer unbeatable, and he would not fight dangerous black contenders like Pittsburgh's own Charley Burley who were easy to bypass because the public seemed unaware of them. Black fighters in Greb's time were relatively scarce, but he made it a practice to take on all comers. At any weight. Off the evidence in the record book -- or, for no-decision fights, the newspaper archives -- it is possible to argue that Greb, rather than Robinson or anyone else, was the best, pound for pound.

6

The return bout with Flowers was Greb's last fight. In the ensuing two months, he had two operations. From conversations with his personal physician, Dr. Charles S. McGivern, he knew that he was risking the sight in his left eye by refusing to have the blind eye taken out. In September, he agreed to let a specialist from Vienna, Dr. Gustav Guist, remove it and put in a glass one. For the surgery, he went to Atlantic City. Newspaper reporters somehow got wind of this, but McGivern fed them a story about a cataract operation.

Even with an artificial eye, Greb had not yet decided to retire. Boxing commission doctors were lenient then, and he'd been fighting with only one good eye as it was. He'd been driving with one eye, too, and he drove the way he fought -- recklessly. In early October he smashed up a car, fracturing a small bone between the bridge of his nose and the base of his skull. It was not by any means his first accident. Afterward, he complained of dizzy spells and of not being able to breathe. On October 21st, he was back in Atlantic City and under the knife again. When McGivern took out the broken bone, an undiagnosed blood clot hemorrhaged. With his fiancée, a Miss Naomi Braden, at his bedside, Greb died the next day.

He was 32. Pittsburgh newspapers devoted entire pages to his passing. Thousands of mourners attended a two-day visitation at the East End home of Ida Edwards; thousands more accompanied the casket to St. Philomena's Church in Squirrel Hill for the funeral. Gene Tunney, who a few weeks earlier had won the heavyweight championship from Dempsey, was an honorary pallbearer.

Tunney outlived Greb by fifty-two years. Tiger Flowers -- the two parts of that name seem to cancel each other out -- survived him by thirteen months. Flowers died as Greb had, from the unintended effects of an operation. In November of 1927 he underwent surgery for the removal of scar tissue near his right eye. Several hours later, his heart stopped beating.

7

Harry Greb's mystique has endured for most of a century. There is something about him, something beyond his accomplishments in the ring, that appeals to romanticists. He's a kind of underground cult figure. Even in Pittsburgh, where he was once as well-known as any Pittsburgher could be, the mention of his name to the average person, even the average adult male, even the average sports-page reader, or even, in fact, the average sportswriter, would not, in all likelihood, ring a bell. And yet down through the years there have always been Harry Greb followers, Harry Greb addicts, Harry Greb idolaters -- call them whatever you like.

And they come from all over. Bill Paxton, a Chicagoan, started a Harry Greb website about the time he started writing his book, and soon it was getting roughly 12,000 visitors a year, he said. What that would break down to is something like 33 hits a day and 230 a week. Taking into account the reality that baseball is still a centerpiece of the culture while boxing has become a fringe sport, like track and field, Greb's hold on the imagination compares with Roberto Clemente's. What Greb and Clemente seem to share is that indefinable quality called charisma. Either you have it or you don't, and Greb had it -- still does. Because Clemente died a hero's death, in an airplane loaded with food and supplies for the survivors of an earthquake, he is deified, whereas Greb was no saint. It is nevertheless instructive that the subtitle of Bill Paxton's book is "Biography of a Tragic Hero."

That is how people think of Greb if they think of him at all -- as a tragic hero. For whatever reason. If it's heroic to fight with one good eye, Greb did that. But fighting with one good eye could also be thought of as foolhardy. And though Greb died young, which is always, or almost always, tragic, his career was essentially finished at the time. Unlike the great Australian fighter Les Darcy, who died considerably younger, he had more than fulfilled his destiny. Bill Paxton quotes a newspaper story relating that in the weeks after his second title fight with Flowers, Greb spoke often of death. He believed that, for him, it was close at hand. Clemente, we know, was equally fatalistic. It may be that tragic heroes have a feeling for such things.

Greb is brought back to life in a four-and-a-half-minute silent film that shows him training for his fight with Mickey Walker on a bright summer day in 1925. It opens with Greb facing the camera. He smiles, looking faintly embarrassed. His eyes are slit-like . . . opaque. The camera backs off just a little to show him punching the air a few times. He is wearing three-ounce gloves. He flexes his biceps. Red Mason comes into view, standing and watching while Greb hops around on his toes, shadow boxing, looking fast but not especially graceful. He's in tight-fitting dark woolen trunks. Swiftly, with his eyes on the floor, he skips rope. The minute he is through, a young woman -- Naomi Braden -- steps out of nowhere and wipes off his face with a towel. For her it's the briefest of cameos.

They're on the open-air rooftop of Madison Square Garden, where Philadelphia Jack O'Brien, the old light-heavyweight champion, operated a gym.. Before an audience of a dozen or more men and boys, some in street clothes, others wearing swimsuits, Greb goes to work on the speed bag. There is wonderment in the faces of the spectators. Another dissolve, and Greb lies flat on a rubbing table. He does some sit-ups, touching his toes. With the hands-on assistance of a battle-scarred O'Brien, he kicks both legs above his head. Like the teenagers in the speed-bag crowd, O'Brien is wearing a swimsuit with a top. It is 1925, remember.

Facing the camera once more, Greb turns his head from side to side. Calisthenics? It's hard to say. But here comes the part we have waited for. Using cushions -- sixteen-ounce gloves -- Greb spars with O'Brien. Only it's make-believe sparring -- lots of motion but no exchange of blows, the punches falling short by design. As when he shadow-boxed, Greb is constantly on his toes, looking quick but not stylish. It is over too soon. Abruptly, we are watching Greb and O'Brien play handball, Greb still up on his toes, bouncing around.

And that is the end of the training session. Greb is ready now for his close-up, looking marvelously debonair -- never mind the flattened nose -- in a pale-colored lightweight summer suit. He wears a necktie of regimental stripes. His straw hat is a skimmer, which he jauntily tips. Again, the self-conscious smile. Fadeout. Just an image on a screen, a glimpse in black and white of the fabled Harry Greb, but it's enough. The charisma shines through.

CHAPTER 5

CANNON FODDER

Harry Greb always had stablemates, but the turnover was high. Greb had a habit of beating them up in the gym. "He never showed mercy to anybody he trained with -- he couldn't keep his hands still," the old trainer Nate Liff once explained to me.

Greb liked small, fast sparring partners. The most durable of his punching bags were Johnny Ray and Cuddy DeMarco. Ray was from the Lower Hill, DeMarco from Charleroi, a Mon Valley steel town. They were masterful boxers.

Ray, whose right name was Harry Pitler, and whose brother Jake was a baseball player, an infielder with the Pirates, almost had to be masterful. Self-preservation demanded it, for he was not by any definition a heavy hitter. Nate Liff, describing his style, said, "It was jab, jab, jab. He didn't exchange punches. He'd jab, hook, and wait for a chance to slip in a right."

His footwork and generalship were superb. The tricks he knew, and the techniques he acquired, he later taught Billy Conn. Trained and managed by Ray, Conn became a champion. Ray, although never quite good enough to win a title himself, had close fights with champions -- three no-decision matches with Johnny Dundee and two with Johnny Kilbane.

In 1916, Ray boxed Kilbane for the featherweight title at the Power House Auditorium on Penn Avenue in Lawrenceville. Under the prevailing rules for a no-decision fight, a challenger could win the title by a knockout or he could win it on a foul. Aware that he wasn't going to knock Kilbane out, Ray tried the second option, claiming he'd been hit low. His act did not convince the referee. Jim Jab wrote in the Pittsburgh Press that Ray "undoubtedly shaded" Kilbane, but Kilbane, of course, retained his title. When they boxed the next year in Philadelphia, the decision on that occasion, in the opinion of Jim Jab, "undoubtedly" belonged to Kilbane.

Jim Jab was not a man to equivocate, and he was capable of making fine distinctions. When Ray boxed Dundee at Motor Square Garden in 1921, two years before Dundee became the featherweight champion, there were spectators who felt that he deserved a draw, but Jim Jab decreed that he had lost -- "by a shade." Later that year, Ray "undoubtedly sustained a trouncing" at the hands of Rocky Kansas, whose next fight was with Benny Leonard for the lightweight championship. (Kansas had Leonard on the floor but lost the decision. After Leonard retired, Kansas won the title from his successor, Jimmy Goodrich.)

According to Nate Liff, there was mutual dislike between Ray and Harry Greb, a dislike so strong that their manager, Red Mason, kept them separated except when they sparred with each other. In 1920, Ray parted company with Mason to fight for a rival manager, whereupon Greb, in the role of errand boy, recruited a long-time enemy of Ray's, Johnny Kirk, to fight for Mason. Kirk (born Casper Curkowski in Poland) was from Lawrenceville. He had boxed Ray six times, the bad blood between them increasing with each fight. When they squared off again at Exposition Hall, with Mason in Kirk's corner and Greb at ringside, there was trouble from the opening bell..

In the first round, according to Jim Jab, the fighters exchanged "scurrilous epithets." They "fouled each other incessantly," and the referee, Louden Campbell, was powerless to stop them. When Ray, who may or may not have been hit low, dropped to the canvas, his face clenched in agony, Campbell allowed him recovery time. In some measure, at least, Ray's acting skills had improved since his fight at the Power House with Johnny Kilbane.

The flash point, when it came, was a harmless looking gesture by Kirk. At the bell for the end of the second round, the fighters happened to be in Kirk's corner. As Ray turned away, Kirk tapped him lightly on the shoulder and said, perhaps sardonically, "Good work." Infuriated, Ray spun around like a top and hit Kirk on the jaw, whereupon Kirk hit Ray on the jaw.

Instantly, a full-scale riot broke out. Everyone in the building (or so it seemed) made a rush for the ring, Harry Greb in the forefront. One of Ray's new stablemates, Jackie Lightning, a flyweight just an inch or two more than five feet tall, was foolish enough to take a pot shot at Greb. Later, Greb denied that he then knocked Lightning unconscious. But somebody did, and there were no other suspects.

Long before Lightning could open his eyes again, a police squad was clearing out the hall. In court the next morning, Ray tried to blame the disturbance on Kirk, but the magistrate, a man named Sweeney, had been at the fight himself and said, "Uh, no, I was there, and I saw the whole thing, and it was *you*, Mr. Ray, who started it." He fined Ray ten dollars.

With no Johnny Ray to kick around, the sparring partner Greb now abused more frequently than any of the others was DeMarco, a good-natured sort. DeMarco was 18 when he first signed with Mason, and Greb worked him over from the start. Unaccountably, they became the best of friends, at one time sharing an apartment at the Morrowfield in Squirrel Hill. Sportswriters called DeMarco "the Sheik of Charleroi," and he was every bit as handsome as the reigning movie sheik, Rudolph Valentino. In later life, DeMarco blamed Greb for the misshapen nose that had a blurring effect on his profile. "I fought five champions," he told a biographer of Greb, Jimmy Fair, "but none of them messed me up the way Greb did. He was the fastest fighter I ever saw. And you couldn't outguess him. I feinted Billy Petrolle and Kid Kaplan and Joe Dundee all over the ring and drove them crazy, but every time I tried it on Greb he knocked me on my can."

Joe Dundee, a welterweight, and Kaplan, a featherweight, were two of the five champions Cuddy fought. He lost to Dundee, held Kaplan to two draws, lost on a foul to Jimmy Goodrich, boxed two no-decisions with Mike Ballerino, a junior lightweight champion, and decisioned Jack Bernstein, a junior welterweight champion. He boxed a draw with Petrolle, not a champion but a very good lightweight, and lost to him once by a knockout.

DeMarco's 339 fights exceed the total for Greb. In a single year, 1925, he supposedly boxed sixty-seven times. During one burst of activity, he had four fights in five nights in four different states. He boxed in Australia, Europe, and South Africa. He boxed in Alaska before Alaska was a state. How many fights he won and how many he lost will be forever uncertain (the no-decision requirement), but he claimed to have won his first 112 before boxing to a draw with somebody, and then 38 more before his first defeat.

Two fights he definitely won were with Jack Zivic, who had beaten Johnny Ray, and one fight he definitely lost, but shouldn't have, was with Tiger Joe Randall in McKeesport, the Tiger's hometown. As the fourth round ended, Randall uncorked a punch after the bell. DeMarco's hands were down, and so, in the next instant, was he. When he failed to come out for round five, the referee called it (unfairly) a TKO.

One night in Johnstown, DeMarco pulled a Tiger Joe Randall on Greb. As Jimmy Fair told it, they were boxing an exhibition, and DeMarco saw his chance to even a few scores. He had taken Greb's abuse in the gym without complaint. This was different: there were spectators. Because Greb outweighed him by thirty pounds or so, he knew he would have the crowd's sympathy, and he knew that Greb knew it, too. As soon as they touched gloves, a gesture that said, "This is only for fun," DeMarco banged a right to Greb's jaw. Everything he had went into that punch, and the middleweight champion was sprawled on the floor.

There was murder in Greb's heart when he got to his feet, but then he hesitated, thinking of the crowd. "If you slug me, they'll mob you," DeMarco reminded him. With an effort, Greb managed to hold back. He had some words for DeMarco, of course, and once, forcing a clinch, he used the laces of his gloves to good effect. While he was doing this, he smiled at the fans, insincerely.

Greb's flare-ups were just that -- flare-ups. He was quick to lose his temper and almost as quick to get over it. Red Mason always said that Greb was envious of DeMarco. "When they both dressed up," Mason explained to Jimmy Fair, "Cuddy would get all the girls."

Dapper, amiable, genteel, DeMarco spent most of the half-million dollars he earned in the ring on clothes and automobiles. After losing all that was left in the stock-market crash of 1929, he established his own business as a salesman of men's apparel. Punches to the Adam's apple had damaged Cuddy's larynx. "I've heard that my voice sounds as if it's coming out of a well," he would say -- and it did. But his sales message always got through. His line of patter was smooth and, above all, grammatical. In the sentence about his voice, note the meticulous use of "as if" rather than "like."

No mere behind-the-counter clerk, Christopher Furey Constantine DeMarco called on his clients in person, and they included such men of substance as Richard King Mellon, Governor George Earle, and Senator Joe Guffey. He could walk in on Mellon without an appointment. The financier and civic leader was "retiring to the point of shyness," DeMarco informed Jimmy Fair, "but a very fine chappie."

Their meetings took place in the big Mellon Bank downtown -- "the most beautiful bank in the world." Many years later, when Mellon's corporate managers allowed it to become a short-lived Lord & Taylor department store, the renovators destroyed its magnificent interior. But Richard King Mellon's office had been in that building, and there Cuddy went to show him samples of cloth.

After Mellon made a selection, all that remained was for Cuddy's tailor to take his measurements. And his measurements were those of an athlete. "You would never suspect it," Cuddy told Fair, "but Mr. Mellon is a clever boxer and a stiff, accurate left-hooker. He could give a lot of preliminary boys some trouble for a couple of rounds." One is left to infer that Cuddy had boxed with Mellon or had watched him box somebody else.

Cuddy took pride in his vocabulary, his alertness, and his skill at repartee. None of this was to last. Like many another old pug, he ended his days in a mental fog. Three hundred and thirty-nine fights explain why, not to mention the ill luck of having sparred too often with Harry Greb.

CHAPTER 6

SHRIMP SLAPPERS

"Boxing is going over so big locally that even 'shrimp' slappers fill the Braddock Bowl," wrote Jim Jab, the phrase-making fight critic of the Pittsburgh Press, in 1929. A flyweight match between Willie Davies of Charleroi and Frankie Genaro, the champion, had packed them in. Davies, with his "will-o'-the-wisp ways," was an easy winner, but they were boxing over the weight, so Genaro did not lose his title.

After about 1950, "shrimp slappers" -- fighters who weighed below 130 pounds -- became vanishing Americans. In truth, there were never very many, but Pittsburgh had more than its share. The first good ones were Jack McClelland and Patsy Brannigan.

In 1904, in St. Louis, McClelland won a fifteen-round non-title bout from Abe Attell, the featherweight champion. According to the St. Louis Republic, "a grueling, slashing fighter" (McClelland) outfought "a wary dancing master" (Attell). Boxing historian Douglas Cavanaugh has written that McClelland was better than just good. He was Pittsburgh's first *great* fighter. If so, he was Red Mason's first great fighter too, but Mason later managed an even greater one, Harry Greb. Up in New Castle, Jimmy Dime had a good or great fighter in Jimmy Dunn, who twice held McClelland to draws.

McClelland was active from 1896 until 1912. Brannigan, by one account, started boxing at age 11 in 1898. Over a stretch of twenty years, he claimed to have had more than 600 fights. A semi-official record shows 239, of which 102 were no-decisions. He lost only eight and was never knocked out or knocked down. Brannigan and Young Ziringer, a North Side neighborhood rival, boxed each other again and again. The confirmed total of fifteen times is probably incomplete.

There is no way of telling how no-decision fights turned out except by a close search of newspaper files. Reviewing Brannigan's six-rounder with featherweight champion Johnny Kilbane on New Year's Day, 1915, at the Gardens, Jim Jab left the impression that Kilbane could have cakewalked to victory. "By superb feinting, he drew poor Patsy into numerous assaults, and then teased him with sly jabs." Only once did the cat-and-mouse game get rough. "In the third chapter, Brannigan made some gore trickle. But Kilbane put on more steam and rocked the gutty redhead with stiff slams, a right uppercut being his trump card."

Gutsiness and "pluckiness" -- another of "poor" Patsy's qualities -- are usually no match for skill. "Brannigan persisted in falling into traps laid by the titleholder." It could be said, nonetheless, that he tried -- "tried his best to introduce pepper into the set-to." Kilbane did not, "unless it was in the final inning, when he opened up and showed his class." Throughout the fight, he ignored "jeers and catcalls" from the Pittsburgh crowd. "Champs," explained Jim Jab, "don't have to exert themselves. So long as patrons go to see them, they will dilly-dally."

Kilbane's dilly-dallying, let the record show, convinced the boxing writers from the Pittsburgh Post and the United Press that Brannigan had won the fight easily. If the champion also dilly-dallied in meetings with Brannigan in Akron, Canton, Youngstown, and Scranton, less exacting observers than Jim Jab failed to report it. The fights in Akron and Canton were close; in Youngstown and Scranton, Brannigan took a beating. His fights with bantamweight champions Johnny Coulon in Johnstown and Jimmy Walsh at the Gardens were no-decision affairs like the ones with Kilbane. According to the newspapers, Brannigan had the edge over Coulon and battled Walsh to a draw.

Brannigan, it was said, never drank, smoked, or used off-color language. For years after leaving the ring, he worked as an elevator operator in the City-County Building. He was 73 when he saw his last fight, a Civic Arena match between Sugar Ray Robinson and Wilf Greaves. One after another, all the old boxers in town were introduced to the crowd before the main event -- all the old boxers except Brannigan. He shrugged and said, "Nobody remembers me."

Four weeks later, on January 5, 1962, while walking along the railroad tracks near Jacks Run Tower in Bellevue, he was hit by a freight train and killed. In a grim sort of way, it seemed fateful. Brannigan's manager had been Jimmy Dime, and only a year and a half before the accident at Jacks Run Tower, another well-known fighter from Jimmy Dime's stable, one-time middleweight champion George Chip, was hit by an automobile in New Castle and killed.

One of Brannigan's contemporaries was Johnny Ray. They boxed each other seven times. Ray had seven fights with Johnny Kirk and six with Patsy Scanlon, his stablemate. He boxed another Pittsburgh featherweight, Dick Loadman, five times. Loadman and Scanlon boxed each other six times. All of these fighters were like one big happy but disputatious family.

Patsy Scanlon was a redhead who came from the Point, where the Allegheny and Monongahela rivers meet to form the Ohio. In Patsy's time the Point was an Irish neighborhood. One of his boyhood friends was a future mayor of Pittsburgh and governor of Pennsylvania, David L. Lawrence. There's a photograph of the Point as it looked around 1900 in Stefan Lorant's pictorial history of Pittsburgh. Two narrow streets, oddly light in color, bisect a dark, dismal cluster of warehouses, freight sheds and railroad tracks, of tenements and shanties, of stunted commercial buildings packed close together. It's a panorama of urban blight.

"We'd go over to the Point and visit Patsy Scanlon's mother," said Jim Rooney, who lived on the North Side and whose brother Art got rich enough playing the horses to buy a franchise for Pittsburgh in the National Football League, "She'd give us tea and Irish cake." Irish cake was bread -- heavy, coarse white bread with raisins in it. "'Five in a bed, and we ate apple pie with a spoon' -- that's what Patsy used to always say. The houses they lived in! No carpets on the floor. No bathrooms. No hot water. There'd be a big wooden barrel under the rainspout. On winter mornings, to get a pan of water to cook with, first you had to break the ice.

"In those days," Jim Rooney continued, "people went to bath houses. A dime to get in and a dime for a bar of soap and a towel. We were the first family in our neighborhood with inside plumbing, I think, but we had money -- my father always owned a saloon. I don't know how they existed, the poor people back then. There wasn't any welfare, there wasn't any food stamps. The government didn't pay your rent. You got a basket of food at Christmas time from your ward chairman. You got a basket of coal now and then. They put the money in their kicks, the politicians did. We had a ward leader who wore spats. Changed his suit about three times a day."

If you were Patsy Scanlon, you wanted more than Christmas baskets. And one way to get more was to fight.

A gnome-like figure with a wandering nose, he had a sharp left hook. His right, said Jim Jab, was "nigh useless." His most important fights -- no-decisions, of course -- were with bantamweight champions Pete Herman in 1919 and Kid Williams in 1921. The Herman fight was one-sided. Jim Jab depicted Scanlon as "a plaything in Herman's hands." Unlike Johnny Kilbane, Herman gave the crowd its money's worth, handing Scanlon "the worst mauling doled out in moons. Patrick's face," wrote Jim Jab, "was a sight. One lamp was just peeping out, the other was mussed." When the tenth round came, "old friends could hardly recognize him."

Scanlon and Harry Greb -- like Ray, one of his stablemates -- were sparring partners. Someone else Scanlon sparred with was Art Rooney, a two-time runner-up in different divisions, lightweight and welterweight, for the National AAU championship. "Patsy batted the hell out of him," a numbers writer named Woogie Harris remembered. In the 1920s and 1930s, Scanlon was the owner of a combination flower shop and horse parlor in Market Square. He survived the after-effects of prizefighting better than most.

Willie Davies belonged to a subsequent generation. Willie's sister was his sometime sparring partner and she managed him for a while. The intellectual type, he attended night school at Pitt and became a teacher. After losing twice to Mose Butch, the first time by an early knockout, Davies gave incontrovertible proof that a university education develops reasoning power. "The fact is," he admitted, "I just can't beat him." There were not many others he couldn't beat.

Mose Butch was from Panther Hollow, in the valley below the Schenley Park Bridge. Panther Hollow was an enclave of hillside houses and cobblestone streets, of old women in black, of sleepy-eyed cats sprawled on doorsteps. Everybody who lived there was Italian. Everybody had forebears who came from Gamberale, a mountain village on Italy's Adriatic coast. Everybody's last name was either Diulus, Sciulli, Bellisario, DePasquale, or Bucci. Mose Butch was a Bucci.

Lefthanded and built like a fireplug, Butch fought aggressively, always moving in. Five fights between Butch and Jackie Wilson resulted in two decisions for Wilson, two for Butch, and a draw. This was before Wilson won the featherweight title. In 1933, Fidel LaBarba, who'd been one of the better flyweight champions, took a close decision from Butch at Duquesne Gardens, but predicted after the fight that the loser would be "going someplace." For a while it appeared that LaBarba was right. Butch outpointed Chalky Wright, a future featherweight champion like Wilson, but lost to three other champions -- Freddie Miller, Tommy Paul, and Benny Bass -- before finishing up with a 53-21-3 record.

Flyweights, bantamweights, and featherweights were pleasing to watch for their speed and artistry. They provided action, but little violence. Premature endings, as when Butch stopped Davies, as when Tommy Paul stopped Butch, as when Eddie Zivic killed an opponent in the ring, were unusual. "These sprites of slam," noted Jim Jab in a patronizing way, "send over scores of socks -- socks that only ruffle. Yet that doesn't prevent their partisans from howling for a knockout.

"None likely," he assured them with the wisdom of his years as an expounder.

PART TWO
Prime Time

East Liberty hero Billy Conn (right) with former heavyweight champion James "Cinderella Man" Braddock (left). "The Pittsburgh Kid", is rightfully considered one of the greatest of all light-heavyweight champions. He is unjustly remembered by many today because of his famous loss to heavyweight champ Joe Louis. But Conn, like Harry Greb, was a top man in the middleweight, light-heavy and heavyweight divisions and his achievements far outstrip the loss to Louis, a fight he was winning up until the fatal 13th round. (Photo Courtesy of the Conn Family)

"City of Champions" is one of those self-bestowed honorifics like "Gateway to the West" and "Big Apple." A baseball team, let's say, wins a pennant, and then a football, basketball, or hockey team from the same metropolitan center wins something comparable and you have a City of Champions. The rest of the world, meanwhile, refuses to be impressed, but if ever the real thing existed -- a city that lived up to the name -- it was Pittsburgh in the late 1930s and early 1940s, when boxing champions doing their roadwork seemed to throng every highway and byway. In fact, there were only seven, counting Tony Marino, a bantamweight champion without portfolio. Charley Burley deserved to be the eighth but was not, because life is unfair.

CHAPTER 7
THE ONE THAT GOT AWAY

In 1929 two brothers named Hartnett promoted fight shows every week at an arena between Beaver Falls and Rochester. Present one night at ringside, Jack Henry, a 19-year-old Geneva College student who was sports editor of the Beaver Falls News-Tribune, took particular notice of a middleweight in a four-round preliminary.

"A Polish kid from Monaca," Henry said later. "He and the other guy stunk the place out. The Polish kid fought from behind his left shoulder and he couldn't be hit. There was nothing but bare back to hit at. All through the fight the crowd booed. I didn't care. I said to myself, 'This kid is a natural. He's a born defensive fighter.'"

Henry managed fighters himself -- preliminary boys like the Polish kid. Their purses averaged forty dollars a fight. From his own cut, thirty-three and a third percent, Henry paid the wages of the trainers and seconds. It was not a fast way to get rich, but now he had seen a fighter with genuine promise. The Polish kid's name was Teddy Yarosz. Henry asked one of the Hartnett's who his manager was. "A guy from Monaca named Berkman. Owns a barber shop."

Henry found Berkman in the lobby and asked if he'd consider selling Yarosz. Berkman said, "Sure. You can have him for one hundred dollars."

As they spoke, the Hartnett's' matchmaker, Ray Foutts, came into the lobby. Interrupting, he said to Berkman, "I'll make this short. How much do you want for that fighter of yours?" Berkman looked at Henry and then back at Foutts and said, "This guy here wants to buy him."

Foutts said, "Be serious. Henry? He's a sportswriter. And he's not even dry behind the ears."

Berkman, turning to Henry, said, "Where's the money?"

Henry said, "I don't have it on me, but look -- let me make a phone call to Bridgie Weber." Bridgie Weber, a theater manager in Beaver Falls, was Henry's good friend. "Let me make a phone call to Bridgie Weber, and he'll bring you the hundred dollars."

Berkman said nothing, which Henry took to mean that he would wait. So, rushing off to a phone booth, Henry called Weber. "Bridgie," he said, "I'm sober. I'm at the Grand Junction Arena, where I just saw the best defensive fighter I've ever laid eyes on, a Polish kid named Yarosz. He's going to be a champion. Come over here with a hundred dollars, and he's ours. We can take him to England. They score points for defense in England, and he'll never lose a fight." English himself, Henry was familiar with his native land's tribal customs. After giving the matter a few seconds' thought, Bridgie Weber promised to put up the money.

Henry ran back to the lobby and said to Berkman, who was talking with Foutts at the concession stand, "Bridgie's on his way with the hundred bucks." Foutts, Henry noticed, had a smile on his face. Berkman said, "Too late, Jack. I just sold the fighter to Ray for a hundred and fifty."

Bridgie Weber, as Henry described him. was "a big, powerful guy with a quick temper." (Henry himself was a small, frail-looking guy with an equable temper.) When Bridgie arrived with the cash and learned from Henry that their deal had fallen through, he was anything but pleased. "He went looking for Berkman and punched him," Henry recalled. "And then he punched Foutts. He messed those guys up pretty good."

But Foutts had Teddy Yarosz, and five years later, in 1934, Yarosz won the middleweight championship.

Thaddeus Yarosz was second-generation Polish. There were two other boxers in the family -- Teddy's older brother, Ed, and his younger brother, Tommy. Their father, who thought that prizefighting made no sense, took an ax one day and chopped up every boxing glove in the house, but Teddy and Eddie and Tommy were not to be so easily sidetracked.

Teddy, in his first three years as a pro, won fifty-five fights in a row and then boxed a draw with Eddie Kid Wolfe in New York. Earlier, he had beaten Wolfe in Detroit. After their draw, Yarosz won three more fights, and then he lost to Wolfe at Motor Square Garden, his first defeat. Four weeks later, they boxed to another draw.

When Yarosz boxed Vince Dundee for the middleweight title, he had lost only to Wolfe -- the decision was questionable -- and to Young Terry in Newark, also with room for dispute. He had mopped up the competition in Pittsburgh, beating Jimmy Belmont three times, Tiger Joe Randall four times, and Buck McTiernan. He had beaten Tommy Freeman, Pete Latzo, and Ben Jeby, all former champions, and he had beaten Dundee twice, both times before Dundee was champion.

A crowd of 25,000 at Forbes Field, the largest ever for a fight in Pittsburgh up to then, saw Yarosz win the title by once again outpointing Dundee. The decision was not unanimous. Penalizing Yarosz for slaps with an open hand, one judge, Leo Houck, the boxing coach at Penn State, voted for Dundee.

It was often hard to tell whether Yarosz had won or lost. His style perplexed boxing writers like Ed Van Every of the New York Sun. "If there can be such a thing as a right jab in the repertoire of one who does not fight in a southpaw stance, then the new champion has it," Van Every observed.

Yarosz was a disconcerting opponent. "He stabs and chops and then goes for cover, and you can't hit him anywhere except on the shoulders," Billy Conn complained. He never stopped moving and he was always on his toes. His punches rarely hurt. "He throws a lot of them, though, and he can sting you," said Bunny Buntag, who managed Buck McTiernan.

When Al Quaill boxed Yarosz, he deliberately stuck out his chin, daring Yarosz to take a shot at it and leave himself open for a counter punch. Yarosz did as expected -- he left himself open -- but never long enough. "I'd miss him by that much," said Quaill, holding a thumb and a forefinger a fraction of an inch apart. Quaill lost a ten-round decision to Yarosz but came out of the fight unmarked. "He hits about as hard as a strong 12-year-old kid," Quaill said derisively.

On New Year's Day 1935, Yarosz went to Scranton for a non-title match with Babe Risko. Three times in the first round, Risko knocked him down. Yarosz had a chronic trick knee that was giving him trouble. He wobbled and limped through the next six rounds, and Ray Foutts stopped the fight. X-rays of the knee revealed a torn cartilage.

By early summer, Yarosz appeared to be fit. Preparing for a September title defense against Risko at Forbes Field, he knocked out a couple of stiffs. (Knockouts for Yarosz were infrequent -- only nine in 127 fights.) Against Risko, his knee held up for just the first three rounds. In the fourth, it buckled. He was still on his feet at the end of the fifteenth, but though the crowd booed the decision, Risko clearly had won, failing only to look good. "Perhaps it is a sad commentary on the ability of the new champion," wrote Chester L. Smith in the Pittsburgh Press, "that he couldn't knock out a man with a broken leg." As for Yarosz, Smith went on, the probability was that he would never fight again.

He fought for another seven years. Back in Forbes Field in September of 1936, after Risko had lost the title to Freddie Steele, Risko and Yarosz met for the third time. Looking physically sound, Yarosz won a ten-round decision. He jabbed, slipped punches, and created tie-ups like the Teddy Yarosz of old, but Lester J. Biederman, at ringside for the Pittsburgh Press, wrote, "It was not a great fight to watch."

Of course it was not. Fights involving Yarosz were hardly ever great fights to watch. His art did not appeal to the masses. Only critics as discerning as Nat Fleischer appreciated what Teddy could do. In January of 1937 Yarosz won a ten-round decision from Solly Krieger in Madison Square Garden, and the all-knowing editor of Ring magazine was impressed. "Seldom since the days of Young Ahearn, Packey McFarland and Mike Gibbons," Fleischer wrote from the depths of his vast connoisseurship, "has a New York crowd seen such splendid, masterly, defensive boxing."

Against chance-taking sluggers like Krieger, Yarosz was always at his best. The crafty Ken Overlin posed a more difficult challenge, but in their ten-round bout at Duquesne Gardens Yarosz kept Overlin from establishing a rhythm with short right hands to the body and ended Overlin's 31-fight winning streak.

Billy Conn's 33-fight winning streak barely survived a twelve-rounder with Yarosz on June 30, 1937, at Forbes Field. Conn was 19, a child prodigy. Inclined to be sluggish at the start of every fight, he came from "a mile behind," wrote Chet Smith, to out finish Yarosz in "one of the most vicious middleweight hooligan brawls" that Pittsburgh ever had witnessed.

Weakening under Conn's late assault, Yarosz back-pedaled and hung on, tactics guaranteed to antagonize a fight crowd. Not this one. At the announcement that Conn was the winner by a split decision, a cascade of boos and seat cushions descended on the ring. In the onlookers' estimation, Conn had waited too long to cut loose.

The rematch, scheduled for fifteen rounds at Duquesne Gardens in September, gave him more time to accelerate. Once again Yarosz took an early lead. His "flashy boxing," noted Regis Welsh, who covered the fight for the Press, "bewildered Conn" for eleven rounds. But then Yarosz faded as Conn began to land with his right. In the fourteenth round, completely done in, Yarosz missed a punch and fell on his face. In the fifteenth, wrote

Welsh, Conn had him close to a knockout, "buffeting Yarosz from rope to rope." Seconds after the final bell, Yarosz collapsed in his corner.

Again Conn had won -- again by a split decision. Again he had changed the course of a one-sided fight. And the response from the crowd, which had been "wild with excitement" in the final minute of the last round, was an unnatural calm. There were no cheers; there were no boos; there was no hail of seat cushions. "Slumped over like a dead man," Yarosz was being given restoratives. He remained in his corner for fifteen minutes, a doctor at his side, and then needed help to reach the dressing room.

Throwing away his scorecard, on which Yarosz was far ahead, Regis Welsh declared the fight a standoff. "They don't carry winners out of the ring in a state of exhaustion," he wrote. "Neither do they award decisions to a fighter who has won only five out of fifteen rounds." One thing Welsh knew for sure: "There should not be a third fight. Let's have no more of it."

Yarosz and Conn now detested each other. They did fight a third time, but not for another ten months. Meanwhile, both had regressed. Yarosz had lost to a Frenchman, Carmelo Candel, in Paris and to Carmen Barth in Cleveland. Solly Krieger had given Conn a bad lacing. But Jake Mintz, making matches for the Rooney-McGinley Club, brought Conn and Yarosz together again on July 25, 1938, at Forbes Field.

Only weeks before the fight, Yarosz and Ray Foutts had parted company. Yarosz, dissatisfied with the terms Foutts had accepted from the promoters -- twenty-five percent of the gate receipts less four thousand dollars, a deduction Foutts agreed to so that Mintz could assemble a strong supporting card -- said he would not fight for that kind of money. "Then do as you please," Foutts told him, and, in the words of the boxer, took a walk. Their contract expired on June 30th, twenty-six days before the fight, and was never renewed.

Chet Smith wrote a column in which he obliquely accused Yarosz of ingratitude. Smith was disdainful of the prize-fighting business, but liked Foutts, a portly and genial tavern keeper from East Liverpool, Ohio. Over the years, Smith argued, Foutts had made Yarosz "the highest-paid middleweight in the country."

Normally unassertive, Yarosz replied in a letter to Smith. "The money angle," he said, "was a minor issue." He acknowledged that Foutts "drove hard bargains." Their association had been "mutually profitable." What came between them finally, he wrote, was Foutts's "general attitude" toward him. Beyond that, he did not elaborate.

A crowd of 10,850 attended the fight, paying, at Depression-decade ticket prices, $18,782. Yarosz's end came to about $3,700, which was $700 more than Conn's guarantee. Considering the times, Foutts had made a pretty good deal.

Yarosz entered the ring with a new manager, his brother Ed. Conn had only his seconds to advise him. His teacher and manager, Johnny Ray, was in the hospital with an unexplained illness, and the absence of a steadying hand became instantly apparent. Almost as soon as he answered the bell, Conn was rabbit-punching, kidney punching, and hitting low. Yarosz, before the fight, had infuriated Conn with a harmless little show of bravado. "Having beaten him twice," he said, "I can do it again." He responded to Conn's rough-house tactics by thumbing, gouging, and heeling. More often than not, both fighters kept punching after the bell.

The referee, Freddy Mastrean, was an ineffectual spectator. His pleas for a clean fight went unheeded. In what little actual boxing there was, the advantage belonged to Yarosz, who would jab Conn off-balance and sometimes follow up with a right. So it went for the whole twelve rounds (a compromise distance; Yarosz had wanted fifteen, to show he could fight that long without falling apart, and Foutts, doing him one last service, had held out for ten). Repeatedly tied up when he attempted to work inside, Conn lost his head, but for every dirty trick he knew, Yarosz had two or three. In the end, wrote Chet Smith, "Conn's white-faced venom brought about his defeat."

Smith wrote Conn off -- too soon, as events proved -- with the assertion "He has shown that he hasn't the mental makeup to be a champion, or even a contender." Regis Welsh wasn't so certain. "Conn," he maintained, "has fought and beaten greater fighters than Yarosz, who has only ring sagacity and a tantalizing boxing style." What was lacking in Conn was self-discipline. Succinctly, Welsh identified the problem. There was "too much Irish" in Conn.

And too much mileage on Yarosz. At 28, he'd been boxing for nine years. Even so, he was still a magician when it came to protecting himself. His brother Ed now matched him with Oscar Rankins, a keg of dynamite. Placed off limits for Yarosz when Foutts was his manager, Rankins had hit

Conn with a punch so mind-warping that, though Conn won their fight, he remembered nothing about it. In ten rounds at Motor Square Garden, Rankins hit Yarosz on the chin several times, but always when Yarosz was moving away. Willie Davies, a judge, gave Rankins his vote on aggressiveness, but the referee and the second judge favored Yarosz by substantial margins. Regis Welsh saw the fight the same way, adding, however, that Rankins' best days were "far behind him."

Yarosz was every bit of 5 feet 10 and, with the extra weight that maturity brings, no longer a middleweight. At his new weight of 175, he proceeded to box rings around Archie Moore, whose best days were still ahead of him, and Al Gainer, ranked eighth in the world. Where Foutts, like the managers of other top-rated white fighters, drew the color line without ever admitting it, Teddy's brother Ed did not discriminate. During his last three years in the ring, Yarosz took on a succession of tough black opponents -- Rankins, Moore, Gainer, Ben Brown, Lloyd Marshall, Nate Bolden, Turkey Thompson, Jimmy Bivins, and Ezzard Charles. He handled them at first with his customary deftness, but more and more often the ring sagacity and tantalizing style were not enough.

Ben Brown decisioned Yarosz twice. Marshall, Thompson, and Charles had him down for short counts. His return match with Marshall, which he won, provoked a diatribe from Regis Welsh. After watching the two fighters gouge, thumb, trip, butt, heel, and wrestle for ten rounds, he blistered their performance without mercy and pronounced the sorry affair "a disgrace to sportsmanship."

Significantly or not, Yarosz never boxed again in Pittsburgh. Regis Welsh was in Cleveland to see him fight Jimmy Bivins and beheld "the senile wraith of a once-clever champion flitting and floundering around the ring." Against the 20-year-old Charles in Cincinnati, the senile wraith "fought a strictly defensive battle and landed only three good punches all night." Except for an eight-rounder with Joe Muscato in Rochester, New York -- Yarosz lost that one, too -- the book was now closed.

Jack Henry's managerial career had ended a year or two earlier. Henry went on to become, successively, a sportswriter for the Pittsburgh Sun-Telegraph, a sportscaster, a journalism teacher, and a stockbroker. But boxing was always in his blood. Growing up in London, he had studied the fight posters at the entrance to the Black Friars Arena, forbidden territory for the young. In the forbidden, of course, there is mystery and allure. When he was nine, his family moved to the United States, settling down in the Beaver Valley town of New Brighton. There he read in the paper one day that Harry Greb, regarded by the English as the greatest fighter, pound for pound, in the world, was training in the area for a fight in Beaver Falls with the Zulu Kid (who was neither a Zulu nor a kid). Young Jack skipped his classes -- "played truant," as the English would say -- and went to the gym. In storybook fashion, Harry Greb noticed and took a liking to him. On the night Greb boxed the Zulu Kid, the immigrant fourth-grader carried his bucket and sponge.

It was Henry's introduction to the custodial end of the boxing business. As his education progressed, he learned the duties of a second and a trainer. He learned to evaluate fighters. He learned to be a manager. And he learned, in a place called the Grand Junction Arena, where opportunity passed him by, that money talks louder than promises of money.

CHAPTER 8
THE FORGOTTEN CHAMPION

Not even the old-timers ever talked about Tony Marino, Pittsburgh's forgotten bantamweight champion. It says in the Ring Record Book that Marino held the title for sixty-two days in 1936. Neither the New York State Athletic Commission nor the National Boxing Association endorsed such a claim, but Nat Fleischer, the Ring Record Book's editor, had decided that Marino deserved recognition, and Fleischer's pronouncements came from on high.

Boxing-commission politics make dreary reading. This plus the fact that fights between 118-pounders rarely interest the public may account for the neglect of Marino. In any case, the twists and turns in his story, along with an unhappy ending, are not generally known or remembered.

Marino grew up to his full height of 5 feet 3 in Duquesne. He worked in the steel mills and sometimes, when he could, as a house painter. His older brother, also a bantamweight, boxed under the name of Tommy Ryan in the 1920s and once had a title fight, losing a fifteen-round decision to Abe Goldstein. Tommy's advice to his sibling was "Forget about boxing," but no amount of persuasion could change the kid's mind. At the age of 19, Tony won the Pennsylvania amateur flyweight championship and immediately turned pro. After two years, he had lost only two fights. Willie Davies and world flyweight champion Midget Wolgast had too much know-how for Marino.

Even in the 1930s it was difficult for fighters of Marino's physical stature to get work. American males were getting taller and heavier. So, in order to find opponents of his own size, Marino hopped a freight for California. He spent the next two years, 1934 and 1935, on the Pacific Coast, boxing Mexicans and Filipinos and also, again, Midget Wolgast -- in this case with the same result as before: Wolgast won a ten-round decision. Against the Mexicans and Filipinos, Marino's record was four wins, five defeats, and two draws. Still hopeful, he came back East to see what he could do in New York with a new manager, Charley Cook.

The partnership was only two months old when Willie Felice knocked him out, but Marino won a return bout and then he decisioned Lou Salica.

Winning this one meant instant prestige, for Salica had been the NBA bantamweight champion -- admittedly for just a short while. The division, as it happened, was in a state of flux, all because Panama Al Brown, the universally acknowledged champion, had left the United States to campaign exclusively in Europe. Out of sight, out of mind. Both the New York commission and the NBA stripped him of his title. The NBA, going further, declared Sixto Escobar the champion. Escobar, a Puerto Rican, quickly lost the title to Salica but just as quickly got it back, winning their return match.

Meanwhile, Panama Al Brown's wanderings took him to Valencia, Spain, where he lost a fifteen-round decision to Valencia's Balthazar Sangchili. Panama Al was nearly six feet tall and Sangchili nine inches shorter, but Sangchili overcame the logistical problem. Supported by Nat Fleischer, he claimed the title. New York refused to go along, and the NBA reaffirmed that Escobar was the champion.

In due time, reason prevailed. There would be a dispute-settling fight between Sangchili and Escobar. First, though, Sangchili wanted a tune-up. He signed for a match with Marino, to be held on June 29, 1936, at Dyckman Oval in New York City over the championship distance of fifteen rounds.

Over ten rounds or twelve rounds, Sangchili would have won. For the first thirteen, the Spaniard gave Marino what the Pittsburgh Press story described as "a terrific lacing." Marino had been down four times. In round fourteen, fighting desperately, he landed two good punches, a left to the body and a right to the jaw. Sangchili had to be carried from the ring.

Fleischer, who summed up Marino as "a smart, flashy boxer, not too strong" (which doesn't explain why Sangchili needed help to get to his dressing room), awarded him the title. The newspapers said that all he had done was qualify for a title bout with Escobar. They met at Dyckman Oval on August 31st, and Escobar won when the ringside physician, over Marino's objections, ordered the fight to be stopped at the end of the thirteenth round.

In this fight, as in the one with Sangchili, Marino kept bouncing up from knockdowns. There were five of them, all in the second round. The correspondent for the United Press, George Kirksey, wrote that Marino was out on his feet. Recovering, he "courageously fought back" from the third through the thirteenth, while Escobar opened cuts over both of his eyes and sliced up his mouth as well. The crowd of 8,500 applauded Marino for his valor.

A little over a month later he was back in the ring, and back in his hometown, for a return match with Sangchili at Motor Square Garden. Marino hadn't boxed in Pittsburgh since leaving for California. "Only the gamest of the game," Regis Welsh wrote in the Pittsburgh Press, could have absorbed the beating he took. Sangchili was on top of Marino all night, Welsh reported, crowding him "every inch of the way." Marino "kept coming," but the decision, a lopsided one, went to Sangchili.

For whatever it may be worth, Sangchili never won another fight. He lost his next five, all by decision, and then retired. Marino returned to New York, dropped down to eight-rounders, and put together a four-fight winning streak over the next eight weeks.

Almost without letup, his mother had been urging him to quit. Home for Christmas, he told his three brothers -- there were also six girls in the family -- that he would do as she wished after one last payday. He had signed for an eight-rounder with Indian Quintana, like Al Brown a Panamanian, to be held on January 30, 1937, at the Ridgewood Grove Club in Queens. Writing to his mother, Marino promised, "I will have good news for you after the fight."

It went the full eight rounds. Quintana floored Marino five times. As he sat in his corner waiting for the announcement that Quintana had won the decision, Marino lost consciousness. He was rushed to a hospital, where two days later he died of a cerebral hemorrhage. He was 24 years old. Marino's legacy to boxing, it has been noted, is the three-knockdown rule. Passed by the New York commission within a week of his death, and subsequently adopted by the NBA, it empowers the referee to stop a fight after one contestant has been down three times in a single round.

Few fight fans are aware that Tony Marino was one of Pittsburgh's champions. Fewer still know of his unwitting contribution to safety in the ring.

CHAPTER 9

THE FIGHTINGEST ZIVIC

Welterweight champion Fritzie Zivic nurtured his "dirty fighter" reputation to such an extent that it ultimately overshadowed his enormous talent. He beat a large number of Hall of Fame fighters and many of his opponents, including Sugar Ray Robinson, Billy Conn, Jake LaMotta, Ike Williams, Beau Jack, Sammy Angott and Charley Burley all gave testimony regarding his skill and intelligence in the ring. (Photo courtesy of Douglas Cavanaugh)

Ferdinand Henry Zivcich, better known to the public as Fritzie Zivic, was the fifth and youngest son of a Croatian immigrant who settled in Lawrenceville around 1890, went to work at the Black Diamond steel mill, sent for his Slovenian sweetheart, Mary Kepele, and married her. All five Zivcich brothers learned to box. Four of them persevered at it, none with as much success as Fritzie, welterweight champion of the world from October 4, 1940, to July 29, 1941.

Fritzie Zivic's distinctive logo was his bashed-in nose. Through good times and bad, he maintained an agreeable light-hearted jauntiness. Zivic had wit, personality, and a flair for after-dinner speaking. The stories he told, in a high-pitched, staccato voice, often poked fun at his own vulnerabilities.

The most reliable record book credits Zivic with 233 fights. By his own count, there were more. According to the book, he lost sixty-five, with ten draws. He was capable of beating such highly esteemed brawlers as Henry Armstrong, Jake LaMotta, Lew Jenkins, and Sammy Angott, all world champions, and of failing to beat ham-and-eggers. Like a good many others in the boxing business, Zivic kept at it too long. When he got around to quitting, after eighteen years, his only stock in trade was his name.

From one appearance to the next, Zivic in his prime could be two different fighters. Dependably, though, he went about his work in a prowling, unhurried, business-like fashion. James P. Dawson, boxing critic for the New York Times, called him "one of the strongest, craftiest, gamest fighters" of the talent-rich 1930s and 1940s.

In the Pittsburgh tradition established by Harry Greb, he took a cavalier attitude toward the Marquess of Queensberry rules. He choked his opponents, thumbed them, spun them by the elbow, used the laces of his gloves, and hit low. That he paid so little attention to the amenities was a paradox in his nature, for on purely social occasions he exuded good will. Even in the ring, he was always courteous. After choking somebody, or hitting low, he never forgot to say, "Pardon me."

Sugar Ray Robinson testified that he learned more in ten rounds with Zivic than in all of his other fights put together. "He lets you lead and then he bangs you with a left hook," Robinson said, almost as if he were shocked by such duplicity. Zivic, looking at it from a loser's perspective, accepted Robinson's compliments modestly. As he told a reporter long afterward, "I tried every trick I knew on the guy. But it wasn't enough."

"Did you choke him, Fritzie?" the reporter asked.

"I choked that son of a gun ten feet in the air," Zivic answered.

"Really? How did Robinson take it?"

"He hollered bloody murder," Zivic said.

Billy Conn was 19 and Zivic a seasoned campaigner when they boxed at Duquesne Gardens in 1936. Like Robinson, Conn won, but not without paying a price. "He put a face on me," Conn said succinctly. "My mother didn't recognize me for five days."

Charley Burley said of Zivic, "In our first fight, he gave me two black eyes. In close, you know, he would just . . . I mean, he was *rough* in close." Zivic won their first fight and lost the next two.

Henry Armstrong's style was made to order for Zivic. A barrel-chested little man with spindly legs, Armstrong knew only one way to fight. He lowered his head and moved forward, punching with both hands. In all three of their fights, Zivic butchered him.

The first, in which Zivic won the welterweight championship, and the second, in which he retained it, were at Madison Square Garden. No title was at stake when they met for the third time, in San Francisco. The decision that night went to Armstrong, but his head, as Zivic described it many years later, "was puffed up like a balloon."

Zivic was still fighting -- barnstorming, actually -- and Armstrong had retired to become a manager when their travels brought them together in 1946. Winding down his career, Zivic was in Kansas City to box an untested prospect from Armstrong's stable of journeymen, Levi Southall. Before the weigh-in, Zivic asked Armstrong how good the kid was. "He's a pretty fair fighter. He'll probably outpoint you," Armstrong said.

Zivic was never the worrying kind, but he felt reassured after taking one look at Levi. "He had a neck like a rooster -- size nine," Zivic recalled. "I gave him a little choke in the first round, and he left his feet." Zivic won an easy decision, and Armstrong, his confidence in Levi's future greatly diminished, advised him the next day to forget about boxing and find a job.

Al (Bummy) Davis was a neighborhood bully from the Brownsville section of Brooklyn who fouled more often than Zivic did and with less regard for appearances. They boxed at Madison Square Garden a month after Zivic won the welterweight championship in October of 1940. Art Rooney, the owner of the Pittsburgh Steelers, was there. "I knew everybody so well, those New York guys," he said, "and they were talking about how dirty Bummy was. I said, 'Well, he'll meet his match. If he wants to fight nice he'll meet his match, and if he wants to fight dirty he'll meet his match.'"

Davis elected to fight dirty, and the rough stuff began right away. Near the end of the first round, according to Zivic, Bummy turned his head and looked at the Garden's three-minute clock to see how much time was left. "I couldn't believe it!" Zivic said. "I'd been waiting nine years for a fighter to do that. I wound up, and *wham!*" Davis, he added, was saved by the bell.

Or maybe not. Announcer Sam Taub's blow-by-blow account of the fight, much of it transcribed by Allen S. Rosenfeld in his biography of Zivic's home-town rival, Burley, indicates that the knockdown came much earlier in the round and that Davis got to his feet right away. Zivic was always an entertaining story-teller.

At the start of the second round, Davis came out swinging -- low. Zivic kept track of how many times he was hit below the belt, counting to seventeen before John J. Phelan, chairman of the New York State Athletic Commission, stood up and shouted for the referee to disqualify Davis. When the referee complied, Davis kicked him on both shins. He then attacked Zivic and had to be dragged to his corner. Deploring the whole affair in Ring magazine, boxing's official conscience, Nat Fleischer, said that in his thirty-five years of association with a sport not renowned for the genteel behavior of its practitioners, he never had seen anything like it.

The New York commission suspended Davis for life and fined him $2,500. "Life," it turned out, was not a word to be taken literally. In another eight months, with Davis now in the Army, he and Zivic were at it again, this time at the Polo Grounds in a benefit show for servicemen. The deportment of both fighters was exemplary. Zivic led all the way and won by a technical knockout when Davis could not survive the tenth round.

A charitable fellow, Zivic asked leniency for Bummy at a subsequent hearing to formally reinstate his license. In one sense, Zivic respected Davis. Before their first fight, Bummy had beaten two former lightweight champions, Tony Canzoneri and Lou Ambers. After the second fight, he knocked out Bob Montgomery, a lightweight champion in the making. And he distinguished himself one last time. When four-armed hold-up men came into a bar where he was having a few drinks, Bummy tore into them, hammering one of the thugs to the floor. Predictably, though, two fists were no match for four guns, and Bummy took a bullet in the neck, along with bullets in two other places. The bullet in the neck turned out to be fatal.

"He was a good kid," Zivic said, either meaning every word of it or refusing to speak ill of the dead.

In Lawrenceville, the Zivcich family lived in a small brick rowhouse at 4925 Plum Alley, conveniently near the Black Diamond steel works. "When you grew up in Lawrenceville," Fritzie once told me, "your only choices were to fight or stay in the house. The kids at school made a fighter of me the first time they heard that my name was Ferdinand. I changed it to Fritzie on my own."

`` So Fritzie it was -- Fritzie *Zivic*. Fritzie and his brothers, who also became Zivic's, did their recreational fighting at the Lawrenceville Boys Club and at the Willow Club in Lawrenceville, where white-haired Jack Metz was the boxing coach. Metz taught boxing as a theorist. He never had boxed himself, never at all. Dozens of his fighters became amateur champions; if or when they turned professional, he never spoke to them again. It happened to Fritzie Zivic. It happened to all of his brothers -- Pete, Jack, Eddie. and even Joe, Jr., a pretty good sandlot baseball player who had only one pro fight.

Pete Zivic, a flyweight, and Jack Zivic, a featherweight, boxed for the U. S. in the 1920 Antwerp Olympic games. Both reached the quarterfinals, where Pete lost to a Dutchman and Jack lost to a Dane. Pete, who called himself the oldest, smallest, and smartest of the Zivic's, turned pro the next year and came home from his first fight with a conspicuous black eye. His appearance so distressed the boys' mother that she burned all the boxing gloves in the house. After Pete got into the money -- a thousand dollars for main events, sometimes more -- her attitude eventually changed.

Compared with what Jack, and later Fritzie, were able to demand, a thousand dollars was small change. Jack, by knocking out Lew Tendler with repeated left hooks, became a leading contender for the vacant lightweight title -- Benny Leonard, the champion, had just retired -- but Tendler won their rematch, and won it easily. The following year, 1926, Jack boxed a draw with Tommy Freeman, who would go on from there to win the welterweight title. Against other champions and future champions, Jack was less successful.

Pete Zivic had five fights with bantamweight champions, losing four times to Bushy Graham and once to Panama Al Brown. Eddie Zivic, who weighed about 130, boxed four champions in four weight divisions -- Armstrong, Tony Canzoneri, Freddie Miller, and Frankie Klick. He won from Canzoneri, but lost to him also, and lost to the other three as well. Fritzie, watching Eddie lose to Armstrong, began to see that the way to beat Armstrong, the ring's only simultaneous featherweight, lightweight, and welterweight champion, was to nail him with uppercuts when he waded in, as he always did.

Fritzie's first pro fight was in 1931. Fritzie and Eddie were still preliminary boys when Luke Carney, a fight manager who wore three-piece suits and owned a Whippet automobile, took them to Los Angeles in his car.

Boxing up and down the West Coast, the brothers were undefeated in thirty-two fights between them and came back to Pittsburgh as main-eventers.

Whether Fritzie or Eddie was the more promising of the two remained a question. "I'll be honest with you," said Nate Liff, who ran a training camp for boxers in the 1930s, "I always thought Eddie would go farther than Fritzie. But Johnny Ray said to me, 'No, Fritzie will go farther. Eddie's a good fighter, but he won't stand up against other good fighters.'"

Ray, who managed Billy Conn, may or may not have been right. At any rate, while Fritzie progressed, Eddie's career took a grimly ironic turn for the worse, all because he could hit hard. "Unnerved," it was said, by the death of a fighter he had knocked out, a lightweight from Texas named Johnny Page, Eddie could not regain his enthusiasm for boxing. His right was the hand that did Page in, and from then on Eddie used it sparingly. In the end, he declared that, for him, the best thing was to quit.

Fritzie and Eddie looked enough alike to be interchangeable. One time because of a last-minute training injury, Eddie pulled out of a fight in Ohio. Fritzie, to save the show, offered to take Eddie's place. Neither the fans, the other fighter, nor the other fighter's manager, he assured the promoter, would know the difference. "OK," said the promoter, "but we have to give the customers their money's worth. Make it last for at least four rounds." Fritzie agreed, and for four rounds he carefully pulled his punches. At the start of the fifth, he advanced to the center of the ring and touched gloves with his opponent. Puzzled, the guy said to him, "What are you doing that for? This ain't the last round."

"It is for you," Fritzie said, and proceeded to knock him out.

Fritzie was in truth a better fighter than Eddie, Nate Liff decided, and he was also a better fighter than Jack. "But if Fritzie and Jack ever fought," Liff said, "I'd have bet on Jack."

Betting on Jack wasn't always a good idea. After Jack knocked out Tendler in Pittsburgh, Liff made the trip to Philadelphia for the return bout. "Put your money on Zivic," he told all his friends there. But Jack had gone knockout crazy and was wild with his punches. Tendler won all ten rounds, and Liff had to sneak out of town. Ruby Goldstein summed Jack up by calling him "the best fighter I ever licked." (He knocked Jack out in four rounds.)

Inconsistency was Fritzie's great fault. Every winning streak, it seemed, prepared the ground for a losing streak, or, if not that, a totally unexpected defeat. Always, however, the youngest, most durable Zivic carried on, losing important fights (to Lou Ambers in 1935, to Billy Conn in 1936) but working his way back to the top. Again and again the critics said he was through. They said it when Tommy Bland, a perfectly ordinary Canadian boxer, won a ten-round decision from him on Christmas day, 1937, knocking Zivic down in the first and last rounds. In the papers the next morning Zivic read that he should "bow to the inevitable" and retire. He understood why the sportswriters were thinking that way. "See," Zivic said, looking back on the episode thirty years later, "I'd been sick, I'd had the pneumonia. July, August, and September -- fifty-four days -- I was in the hospital. And when Tommy Bland beat me, the papers said I'd never be any good again. They said the pneumonia had hurt me too much."

But Zivic suspected that the papers were wrong. He knew that his real problem had not been pneumonia, but peanuts. "That's right -- peanuts," he said. "I had a peanut business called the Fritzie Zivic and Son Peanut Company, and it was taking too much of my time. Early in the morning, I'd get up and do my roadwork, and for the rest of the day I'd have to run around town hustling peanuts. I was working too hard."

Dismissing the peanut company from his mind, Zivic won a fight in Chicago. Two months after that, Tommy Bland came back to Pittsburgh, and Zivic knocked him out in the eighth round.

The critics stuck to their guns. Over the next sixteen months, Zivic lost only three fights out of thirty, but two of the three were to Charley Burley, and once more they said he was finished. After losing to Burley for the second time, Zivic won six in a row, but then came another setback. Out in Chicago, he boxed a rabbi's son from Dubuque, Iowa, Milt Aron. Seven times in the first seven rounds, Zivic had Aron down. Seven times Aron got up. Shrugging, Zivic turned to the crowd and said, "What am I gonna do?" What he did was lose in the eighth, by a knockout.

In Chicago again, not long afterward, he won a close, rough fight with Johnny Barbara. His purse was a mere $250. He took the Broadway Limited back to Pittsburgh and went from Penn Station to the Lyceum gym. Joe Luvara, who sometimes worked in Zivic's corner, was waiting for him there. "Oh, he looked awful," Luvara recalled. "He looked like he'd been through a meat grinder. I was putting hot packs on his face when the phone rang. A promoter in Philadelphia was calling. He wanted a return match -- in ten days. Me, I'd have run. But Fritzie took the return match for $750. And, yeah, Fritzie won."

Luvara had the details wrong. It was twenty-five days between the first fight and the second, not ten, and the winner was Barbara. Immaterial. The point of the story is that Zivic believed fighters should fight. Six months later, he was welterweight champion.

In the interim, he had won from Sammy Angott, the National Boxing Association's lightweight champion, knocking Angott down in the sixth round. Both fighters were over the lightweight limit. Boxing Armstrong for the welterweight title -- Armstrong was ready to make a defense, and his manager, Eddie Mead, thought that Zivic would fill the bill -- Fritzie was a 4-1 underdog. Armstrong had given up the featherweight championship and had lost the New York version of the lightweight title to Lou Ambers, but had made a good try for the New York version of the middleweight title, holding Ceferino Garcia, the bolo-punching Filipino, to a ten-round draw. In later years, when Zivic was on the banquet circuit, he often amused the crowd with a humorous set piece about the night he fought Armstrong. It went like this:

"I thought I could lick Armstrong because of his aggressiveness. You could close your eyes and hit the guy -- he was always on top of you. The only thing you needed was condition, and I was in very good shape. I was busted, too, which made it easy to stay that way. My biggest purse up to then had been thirty-two hundred dollars for beating Angott.

"On the afternoon of the fight, a lot of my friends from Pittsburgh came around, and when I'd go to shake hands with them, they'd bow their heads and say, 'Good luck, Fritzie. Don't get hurt.' So, while I'm taking my walk after the weigh-in, I'm thinking about this, and I'm concerned.

"I walk down to Fifty-seventh and Broadway, and there's a display room full of Cadillacs. In two minutes, I've forgotten about Armstrong. I went in just as I was, wearing an old leather jacket and a beat-up pair of pants, and the salesman tried to give me the brushoff. But I told him, 'Listen, tomorrow I'll be the welterweight champion and I'm coming in here to buy one of these.'

"That night at the Garden, Armstrong came out for the first round and he hit me with everything he had -- hooks, uppercuts, elbows, head, thumbs, the works. And my Cadillac started going farther and farther away. It was in East Liverpool, Ohio, or someplace.

"Second round, same thing. Third and fourth rounds too. Worst beating I ever took. I thought I was fighting four men instead of one. So finally by the sixth round my right eye was closed and the Cadillac must have been in Honolulu.

"I thought to myself, 'I'll never go fifteen rounds. I'd better give him the same stuff back.' In the seventh, he hit me with a low punch, and I butted him. Then I gave him the thumb, and Arthur Donovan, the referee, stepped between us for a moment. He said, 'Boys, if you want to fight like this, go ahead.'

"The rest of that round, we must have fouled each other twenty times, but I always said, 'Pardon me.' Out there in Honolulu, the Cadillac turned around. I had him busted up pretty good by the eleventh round, and the Cadillac was back in the States. By the fourteenth, it was pretty close to East Liberty, and in the fifteenth it backed right into my driveway.

"With six seconds to go, I hit Armstrong with a right, and he fell flat on his face. The bell saved him.

"When they said, 'The winner and new champion,' I said to myself, 'Well, I've got a Cadillac now.' But the next day a high-pressure salesman looked me up, and darned if he didn't sell me a Packard."

Three months later, in his only successful title defense, Zivic beat Armstrong again, the referee stopping the fight in the twelfth round. They drew the biggest crowd ever at Madison Square Garden, 23,190, and Zivic's share of the purse came to $19,836, a small fortune in 1941. It wasn't all his to keep. By the terms of the contract, according to Zivic, Eddie Mead had to be cut in for twenty-five percent. "That was the agreement I made to get the original title fight," Zivic said. "Mead got twenty-five percent of everything I made as champion. It cost me twenty-six thousand dollars altogether."

Zivic said that four days before his first fight with Armstrong, Mead offered him fifteen thousand dollars to "take it easy." "I'll think it over," Zivic said he told Mead, adding, "I'd have refused then and there, but I thought he might claim that Armstrong had hurt his hand or something and call off the fight. So I said I'd think it over, and never got back to him."

Zivic revealed this after Mead had died. Armstrong denied any knowledge of such an offer, but Armstrong and Zivic remained on good terms. At a testimonial dinner for Zivic in the late 1970s, Armstrong delivered a flowery oration, saying, "We fought as true champions and never faltered."

Whatever way the money was split, Zivic's ten months as champion were profitable. Lucrative non-title bouts included the pair with Bummy Davis and a ten-round draw with Lew Jenkins, the New York State Athletic Commission's lightweight champion. There were lesser non-title bouts as well, and, true to form, Zivic had occasional off nights, as when Mike Kaplan decisioned him in Boston. Kaplan had won forty-eight of fifty previous fights, but one of the two he lost was to Zivic (by a split decision), and all Zivic could do was state the obvious: "It doesn't look too good for a champ to get beat."

Worse was to come. Apathetically, the champ lost his title to someone who wasn't even a rated contender. Against Freddie Red Cochrane in Newark, New Jersey, Zivic waited so long to get started that Cochrane was still ahead after fifteen rounds.

The return match he promised Zivic "any time you want it" finally took place almost a year and a half later, at Madison Square Garden. Zivic won. He did not, however, regain the championship. With the United States at war, Cochrane had enlisted in the Navy, and the fight was a benefit for the United Services Organization, a friend to every soldier and sailor. Could any patriot begrudge Cochrane the one small stipulation he made, requiring Zivic to exceed the welterweight limit of 147 pounds? Cochrane hung in for the full ten rounds, but plainly wouldn't have lasted the championship distance of fifteen.

In Newark, Zivic had let the title slip away for a purse of only five thousand dollars. As just another contender, he was making real money again. His two fights with Ray Robinson drew well at Madison Square Garden (Robinson won the second one, too, won it decisively by a TKO in the tenth), and so did two fights there with still another lightweight champion, Beau Jack (Zivic lost two close decisions). Ex-champ Lew Jenkins came to Pittsburgh for an encore with Zivic, and Fritzie stopped him in ten. Halfway through that fight, Jenkins called Zivic a name. Calmly and deliberately, Zivic stepped on his foot. Jenkins looked down, presumably to see if the foot was still there, and Zivic took prompt advantage, as he had against Bummy Davis, or said he had. Jenkins never fully recovered.

Subsequently, Zivic and Carmen Notch, his former sparring partner, sold out Duquesne Gardens. Notch had held the washed-up Jenkins to a draw, but Zivic put the upstart in his place, although it wasn't easy, winning a slam-bang ten-round decision.

After that, he embarked on a four-fight series with Jake LaMotta, who had just given Robinson his first defeat. LaMotta used to say that of his six fights with Robinson he won all but five. Zivic could say, although he never did, that of his four fights with LaMotta he won all but three.

The first two were in Pittsburgh, followed by one in New York and one in Detroit. In the first fight, LaMotta got the decision, but the sportswriters, most of them, thought Zivic had won. In the second fight, Zivic got the decision, but the sportswriters thought LaMotta had won. Over the long haul, LaMotta was too big and strong for Zivic. He was also too young -- 22 to Zivic's 30 the last time they met. Even so, the third fight was close -- one judge voted for Zivic -- and the last one, in which Zivic bruised a knuckle on his left hand in the second round, was at any rate not uneven.

Many times Zivic proved that there was no one he wouldn't fight. "Just as long as I get paid," he would say. Joe Luvara put Zivic in a class by himself as a warhorse. "He never asked a question, never asked if a guy could punch," Luvara said. "He boxed LaMotta when LaMotta was a middleweight. Four times. And Charley Burley. How many welterweights would fight Charley Burley?" Not Robinson. Not Armstrong. "Fritzie boxed Burley three times. He was a fighter."

In the furtherance of his own economic interests, Zivic made sure there would not be a fourth fight with Burley by purchasing his contract, a maneuver known in the corporate world as a leveraged buyout. But Luvara had it right. Ray Robinson was unbeaten, and beginning to look unbeatable, when Zivic agreed to fight him the first time. "I'll eat the guy up," he said to Luvara. He didn't do it -- nobody did -- but he took a few bites out of Robinson. And, knowing from first-hand experience what to expect, he was not in the least reluctant to box him again.

Milt Aron, Zivic always said, was the hardest puncher he ever fought. That did not keep him from jumping at the chance for a return match. He had claimed a fast count when Aron knocked him out in Chicago. "It should have been put to a boogie-woogie beat," Zivic said. The return match, Zivic's first fight after losing his title, took place in Pittsburgh. Once more Aron was the first to go down, and this time he stayed down, knocked out in the fifth round.

Year after year, it seemed, Zivic boxed the reigning lightweight champion. Bob Montgomery was the last of four, and though Zivic came on strong at the end, he lost. After that defeat, even Nat Fleischer pronounced him washed up. "Zivic's days as a fighter are over," he wrote -- prophetically in the sense that Zivic never again beat a top-flight opponent.

And yet there was one more shining hour in Madison Square Garden. At the age of 18, Billy Arnold, a morning glory from Philadelphia, was undefeated in thirty-one fights, winning twenty-six of them by knockouts, and his advisors thought of Zivic as a steppingstone. They miscalculated. On January 5, 1944, in a bout that was limited to eight rounds because of Arnold's tender years, Zivic handled him easily, ending forever any dreams of the big time the kid may have had.

Zivic by then was a corporal in the Special Services section of the Air Force, granted special permission to take a fight here and there when he was offered one. In return, he boxed exhibitions for the troops and donated money to the entertainment fund at his base, Camp Normoyle in Texas. Against so-so opposition for the most part, Zivic had twenty-seven fights as a serviceman. One of those fights was with Ossie Harris, at Duquesne Gardens. He had beaten Harris twice, but this time he lost (he was losing now with regularity). He never boxed in Pittsburgh again, but he boxed almost everywhere else, continuing to fight, and continuing to lose, after his discharge from the Air Force at the end of the war.

There was only one reason. Zivic needed cash. For every dollar he made in the ring, he was losing two or three as an entrepreneur.

In 1941, Zivic had bought Hickey Park, an open-air wooden arena in Millvale, for twenty-seven thousand dollars and promoted fights there during the summertime. He told his good friend Joe Pavlak, a newspaperman from upstate New York who wrote an informative, privately-printed biography of Zivic, that to keep Hickey Park in repair cost him ninety thousand dollars. While Zivic was in the Air Force, his wife, the former Helen Stokan, promoted at Hickey Park. Helen Stokan was from Lawrenceville, too; her brother Lou had been one of Fritzie's trainers. Helen knew how to make matches, but regardless of who ran the place, Hickey Park was a losing proposition.

After Luke Carney died, Zivic became his own manager. He managed other fighters as well. Coming and going, there were seventeen, not counting Burley. Only two -- Juste Fontaine and Charley Affif, who was billed for a while as Young Zivic -- ever amounted to much, and Affif never boxed for decent purses until after Zivic grew impatient and sold his contract.

Zivic once estimated that his earnings in the ring totaled half a million dollars, but by the late 1940s he was broke. Nobody in town had a bigger collection of bad checks. A friend once advised him, "Times are pretty good now, but there's going to be another depression. Put ten thousand dollars away every year, and in ten years you'll have a hundred thousand dollars." Zivic's answer was, "Yeah, that's right. But if times are still good in ten years, I'll be stuck with all that money."

By his own admission "too fast with a buck," he could never say no to a moocher. "What the heck," he explained. "You give this guy a hundred, another one a thousand, and somebody else gets you for five thousand." Four thousand is what he blew on a birthday party for Juste Fontaine. To handle the crowd, he rented an entire hotel floor. "Half the people that showed up I didn't even know," Fritzie said. At a celebration in Lawrenceville when he returned from New York as champion, he filled a market basket with fifty-cent pieces and threw them to his well-wishers -- mostly kids -- from a second-floor window above the Stokan brothers' saloon. He was fast with a buck and equally fast with a half-buck.

Ignoring suggestions that he ought to retire, Zivic boxed eighteen times in 1946, always on the road. One of those fights was with Russell Wilhite, the pride of Memphis, Tennessee. No way he could lose to anybody named Russell Wilhite, Zivic reasoned, and his opinion was fully shared by the promoter. As Zivic told the story to Myron Cope for a magazine piece years later, he accepted five hundred dollars over his agreed-upon purse to make certain that Wilhite lasted until at least the eighth round. "I knew I was in trouble," Zivic said, "when I jabbed the guy on the shoulder and he almost went down."

Somehow Zivic managed to keep Wilhite vertical for four rounds. In the fifth, he simply couldn't restrain himself. With a punch that was little more than a tap, he put Wilhite down for the count. Afterwards, escorted by several bodyguards, the promoter came around to Zivic's dressing room and stood outside demanding to see him. Well aware of what his visitors were there for, Zivic took five hundred dollars out of his wallet and slipped it under the door.

Starting in 1947, he tapered off. His last two fights (he won both, against pushovers down in Georgia), were in 1949. Desperate for money, he sold Hickey Park. He moved from a big house in Mount Lebanon to a smaller one. No job was beneath his dignity. Always with good cheer, he dug ditches, tended bar, sold wine, cars, and insurance, worked in a steel mill, was master of ceremonies in a night club, and had a disc-jockey show on the radio. He ended up in the boilermakers' union, working on major construction projects. In the leanest of years, he provided well for his family. His two sons and his daughter went to college; all three were successful in their business and/or professional lives.

Probably no other Pittsburgh fighter was ever more popular than Zivic. With Harry Greb and Billy Conn, he formed a bar-room pantheon. In saloons all over town, their photographs -- and, at one place, a floor-to-ceiling mural, painted by a Carnegie Tech art student -- were part of the décor. They encapsulated, for fight fans, the Pittsburgh qualities of determination, physical courage, and unpretentiousness.

Pittsburghers place high value on unpretentiousness, and it was characteristic of Zivic that, after changing the name of Hickey Park to Zivic Arena, he kept on calling it Hickey Park. When he was getting the breaks, he never gloated; when he was down on his luck, he never complained. Inside the ring or out of it, he knew how to roll with the punches.

CHAPTER 10

THE PITTSBURGH KID

He who fights and runs away lives to fight another day;
He who fights and stands his ground may not last another round.
-- George Benton, middleweight boxer.

By the age of 23, Billy Conn had been up against nine world champions in three weight divisions and had beaten them all. Nobody ever talked about that. "Nobody remembers the fights I won. Nobody. Nobody," he complained in his old age. "All I ever hear is, 'Billy, you cost me money when Joe Louis knocked you out.'"

It's a Pittsburgh legend, the cautionary tale of how Conn had the heavyweight championship all but won and then made the mistake of his life. It's the stuff of periodic rehashing, a fight that lives on in folklore with an ending right out of Greek tragedy, or at any rate Eugene O'Neill.

Except for the first fight between Muhammad Ali and Joe Frazier, there may never have been its equal, in the history of the ring, as theater. There may never have been its equal for sustained excellence. "Men had been slugging it out for eons, and there had been 220 years of prizefighting," Frank Deford wrote, "but this was it. This was the best it ever had been, or would be, the 12th and 13th rounds of Louis and Conn on a warm night in New York just before the world went to hell."

It was June 18, 1941. In Europe and Asia, huge parts of the world had been going to hell for quite some time, but that is neither here nor there. For Louis and Conn, 54,487 cash customers, paying a top price of one hundred dollars a ticket in Depression-era money, filled the Polo Grounds. Conn went into the ring outweighed by thirty-two pounds, but from the seventh round on he took the fight to Louis, confusing him, out boxing him, beating him to the punch. His comeuppance in round 13, demonstrating where hubris can lead you, obliterated all the rest of his career.

Conn had seventy-seven fights and lost twelve. He lost five of those twelve before he was 18 years old. He had beaten four world champions before he was 20. He had beaten four more world champions and held a title of his own before he was 22. After that first Louis fight -- there was a return match in 1946 -- none of this seemed to register with the public.

` And that is because the first Louis fight was more than just a fight. It was seen as an object lesson in the danger of overreaching. It proved that all the old verities were still in effect. Don't change horses in the middle of a stream. Dance with the one who brung ya. Don't bite off more than you can chew. A bird in the hand is worth two in the bush. Pride goeth before a fall.

Recklessly, Billy Conn had paid no attention to these time-honored admonitions. He had not played it safe or hedged his bets. He had put up a spectacular fight and he was winning it. He'd been too quick for Louis -- dancing, circling, moving inside to throw fast combinations and then pulling away. In the twelfth round he staggered Louis. It gave him ideas. Now he would finish the job. Before the bell for the thirteenth, he told his manager, Johnny Ray, "I've got him. I'm gonna knock him out."

"Box," Ray said. "Stay away."

"No, I've got him," Conn answered.

"OK, then," Ray said as the one-minute rest period came to an end. "You're on your own."

On his own, brimming over with self-confidence, Conn blew his chance of replacing the heavyweight champion who may have been the best of them all. Instead of boxing, instead of staying away, he went out and slugged. All by himself, and with thrilling audacity, he fatally re-enacted the charge of the Light Brigade, plunging headlong into the fight game's mythology.

His thoughts about this -- the what-ifs, the how-comes, the woulda's and shoulda's and coulda's -- were never easy to fathom. In the dressing room after the fight, he was sitting on a table with his head bowed, sportswriters pressing in on all sides, when Jesse Abramson of the New York Herald Tribune asked the question on everybody's mind. Why did he change his tactics and trade punches with Louis in the thirteenth round? Smiling -- a few minutes earlier there had been tears in his eyes -- Conn looked up and said, "What's the use of being Irish if you can't be dumb?" A comedian's line.

Another answer he gave, years later, sounded goofily romantic: He was thinking of his future wife, Mary Louise Smith, and how much prouder it would make her if he knocked out Joe Louis instead of just winning from him on points. He told that, or something like it, to Frank Deford, and

Deford weaved it into a love story, "The Boxer and the Blonde," a marvelous job of writing spread out over twenty-six pages in Sports Illustrated. The longest profile the magazine ever had run; it generated a mountain of fan mail.

But ask yourself this: would a fighter who is trying to win the heavyweight championship take a moment between rounds to daydream about his girl? In any case, the never-ending interrogation wearied Billy Conn. "Look," he told a questioner, clearly exasperated, "when you hurt a guy, and he's holding on, you naturally try to knock him out. That's your business. That's what you're supposed to do." As for wanting to impress Mary Louise . . . "That was a bunch of baloney. I'm fighting for the championship and I'm thinking about my girl? I'd have to be crazy. I'd have to be an absolute nut. I was thinking about winning the fight."

His answer to Jesse Abramson -- equating the fact of his being Irish with stupidity -- was spontaneous. Conn grew up on the streets of East Liberty, a typical Pittsburgh working-class neighborhood; he belonged to a time and place in which ethnic humor, verging on insult, was a staple of conversation. Art Rooney had a friend called Nigger Smitty (who was Jewish, not black) and another called Dago Sam. If they resented these monikers, no one was any the wiser. Eastern Europeans were hunkies, Lebanese and Syrians were sand scratchers, Germans krautheads, Jews any number of things. There were lace-curtain Irish (the social climbers) and shanty Irish (the ones at the bottom of the heap). That was the way people talked; it was part of the vernacular.

Ethnicity was one source of nicknames, variation from the physical norm another. There were men called Fatso, Porky, and Jumbo, Shorty and Stumpy, Peg leg and One Eye and Balloon Head. A slur was not a slur but simply an identification tag, casually bestowed and, by the thick-skinned, casually accepted. Vietnam and the Civil Rights movement changed all that. Obscenity -- taboo on the more decorous levels of society until the 1960s -- became perfectly OK, even fashionable. Obscenity was not offensive or pornographic; war was, killing was, bigotry was. Obscenity proved that you understood this. It was a statement of sorts, like wearing your hair long or being an unabashed slob. But ethnic slurs, racial epithets, sexist (as opposed to sexual) language -- that kind of talk was out of bounds and remains so.

Billy Conn's speech habits were formed in his youth. If people minded (and some did), he never worried about it. In his obituary of Conn for the Pittsburgh Post-Gazette, the talented sportswriter Gene Collier called him "as blunt as a knuckle." Mary Louise used a different metaphor: "He cut through the mustard. He got right to the point."

He cut through the mustard with Fred Apostoli in their second fight, which Conn always said was his toughest, passing over the two with Joe Louis.. His fight with Oscar Rankins may have been tougher still, but Conn had no recollection of that one after Rankins knocked him down in the second round. Anyway, getting back to Apostoli, there was some thumbing and butting and trash talk in the clinches. Conn started calling Apostoli "dago" and Apostoli started calling Conn every name he could think of. In Billy's corner between rounds, his seconds, both Italian, paid no attention to his cuts and bruises, which were numerous; instead, they shouted at him to clean up his language. Conn took this abuse as long as he could, and then, instinctively, he cut through the mustard. "I'll tell you what," he suggested. "You two dagos go over and work in Apostoli's corner." Glancing at Johnny Ray -- an alcoholic whose real name was Harry Pitler and who had sedated himself with a few stiff ones before the fight -- he added, "And take that drunken Jew with you." Conn's nickname for Ray was "Moonie," short for "Moonshine."

While no Irishman on record ever publicly objected to Conn's denigration of the national IQ, his forthrightness much later on his only visit to the Emerald Isle left a newspaper reporter speechless. "Billy," the reporter had said to him, "you're a god over here. The people all love you. Now, tell me: what do you think of Ireland?" So Conn told him. He said, "I'm glad my mother didn't miss the boat."

His mother's name was Margaret McFarland, and she was Irish, all right, but the boat she didn't miss had left from England, where the McFarland's were living at the time.

Billy called his mother Maggie. He called his father, William Conn, Sr., "Westinghouse," because he worked as a steamfitter at Westinghouse Electric and spoke of the place as a kind of heaven on earth. When Billy was 13, his father gave him a tour of the plant. Rhapsodically, he told the kid, "Son, this is your future. This is where you'll be spending your life."

"It scared the hell out of me," Billy recalled.

He decided then and there that he'd be spending his life somewhere else. Presenting himself shortly afterward at Johnny Ray's gym in the Conns' own East Liberty neighborhood, he declared his intention to be a prizefighter. "I want you to teach me," Billy said.

"OK," answered Ray, handing him a broom. "First let's see if you know how to sweep the floor."

Ray did not manage amateurs. Amateurs boxing amateurs did not learn anything and meanwhile they were getting hit. For getting hit, you should always be paid. Ray kept his eighth-grade dropout learning basics for three years and then put him in, when he was 16, with an experienced professional named Dick Woodwer down in Fairmont, West Virginia. "I got two and a half bucks and a licking," Conn remembered.

He was right about the licking but not about the two and a half bucks. The amount Ray handed him before the ride back to Pittsburgh was fifty cents.

"Where's the rest of it?" Conn asked.

"You lost and you had something to eat," Ray reminded him. He was deducting his managerial fee -- fifty percent -- plus the cost of the pre-fight meal.

Lickings in four of Conn's next twelve fights were to follow. After that, hardly anyone licked him. His record at the end of two and a half years was thirty-four wins, five losses, and one draw. In 1935 Teddy Movan, a good-looking prospect from McKeesport, beat Conn twice. In 1936 Conn beat Teddy Movan twice. He won five close fights from another home-town rival, Honey Boy Jones, and got a split-decision win over Fritzie Zivic, a contender even then for the welterweight title. It was Conn's first important main event. Always a slow starter, he lost the opening rounds but out finished Zivic. "The early rounds don't matter," Conn used to say. He had an unusually slow pulse, an unusually slow heartbeat. He never ran out of gas. His opponents did.

After passing his test with Zivic, Conn won decisions from three former middleweight champions, Babe Risko, Vince Dundee, and Teddy Yarosz. He beat Yarosz two out of three. Matched with the paralyzing puncher Oscar Rankins, he took a right to the jaw that knocked him silly. Down for a count of nine in the second round, he did not remember getting to his feet and winning another split decision. In the dressing room afterward, under the impression that he had lost by a knockout, he apologized to Johnny Ray. He continued to think he had lost, in spite of Ray's assurances to the contrary, until he read about the fight in the papers the next day.

When they were old pugs reminiscing, Conn mentioned Rankins to Joe Louis. He said, "I boxed that guy before I could vote." Louis knew all about Rankins, having sparred with him several times in the gym. "Didn't your manager like you?" he asked.

Between Conn's first two fights with Yarosz came a learning experience. Ray took him out to San Francisco, and he lost a close decision to Young Corbett III. Young Corbett III wasn't young and his name wasn't Corbett. It was Rafaele Giordano. He came from Italy but had settled in San Francisco, where fighters had been calling themselves Young Corbett ever since the original Corbett, a San Francisco bank clerk, won the heavyweight championship in 1892 by knocking out John L. Sullivan. Young Corbett III was a ripe 32. He'd been fighting since 1919. In 1933, he had won and then lost the welterweight title. He had beaten, among others, Mickey Walker, Gus Lesnevich, Ceferino Garcia, and Jackie Fields, all champions, and Jack Zivic. Getting up from another knockdown, Conn out finished Corbett, just as he out finished everybody, but this time it wasn't enough. Corbett, a ring-wise southpaw, had too many slick moves for Conn.

By Johnny Ray's lights, the outcome was irrelevant. The ten rounds with Corbett had been educational. It helped Conn to get past Yarosz again six weeks later, and then in a return match with Corbett at Duquesne Gardens, he won as he pleased, looking dominant.

Conn at the age of 20 was not a show-off -- just the reverse -- but success has its rewards. In "Billy Conn, the Pittsburgh Kid," Paul F. Kennedy writes that he bought a new Cadillac and started wearing "expensive clothes." Conn was particular about clothes all his life; he dressed in the conservative, traditional way that never went out of style. In his new duds he was strikingly photogenic -- too good-looking to be a prizefighter, everyone said. He was six feet tall; he had chiseled features, wavy black hair, a white-toothed smile. William Conn, Sr. -- "Westinghouse" -- accused him of putting on airs.

William Conn, Sr. would fight anybody. "Oh, what a brawler he was," an old friend of his remembered. "He'd go to the Krakkers Hotel in East Pittsburgh and clean the whole place out." On Thanksgiving Day, 1937, William Sr. and William Jr. began to argue about William Jr.'s attitude, and the argument turned into a fist fight. They went outdoors and stripped to the waist. And William Jr. was having the best of it when his two younger brothers, Jackie and Frank, pitched in, Frank on the father's side, Jackie on Billy's. Somebody called the cops, who put an end to the melee. Afterward, Kennedy writes, the combatants and all the rest of the Conns -- Maggie and the daughters (three of them) -- sat down to a peaceable Thanksgiving dinner.

There remained the uneasy impression that Billy was perhaps too full of himself. Underestimating an opponent had never been one of his faults, but he still had some lessons to learn. Expecting an easy time of it, he trained in a rather cursory way for his fight at the Gardens on December 16th with rough and ready Solly Krieger, and the price he paid was a one-sided defeat. Krieger knocked Billy down and punched him around for twelve rounds. Never again, Billy promised himself, would he go into a fight out of shape.

From then on, until Louis knocked him out, the only fight he lost was his third one with Teddy Yarosz. They were like two guys in an alley that night, observing no rules. Johnny Ray was in the hospital with what everyone knew was an alcohol-related illness, and Conn needed him. Conn always said of Ray that, "even drunk," he knew more about boxing than other trainers did when they were sober. "He'd spot what you were doing wrong in a minute. He had a pay phone on the wall, and he said to me, 'See that phone? Who's gonna get to it quicker, the guy who walks straight to it or the guy who takes a roundabout route? That's the way it is with punches. A straight punch gets there first.'"

Shown how to do it, Conn could get there first with his jab, his straight right, or his left hook. Conn was the most picture-perfect Pittsburgh champion. He boxed in the upright classical style, but with a certain high-spirited abandon. Somewhere or other, Jack Palance, the sinister-looking movie villain who had once been a prizefighter himself, sparred a couple of rounds with Conn. "He was like a feather in the wind," the actor said. A feather in the wind, but not as harmless. He was ready at all times to attack. He attacked when he was hurt and he attacked when his opponent was hurt. He could outbox heavier hitters and outfight opponents with boxing skills equal to his own. He was never a knockout puncher, but he hit just hard enough to keep all the knockout punchers respectful.

Ray Actis was a knockout puncher, and he had Billy down in the third round of their fight in San Francisco two months after the Conn-Yarosz fiasco. In the next round, Actis was down. In the eighth round, with Actis out on his feet, the referee stopped it.

Next, Billy got the return match he wanted -- a twelve-rounder at Duquesne Gardens with the National Boxing Association's new middleweight champion. Out in Seattle, Solly Krieger had taken the title from Al Hostak. Against Conn, he would not be defending it: both fighters exceeded the middleweight limit of 160 pounds. Otherwise, there would have been another new champion, for this was not the Conn who had lost to Krieger in their earlier fight. Krieger may have won a round or two, but no more.

And so now all of a sudden Conn was a marquee fighter. He had beaten former champs and future champs but never before a current champ like Krieger. He was ready for New York, ready to be matched with the other current middleweight champ, Fred Apostoli. An aggressive pit bull of a fighter, Apostoli had beaten Krieger twice, the second time by knocking him out. He was the "real" middleweight champion, everyone knew -- the New York State Athletic Commission's champion.

The bout with Apostoli, a Mike Jacobs promotion, would be Conn's first appearance in Madison Square Garden, and the Pittsburgh saloon keeper Owney McManus chartered the first of his Ham and Cabbage Specials, so called. The Ham and Cabbage Special -- a private railroad car, or sometimes two private cars, attached to a New York-bound express train and filled with admirers of Conn, mostly but not exclusively Irish -- became a fixture from then on for Conn's big fights in the big town. The more uninhibited passengers wore leprechaun hats and paper shamrocks. They provided their own refreshments, mainly liquid. No ham or cabbage was served.

Conn and Apostoli treated New York to an entertaining fight. Making use of his advantage in height, weight, and quickness, Conn won the decision in ten rounds. He had outgrown the middleweight division, so Apostoli's title, like Krieger's in Pittsburgh, was not at stake. New York didn't care. New York's Irish, and some non-Irish too, went wild over Conn. His looks and his fighting spirit dazzled them. The fact is that Conn was more popular in New York than in Pittsburgh, where Zivic and Yarosz had sizable followings and where anyone who understood boxing could tell you how good Charley Burley was. Back home, it was nothing unusual for Conn to hear boos.

Among the many New Yorkers who took a liking to Conn was Frankie Carbo, a mob guy and businessman. Frankie Carbo entered into partnerships with the always compliant managers of promising young fighters, partnerships which the managers hadn't sought. One day while Conn was training at the Pioneer Gym in New York, preparing for his return match with Apostoli, who should walk in but Carbo. "I've got a piece of your fighter," he announced to Johnny Ray. Henceforth, he said, he was cutting himself in on all of Conn's earnings in New York.

To Carbo's great surprise, Ray answered, "No, you aren't." While there never has been any firm confirmation of this, in all probability Ray then got in touch with Milton Jaffe, who handled money matters for Conn and Ray, and Jaffe got in touch with Art Rooney, who had been his business partner toward the end of the Prohibition era. Together, they owned a floating casino in the Allegheny River on which gambling and booze were available. More to the point, through his connections as a boxing promoter, Rooney knew the mobster Owney Madden.

In the 1930s, with a fight manager named Bill Duffy, Madden had guided the inept Italian giant Primo Carnera through a series of fixed fights to the heavyweight championship. While their man mountain held the title, they brought him to Pittsburgh as a favor to Rooney for a charity exhibition bout at St. Peter's School on the North Side. St. Peter's was where Rooney had gone to grade school; the North Side was where he continued to live. The proceeds from the exhibition went to the Depression-battered parishioners of St. Peter's Church, where Rooney was a daily communicant. It is more than likely, therefore, that Ray spoke to Jaffe and Jaffe spoke to Rooney and Rooney spoke to Duffy and Duffy spoke to Madden. What Conn himself verified is that two days after the visit from Carbo, one of Madden's enforcers, a man named Cockeye Dunn, came around to the Pioneer Gym and told Ray not to worry: there would be no further trouble from any mob guy, least of all a small-timer like Carbo.

Conn's rematch with Apostoli sold out Madison Square Garden. Before their first fight, Conn never wore a mouthpiece. "I got one the next day," he said. The second fight -- fifteen rounds instead of ten -- made the first fight seem tame. It was like a trip through hell, but the result was the same as before: a close but unanimous decision for Conn.

Showing the after-effects, he came home to Pittsburgh with his head wrapped in bandages. A Pittsburgh Press photographer was waiting for him at Pennsylvania Station and took a picture that ran on page one with the caption: "If This Is the Winner, What Does the Loser Look Like?" Conn thought that was hilarious. The loser, he liked to recall, did not have a mark on him. And the winner, he would add, went from the railroad station to Mercy Hospital for two days of rest and repairs.

Leased out, in effect, to Madison Square Garden and Mike Jacobs, Conn returned by popular demand for a third fight with Krieger, winning easily in twelve rounds. They were to meet one last time -- at a parking lot in Miami years later. Krieger parked Billy's car, and Billy handed him a twenty-dollar tip. The whole sorry business was depressing to Billy. "I felt like crying," he said.

Conn felt true compassion for anybody who worked. He knew that some men, and Krieger may have been among them, wanted nothing more than to work -- nothing more than to have a job and a paycheck -- but he never understood why. Sure, training for a fight was work -- hard work, tedious work. Billy knew that, too, but training didn't make you a human ant. Somehow it wasn't drudgery, like putting in eight long hours a day at the Westinghouse plant, where his father had taken him for a glimpse of the promised land. He thought of boxing -- his chosen profession -- as the lesser of two evils. No one with any sense would be a fighter, he said, but it was better than working at Westinghouse, better than working in a steel mill.

Two months after beating Krieger, he was fighting Melio Bettina for Bettina's light-heavyweight championship. Like Young Corbett III, Bettina was a southpaw. He came from Beacon, New York, twenty or thirty miles up the Hudson River. The town's population included many Italians, and the ones who had ringside seats at Madison Square Garden on the night of the Bettina-Conn fight rolled out a banner: "Bring Home the Bacon to Beacon." Conn, waiting for the bell, glanced down at these hopeful partisans and made a prediction: "There's gonna be a lot of hungry dagoes in Beacon tonight."

Over the first five rounds, which Bettina won, it seemed probable that Beacon would get its bacon and Conn would be eating crow. He was lucky: ten rounds remained -- time enough to dissect Bettina's style. Coming back strong, Conn earned the decision, a close one disputed by the loser.

There would have to be a return match, even while Conn, Ray, and Mike Jacobs were looking farther ahead. At 21, Billy was still almost gaunt. In none of his fights had he weighed more than 170 pounds and a fraction. The light-heavyweight limit was 175. And yet if Ray and Jacobs had their way -- if Conn himself had his way -- he would soon be fighting as a heavyweight. It was gratifying to be the light-heavyweight champion, but the heavyweight division, Conn reminded Ray, was where the money was. It was also where Joe Louis was, a champion bereft of challengers.

Since his first-round destruction of Max Schmeling -- ample repayment for the only defeat on his record -- Louis had been reduced to what the sportswriters dismissed as a bum-of-the-month agenda. He had knocked out John Henry Lewis, the light-heavyweight champion before Bettina, sending him into retirement. John Henry was going blind, so when Louis made it short and sweet, knocking him out in a minute or two, it was viewed as an act of mercy. He had knocked out Jack Roper and Tony Galento, who could see well enough, but were retreads. What Louis badly needed was someone like Conn, someone new and exciting.

There was an X factor, though -- Conn's size, or lack of it. Mike Jacobs' plan was to give him a tryout -- to see how he looked against a heavyweight who wasn't a battleship. Broadway plays always opened in the sticks (defined as anywhere but New York), so Jacobs (who brokered or scalped tickets for Broadway plays) outsourced Conn to Philadelphia for a fight with Gus Dorazio. When they met, on August 14, 1939, the thirteen-pound difference in the weights was no problem for Conn. He passed his test impressively, winning in the eighth round by a TKO.

For Conn, Ray, and Jacobs, that settled it. Billy's destiny was now clear. He would fight his way to the top of the heavyweight heap and then take on Louis. In the meantime, there were promises to keep. Pittsburgh deserved a title fight and Bettina deserved a return bout. It would be held at Forbes Field in September, with Jacobs promoting. Pittsburgh was Art Rooney's promotional turf, but Jacobs could move in on anyone.

He'd be coming to Pittsburgh at something of a sacrifice, actually. In Yankee Stadium or the Polo Grounds, the crowd would have been larger than the 18,422 who paid their way into Forbes Field. At least the gate receipts -- $62, 892 -- broke the Pittsburgh record. With the war heating up in Europe, America was re-arming, which meant that the steel mills were making steel, which meant that for Pittsburgh the Depression was over. There was one other reason for Jacobs to be satisfied -- Conn's performance. After a characteristically slow start he dominated the fight, winning the last nine rounds at a fast gallop. Whether Bettina could go fifteen was the only question, and he just barely managed it. "People think Billy can't hit," Bettina said afterward. "Well, he stings you; he wears you down."

Conn made two more title defenses, both against the number one contender, Gus Lesnevich. The first of these fights was in Madison Square Garden, and Conn won as expected. True to form, he started out sluggishly and then accelerated. The newspaper critics were complimentary but seemed to be more interested in a fight on the undercard and its aftermath.

Jackie Conn, Billy's 17-year-old brother, had been boxing for several months. The only real thumping's he took had come at the hands of Billy, not all of them in the ring. Billy used Jackie as a sparring partner, but there were also bare-knuckle fights between them, with Jackie getting the worst of it. The bare-knuckle fights were triggered by Jackie's bold raids on Billy's new wardrobe and by his contraband joy rides in Billy's new Cadillac.

Jackie was two or three inches shorter than Billy, and he carried a lot of baby fat. Even so, when he hit somebody on the chin there were instantaneous results. A much better street fighter than he could ever hope to be with the gloves on, he thought of himself, despite all the evidence, as a future champion. "I'll lick *you* some day, Billy," he would threaten, but his aspirations ended in Madison Square Garden on the night of the first Conn-Lesnevich fight when a college boy called Mutt Wormer knocked him out in the first round.

As reported in the New York Post, Jackie's seconds half-carried him to Billy's dressing room, where he collapsed on a rubbing table and "wept as if his heart would break." Billy, after his own peculiar fashion, tried to console him. "Now, listen," he said. "You're through, see? You're hanging up your gloves right this minute. I'm not going to have guys like Mutt Wormer knocking you out. If anybody's going to lick you, I'll do it myself." He said that Jackie was disgracing the whole family. Then he ordered him to go take a shower.

Jackie stopped blubbering and followed instructions, but the next thing anyone knew he was banging his head against the wall of the shower room. "Fished out," as the New York Post writer put it, he started picking up chairs and throwing them. "I'm *not* through fighting!" he shouted at Billy. "You *can't* make me quit!"

In obvious need of sedation, Jackie spent the night at Polyclinic Hospital, missing his brother's fight with Lesnevich. Jackie himself never fought again except on asphalt or concrete. In the Pittsburgh Sun-Telegraph one day, he was pictured after duking it out with three slightly older guys. All four of them, arrested and taken to court, were looking up at a magistrate and into the camera. It appeared that Jackie's three adversaries would be wearing dark glasses and taking their meals through a feeding tube for some time to come. On his own round, cherub-like countenance there wasn't so much as a scratch.

Before beating Lesnevich again in a Mike Jacobs promotion at Olympia Stadium in Detroit, Billy had a tune-up fight with Henry Cooper and won in twelve easy rounds at Madison Square Garden. The return match with Lesnevich duplicated their first fight. Only because Conn took it easy in the closing rounds was Lesnevich on his feet at the final bell.

Conn waited a few weeks and then officially surrendered his light-heavyweight title . His first fight as a heavyweight was with Bob Pastor, who'd gone the distance with Louis -- ten rounds -- and then another ten rounds in their return match before the inevitable knockout. Conn had put on some weight, but not much. One hundred and eighty pounds was about the most that his lithe frame could accommodate. He did not seem to punch any harder. True, his fight with Pastor went into the books as a knockout, but the punches that floored Pastor three times may have been low.

It was easy to see that Pastor thought they were low. When the referee counted him out in the thirteenth round he was flopping around on the canvas, "clutching at his groin." Hitting low had cost Billy the previous round and a warning from the referee a round or two before that. The knockout punch, a left hook like the others, was "dangerously close" to being low, the referee said. Boxing adjudicator Nat Fleischer, sitting at ringside, pronounced it fair, and Conn called Pastor a crybaby.

Talking about the Pastor fight a long time afterward, Conn enlarged on the subject of pugilistic ethics. "You're not an altar boy in there," he said. "You do what you can to win -- hit 'em on the break, backhand, all that rotten stuff. What are they gonna do -- shoot you for it?" He sounded like Fritzie Zivic or Harry Greb.

Conn's fight with another good journeyman heavyweight, Lee Savold, was memorable for one thing. It changed his appearance. For eight rounds, he'd been satisfied just to outbox Savold, and the fans in Madison Square Garden were getting restless. They wanted more action. "So in the ninth I mixed it up, and he broke my nose," Conn recalled. "I said the hell with this and went back to boxing for the last three rounds."

The broken nose didn't ruin Conn's looks. In a way, it may have improved them. Case in point: Marlon Brando's broken nose. Also the result of a punch (Brando liked to box just for exercise), it enhanced his market value in Hollywood. As the producer's wife, Irene Selznick; explained, "The broken nose gave him sex appeal. He was too beautiful before."

Conn's win over Savold, added to his knockout of Pastor, made a title fight with Louis certain for the following summer. In the meantime, with a series of tune-ups on his schedule, he'd be dealing with two major distractions. Maggie, his beloved mother, was dying of cancer, and he had fallen hard for Mary Louise Smith. The trouble there was that Mary Louise's father, Greenfield Jimmy Smith, disapproved. In the first place, as he pointed out, Mary Louise was still just a teen-ager. In the second place, although Greenfield Jimmy had nothing against Billy as a person and nothing against prizefighters per se, he was resolved not to have one for a son-in-law.

Without exactly meaning to, Jimmy himself -- a former major-league baseball player who owned an upscale, membership-only restaurant and bar in Shadyside -- had brought Billy into his daughter's life through a casual invitation to the Smith family's summer place on the Jersey shore. For Billy, it was love at first sight. Smitten, he told the young charmer, "I'm going to marry you some day." Mary Louise raised an eyebrow at that, but the longer she thought about it the better she liked the idea. Not so her father.

A combative little guy just 5 feet 9 inches tall, Jimmy Smith was in the habit of backing up his words. As a utility infielder for John McGraw's New York Giants, he could always be found in the thick of things when an inside pitch or a slide into a base provoked fisticuffs. Frank Deford wrote that he faced down a whole dugout full of Brooklyn Dodgers, offering to fight them either one at a time or collectively.

To separate Mary Louise from Billy, Greenfield Jimmy packed her off to Rosemont College, a girls' school in Philadelphia. Intermittently, the lovebirds kept in touch. Before his fight at Philadelphia's Shibe Park with Dorazio -- the tryout arranged for him to see if he could handle heavyweights -- Conn bought twenty ringside tickets and had them delivered to Rosemont so that Mary Louise could be there with her college friends. But the Rosemont nuns had a nine o'clock curfew, and Billy's premium seats remained empty.

Getting ready for Louis, with Savold taken care of, Billy had four fights away from New York. They were all against nonentities and none went the distance. He dispatched Ira Hughes in the unlikely venue of Clarksburg, West Virginia, Danny Hassett in Washington, D.C., the Swede Gunnar Barlund in Chicago Stadium, and Buddy Knox at Forbes Field. Art Rooney and Barney McGinley co-promoted that one with Jacobs. Nobody expected a close fight, and it wasn't -- Conn won by a knockout when Knox was unable to answer the bell for the eighth round after going down three times in the seventh -- but the crowd of 27,042 was a new record for boxing in Pittsburgh.

Two days later, on May 28, 1941, Billy and Mary Louise drove to Brookville in northern Pennsylvania and took out a wedding license. Jimmy Smith was beside himself. He told a bishop what he would do if any Catholic priest in the Diocese of Pittsburgh married his daughter to Conn, and the bishop listened respectfully. Could no one stand up to this guy? Billy wondered.

In a newspaper interview, Jimmy said that the next fight Billy lost would not be to Louis but to him. No pug was going to marry his beautiful Mary Louise. Billy, putting Jimmy out of his thoughts, set up a training camp near Pompton Lakes in New Jersey.

The notion that Conn had a chance to beat Louis seemed insane. Opponents his own size did not have a chance against Louis, but public interest in the fight was enormous. For several days before June 18th, chartered trains in addition to the Ham and Cabbage Special carried thousands of believers in Conn from Pittsburgh to New York. If he felt any pressure, the object of all this enthusiasm kept it well hidden. On the afternoon of the fight, he almost gave Johnny Ray a heart attack by rough-housing with Jackie in his hotel room. They were down on the floor wrestling and punching each other when Ray walked in and put a stop to it..

Back in Pittsburgh that night, it bears repeating, the Pirates and the New York Giants suspended a game at Forbes Field before the start of the fourth inning so the players and spectators could listen to an amplified radio broadcast of the fight.

All over America people listened. Conn, when he took off his robe as he waited for the bell, looked pale but not pasty, thin but not frail. Louis seemed massive and calm. His smoothly muscled superstructure was glowing like polished brass. Conn had weighed in at 169 pounds -- below normal even for him -- and Louis at 201. The ring announcer, for propriety's sake, added a little something to Conn's weight, bringing it up to 174, and subtracted a bit from Louis's, reducing it to 199 ½.

In 1935, before he had won the championship, Louis boxed a German named Hans Birkie at Duquesne Gardens. The 17-year-old Conn took care of his resin box, and Louis paid him the standard fee -- two dollars. For this fight, Conn would be getting seventy-seven thousand and change.

He was tense going out for the first round. He was not afraid of Louis -- Conn wasn't afraid of anybody -- but in all of his fights he needed time to get started, and if a puncher like Louis tagged him early, that could be fatal. Gloves held high, he skipped around nervously and slipped, almost falling over backward. Either the canvas was wet or the soles of his shoes were too slick. Before the round was over, Conn slipped again, both feet skidding out from under him, and he landed ignominiously on his back.

If the first round was not good for Conn, the second round was worse. He took some shots to the body and head. But then in their first real exchange he held his own. Louis had a fast pair of hands, but Conn's were faster. Sure of himself now, he started fighting all-out in round three, swooping in on Louis and connecting with left hooks. Conn's left hook was as quick as his jab, and he was leading with it. He took some punches too, but whenever Louis landed hard, Conn tied him up. Between the third round and the fourth, he said to Johnny Ray, "This is a cinch."

The rest of the way, he fought with growing confidence. He never ran from Louis but was calibrating his movements to stay out of range, setting the champion up for sudden strikes. Inside, toe to toe, he could hit faster than Louis, and in their brief, fierce exchanges that is what he did, relying on his speed to make a clean escape. In the fifth round, though, and the sixth, the momentum changed. Louis was now hammering Conn. In the seventh Conn again took control. At the bell that ended the ninth, he had a few words for Louis. "Joe," he said, "you're in for a fight." Louis answered, "I know it."

The tenth and eleventh were big rounds for Conn. He was up on his toes, circling to his left, away from Louis's hook, landing punches in flurries and then disengaging. Louis seemed sluggish and hesitant. Conn slipped again in the tenth, falling into the ropes. With a glove on the middle strand, he dangled there for a moment, defenseless. Ever the true sportsman, Louis stepped back, refusing to take advantage.

At the end of the eleventh, Conn loped to his corner exultantly, waving a glove. He went out for the twelfth full of fire. A left hook caught Louis on the chin and made him pirouette into a clinch, one foot off the floor. With his arms around Billy's neck, Louis hung on to keep from going down. Conn belabored him for the rest of the round, punching from all angles. Louis, it appeared, was in trouble. But when the bell rang, ending the round, it was Conn who seemed disoriented; he took a step toward Louis's corner instead of his own.

With three rounds to go, he had the lead on two cards. One of the judges, inexplicably, thought the fight was even. Louis's handlers were telling him there was only one way he could win -- by a knockout. Johnny Ray, meanwhile, was trying to tell Conn something different. *Box. Stay away..* But, for once, his star pupil wasn't listening.

At the start of the round that would freeze his identity for all time, the thirteenth, he did not immediately tear into Louis. He fiddled around for at least a full minute, and only then did he come off his toes and start throwing punches recklessly, using his right as much as his left but sometimes doubling up on his hook. There was no moving in and moving out. Flatfooted, he stood in front of Louis and kept up a barrage. He threw seventeen punches altogether and most of them landed.

But suddenly, over a left hook that missed, Louis drove a murderous right, and Conn was hurt. He tried to clinch. He couldn't hold Louis off, and now it was Louis landing punches without a return. Watching the fight film half a century later, Conn said, "He hit me twenty-five good shots." The twenty-fifth put him down. He dropped to the canvas heavily and for seven or eight seconds was motionless, curled up on his right side,. Then the instinct that born fighters have, the propellant that seems to act on its own, took effect. Pushing himself up, he wobbled to his feet. It wasn't soon enough. Eddie Josephs, the referee, had counted him out. With two seconds left in the round, the fight was over, and just as well for Conn. He sobbed all the way to his dressing room.

At the Waldorf Hotel, in midtown Manhattan, Mary Louise had listened to the fight with her aunt Catherine. To put that more accurately, Aunt Catherine listened while Mary Louise sequestered herself in the bathroom with her rosary beads, emerging between rounds to hear a strangled synopsis of Don Dunphy's blow-by-blow description ("My God, Mary Louise, he's winning, he's winning!")

Conn, after dealing with the sportswriters, wept some more, showered, got into his street clothes, and walked five miles from the Bronx to the Waldorf with Johnny Ray. Here and there as they passed through Harlem, jubilant Louis fans recognized Billy and called out condolences. When Mary Louise answered his knock at the door, he stood in front of her alone, having parted with Ray, and forced out the words, "I did my best." The tears were back in his eyes. "Billy," she said, "it's all right."

Billy and Mary Louise intended to be married on June 20th, two days after the fight, at the Smith family's church, St. Philomena's in Squirrel Hill, but the father of the bride profanely refused to give his blessing and somehow it postponed the ceremony. By one means or another, Jimmy Smith had a way of getting things done.

Billy's mother died on June 28th. The day after the funeral, Billy and Mary Louise eloped, having found a priest who feared neither bishops nor Jimmy Smith. Father Francis Schwindlein tied the knot at St. Patrick's Church in Philadelphia. Mary Louise had recently turned 18. Billy was 23.

Predictably, a heightened period of estrangement between the newlyweds and Jimmy Smith followed the nuptials. Jimmy told a sportswriter, "I'll punch the hell out of that fellow," meaning Billy, not the priest. "I'm trying to raise a decent family," he said. "I don't want my daughter mixed up with a prizefighter."

The rest of the country was a bit more open-minded. Republic Pictures enticed the honeymooning pair to Hollywood, where Billy played a fictionalized version of himself in a prize-fight movie called "The Pittsburgh Kid." It was shot in two weeks and Billy got $25,000 for a performance of which he said later, "I'd rather not talk or think about it." With $17,000 from his earnings, he bought a house in Squirrel Hill, and the story was that when unwelcome visitors made an appearance they would find themselves watching a re-run of the movie.

Billy may have been a wooden actor, but Warner Brothers asked him to play the lead in "Gentleman Jim," a movie about the debonair nineteenth-century heavyweight champion James J. Corbett. He did not for a moment consider it, and Errol Flynn got the part. Billy had a low opinion of acting and actors. He refused to let Mary Louise accept a bit part in "The Pittsburgh Kid," and when the screen writer Budd Schulberg offered him a role in "On the Waterfront," the 1954 classic about dockside union racketeering, Billy answered with finality, "One stink bomb is enough."

Marlon Brando won an Oscar in "Waterfront" as a washed-up boxer named Terry Malloy. There's a scene full of pathos in which Terry's brother, played by Rod Steiger, tells him, "Kid, when you weighed 168 pounds, you were beautiful. You could have been another Billy Conn." The real Billy Conn was watching the film at the Stanley Theater in downtown Pittsburgh, and as soon as the line was spoken, he used to say, some loudmouth in the audience called out, "He's a big enough bum as it is." Billy took delight in telling jokes on himself, even if he had to make them up.

In the months between the Japanese attack on Pearl Harbor and his induction into the Army, Conn had three fights, winning handily enough from Henry Cooper again in Toledo, J. D. Turner in St. Louis, and Tony Zale, the middleweight champion, in New York. In none of the three did he resemble his old self. Zale got in one good punch, his trademark left hook, at the start of the first round, and from then on Billy fought going backwards. Zale stumbled after him, swinging and missing while being peppered with jabs and hooks. Wanting more action, the crowd in Madison Square Garden, where Conn had previously heard only cheers, booed.

"Boxing," wrote the novelist Joyce Carol Oates, the most perceptive observer of fights and fighters who ever wore a skirt, "consumes the very excellence it displays. To expend oneself in fighting the greatest fight of one's life is to begin by necessity the downward turn that the next time may be a plunge, an abrupt fall into the abyss." From round seven through twelve against Louis, Conn fought the greatest fight of his life. Not until their return bout five years later would there be an abrupt fall into the abyss, but on June 18, 1941, Conn rose to the mountain top and then, by necessity, took the downward turn.

For a boxer so young, his climb had been astonishing. Old-time trainer Ray Arcel said that people didn't realize how good Conn was. Joe Louis had an accurate idea. Conn, Louis said, was the best light-heavyweight he ever saw. Boxing men like Teddy Brenner and Harry Markson of Madison Square Garden said the same thing. Nate Liff, who saw Harry Greb fight -- who worked in his corner, swinging a towel -- said that Greb-Conn "would be a toss-up." Johnny Ray, Greb's old sparring partner, gave Conn the edge over Greb. Conn himself, the chances are, would have disputed that. He was only eight years old when Greb died, but he "knew" -- just knew -- that Greb was the greatest fighter who ever lived. After the death of his mother Conn saw to it that she was buried as close as possible to where Greb had been laid to rest in Pittsburgh's Calvary Cemetery.

In March of 1942 Conn enlisted in the Army, having changed his mind about going into the Navy as a chief petty officer when he learned from Lieutenant Commander Gene Tunney that, like it or not, chief petty officers wore bell-bottom pants. Conn had no use for bell-bottom pants or for Tunney, who rubbed him the wrong way. Tunney once told a New York sportswriter that Conn would lose to Sugar Ray Robinson if they fought. A day or two later, Conn was in Mike Jacobs' office when Robinson walked in. "Let's go down to the parking lot and settle this," Conn said. Robinson answered, "Billy, it was Tunney who said that, not me."

The Army sent Conn to Fort Campbell in Kentucky for basic training and then made him a boxing instructor first class. Joe Louis was in the Army too, but the War Department gave its permission for a second Conn-Louis fight to be held at Yankee Stadium in June. Although the Army Emergency Relief Fund was to get an undisclosed percentage of the gate receipts, there would still be enough to go around, and Conn looked forward to another big payday. Then fate took a hand. An off-the-books, highly impromptu bare-knuckle fight in the kitchen of Jimmy Smith's house in Squirrel Hill unexpectedly pre-empted the Army-sanctioned affair.

Excused from his military duties at Fort Wadsworth on Staten Island, Billy had started training for the return match with Louis. Early in May, Mary Louise gave birth to a son, David Phillip. Billy obtained a three-day pass and came home for the christening. He had neither seen nor spoken to Jimmy Smith since the wedding, but Art Rooney, David Phillip's godfather, got them together for a handshake and a pledge to forget their differences. After the christening at St. Bede's Church in Point Breeze, Jimmy invited everyone to a bury-the-hatchet party at his house, where the truce brought about by Art Rooney disintegrated.

Late in the afternoon, with the men all gathered in the kitchen, Jimmy brought up the subject of Billy's irregular church attendance. Billy was sitting on the stove. He said something back, whereupon Jimmy offered to punch him. More than forty years afterward Art Rooney told Frank Deford, "I can still see Billy coming off that stove."

Greenfield Jimmy met him in full flight, and when at last they were separated Billy's left hand was broken. He had bounced it off Jimmy's head. There were scratches and lacerations all over Billy's face; not even Joe Louis had done as much visible damage. Billy's opponent, middle-aged Jimmy Smith, was unscathed. From then on for many years, Louis would ask Billy whenever they met if his father-in-law had beaten him up lately.

With Billy's left hook inoperative, Conn-Louis II was put on hold until after the war. In the meantime, the Army assigned Billy to a traveling special-services unit. It went from camp to camp in the United States and from command post to command post in the European Theater. Putting on the gloves with company, battalion, and regimental champions, Billy took care not to show anybody up.

He had one close call with death -- as a passenger aboard a small transport plane which developed trouble of some kind on a flight across the Mediterranean Sea. Billy promised God that if the plane landed safely he would give five thousand dollars to Sacred Heart Church in East Liberty for a statue of the Blessed Mother and five thousand dollars to Art Rooney's brother Dan, a Franciscan priest, for the order's missionary work. The pilot brought the plane down in Marseilles without mishap, and Billy kept both of his vows.

His commanding officer, a professional golfer named Horton Smith, reminded him a little of Tunney. "He wanted me to salute and call him sir," Billy said. Saluting and stirring people was not his style, not at all, and Captain Smith threatened to bust him from corporal to private. Just in time, duplicating the way that George Patton's Third Army relieved the American troops at Bastogne, a civilian, Bob Hope, rescued Billy. The actor and entertainer were in France with another special-services outfit. He knew all the generals. With a few well-placed words, he was able to get Billy transferred from Horton Smith's unit to his own.

After getting out of the Army in September of 1945, Billy spent some time with his family, which now included a second son, Billy Junior. He learned that his first-born's name, at the behest of Jimmy Smith, had been changed from David Phillip to Tim -- which sounded "more Irish," the doting grandfather explained. Jimmy, it turned out , was ready to let bygones be bygones, and slowly the tension between father-in-law and son-in-law changed into genuine friendship.

Billy's three and a half years in the Army had been poor preparation for his 1946 fight with Louis, to be held at Yankee Stadium on June 19th. He was twenty pounds overweight and his timing was off. So bad did he look in a couple of exhibition bouts that Milton Jaffe took him to Hot Springs, Arkansas, where know-it-all sportswriters from the East seldom ventured.

Remarkable for the easy-going ways of its law-enforcement officers, Hot Springs was a resort town with mob-controlled gambling and horse racing. Owney Madden lived there in retirement -- married to the postmaster's daughter, taking the baths, walking his dog, cultivating his garden, and contributing often to charity. The chief of police was his next-door neighbor. Tourists from the North, along with hustlers and racketeers, congregated in Hot Springs during the winter months, but nothing about the place or its setting in the hills appealed to Conn. When Nate Liff, who ran his training camp, assured him that western Arkansas was "God's country," Billy answered, "I wouldn't give you an alley in Pittsburgh for it."

In April he moved his training site to Greenwood Lake in New York. It was clear to anyone who knew boxing that his once exceptional skills were completely gone. Johnny Ray -- drunk most of the time -- was of no use to him at all. As for the showing he made against Louis -- witnessed, unfortunately, by more people than ever had seen a fight, a television audience of 146,000 plus the 45,266 ticket buyers in Yankee Stadium -- the less said the better. There were those who believed, without any evidence for it, that he went into the ring unknowingly drugged. At 182 pounds he was too heavy and too slow. Louis looked almost as bad but could still punch. He knocked Billy out in the eighth round. Conn's only other knockout defeat was in the first Louis fight.

At 28, he was finished. His purse -- twenty percent of the box-office net -- came to $325,998.22, the equivalent of several million in today's currency. There were debts and taxes to pay, and his management team, Ray and Jaffe, got one-third off the top, but he had earned more than half a million dollars in the ring all told and would never have to work in the usual sense of the word

For six months or so, he secluded himself from the public, emerging at last to front for some Oklahoma oil men. They persuaded him to go through the motions of a comeback. He made appearances in Macon and Dallas, knocking over a couple of stiffs, and boxed a six-round exhibition with Louis in Chicago. What finalized his decision to retire was a sparring session at the Lyceum Gym with Charley Affif, a middleweight contender at the time. Conn didn't do very well. Afterward, he said to Affif pleasantly., "When a bum like you can hit me, I know I'm finished,".

Eventually the oil-well venture played itself out, and Conn allowed the use of his name by a car dealer. On the side, he managed a few fighters in a half-hearted way. He was too impatient with them to be successful.

In 1966, Carlos Ortiz, the lightweight champion, defended his title against Sugar Ramos in a bull ring in Mexico City, and Bill Daley, the champion's manager, arranged for Conn to referee. Behind in the scoring, Ortiz opened a cut over Ramos's eye. It was bleeding badly, so Billy stopped the fight, as he should have done. The spectators, unhappy about it, pelted him with bottles, rocks, and pesos. It was no sure thing that he would leave the bull ring alive. "I had some bad moments in the thirteenth round with Louis," Billy said, "but this was worse." He'd had some even worse moments in a disabled airplane during World War II and had bargained with the Lord; what saw him through this time was the Mexican Army. Between a double line of soldiers, he scrambled to the safety of an automobile escort.

This was after Milton Jaffe, who owned a piece of the Stardust, a gambling and entertainment palace in Las Vegas, had put Billy to work out there as a "greeter" -- a glad-hander. It didn't last. Billy wasn't cut out for that sort of thing, and he hated Las Vegas, as did Mary Louise and the kids (with the addition of a third son, Michael, and a daughter, Suzanne, there were now four). Inside of three years they returned to Pittsburgh. The time was not far off, Billy predicted, when Las Vegas would be destroyed by a thunderbolt sent down from on high.

Public appearances were distasteful to him, but once when Joe Louis was in town they went to an affair in a union hall, and Billy took along the film of their first fight in a shopping bag. While he watched it with the union members, Louis ducked into the bar, sticking his head out every few minutes to ask what round it was. At the start of the thirteenth, he grabbed a chair in the back row and sat there unnoticed in the dark until the knockout. Then he jumped to his feet and shouted, "Good-bye, Billy!" Billy didn't seem to be amused.

For the most part, Billy hung out with a few close friends, among them the affable 6-foot-3, 270-pound Joey Diven, who parlayed his celebrity as one of the great undefeated bar-room and street fighters into a political career of sorts. There were scrapes from time to time -- with a pal named Jack Cargo they wrecked the Gaslight Club in Shadyside one night after Joey had bounced the bouncer -- but nothing that couldn't be squared with the cops.

Mayors, county commissioners and the like would make room for Billy on their payrolls. His only obligation was to pick up his check. He disdained any job that made demands on his time but would put in a good word for friends. Once when Jack Lynch, the county controller, balked at hiring Cargo with the explanation, "Gee, Billy, he wouldn't ever show up," Billy said to him, "Well, look at it this way -- would you want him around?" For all of its beautiful simplicity, his reasoning left the controller unmoved.

When there were big fights in New York, the promoters would sometimes ask Billy to come in from Pittsburgh and help with the publicity -- answer questions from the sportswriters, talk about the merits of whoever was going to be in the main event, and so on. Often his observations were not in the promotion's best interests, for, with few exceptions, Billy did not think much of the fighters who came along after the 1940s. Naively, a reporter once asked him if modern-day boxers skipped rope. "Yes, but they should hang themselves with it, as bad as they are," Conn said. Another time, when a fighter explained that he always allowed his sparring partners to hammer away at his midsection "because it tightens your stomach muscles," Conn rolled his eyes. "That doesn't tighten your stomach," he said, "it loosens your brain."

At a training camp in the Catskills before the fight between Jerry Quarry and Joe Frazier, I stood next to Conn near the ring while Quarry sparred. Quarry was Irish, the first Irish heavyweight contender since Conn, and so that was the promotional gimmick. Unlike Conn, Quarry boxed with his hands low, allowing them to dangle. Only amateurs and fools boxed like that, Conn believed. He called Quarry over at the end of a round and, in tones that were almost fatherly, advised him to hold his hands up. Quarry told Conn he knew what he was doing and walked away -- a vaudeville hoofer rejecting a tip from Gene Kelly. Disgusted, Conn said to me, "I hope that bum gets knocked out in the first round." I was standing at Conn's left. On his right was Quarry's youngest brother, age six or seven, who couldn't believe what he was hearing. He looked up at Conn and asked, "Do you think my brother's a bum?" "A *big* bum," Conn answered, and went off in search of the limousine driver who had brought him to the camp from New York.

Quarry did get knocked out, but in the seventh round, not the first. Conn wasn't present at the fight, having given away his complimentary tickets.

He attended banquets, sometimes taking questions from the audience. At a dinner in Rochester, New York, someone asked for his opinion of a popular home-town lightweight. "Never heard of him," Billy said. "Who is he?" "The guy sitting next to you on the dais," he was told.

Late in life, unwillingly, Billy endured a testimonial dinner for himself at the Pittsburgh Hilton. There were too many speakers and all of them talked too long. When at last the toastmaster called on Billy -- "And now we will hear from the guest of honor" -- he got to his feet, accepted an envelope with a check in it, said, "Thank you," and sat down. Tickets for the affair were fifty dollars. A man who had bought six approached Mary Louise and asked if she could give him a copy of Billy's speech.

In "The Boxer and the Blonde," Billy and Mary Louise live happily ever after. And that is the way it was until Billy started having memory lapses and showing other signs of confusion. Dr. Paula Trzepacz, an associate professor at the University of Pittsburgh's school of medicine, determined after an examination that he was suffering from pugilistica dementia, which is similar to, but not identical with, Alzheimer's Disease and is irreversible. He was 75 when he died, after months of confinement at the Highland Park Veterans Hospital.

While he was still living at home in the early stages of his decline, he'd had one last spur-of-the-moment fight. Returning from Saturday night Mass at St. Philomena's, Billy and Mary Louise stopped off to buy coffee at a convenience store. A holdup man in his mid-twenties followed them in. "Give me your money," he said to the cashier. Under a hooded black sweatshirt, he appeared to be pointing a gun. Mary Louise, at a signal from Billy, started for the door. The cashier seemed petrified. To get his attention, the holdup man leaned across the counter and punched him in the face. At this point Billy took over. He stepped toward the intruder and sent him reeling with a magically restored left hook. Then he wrestled the guy to the floor. It was not a clean knockdown, but the holdup man knew he was dealing with a pro. He struggled to his feet, ran outside, and was gone.

Billy Conn was 72 then and deteriorating physically. The young thug, as far as anyone could tell, had a deadly weapon. So why would Billy take such a gamble? Who knows, except that when Billy thought he should do something, he went ahead and did something.

He cut through the mustard without any dithering. Without extensively weighing the consequences. Neither the fists of Joe Louis nor the threat of a holdup man's bullet gave him pause.

CHAPTER 11

FELLOW TRAVELERS

Sammy Angott and Jackie Wilson were nomads, boxing where opportunity led them.

Wilson, a featherweight, wandered all over the globe. He would stay in one place for months at a time, moving on when the supply of opponents gave out. He boxed in Australia, he boxed in the British Isles. He boxed in Southern California, which was teeming (and still is) with fighters as small as he was -- Mexicans, for the most part, but Orientals too. Everywhere else in nutrition-wise America, flyweights, bantamweights, and featherweights had become a collective endangered species.

Lightweights like Angott were plentiful enough, but though Pittsburgh was Angott's home base he did not have the following that bigger men did -- Fritzie Zivic, for example, and Billy Conn. Never thought of as a red-hot local attraction, Angott barnstormed. All five of his title fights -- and all four of Wilson's -- took place on the road. Even the second Wilson-Angott fight was held, for some reason, in the Middle West -- Milwaukee. Angott, making use of his size advantage, won the decision. Three years earlier, in 1935, he had outpointed Wilson at Hickey Park in Millvale.

Both future champions were building up to contender status at the time of this first fight, Wilson more slowly than Angott. On his invasion of England, Ireland, and Scotland, he lost only once in thirteen fights. In Australia he did not lose at all, winning ten out of ten. Angott continued to fight in Pittsburgh from time to time, but his manager, Charley Jones, originally from McKeesport, had moved to Louisville, where he could spend his afternoons at Churchill Downs. Jones was an accountant who liked to play the horses. It was in Louisville that Angott won the first of his three lightweight titles, the National Boxing Association's version.

Right name Salvatore Engotti, he lived in Washington, Pennsylvania, his birthplace. Engotti/Angott was not a pleasing fighter. Stubby and tenacious, he grabbed and held, pushed and pulled, staying on top of an opponent and giving him no room to punch. Nat Fleischer called Angott "the first unpopular lightweight champion." He was clever and he threw combinations, but mostly he worked inside, relentlessly digging away.

Wilson, by contrast, was slick, fast, elusive. In the featherweight division, only Willie Pep excelled him as a stylist. Eddie Shea, a heavy hitter from Chicago, expected to beat Wilson when they boxed at Motor Square Garden in 1933. "The only time you'll touch Jackie," Pittsburgh trainer Nate Liff told him, "is when the two of you shake hands before the fight." That was about the way it turned out.

Both Wilson and Angott had long careers. Wilson's first fight was in 1930, his last one in 1947. Between June of 1932 and July of 1937 he was undefeated. Angott boxed in three different decades, the thirties, forties, and fifties. Like many another practitioner of the arts, neither of them knew when to quit.

In and out of their divisions, they fought the best. Until Angott turned the trick, no one had beaten Pep. All in all, Angott had twenty-four fights with seventeen world champions, winning more often than he lost. One champion he lost to -- three times -- was Sugar Ray Robinson, each fight going the distance.

In an upside-down way, Angott was responsible for Fritzie Zivic's shot at the welterweight title. Eddie Mead, who managed the champion, Henry Armstrong, happened to be in town the day that Zivic and Angott were to box at Forbes Field -- August 28, 1940. Mead was en route from the Pacific Coast to New York, where Armstrong would make his next title defense, and he attended the Zivic-Angott fight, planning to choose one or the other as Armstrong's challenger. When he left after four rounds to catch a train, Angott was leading. To Mead, it seemed clear that he would be the tougher opponent for Armstrong. "We'll take Zivic," he said upon arriving in New York, and though Zivic had come on fast to win the decision from Angott, five weeks later he was fighting Armstrong, and beating him.

Angott's NBA lightweight title was not at stake in the Zivic fight. He had won it five months earlier by virtue of a fifteen-round decision over Davey Day. Lew Jenkins, a scrawny Texan with a knockout punch, was the New York State Athletic Commission's champion until he and Angott got together in Madison Square Garden on December 19, 1941, and Angott wrapped him up like a Christmas present. "Easiest fight of my life," Angott said. Jenkins, struggling to get out of clinches, needed the wiles of a Harry Houdini. He tried at one point to flip Angott over his head, almost succeeding. Angott lost a round on a foul, but he could spare it. Of the other fourteen, he won all but one.

In Angott's only fight as consensus champion, his opponent, Allie Stolz, forfeited two rounds for low blows, and Angott, getting up from a knockdown, won the decision, a disputed one. "They stole it from me," Stolz said. Over the weight, Angott beat future champion Bob Montgomery twice, lost to Robinson, and beat Aldo Spoldi, the Italian champion. He then announced his retirement. A hand he had broken in his second fight with Montgomery was giving him trouble.

Two months later, with his hand on the mend, Angott had a change of heart. Returning to the ring, he ended Willie Pep's winning streak at sixty-two fights. By his own admission, Pep failed to land a single clean punch, so successful was Angott at tying him up. Angott's pressing tactics could neutralize speed. Against someone like Armstrong, his next opponent, pressing tactics were not as effective. Armstrong simply met him head-on and won the decision.

The New York boxing commission had awarded Angott's lightweight title to Beau Jack, a shoeshine boy from Georgia who was knocking everybody out, but the NBA withheld its recognition and sanctioned a title match in Hollywood between Angott and Slugger White. Angott won. When the two champions, Angott and Jack, met in New York on January 28, 1942, the result was a draw.

Shuttling back to Hollywood, Angott then lost the NBA title to a 5-foot, 3-inch Mexican southpaw, Juan Zurita. After five more fights, three of them defeats, two at the hands of a future champion, Ike Williams, he announced his second retirement.

It lasted nine months, until August of 1945. He had not fought in Pittsburgh for almost four years, but now he was back again, appearing every few weeks at the Gardens. He boxed a draw there with Gene Burton and stopped Ike Williams in six. Williams had won their first two fights on split decisions. In this one, Angott's body blows were the difference.

Seemingly rejuvenated, he won his next two fights, both with Danny Kapilow, and then he overreached. In his third meeting with Robinson, before a sellout Gardens crowd of seven thousand (who had come to see Sugar Ray), he took a pasting. "Robinson is a great fighter, the best I ever saw," said Charley Jones afterward. Angott, who had been down twice, nodded. There was silence for a moment, and then Angott told the reporters, "I only wish I was a few years younger." Four months later, in Washington. D.C., Beau Jack knocked him out, doing what nobody else ever had.

But at 31 Angott was not yet finished. He actually won his next twelve fights, mostly in tank towns. Twice, though, he boxed in Chicago, outpointing Johnny Bratton, a future welterweight champion, for the second time. He never beat another first-rater, and in 1949 he started losing now and then to nobodies. In 1950, he retired again, for keeps, and took up managing, without much success.

Jackie Wilson came to Pittsburgh from Arkansas during the great black migration of the 1920s, still just a kid. In one of his first main events, he held the flyweight champion, Midget Wolgast, to a draw. Four years after turning pro, he had beaten Western Pennsylvania's two best little men, Willie Davies and Mose Butch, and most of the good little men between New York and Chicago.

Wilson beat Freddie Miller, the NBA featherweight champion, and Mike Belloise, the New York commission's champion, two weeks apart in non-title bouts at Duquesne Gardens. From then on, and he boxed for another ten years, his only fights in Pittsburgh were with Armanda Sicilia and Emil Joseph in 1939 and Willie Pep in 1943. Pep was the New York featherweight champion but had just lost to Angott. Wilson had won and lost the NBA title. Though they were fighting over-the-weight, the bout was a twelve-rounder, and Pep won. When he again beat Wilson three years later in Kansas City, he had still not lost since his fight with Angott and was the undisputed holder of both featherweight titles.

Another champion Wilson could never beat was featherweight Leo Rodak. Of their seven fights, the Chicagoan won four (the first three were draws). When Wilson won his NBA title from hard-hitting Richie Lemos in Los Angeles, Richie's hometown, he was 32 years old and almost spent. Calling on all the remnants of his skill, he out boxed Lemos easily and then won their return match the same way.

Simply by not defending it, he held the title for more than a year. In over-the-weight bouts, he won from the undistinguished Abe Denner and from Ceferino Garcia, the washed-up former middleweight champion, and, in his only New York appearance -- at St. Nicholas Arena -- lost an eight-round split decision to Terry Young. From the fifth round through the eighth he fought with what X-rays later revealed to be a broken bone in his left forearm. At last on January 18, 1943, Jackie Callura, of Hamilton, Ontario, succeeded him as featherweight champion by winning a fifteen-round decision when they met in Providence, Rhode Island. According to a wire-service story, Callura "wrestled, shoved, and lunged his way to victory." Two months later in Boston Callura did it again.

Consecutively, Wilson had four managers -- Pete Reilly, Harry Burnkrant, Bill Daley, and Jack Laken, who steered him to the title. He appears to have been an unobtrusive sort. Nate Liff remembered him as "quiet, quiet -- a gentleman." His decline was prolonged and pathetic. By 1946, fighting up and down the West Coast, he was losing to almost everybody and, for the first time since 1932, when he was still learning his trade, getting knocked out. Wilson lost sixteen of his last eighteen fights, and in four of them he wasn't able to finish.

Most boxers -- there never has been an adequate explanation for this -- live to a ripe old age. Jackie Wilson died at 57, all but forgotten. He died in obscurity; a Pittsburgh champion forever rootless.

CHAPTER 12

PARIAH

The most deserving Pittsburgh fighter who never had a chance to win a championship was Charley Burley. His story can be summarized in two words: excellence unrewarded. For reasons having to do with economics and discrimination, but mostly economics, no titleholder in either the middleweight or welterweight division would take the huge risk of losing to Burley. He was too good for his own good, and yet there is one more way to explain why Burley remained the permanent outsider, shunned not only by the managers of the fighters on top, but by promoters as well. And it isn't race.

Sure, pigmentation had something to do with why he was ostracized. He was black, or, rather, half black. His mother, a white woman named Angeline O'Brien, came to this country from County Cork in Ireland, but her American husband was black, and black always cancels out white. It's the way things were, and still are. And in Burley's day boxing was still not quite an equal-opportunity sport. The de facto segregation that kept major-league baseball, professional football, and intercollegiate team sports the province of whites only had never existed in boxing, but the champions were nearly always white. That was how the ticket buyers wanted it, or so the promoters believed. Look how long it took Sugar Ray Robinson, for all of his ability and for all of his appeal, to win a title -- more than six years.

Nevertheless, between 1926, when Tiger Flowers took the middleweight championship from Harry Greb, and 1950, the year Burley at last called it quits, many black and Hispanic boxers were getting title shots and, like Flowers, making the most of it. Why Burley was not among them never mystified the men of his profession. He represented what the boxing historian Douglas Cavanaugh has termed "a maximum risk/minimum gain option." That is to say, he was a dangerous opponent for any champion, and he did not, for reasons having to do with the calmly professional way he approached his job, excite the public. In short, he was not a box-office attraction. No middleweight or welterweight in the world could expect to have more than an even chance against Burley, if that, and he'd be working for what amounted to chump change..

So, right to the end, Burley kept winning fights against fellow outcasts or the occasional over-ambitious striver in places like the second-floor Aragon dance hall in Pittsburgh's downtown, where the top ticket price was three dollars or so and where crowds of a little over a thousand could fill all the seats.

Burley boxed for peanuts at the Aragon and for never much more than that anywhere else. Instead of riches, he piled up accolades -- often the same one, repeated verbatim. Archie Moore called him "the greatest all-around fighter I ever saw," either knowing or not knowing that Eddie Futch, the legendary trainer, also was calling Burley "the greatest all-around fighter I ever saw." Is there any other way you can say it?

Among the fighters Moore had seen from the receiving end of their punches were Muhammad Ali, Rocky Marciano, and Ezzard Charles. Eddie Futch had no peers at evaluating a fighter's assets and liabilities, and all he could find in Burley were assets. "He was a remarkable craftsman and a terrific puncher with either hand," Futch told the journalist Allen Barra. "He had a number of weapons going for him, and if he had to make adjustments to his opponent's style, he could do it quickly. It's a pity," Futch added, "that there aren't any films to show posterity how good Burley was."

As it happens, there is one -- of his fight in 1946 with a top-notch light-heavyweight, Billy Smith, in Oakland, California. The weights as announced from the ring that night were 160 for Burley and 172 for Smith. Burley's actual weight was 148. They had boxed in Oakland only six months before. Burley won that fight and he won the return match.

No round of the second fight is shown in its entirety, but parts of all ten are shown, and Smith doesn't land a single hard blow. Burley never gives him anything to hit. He was artful at the game called bait and switch, skipping out of his corner at the start of each round with an eagerness that belied his intentions, for instead of taking the fight to Smith, he would wait for a chance to counter-punch. Left shoulder forward in a sideways stance, he fought with his hands low, keeping just out of range and pulling back from Smith's leads or hopping back instead of blocking them. Burley was amazingly agile and fluid. He feinted with his head and with his shoulders. Smith, looking foolish and frustrated, would swing and miss and leave himself open, and Burley would jump in with a left hook to the body or an overhand right to the head. He used his left jab defensively, to take Smith out of his rhythm.

Archie Moore became an expert on Burley in 1944, when the paths of these wanderers, who traveled far and wide looking for chances to make a buck, crossed in Hollywood. Burley, exempt from military service because of a perforated eardrum, had a wartime job in a San Diego foundry. Having agreed to fight Moore as an eleventh-hour substitute, the story goes, he made a hurried trip home to pick up his equipment and then hopped a bus to Los Angeles, 125 miles away. Pure hokum. He'd signed a contract for the fight days before, maybe even weeks before -- long enough, anyway, for posters to be printed. In beating Moore easily, he bounced him off the canvas four times.

Allen Barra quotes Moore as saying, "Charley Burley could do things that nobody else could do. I caught him leaning way back. He was clear off balance. He didn't have any leverage in that position, but he almost took my head off with a monster left hook. He suckered me in beautifully."

Eight years later Moore would be the light-heavyweight champion. Burley, the younger of the two, would be picking up trash. About the time that Moore got into the money, his long quest for recognition behind him, Burley took a job with the City of Pittsburgh's sanitation department. In his last fight, temporarily leaving the garbage truck, he traveled down to Lima, Peru, and knocked out Pilar Bastidas, light-heavyweight champion of South America.

Bastidas, of course, kept his title, the existence of which was largely unknown on the other six continents. I have said that Burley never fought for a title. To be exact, he never fought for a title worth having. During his sojourn on the Pacific Coast, he won the middleweight championship of California from Jack Chase, another good black fighter the good white fighters avoided, knocking Chase out in the ninth round.

The only white champions Burley could entice into a ring were champions in the making, Fritzie Zivic and Billy Soose. Both lost to Burley when they were still on the rise, doing no harm to their own careers but damaging Burley's irreversibly. Suddenly no white contender -- no white contender whose manager gave a thought to his welfare -- wanted anything to do with Burley. Eventually, even Zivic steered clear of him, and Zivic, it always had seemed, would take on anybody.

The way he ducked Burley -- by purchasing his contract and becoming his manager -- was ingenious. Burley had beaten him twice in a row after losing the first of their three fights on a questionable decision, Enabled as Burley's manager to call the shots, Zivic was thus in a position to ignore any public demand for a fourth fight between them.

Only there wasn't any public demand. The fact is -- and it explains the neglect of Burley a lot more than racism does -- that he lacked what Ray Robinson had: star quality. All really knowledgeable fans delighted in watching Burley. In the words of Archie Moore, "He could feint you crazy. When you threw a jab, you'd better hit the guy, because he'd counter." Exactly, but for the great majority of fight watchers, that was the rap against Burley. He wouldn't lead, except when he had an opponent hurt, and then, as Moore put it, his punches came as rapidly as machine-gun fire. Ordinarily, though, he was patient and systematic, and prudent counter-punchers, even great ones, don't draw.

Being black merely compounded the problem for Burley. In the 1940s there were other black fighters too good for their own good, and they fought one another to make a living -- fought one another again and again. Collectively, they were known as the Black Murderers' Row, and Burley was one of them. Burley had seven fights with Holman Williams of Detroit, winning three and losing three with one "no contest." Williams was Burley's equal as a defensive artist but didn't punch as hard. Burley fought Jack Chase three times, Cocoa Kid twice, and Bert Lytell twice. He tangled with heavier black fighters -- Moore, Lloyd Marshall, Jimmy Bivins.

J. D. Turner, who lasted ten rounds in a losing effort against Billy Conn, was 6 feet 3 and weighed 225 pounds. Burley, 5-9 and 151 ½, dispatched Turner in six. "I had a hard time reaching him, but I worked on the belly until I made the other part fall," Burley told me. Actually, the fight came to an end with Turner in his corner. Battered and bloodied, he failed to answer the bell for the seventh round.

Marshall, Bivins, and Ezzard Charles were just a little too much for Burley. One successful white fighter whose manager barred no one was Georgie Abrams, a middleweight with three wins over Soose. "Burley Easily Beats Abrams," read the headline in the Pittsburgh Press, disregarding the fact that the official decision when they boxed at Hickey Park in Millvale on July 29, 1940, was a draw.

Something else that worked against Burley was his refusal to "do business" -- purposely lose a fight to advance his career. In the mob-controlled days of boxing, a fighter might go in the tank to facilitate a gambling coup or to set up a big-money return bout. As recompense, besides a payoff, there would be the confident expectation of benefits to come -- benefits in the way of desirable matches.

None of Burley's managers seemed to have any clout. Including Zivic, there were probably a dozen or more. So many years have gone by that it's hard to reconstruct their comings and goings. Chappy Goldstein was the manager who sold Burley's contract to Zivic. How much Zivic paid remains a secret, but two years later he passed Burley on to Tommy O'Loughlin for five hundred dollars, fair market value. O'Loughlin promoted fights in Minneapolis, where in 1941, shortly before the Japanese bombed Pearl Harbor, Burley and his wife Julia went to live. Bobby Eaton managed him there, apparently as a front man for O'Loughlin.

One thing his managers had in common. All except Zivic, who hired an agent, Schnitz Silverman, to book fights for Burley, considered him "difficult." "He was never satisfied," one old-timer recalled. Small wonder: Burley's largest purse was three thousand dollars for his second fight with Smith. A crowd of twenty thousand at Forbes Field saw Burley's third fight with Zivic; his purse that night was fifteen hundred dollars.

Promoters explained that Burley didn't bring in the customers. About the only place where he could walk down the street and be recognized was the mostly black Hill district. Burley grew up there, biographer Allen S. Rosenfeld writes, in several different locations. After his father, a coke-oven worker in Westmoreland County, died of a miner's disease, the widowed Angeline moved with Charley and a younger sister to Pittsburgh, where three older sisters were living. Burley attended a Hill district high school, Fifth Avenue, and worked for a butcher in the Jewish section of the Hill, plucking chickens. He learned to box at the Kay Boys' Club.

Burley had bronze-skinned good looks, and he retained those good looks after years in the ring because he never took a punch in order to land one. In the way he dressed and deported himself, he radiated style. One of the neighborhood kids was August Wilson. For a New Yorker piece by the drama critic John Lahr, Wilson described Burley as a "role model for manhood," unforgettably impressive "in his Friday-night regalia -- hundred-dollar Stetson, cashmere coat, yam-colored Florsheim shoes." He was one of those black men, Wilson told Lahr, who "elevated their presence into an art." The lead character in Wilson's play "Fences," an embittered black baseball player too old to profit from the integration of the major leagues in the late 1940s, is patterned after Burley, Wilson said.

Burley himself did not seem embittered so much as forbearing. In 1983, pensioned off by the city, he was living near Pitt Stadium in a small brick duplex. "I've been through the mill," he said to me there one day in a patient, long-suffering tone. "I had a stroke a couple of years ago. I've been in the hospital. I've been back and forth to the doctor. The stroke stressed me up. I can't remember certain things."

I was asking him to review some of his fights. "Julia," he called to his wife, "bring out the record book." In a minute she appeared with a cardboard box full of newspaper clippings, loosely stuffed into a disintegrating scrapbook. "Charley," she said, "you don't have a record book. And these clippings are as old as Methuselah." Burley reached out for the cardboard box and said, "That's OK, I'm as old as Methuselah myself." His heavy-lidded eyes and grizzled mustache, drooping at the corners, gave him a world-weary look.

There was documentation in the scrapbook for the kind of luck Burley had. When luck came his way, mishap would inevitably follow. He could count on it. One day Burley hit the numbers for $1,012. The numbers writer, after paying him three hundred dollars, welshed on the remainder of the bet, so Burley went to court. The story was in the paper. A judge, deciding quickly, found the numbers writer guilty, but his crime -- operating an illegal lottery -- was against the Commonwealth and not against Burley. The court had no interest in whether Burley got the rest of his money. He couldn't win.

Inside the ring, everything worked right for Burley. Outside the ring it was just the reverse. As an 18-year-old amateur, having lost to another promising Pittsburgh fighter, Leo Sweeney, in a match that decided the 1936 National AAU welterweight championship, Burley passed up the Olympic trials to compete in the Spanish People's Games, sponsored by the government of Spain in opposition to the big propaganda show the Nazis were putting on in Berlin. Almost as soon as the American team arrived in Barcelona, the Spanish Civil War broke out.

Burley heard yelling and shooting from his hotel room one night and went to the window. A bullet came whistling past his head. "It missed me by inches," he said. With the other American boxers, he hunkered down in the hotel until the games were called off. Six days later, he managed to board a ship for the United States.

Burley turned pro that fall, won seventeen of his first eighteen fights, and then lost to Zivic. Or maybe not. As Regis Welsh, the great Pittsburgh Press boxing writer, phrased it, "Burley gave Zivic a thorough going over, but Zivic got the decision." Burley had mixed feelings about Zivic. "Inside, he was thumbing me and everything," Burley said. "He couldn't help himself, you know. That was his way. Lord knows I hate to talk about these things. We've lost him" -- Zivic had recently died of "Alzheimer's disease," most likely a euphemism for pugilistica dementia -- "but God loves the truth. He was a dirty fighter but a good guy -- as boxers go. We have some rough ones, you know."

Their second and third fights were not even close. After the second fight, Harvey Boyle wrote in the Pittsburgh Post-Gazette, "Burley won it by a country mile." Harry Keck, in the Pittsburgh Sun-Telegraph, foresaw "the end of the fistic trail" for Zivic. He had taken "a one-sided beating." More than two years later, with the end of the fistic trail nowhere in sight, Zivic became the welterweight champion by giving the celebrated Henry Armstrong a one-sided beating. Meanwhile, he had lost again to Burley. "Zivic never retreated so much in one bout at any time in his long career," noted Regis Welsh.

Re-reading the frayed and faded clips, Burley said, "I didn't have no trouble with Fritzie after the first time because I learned how to fight him. He had a very good uppercut, but I moved my left into it." Demonstrating, he extended a broad, sinewy forearm and blocked an imaginary uppercut. "I jabbed him and beat him to the punch. I always had a way to get out of everything and keep my left in his face and maneuver so that he couldn't ever really unwind." With a shrug, Burley added, "But Fritzie got the chance to fight Armstrong. It's your manager, I guess."

Late in Armstrong's tenure as welterweight champion, Burley's manager was Zivic, whose purchase of his contract from Goldstein was plainly a conflict of interest. Not that Eddie Mead, Armstrong's manager, ever looked upon Burley as an opponent he wanted. This he had made clear when

Chappy Goldstein managed Burley. As for Zivic, in the aftermath of his fight with Armstrong, Regis Welsh asked if he intended to fight Burley again. Zivic walked away without answering, so Welsh put the question to Luke Carney, Zivic's manager, whose reply, Welsh wrote, was unprintable.

Later, Zivic confided to friends that he did offer Burley a title match, but with one proviso. If Burley won -- "and you'll have to kill me," Zivic told him -- he wanted fifty percent of Burley's purses as champion instead of the thirty-three and a third percent he'd been getting.

"Burley wouldn't go for it," Zivic said.

Zivic won a return match with Armstrong and then blew a decision to Freddie Red Cochrane in his next title defense. With the championship gone, he kept an old promise by selling Burley's contract to O'Loughlin.   For Burley, the change was no improvement. Routinely, O'Loughlin tried and failed to get a championship fight with Cochrane. (Zivic never got one, either. His return bout with Cochrane was over the weight.) After Robinson won the title, Burley said to him, "Ray, you and me would make a good fight." Robinson and his manager/mouthpiece, George Gainsford, kept their thoughts about that to themselves. Half-humorously -- and not for publication -- Robinson once told some reporters, "I'm too pretty to fight Charley Burley."

There was never any talk of a return match between Burley and Billy Soose when Soose held the middleweight title. It was in Burley's twenty-fifth fight that he decisioned Soose, who had beaten him in an amateur bout. Burley always felt that too much was made of the fact that Soose had an injured right hand when they met as professionals. "Soose Outclassed" said the headline in Burley's scrapbook.

Burley was having trouble with one of his own hands, the left. After his TKO win over the Canadian Sonny Jones at Motor Square Garden in January of 1939, he went into the hospital for bone-graft surgery and wore a cast for five months. Then in his first fight after the layoff, he lost a split decision at Hickey Park to Jimmy Leto, a tough New Jersey welterweight who had beaten Zivic. Before the end of the outdoor season, having repeated his own win over Zivic, Burley fought Leto again at Hickey Park and methodically outpointed him.

Of Burley's seven fights in Minneapolis for Tommy O'Loughlin, he won six by knockouts. The seventh was with Holman Williams. Burley won that fight, too, but it went the distance, ten rounds. The ease with which Burley handled J. D. Turner before a Minneapolis crowd gave O'Loughlin a whimsical idea. He offered Conn, who only two months before had failed to put Turner away, $7,500 and 35 percent of the gate receipts for a fight in Minneapolis with Burley. Conn would soon go into the Army, but his manager, Johnny Ray, was negotiating for a return bout with Joe Louis, a come-from-behind knockout winner over Conn in their heavyweight championship match the previous June. For that fight, Conn had earned about ten times the amount O'Loughlin was now guaranteeing him. Johnny Ray answered disdainfully. He sent an envelope containing a "United States of Anemia" three-dollar bill to O'Loughlin.

Soon afterward, O'Loughlin got Burley a fight in New York -- at St. Nicholas Arena with Showboat Bill McQuillan, an audition, he hoped, for a Madison Square Garden engagement. In just a little over a minute, Burley knocked McQuillan stiff, but the Garden date never materialized. Burley had scared off any welterweight or middleweight contenders who may have been paying attention. Next, Burley tried Chicago, where he flattened a trial horse from Detroit, Joey Sutka. Predictably, nothing came of it.

His last fight in Minneapolis was on April 30, 1942, with a middleweight journeyman, Sonny Wilson. On the same card, Sugar Ray Robinson boxed an equally undistinguished opponent, Dick Banner. Burley knocked out his man in two rounds and Robinson did the same thing to Banner. In "Charley Burley, the Life and Hard Times of an Uncrowned Champion," Allen Rosenfeld reprints what the ringside reporters had to say, and the consensus seems to have been that while Robinson was flashier and in some ways the superior stylist, Burley appeared to hit harder and gave the impression of being more durable.

Afterward, for a while, O'Loughlin was full of big talk about a Burley-Robinson dream match in Minneapolis, but Burley knew better than to count on it. He collected his purse for knocking out Wilson -- one hundred and fifty dollars (Robinson pocketed one thousand) -- and signed for a May 25 ten-rounder in Pittsburgh with Ken Overlin, a tricky former middleweight champion. It would be part of a Forbes Field extravaganza headlined by Zivic and Lew Jenkins, who had lost the lightweight title to Sammy Angott a few months earlier.

But complications developed. Overlin, with World War II heating up, had re-enlisted in the Navy and couldn't get leave. Substituting for him, Ezzard Charles, a 20-year-old high school senior from Cincinnati, gave Burley an unexpected licking.

Ezzard Charles was no ordinary high school senior. True, he had just lost to Kid Tunero, a savvy and experienced Cuban fighter. He had lost to Ken Overlin also, but had later held Overlin to a draw, and he had knocked out Anton Christoforidis, a former NBA light-heavyweight champ. He had knocked down and outpointed Teddy Yarosz, the former middleweight champion from Monaca. In time, he would be the heavyweight champion. He was rangier than Burley -- much the bigger man. And yet his mastery in the ring that night surprised everybody. The schoolboy, in this instance, looked like the professor. In the final round, he dropped Burley to one knee for a count of three.

Burley laid off for no more than a week or two before agreeing to fight Holman Williams again, this time in Cincinnati. And then the Rooney-McGinley Club offered him a rematch with Charles at Hickey Park. Burley said yes to that, too. So, on June 23rd he boxed Williams, winning with no trouble, and on June 29th, back in the ring with Charles, who by this time was finished with book learning, he lost another one-sided decision.

"Those big fellas, ya know, they had the reach on me. I'd have to box and move, bob and weave," Burley said when I talked to him about Charles. In that return match, he boxed and moved and bobbed and weaved and hung on. Never again would he fight Charles, but he willingly took on other good black light-heavyweights. Under the auspices of O'Loughlin, he transferred his household from Minneapolis to San Diego and boxed up and down the Pacific Coast as far north as San Francisco for sixteen months, making two sorties to New Orleans for fights with Holman Williams. He also boxed Williams in Hollywood and Buffalo.

Besides Burley, O'Loughlin had Elmer (Violent) Ray, a 200-pound heavyweight, in his stable. It was easier to get matches for Ray than for Burley, and Burley may have felt some resentment. Eventually, he severed his ties with O'Loughlin, but not before a memorable sparring session with Ray in a Los Angeles gym. Harry Otty describes it in "Charley Burley and the Black Murderers' Row." Otty writes that every time Burley sparred, an appreciative crowd would gather, and Ray, on this occasion, attempted to steal the show. One of the hardest hitters in the heavyweight division, he started throwing powerful overhand rights, which Burley pulled away from or slipped. About the fourth time he tried this, Burley let the punch fly over his shoulder and countered with a right of his own. They were wearing sixteen-ounce gloves, but Ray hit the deck with a thud. Burley waited several minutes until Ray's eyes were refocused, pointed a glove at him -- "You asked for it," he was saying tacitly -- and left the ring.

Some sixth sense told Burley when to expect a punch. It was what made him so hard to hit. He said that no one except Lloyd Marshall, who put him down for a count of three, ever knocked him off his feet. In the same fight, Marshall dropped him to one knee, as Charles, Jack Chase, and Mike Barto, a left-hooker from New Kensington, had done. Barto caught Burley cold, in the opening minute of the first round; Burley knocked him out in the fourth.

In more than one hundred fights, mostly with men who outweighed him, Burley lost twelve times. His last significant wins were over Billy Smith the second time and Bert Lytell. Not even Lew Burston, a New York manager who belonged to the inner circle, could get him fights. He "started drinking a little," he said. In 1947, 1948, and 1949, he boxed only five times and lost two of those fights -- to Lytell in Baltimore and to Doc Williams, no relation to Holman, in New Orleans. He was out for a while with pleurisy. He was out for a while with pneumonia. His hands hurt. He was 32 -- old age for a pug back then -- and had done no serious fighting in seven months when co-promoters Joe Brusco and Bill Dumer matched him with Chuck Higgins, an upwardly mobile young knockout puncher from Ellwood City with a 33-1 record. The date was February 2, 1950, and the venue was the Aragon ballroom.

Carl Hughes, the boxing writer for the Pittsburgh Press, was off on another assignment, and an unqualified novice filled in for him. Burley, he declared in his pre-fight story, was too far over the hill to be a suitable opponent for Higgins. A more idiotic statement never appeared in the Pittsburgh Press sports section, and after Burley's quick first-round knockout of Higgins -- all it took was a feint, a left uppercut, a right-hand chop, and a left hook -- I apologized to him for making it.

"Get me a fight with Lee Sala," Burley said, "and we'll be friends." Lee Sala was the hottest middleweight in Pittsburgh. That his manager, Bunny Buntag, wouldn't even discuss a match with Burley was a given. Some thirty years later, Buntag explained his reasoning to another Pittsburgh Press writer, Bill Naab. "I could demand ten thousand dollars to twelve thousand dollars a fight for Sala," he said. "Any time I thought Sala was not a sure thing I'd demand even more to discourage the promoter. So why would I take a fight with Burley for fifteen hundred dollars at the most, maybe get knocked out, and lose everything?"

In 1951, when Sala was training for a fight with Joey DeJohn in Syracuse, Buntag hired Burley as a sparring partner. Burley's job was to show Sala the moves that had baffled Zivic and Archie Moore and almost everybody else he ever fought. They were not transferable. Nate Liff, who worked in Sala's corner, also had worked in Harry Greb's corner, and one day Sala asked him which of the two -- Burley or Greb -- was the better fighter. "Nate, I can't hit the guy," Sala said. Liff always figured that Sala lost to DeJohn because his hours in the gym with Burley had crushed his spirit. "Burley made him think he couldn't box."

For the record, Liff doubted that, as good as Burley was, he'd have beaten Harry Greb.

After disposing of Chuck Higgins, Burley fought only two more times. He knocked out Buddy Hodnett of Detroit at the Aragon -- the paid attendance was a pitiful 727 -- and then came his trip to Peru for a knockout win over the aforementioned Pilar Bastedis.

His job collecting rubbish lasted thirty-two years. Thorough and conscientious, he was the best rubbish man he could be -- maybe the best rubbish man it is possible to be.

He said that in all that time he never felt sorry for himself. "I think I was mistreated in the fight game -- the championship thing -- but I just thank God I'm still here." He was 66 at the time. "The rubbish truck" -- Burley never used the words "garbage" or "trash" -- "was hard work. I had an operation on my leg on account of the rubbish. A barrel hit my leg and cut it, and gangrene set in." He rolled up a pantleg and displayed a thin calf. "They took the skin from one part of my leg and put it on this other part, down here.

"But I always did my job. My wife and kids" -- there were three -- "never wanted for anything. When you work seven years in a row without ever missing a day, that's pretty good. It didn't put a crown on my head, but the money was all straight. And my wife is the greatest woman in the world."

The scrapbook, closed, was on his lap. "Where's that letter, Julia?" he said. "I just got a letter from London. We always get letters from a lot of different places. A fella just wrote from . . . " Julia handed him an envelope. " . . . Cardiff," he said, looking at the postmark. He pulled out the letter and read the first paragraph aloud. "'I am writing to ask for an autographed photo and a copy of your record. I list you the number two all-time great, after Joe Louis . . . '"

"How do they get your address?" I asked.

Burley smiled. "Lord knows. But you appreciate things like that. One fella sent me ten dollars for an autographed picture. I sent him the picture, but I kept the ten dollars."

If the fates owed Burley a little bit more than a ten-spot, Burley wasn't going to suggest it. Again he thanked God for looking after him. "Oh, there's been setbacks," he said. "The stroke. Arthritis. Sugar, too. But sickness comes to everybody. And I never was hurt in the ring -- I'm unmarked. All I want now is a few more years."

A few more years were all he would get. But he lived to be inducted into boxing's Hall of Fame, where Zivic and Conn had preceded him and where Soose would catch up with them later. For once, Charley Burley was able to get his foot in the door.

CHAPTER 13

COLLEGE BOY

Sportswriters swallowed it whole, the story that Billy Soose hated his profession. That was what Soose's manager told them, and that was how they portrayed this erstwhile collegian who was middleweight champion of the world. They wrote that Soose was in boxing for the money, that he didn't like to be hit, that he despised the hangers-on and underworld characters a prizefighter unavoidably met.

Soose smiled at the recollection one day as he sat in the crowded work room of his house near Lake Wallenpaupack in the Pocono Mountains, an 80-year-old senior citizen with a real-estate business and a talent for making rugs. His manager, he said, had a vivid imagination. Soose expressed this thought in what his English professor at Penn State University might have called the vernacular. That is to say, he used an earthier phrase than "vivid imagination." The manager, Paul Moss, was a Hollywood agent and screenwriter unversed in the niceties of the fight racket. When he worked in Soose's corner, wrote the New York columnist Richards Vidmer, he was "pitifully ignorant of what to do."

Moss's value to Soose was in a different sphere altogether. Good-natured and quick-witted, Moss used his publicist's charm on the columnists who derided him, and it kept Soose's name in the papers. He managed Soose for one reason only -- because he liked him. All they had in common other than friendship was their birthplace, Farrell, a Pennsylvania steel town northwest of Pittsburgh.

The belief that Soose was not enthralled with the way he earned his living contained at least a kernel of truth. There were times when Ray Arcel, the trainer Moss hired, saw fit to castigate Soose between the rounds of a fight for dilly-dallying. Soose's reluctance to take advantage of the weaknesses he exposed in his opponents led Frank Graham of the New York Journal-American to make a fatherly suggestion one day. "Bill," the sportswriter said, meaning to be kind, "you don't have the killer instinct. Quit while you're ahead."

Soose agreed that he did lack the killer instinct, although "Killer," for some reason -- sixteen knockouts in sixteen fights may have had something to do with it -- was the nickname he acquired as a sophomore prodigy on the boxing team at Penn State in 1937. He agreed that he fought to "accumulate wealth," as his manager put it. He acknowledged evading punches, on the premise that someday he might have a need for the brain cells he thereby preserved. But he knew that he would know when to quit.

He quit at the end of the Second World War. Coming out of the Navy, he considered his peace-time options. Promoter Mike Jacobs had offered him one hundred thousand dollars for three fights, with the privilege of naming his opponents. But money, just then, wasn't tempting to Soose. He had put aside money from his earnings in the ring. With Moss, he owned the Poconos property they had bought to set up a training camp -- 225 acres of northeastern Pennsylvania forest land. Financially, Soose was secure. He was 30 years old, married, and ready to settle down.

There was also a physical problem. In his sixth pro fight, he had broken his right hand -- separated the tendon between the middle and ring fingers. And remembering now, almost sixty years later, the difficulties that followed, and how the hand continued to bother him even as a naval officer, he said, "I could never do anything with it. It just never, never got better. After every fight, I'd have my hand in a bucket of ice."

Instead of taking the hundred thousand from Jacobs, Soose dipped into his "accumulated wealth," bought out Moss, and built a lakeside resort: twenty-four cottages, a restaurant with a bar, and a marina. Gradually, he bought up more land, until he owned, all told, 490 acres.

"To me, this is God's country," he said. "I've been all over the world, and what could be better than right here? Look at what we have. Deer. Foxes. Bears. Woods. An artificial lake. We don't get tornadoes, we don't get typhoons, we don't get williwaws."

Nor tsunamis, nor volcanic eruptions. Let the record show that the Poconos are a haven from natural disasters of the more spectacular kind. When Soose sold his property in the early 1990s, keeping only the living quarters and enough land for privacy, it was worth in the neighborhood of one and a half million dollars.

Soose died at 83 of a stroke, none the worse, up to then, for his years in the ring. He had aged well. In his prime, he was just over six feet tall, with wide, square shoulders, a slim waist, and long legs. At 80, not much had changed. His bearing was still erect, the combed-back silvery hair still abundant. A small dent broke the symmetry of his button nose. His conversational style was self-assured and direct, good-humored with something of a bantering tone.

"What's your name?" he said one day to the newly-hired waitress at a restaurant not far from his house.

Her name was Linda, she told him.

"May I call you Linda?" Soose asked.

"Sure."

Springing the trap, Soose said, "Well, when may I call you, Linda?"

Linda smiled indulgently and asked if he wanted to know what the specials were.

Divorced, Soose lived by himself on twenty-five acres. His house, painted dark brown and resting on a concrete-block base, was two stories high. Together with a dilapidated shed, it occupied a clearing at the end of a short gravel drive. He continued to hand out illustrated business cards that pictured him as a roguish young desperado in boxing trunks, the hair wavy black and parted high on the left with one short curl out of place. The flip side of the card read: "Mobile home sites for lease" and "Acreage and lots for sale."

His other occupation, nearly dormant by now, was the making and selling of rugs. Soose worked at this trade in a room full of plain wooden furniture -- wooden tables, wooden chairs, wooden cabinets. The rug-making equipment consisted of a knitting machine and an over-sized sewing machine. Photographs and hunting rifles festooned the walls. In a cluttered adjacent storeroom were golf clubs, sheets of plywood, a washer, and a dryer. Nowhere in the house did vulgar ostentation meet the eye.

It is easy to drop out of sight in the Poconos. When Soose died, in 1998, the news traveled slowly. Appearing two weeks after the funeral, a wire-service story in the Pittsburgh Post-Gazette identified him, none too precisely, as a former "New York state" middleweight champion. Actually, Soose was the New York State Athletic Commission's middleweight champion of the world from May 9, 1941, to November 1, 1941, when he vacated his title to box as a light-heavyweight. The National Boxing Association, during that time, had its own, less authentic middleweight champion, Tony Zale -- less authentic because, for one thing, Soose had already beaten him and also because, New York being New York, its championship carried a bit more prestige.

Soose turned professional in 1938, acclaimed in newspaper articles as "the greatest college boxer of all time." In the amateurs, he had lost only six of more than two hundred fights. Of his forty-two professional fights, again he lost six, all by decision. He won thirty-five and there was one draw, the result of a strange occurrence in Los Angeles. Behind on points, former middleweight champion Ceferino Garcia began to attack Soose with his head, cutting him so severely that the referee sent the fighters to their corners. Calling it a draw subverted justice, Soose claimed, but that was the referee's verdict.

The name Soose, originally Soos, is Hungarian. Soose was only one year old when his father, a steelworker, died. He discovered boxing at the age of 14. Passing a house that he thought was abandoned, he heard an enticing sound -- the rat-a-tat-tat of a speed bag. He stopped and went to the door. There were fighters working out. A man he assumed to be the owner of the place said to him, "Make yourself scarce, kid." Soose interpreted this as an invitation to hang around. He appointed himself water boy. A fifty-gallon drum held the water the boxers used for drinking and washing purposes, and Soose kept it full by trudging endlessly back and forth between the house and the tap, which was half a block away. At last the man in charge allowed him to box. He had grown to within an inch of his full height and weighed 103 pounds.

Soose never actually had a teacher. At Penn State his coach was Leo Houck, whose academic credentials included fights with Gene Tunney, Harry Greb, Jack Dillon, Battling Levinsky, Frank Klaus, Billy Papke, George Chip, Johnny Wilson, and Jack Britton, world champions in their time. To the question "What did you learn from Houck?" Soose answered, "Nothing," which no doubt was the literal truth. Long before Houck set eyes on him, Soose was a finished fighter. Once he had made it to the top, Soose took pleasure in repeating what Houck is supposed to have said about him early on -- "He doesn't look like much to me."

If so, Houck's vision was faulty. Among the hordes of good amateur boxers populating Western Pennsylvania in the early 1930s, there was nobody better than Soose. "I won every championship tournament I entered," he said with no concession to false modesty. "I beat five guys in one night in a tournament in Pittsburgh. I beat Charley Burley in the amateurs. Had him on the floor in the first round. Burley was a great fighter

-- he beat me in the pros. Of the six guys who beat me in the amateurs, I won return matches with four."

One guy who beat him was Leo Sweeney, a National AAU champion optimistically referred to in a newspaper article as "the most promising young fighter to come out of Pittsburgh since Harry Greb -- fast as a whirlwind and a clever boxer, with power in both hands." To hear Charley Burley tell it, Sweeney had "the best damned left you'd wanna see." In his first fight with Soose, Sweeney gave him "a pasting," as Soose put it. Soose then beat Sweeney, and after that they continued to take turns. Sweeney would beat Soose and Soose would beat Sweeney. When the series was finally over, each had beaten the other three times.

Sweeney, by the way, found that boxing interfered with his pursuit of less arduous pleasures. After a so-so career interrupted by World War II, he retired with a 9-8-2 record and became a cop instead of the next Harry Greb.

As for Soose, he went off to college. He enrolled at Pitt before deciding on Penn State. Paul Moss had been urging him to switch, Moss being a Penn State alumnus. But what actually tipped the balance, Soose said, characteristically forthright, Penn State "offered" him more.

For his major, he selected pre-med -- and was overmatched. "I couldn't vanquish organic chemistry," he said, making organic chemistry sound like a boxer whose style is not easy to fathom. Physical education was an easier opponent.

Refusing "financial help" volunteered by Moss, he worked for his tuition as a table waiter and furnace attendant and by pulling large crowds into Recreation Hall, Penn State's basketball and boxing arena. Two hours before his match with a Syracuse University middleweight from Pittsburgh who was said to be capable of extending him, five thousand students and townspeople were lined up waiting for the doors to open.

The Syracuse fighter, Tarzan McGivern, went down for the count in the second round. Nobody else Soose boxed as a collegian lasted beyond the first. "Soose ate those guys up," a former classmate remembered.

Plainly, something had to be done. The coaches of the teams on Penn State's schedule threatened a boycott of Soose. They would not send their middleweights out to be slaughtered. From officialdom came the solution to the crisis. The Eastern College Athletic Conference declared Soose ineligible. He'd been getting "expense money" for amateur fights in the summer. "To make it more binding," Soose recalled, "they dusted off a rule that prohibited Golden Gloves champions from boxing in college."

Soose cut short his education and announced he was turning professional. Jack Dempsey offered to manage him. So did Jake Mintz, a Pittsburgh promoter and matchmaker who would one day manage heavyweight champion Ezzard Charles. But friendship and home-town ties won out: Soose signed a contract with Moss.

The next thing he knew he was living in the house of a movie-star couple, Dick Powell and Joan Blondell. Powell, Moss's client, had Pittsburgh connections. He'd been master of ceremonies at the Enright Theater in East Liberty at a time when 2,000-seat movie houses offered stage shows in addition to films. Powell went directly from East Liberty to Hollywood. Musicals were big, and he could sing. He played the juvenile lead in two or three Busby Berkeley extravaganzas, graduated to roles that were more fulfilling, and married Joan Blondell.

Under what Soose called Powell's "tutelage," he quickly adjusted to Hollywood. Not many fighters had such tender, loving care. According to Hearst columnist Bob Considine, Paul Moss was "the sensitive type," known to "faint dead away" at the sight of his boy Soose taking a punch. Fainting was not one of Dick Powell's weaknesses, but his sensitive side revealed itself at Soose's first pro fight. "He covered his face with his hands," Soose remembered.

Certain Hollywood actresses were hardened enough to watch without flinching. After one of Soose's easier fights, Alice Faye and Lupe Velez, scarcely able to contain themselves, jumped from their first-row seats into the ring and planted kisses on his unmarked face. He was anything but thrilled.

Soose's notion of cutting loose was to play gin rummy with Joan Blondell. Powell, as a way of protecting Soose, barred him from the high-stakes card games that went on late at night when friends came to call, but in the morning, after breakfast, the lady of the house would be looking for action. Over a period of several months, Soose won two thousand dollars from her.

Repentant, but not totally so, he offered to give "some of it" back. "Nothing doing," she told him. "You won that money fair and square." On-screen or off-screen, Joan Blondell was the big-hearted, smiling good sport.

Soose had five fights on the West Coast and won them all. He won his sixth fight as well, a semi-final with Al Quaill at Forbes Field. It was Pittsburgh's first look at Soose as a pro and also his first ten-rounder. In the main event, 20-year-old Billy Conn lost a decision to Teddy Yarosz, the slippery, slithery former middleweight champion who demonstrated, on this occasion, an adeptness at dirty fighting. Soose, like Conn, was up against an older, more seasoned opponent, with the difference that Quaill could be hit. All night long, he plodded after Soose, exposing himself to "a rain of punches," as the man on the scene for the Pittsburgh Press described it, and landing very few of his own. He knocked Soose down, in the second round, but Soose took the count on one knee, unharmed. He paid a price, just the same, for his rain-making: Quaill's chin turned out to be harder than Soose's right hand. The clinical term for the damage to his hand, Soose said, harking back to his pre-med days, was tenosynovitis.

Except in moments of recklessness, he was never again a two-fisted fighter. For the rest of his career, the hand gave him trouble. "I went to Chicago and had it operated on. I went up to Maine and chopped wood. I rowed boats. Nothing helped. Whenever I hit a guy with a right hand I felt the pain up to my neck," he said.

Soose hit Babe Risko with a right and knocked him out. Risko had beaten Yarosz for the middleweight title and had lost it to Freddie Steele. "He was open," Soose said. Any time someone was open, there was no way Soose could hold back. He would throw the right hand instinctively, but the limit was one to a customer -- one good one. At Duquesne Gardens one night, Soose hit Charley Burley with a right in the third round and from then on fought him one-handed. Burley got the decision.

Afterward, Soose chopped more wood and started winning again. Before losing to Burley, he had lost a weirdly arrived at split decision to a New Jersey middleweight of no great distinction, ,Johnny Duca. Leo Houck refereed their fight in Lancaster and cast the vote that won it for Duca. One judge had voted for Soose and the other had called it a draw. Under the rules of the Pennsylvania State Athletic Commission back then, the referee's vote was decisive if the judges disagreed. Possibly, as when Houck first appraised him, Soose hadn't looked like much to his one-time coach that night. "In explanation, Houck said, "He was clowning a lot in the early rounds." The commissioner at ringside, disregarding protocol, declared the fight a draw, but was overruled the next day by the rest of the commission, and so Duca was the winner.

Houck had helped Soose train for some of his earlier fights and had worked in his corner two or three times. Never again was there a professional relationship between them. But when Houck died -- in Lancaster, as it happened, on January 21, 1950 -- Soose attended the funeral.

Over the thirteen months after his loss to Duca, Soose more than evened the score, beating him twice -- first in Youngstown and then in a Lancaster encore. Eastern Pennsylvania was familiar territory to Soose. He boxed in Scranton so often that Scranton all but adopted him. When he outpointed Ken Overlin there -- Overlin's middleweight championship was not at stake -- John Kieran of the New York Times called it a home-town decision.

Soose always thought of himself as having "lots of hometowns" -- Scranton (where he boxed six times), State College, Hollywood, Pittsburgh, and of course Farrell. He had one fight in Farrell, winning it by a second-round knockout. Most of his early main events were in Pittsburgh, but New York, in the 1930s and 1940s, was where all the best fighters ended up.

Because of Moss, Soose spent time in Hollywood as well. He took a screen test, in fact, for the Lou Gehrig part in "Pride of the Yankees." "Well, what the hell, I wasn't going to beat out Gary Cooper," he said about that. Once when Robert Taylor made a boxing picture, they shot Soose's footwork for the fight scene. Soose put the gloves on with Taylor, just to teach him a few simple moves, and the studio arranged for publicity stills. Powell, who considered Taylor a rival, pulled enough strings to keep them from being printed, Soose said.

In addition to organic chemistry, Soose could never vanquish Georgie Abrams. They boxed three times and Soose lost three times. The first of these fights was in Pittsburgh, Soose's hometown at the moment. For all it meant to the judges, Pittsburgh might as well have been Pocatello, Idaho. They voted for Abrams. Everybody else, including the referee, thought that Soose was the winner with something to spare.

So good did Abrams feel about getting the decision -- and getting the decision in each of their next two fights -- that for the rest of his life he looked upon Soose as a benefactor. "Bill," he would say when he dropped in on Soose at his Poconos resort, "you made me."

Abrams was not, by Soose's exacting standards, a good fighter. "He was a spoiler -- didn't give you punching room," Soose said. Their third fight took place when Soose was champion, and Paul Moss saw to it that Abrams came in over the middleweight limit of 160 pounds, a wise precaution. Abrams could punch -- he had Sugar Ray Robinson on the floor -- but it was mauling, not hitting, that allowed him to beat Soose.

Only two fighters ever hit Soose so hard that he remembered the feeling. One was Tony Zale. "He hit me in the liver in the first round," Soose said, adding in graphic language that all of his inner organs were in turmoil for several minutes. Zale had a powerful left hook, which he didn't come close to landing for the rest of the night. They were fighting in Chicago. Singer/actor Al Jolson, getting favorable odds, won forty thousand dollars on Soose and threw a party for him afterwards at the Edgewater Hotel.

The other punch Soose vividly recalled, a left hook to the temple, was delivered by an amateur named Steve Branzovich. Soose said it felt like a bullet going through his head. He was never hurt, he maintained, by any of the four fighters who knocked him down -- Quaill, Jimmy Bivins, Ernie Vigh, and Paul Pirrone. "They caught me off-balance," he said.

Soose's disinclination to take a punch to land one annoyed many spectators and boxing writers, New York boxing writers in particular. "Soose can fight until daylight," wrote Jack Miley of the New York Daily News, "and you know that nothing is going to happen."

Soose was nimble, Soose was quick. Against standard-sized middleweights, his height was an advantage. A film of his fight with Zale shows him constantly in motion. His jab was busy, rather than damaging. He would jab Zale off-balance, tie him up, and dig a hard left to the body. He used his right just to remind Zale that he had one, throwing it rarely and without any force. Chances are that no middleweight ever boxed better than Soose, but he was strictly, as he said, a one-handed puncher.

Craftsmen of this type are generally unappreciated. Tami Mauriello, complained Miley, lasted the full ten rounds with Soose despite the fact that he was out on his feet. The first time Soose beat Ernie Vigh (he did it twice), Al Buck pointed out in the New York Post that he was plainly unwilling to gamble.

In Los Angeles one-night Soose eased up against an outclassed Tony Casino at the request of the referee. Instead of trying for a knockout, he played cat-and-mouse with Casino. At one point, Casino was so befuddled that he completely lost track of Soose, who tapped him on the shoulder from behind and said, "Hey -- here I am."

In Overlin, recognized as middleweight champ by New York, Illinois, and California, Soose was up against a defensive artist whose techniques were equal to his own. "And two boxers never make a good fight," Soose admitted. In Scranton, Soose and Overlin made a bad one. During the last three rounds, Soose recalled, "everybody left -- even the judges, I think." Overlin, apologizing for his defeat, said he was "over trained." To the sportswriters, it looked as though he had probably not trained at all. Even so, a majority of them felt as John Kieran did that Overlin had won, and Overlin thought so, too. After dismissing Soose as a legitimate contender, he said to the writers, "That kid can't fight. I can beat him any time, but this was an off night for me."

When they met for the title in Madison Square Garden, Soose having proved his legitimacy at the expense of Zale, Vigh, and Mauriello, Overlin had another off night. Soose "out scrambled" him, as one writer put it, to win a unanimous decision. Again, however, it was Overlin who won in the newspapers -- decisively. And again, it was not an interesting fight.

"They were both lousy fights, to tell you the truth," Soose conceded. Overlin, he said, was almost unhittable. "You'd see an opening, try to sllp a punch in, and he'd block it." In the title match, Overlin jabbed, held, backpedaled, and tin-canned. "The most yawn-provoking fight ever seen in these parts," was how Joe Williams summed it up in the New York World-Telegram. "For 15 rounds," he wrote, "the fighters did nothing." Soose, Williams thought, was "too thin, too cautious, and -- we hate to say the word -- too inept."

The Daily News columnist, Jimmy Powers, didn't agree. "Billy Soose," he wrote, "is the classiest middleweight unveiled in Madison Square Garden in a long, long time. He's smart. He's a fast puncher. He has a grand pair of legs." Powers had been convinced since watching him handle Mauriello that Soose was the best middleweight in the business..

(Historical note: Soose versus Overlin was the first fight ever televised -- by closed circuit in the New Yorker Hotel.)

Soose's only fights as titleholder were over-the-weight affairs with Abrams (the third time around), with Garcia (the unsatisfactory draw), and with Tony Celli (Soose by a knockout). A proposed return bout with Zale never came off. In Soose's place, Georgie Abrams boxed Zale and lost a fifteen-round decision.

Less than six months after winning the title, Soose relinquished it, unable to continue making 160 pounds. The way Soose looked at it, there were no light-heavyweights he couldn't whip. Gus Lesnevich was champion, Billy Conn having moved up to the heavyweight division. When Soose said he could beat any light-heavyweight, he did not exclude Conn, a heavyweight in name only. "Billy's a nice boxer, but I can lick him," Soose would tell anyone who asked. All Conn ever said was that Soose could fight -- "even if he did go to college."

How Soose would have done against Lesnevich, let alone Conn, nobody ever found out, because a month and six days before Soose lost a decision to Jimmy Bivins, a good pocket-sized heavyweight, the Japanese bombed Pearl Harbor. While negotiations for a return match with Bivins were proceeding, the head of the Navy's physical training program, Lieutenant Commander Gene Tunney, telephoned Soose and said, "You've got to get in." Obediently, Soose enlisted. He spent the war years, most of them, on Kodiak Island, off Alaska, rising to the rank of lieutenant.

Joan Blondell wrote to him at least once a week. Paul Moss wrote and called. When the shooting was over, Moss and Soose kept in touch. Around 1950, Moss went to England and wrote the Father Brown television series for Alec Guinness. Back in New York in 1955, he met Soose for dinner at Toots Shor's restaurant. Soose never saw him again. Ten days later, Moss's sister called Soose and told him that Paul had suddenly died.

"He was a great guy and we got along famously," Soose recalled when I talked to him long afterward. They fit well together, Moss and Soose. The manager couldn't bear to see his fighter get hit, and the fighter avoided doing so with uncommon skill.

PART THREE
Storytellers

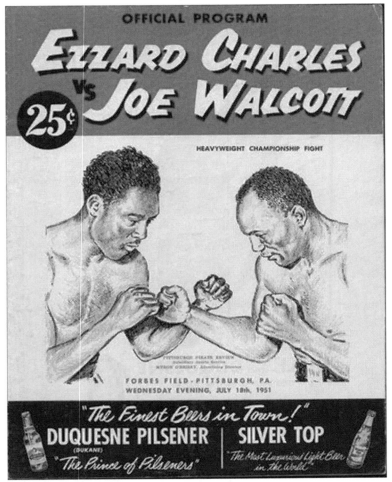

The official program of the July 18, 1951 Ezzard Charles-Jersey Joe Walcott heavyweight championship bout at Forbes Field.

CHAPTER 14
YANKEE DOODLE DANDY

Long after his fighting days were over Jack Johnson became a manager. He brought one of his fighters, Al Gainer, to train at a 27-acre camp in Shaler, PA called Eagles Rest before a bout against light heavyweight champion John Henry Lewis at Forbes Field. (Picture Courtesy of the Library of Congress, LC-USZ6-1823)

In the span of a few years during the second decade of the twentieth century, Nate Liff boxed as a flyweight, bantamweight, and featherweight, had an indeterminate number of fights -- he didn't bother to add them up -- and retired with an unusual record. "I didn't lose any fights and I didn't win any fights," he said, explaining, "Those days, they had newspaper decisions. There were seven newspapers in Pittsburgh. If you bet on a fight, you left it up to a majority of the sportswriters." Which, officially, did not mean a thing. Officially, if a fight did not end in a knockout, nobody won and nobody lost. The result was a "no decision."

Except in the newspapers. In the newspapers, the sportswriters who covered boxing decided who won, and this was all right with Nate. He had faith in their expertise and objectivity. Jim Jab . . . Dick Guy . . . Harry Keck . . . Regis Welsh . . . Nate Liff remembered them fondly. Regis Welsh, in his opinion, was the best -- "the best boxing writer in America. If you read his story, by the time you were halfway down, you thought you was at the fight." Jim Jab was a good writer, too, according to Nate. "A square guy. An honest guy."

Like everybody else in boxing, Nate was aware that Jim Jab led two lives. Since 1880, when he was 16 years old -- a precocious 16 -- he'd been a newspaper reporter. Since 1910, under the name on his birth certificate, Alfred R. Cratty, he'd been a personal-care physician as well, having obtained a degree, at the age of 46, from the University of Pittsburgh medical school. Bearded, distinguished looking, dressed in the height of 19th-century fashion, he covered boxing into his sixties and practiced medicine into his eighties.

BoxRec.com lists nineteen fights for Nate Liff, all newspaper decisions except the one with Young Pinchot, from Charleroi. "A hell of a good boxer," Nate remembered. "He beat me in the newspapers. Maybe six months later, he boxed Joe Lynch, the bantamweight champion, but Lynch won." Not only did Nate lose to Pinchoi in the newspapers, he lost to him also in the ring. According to the record book, Pinchot TKO'd Nate in the eighth round.

The first fight Nate ever saw was at the old City Hall in Market Square, which had a second-floor auditorium that seated no more than a thousand spectators -- a strange location, surely, for the middleweight championship contest between Frank Klaus and George Chip on the night of October 11, 1913. "How I got in," Nate liked to tell the people who liked to listen to his reminiscences, "I brought some oranges with me, and I said to the guy at the gate, 'These are for the fighters.' The fighters' seconds used to take oranges into the ring. They'd squeeze them between rounds and give the fighters the juice."

Harry Greb was on the card that night, having recently turned pro, but he made no impression on Nate, who remembered only Klaus and Chip. Klaus was the champion, Chip the challenger. Klaus was a heavy favorite, and for the first five rounds he looked the part. "He was playing with Chip," Nate said. "Then, in the sixth round, Chip threw a right -- threw it from left field -- and stiffened him."

By his own estimate, Nate was eight years old in 1913. He could not say for sure. It is certain that he died in January 2000, but the date of his birth remains a mystery.

"I was born in Russia," he explained. "They didn't keep no records, Russia -- especially on Jews. I came over to this country as a babe in arms, and every time I asked my mother how old I was, she'd say, 'Well, there was a barn next door to where we lived, and the day after the barn burned down, you was born.'"

So, for a long, long time, Nate would be giving out different dates for his birthday until finally Marian, his wife, said to him, "Look, Nate, why don't you settle on one? Why don't you make it July Fourth?" Liking the sound of July Fourth, Nate went along with her suggestion. "What about the year?" she wanted to know. Nate said, "I'll take a shot at it -- 1905."

There is reason to believe that his shot missed the mark. If Nate entered the world in 1905, it would make him just nine years old when he was boxing as a professional under the name of Frankie Murray. Or Jimmy Avery. Or sometimes Nate Liff. Even in those days, no nine-year-old could have fooled whatever authorities there were, and Box-Rec gives November 16, 1914, as the date of Nate's first fight, a six-rounder with Young Drexler. The newspapers called it a draw.

It is thus improbable that July 4, 1919, when Nate saw the Dempsey-Willard fight in Toledo, was his fourteenth birthday. Nate hitch-hiked from Pittsburgh -- imagine what the roads were like -- showed up at the arena with a bundle of newspapers and got permission to sell them inside. By the time the main event started, he had worked his way down to the first row.

A few months later, Nate was in Canton, Ohio, for Harry Greb's fight there with Greek KO Brown. Greb's manager, Red Mason, said, "Natie, would you like to earn a dollar?" "Doing what?" Nate asked. "Swinging a towel," said Mason. Now, swinging a towel, Nate always maintained, was not an easy way to make a buck. "Keep doing it for ten rounds" -- or, in this instance, twelve rounds -- "you had to be in shape."

Towel swinging is a thing of the past. It's a lost art -- one that Nate would demonstrate by going through the motions with a purely imaginary towel. "In order to get the air to the fighter, you have to swing it *above* his nose, not below," he would say. "Below the nose just won't work."

As it happened, Red Mason got his money's worth out of Nate. "About the sixth round," Nate recalled, "Greb was hitting Brown at will. Mason yells, 'Take him out! Take him out!' Greb yells back, 'You take him out. I'm not gonna break my hands on this bum.' " So Nate earned his dollar, swinging that towel above Greb's nose for the full twelve rounds.

Nate never paid to see a fight -- never for as long as he lived. Whether as towel swinger, newsboy, orange supplier, or you name it, he would always find a way to crash the gate. One time at Duquesne Gardens, when Nate was a grown man, it looked as if he and two companions were out of luck. At last Nate thought of something. He said to the others, "Follow me." To the man at the door taking tickets, he said. "I'm Nat Fleischer. These guys are OK." And the three of them, unchallenged, sashayed through the turnstile.

In only one way did Nate resemble Nat Fleischer, the editor of Ring magazine and compiler of the Ring Record Book. Both were short of stature, but Nate was much handsomer -- black-haired, with regular features. In his nineties, although the hair had turned to silver, it was still plentiful. Nate's posture was that of a West Point cadet, and his pink complexion radiated good health. His career as a fighter had left him completely unscarred.

After retiring from the ring, Nate had a career as a manager -- a very brief career. His only fighter was Jake Mintz, who became the manager, later on, of a heavyweight champion, Ezzard Charles. "I managed Jake Mintz for three fights," Nate said, "and I batted one thousand with him. He got knocked out each time."

Before one fight, Mintz predicted that he would knock the other guy out. Sure enough, in the very first round he put his opponent down. "It got him all excited," Nate recalled. "He came running over to the corner and said to me, 'I told you I'd knock him out!' And while he was saying that, the guy gets up and comes over and knocks Jake out."

Nate often worked as a second. He was one of the busiest trainers in town, but he found his true calling by accident. The way it came about, Billy Conn's manager, Johnny Ray, wanted a quiet, secluded training camp for his fighter, and in 1936 he asked Nate to look around. "So I did," Nate was saying one day, "and I ran into this great big white house on top of a hill. It was in Shaler -- twenty-seven acres. The girl in the office told me they called it Eagles Rest. I liked it so well I leased it for myself."

Nate got hold of a ring and put it up in the shade of some trees. After that, he installed tennis courts, a rifle range, and a badminton deck. He applied for a restaurant license and a liquor license. The restaurant became popular for its steaks. There were ten rooms upstairs, and he rented them to fighters. The main dining room could accommodate a thousand people. Big shots like Ben Fairless, the chairman of U.S. Steel, used it for banquets.

That first summer, Jack Johnson brought a fighter to Eagles Rest -- Al Gainer, who had a match coming up with John Henry Lewis, the light-heavyweight champion, at Forbes Field. Johnson was Gainer's manager and trainer, and he, stayed at Eagles Rest with his fifth wife, the former Irene Pineau, for six weeks.

"Johnson was a very intelligent man," Nate said. "He could speak German fluently. His wife -- a white woman -- would get up every morning and go to church. You couldn't swear around her or anything."

Almost 60 by then, Johnson still appeared in "sparring matches" and "exhibition bouts." He put the gloves on with Gainer one day and blocked every punch his title contender threw. (Gainer hit Lewis often enough but lost a twelve-round decision. Lewis, at the time, was managed by Gus Greenlee, whose earnings as the numbers king of the Hill District enabled him to own the great Negro League baseball team, the Pittsburgh Crawfords. Lewis was a transient from Los Angeles, but Greenlee also managed three good Pittsburgh light-heavyweights -- Red Bruce Honey Boy Jones, and Mose Brown.)

Johnson, after losing his heavyweight championship to Jess Willard in 1915, boxed for another thirteen years. In 1920 and 1921, he had a few fights in Leavenworth Prison, where he was serving time on an old rap, a Mann Act conviction. He boxed in Spain, in Cuba, in Mexico, and in Canada. In 1928, at the age of 50, he boxed in Topeka, Kansas, and Kansas City, Missouri, losing by a knockout both times, and then retired.

After that, always on the lookout for chances to make money, he worked as a boxing promoter, a securities salesman, a beer salesman, a nightclub MC, and a movie actor of sorts, and he was not above lecturing at a flea circus in New York City. If opportunity came his way, he took advantage of it, but he wasted no time on potentially unprofitable associations. "I'd introduce him to people," Nate recalled. "If I said to him, 'Jack, I want you to meet Joe,' he'd walk away. If I said, 'Jack, I want you to meet MISTER

So-and-so, a great admirer of yours,' he'd smile and shake hands. He knew he had a live one."

Nate ran his camp democratically. Though he was partial to Billy Conn, who by 1939 was the light-heavyweight champion, having beaten Melio Bettina at Madison Square Garden in July of that year, Nate granted Bettina's request to train at Eagles Rest for his return match with Conn in September at Forbes Field. Conn, of course, would be using the place too, and Johnny Ray objected to having Bettina share the facilities. He considered Eagles Rest his own turf. Moreover, the weather was brutally hot, and Ray wanted Bettina to train at Hickey Park in Millvale, where the ring had a canvas top. On humid days, and every day was humid, the canvas top kept the heat from escaping. By contrast, the shade trees at Eagles Rest gave protection from the sun without enclosure.

Johnny Ray argued with Nate. Playing his trump card, he shouted, "I've got the light-heavyweight champion of the world!" "Well, that's fine," answered Nate. "Put him in a bottle and cork it, and you'll have him forever." Conn, never fearing, unlike Ray, that he might need an edge to win the fight, laughed. His manager did not.

Eagles Rest made money for Nate, and he liked the job of running it, but in 1943, feeling overworked, he put off renewing the lease and went to Florida with Marian for a six-month vacation. Florida re-energized him. He came back to Pittsburgh full of new ideas for his camp. But Eagles Rest, alas, was now a nightclub. The owner, a man named John Frischemeier, had leased it to somebody else.

"That taught me a lesson," Nate said. Paraphrased, the lesson was this: Never let down your guard. In life, as in the ring, the punch you don't see coming is the one to beware.

CHAPTER 15

THE LAWRENCEVILLE MINSTREL

One thing Bobby Massick never said was, "I could-a been a contender." Instead, he said, "I fought the best and I fought the worst and I lost to them all. One time I fought a guy who had one arm, and he beat me and wanted a return match." Bobby Massick was a welterweight club fighter from Lawrenceville. "If you were born in Lawrenceville, you were born with boxing gloves on" is something else he would always say.

In his old age, Massick had long gray hair, bowed legs, and a nose undiminished by the punches it had blocked. "I started fighting about . . . well, I'm 86, and I was 17 . . . " He left the arithmetic unfinished. The year he was looking for would have been 1925. In 1994, the year he was 86, Massick died.

His best guess was that he'd had "about fifty fights, countin' amateurs and all. When they needed someone to get the hell beat out of him, they got me." Massick took the beatings and retired with a few hundred stories to tell. He told them to his friends at the Elks Club in Braddock and he told them in the columns he wrote for two weekly newspapers, the Valley Mirror in Munhall and the North Braddock Free Press. To make a living, he worked as a linotype operator at one of the large daily papers, the Pittsburgh Press.

Massick never really fought the best. His toughest opponent, Jimmy Belmont, was good, but not one of the elites. "I boxed him about ten times," Massick said. "We were like brothers. I think in most of our fights he let up on me. We boxed outside East Liverpool one time and got a buck-twenty apiece. The promoters ran away with the money.

"Belmont was a puncher," Massick went on. "He knocked out three men in one night at the ballpark in Duquesne. Another time, he fought an ice man, Steve Mezinko. A guy who carried ice. Belmont had boxed him in the gym and found out he could hit. Afterward, Belmont said, 'I don't want no part of that guy.' Mezinko used his own name for a while and then changed it to Steve Ketchel. That was the name he fought under. So finally some promoter matched Belmont with Ketchel, and Belmont didn't know who it was. When he got in the ring and looked across at the other corner, he said, 'Oh, my God -- Mezinko!' Well, the first round started and Belmont hit Mezinko one time and that was it.

"Belmont knocked out Buck McTiernan twice and won a decision from him. He was built like an Adonis, Jimmy Belmont. A good, kind-hearted guy, too. He fought Jackie Fields and got a draw. In his next fight, Jackie Fields won the welterweight title. Belmont won a decision from Babe Risko in Cleveland. He fought Teddy Yarosz. There's three world champions right there."

Six months after losing to Belmont, Risko beat Yarosz for the middleweight title. The mobster Frankie Carbo had an "investment" in Risko, and on the afternoon of his fight with Belmont, Massick said, a conversation took place between somebody or other and Jack Laken, a hard-working itinerant scuffler who was Belmont's manager at the time. Let it be clearly understood, this person told Laken, that Risko was going to win. Laken passed the word along to Belmont, and Belmont erupted. "I'm not laying down for anyone!" he shouted. In the ring that night, he delivered a beating to Risko.

As for Laken, before getting out of Cleveland, according to Massick, he experienced an unusual thrill -- being dangled from the window of his hotel room by visitors who were close friends of Carbo.

"Belmont was from Braddock, and he had a few fights at Meyers Bowl," Massick said. "Meyers Bowl opened in 1929. Belmont and McTiernan boxed at Meyers Bowl. Benny Bass, who'd been featherweight champ, beat a guy named Steve Smith in the first fight there. A Pittsburgh guy, Al Iovino, knocked out Henry Armstrong at Meyers Bowl. It was Armstrong's first pro fight, and he went by the name of Melody Jackson. Al Iovino knocked him out in the third round.

"Meyers Bowl lasted one year. Know why it went broke? They had five thousand seats, a dollar a seat. Apples Meyers and his brother -- the promoters -- got greedy. They raised the ticket price to three-fifty. Those were Depression days. Nobody had that kind of money, and the place folded up.

"I'll tell you another good fighter who boxed at Meyers Bowl -- Willie Davies, a hundred and twelve pounds. After every fight, he'd sing a song . . .

"*I went ten rounds with Dempsey;*

` "*The rounds were mighty fine.*

"*'We were riding on a merry-go-round;*

"*'His seat was next to mine.'*

"I fought a welterweight from Kittanning, Freddy Boylestein. Mike Harding, my manager, said, 'This fella just got out of the hospital. You won't have no trouble at all.'

"I said, 'How much is in it?'

"'Thirty bucks.'

"The fight was in the Holley Building in Wheeling, West Virginia -- up on the eighth floor. I got down there and I see my name on billboards: 'Hurricane Bob Massick versus Freddy Boylestein.' The billboards said that Boylestein had eight straight knockouts. I said to Mike Harding, 'Hey! I'm getting on a train and going back to Pittsburgh.' I said, 'You're leading me to the slaughterhouse.' I said, 'You're crazy if you think I'm fighting that guy.'

"The promoter said, 'Look, we made a mistake. Go through with the fight and we'll give you sixty bucks.' I thought, 'Well, what the hell.' I put it in Mike's hands. He said, 'Go lay down for a while -- take a nap -- and you'll be all right.'

"When I got in the ring that night, the place was packed. In the first round, I happened to hit Boylestein, and down he went. I thought, 'If he only stays there.' But he hopped right up and jabbed and jabbed and jabbed. He could really box. He knocked me down in the sixth round, and the referee says, 'Kid, I think you've had enough.' I got my sixty bucks and blew it all in a speakeasy and came back to Pittsburgh broke.

"I saw Harry Greb in two of his fights at Motor Square Garden. He never stopped punching. The Human Windmill. Could he have beaten Sugar Ray? Hell, yes, 'cause he wouldn't never let up. When a man beats Gene Tunney, the only man who ever beat Tunney, how could Ray Robinson beat him?

"Greb was from Garfield. The Zivic's were from Lawrenceville. The Katkish's were from Lawrenceville, too. They lived at Forty-ninth and Hatfield streets, and the Zivic's lived at Fiftieth Street and Plum Alley. There were five Katkish brothers, all fighters -- Eddie, George, Jack, Joe, and Mike. Eddie won every championship in the amateurs -- national championships. Jack, he was like a bull. Jack Katkish had a chance to fight Jack Zivic for the featherweight championship of Pennsylvania. They were walking down the street one day, and Zivic said, 'Hey, Kattie, let's not go through with this fight. I'd beat your brains out. I know it and you know it.' But Katkish insisted. They were neighbors, they were friends. They boxed at Motor Square Garden and they each got a thousand dollars. They fought like two tigers. And Jack Zivic gave Katkish such a beating that one week later he was in Woodville Hospital.

"The oldest Zivic brother, Pete, had a saloon in Lawrenceville. Two guys from New York City came in -- strangers -- and Pete was at the bar, listening to them talk. One of these guys says to the other, 'Which of the Zivic's do you know best?' 'Pete,' the other guy says. 'How well do you know him?' 'Well, we gambled together, we went out with women together.' Pete's standing right there in front of him, and he says to the guy, 'I'll bet you don't know Pete Zivic at all.' 'How much?' the guy says. Pete slaps a twenty-dollar bill on the bar, and the guy picks it up.

"'*You're* Pete Zivic,' he says."

Pete Zivic's saloon went back to a time in Pittsburgh when it was not out of the ordinary for kids to grow up with boxing gloves on their hands. There was always fresh material then for Bobby Massick, peerless raconteur of the fight game.

CHAPTER 16
CROWD PLEASERS

When the subject of heavyweights who could hit hard came up, somebody always mentioned Harry Bobo. But that was long ago -- Bobo's last fight was in 1944 -- and today his deeds are forgotten.

Bobo derived his nickname, the Peabody Paralyzer, from the high school he attended in East Liberty. The son of a deacon in the Baptist Church, he turned professional at 18 and immediately started knocking guys out. His first three opponents went down in the first round. He was tall, 6 feet 4, and he weighed more than 200 pounds.

After eleven fights, all of which he won, Bobo had eight knockouts -- four in the first round, three in the second, and one in the third. Moving up to the main-event class, he decisioned the more experienced Nick Fiorentino at the Islam Grotto on the North Side in his first ten-rounder. Bobo's manager, Eddie Kapphan, now took a big leap forward, putting him in with Henry Cooper, an accredited trial horse from Brooklyn, in a main event at Duquesne Gardens, and again Bobo won in ten rounds..

Kapphan then overreached. He accepted a Duquesne Gardens ten-rounder with Gus Dorazio, who thought of himself as a title contender. It would be Bobo's thirteenth fight and Dorazio's fifty-fifth. Joe Louis would eventually expose Dorazio as just another Bum of the Month, but Bobo was not quite Joe Louis, and Dorazio gave him a trouncing. As the fight came to an end, Bobo was saved by the bell. .

After that, there were ups and downs for Bobo. At the South Side Market House, he lost to Tony Shucco, once the second-rated light-heavyweight contender. In Baltimore, he decisioned the Swedish champion, Gunnar Barlund. He followed that with four straight knockout wins over palookas, and then came a return match with Dorazio. Bobo won it, but the decision, although unanimous, wasn't popular.

In the summer of 1941 -- 20 years old now -- Bobo won two fights at Forbes Field with Lee Savold, who had been a more troublesome opponent than Dorazio for Billy Conn. The first fight was close -- sportswriters questioned the decision -- but Bobo ended the return bout quickly and decisively, knocking Savold out in the second round.

Between the two meetings with Savold, Bobo was knocked out himself, by Bill Poland in Baltimore. There had to be a rematch, of course. It took place at Forbes Field in Bobo's first appearance after knocking out Savold, and this time he knocked out Poland. When Bobo got into the ring there was always the likelihood that someone would end up on the floor..

Opportunity now beckoned -- a December 1st Duquesne Gardens pairing with the former light-heavyweight champion, Melio Bettina, who had put on a few pounds and was campaigning successfully among the heavyweights. Bettina entered the ring with a seven-fight winning streak and left it, to the applause of the crowd for "a close and exciting contest," with an eight-fight winning streak.

The mandatory return bout had to wait until June. In the meantime, Bobo kept busy. Surprising almost everybody, he got off the floor in the first round and knocked out Lem Franklin, a young Cleveland heavyweight with a punch more feared than his own. The fight packed them in at Duquesne Gardens, and it ended almost as soon as it began -- which made Bobo the favorite in a third encounter with Dorazio, but they were fighting in Philadelphia, Dorazio's hometown, and Bobo lost by a split decision.

Cleveland Stadium was the site of the Bobo-Bettina encore. Bettina's winning streak now stood at twelve, and since his first fight with Bobo he had beaten Dorazio. Getting up from a knockdown in the fifth round, he now won from Bobo a second time. It may be that his southpaw style confused Bobo. Or perhaps there was something else. Just a few weeks later, Bobo knocked out Claudio Villar at Forbes Field, and he never had looked more dynamic. But before he could fight again, the Pennsylvania State Athletic Commission revoked his license. He was blind in his right eye, the commissioners announced.

Precisely how it had happened is unclear. Anyway, his banishment in Pennsylvania was final. Ohio's commission ruled that he could see well enough to throw knockout punches, and he proved it to a Cleveland crowd by flattening Larry Lane in one round. Next, he decisioned Buddy Walker in Columbus. With Joe Louis in the Army, Ohio awarded him the "duration" world heavyweight championship, a synthetic and meaningless title. About a month after the Walker fight, he won a fifteen-round decision in Baltimore from Big Boy Brown, a 260-pound cousin of Louis, and now Maryland, too, recognized him as duration champion.

Ohio and Maryland, it appears, considered one eye sufficient for the kind of work prizefighters do. Bobo held his championship of two states from January 25, 1943, until August 9 of the same year without making a defense, and then in Baltimore's Oriole Park, before a turnout of 9,500, he lost it to Lee Q. Murray by a TKO in the eighth round.

Whether his eyesight was getting worse is hard to say, but he boxed only four more times, decisioning Walker again and Brown again, losing to Walker by a knockout, and winning by a knockout from Johnny Denson, the sort of opponent he was knocking out on undercards at the start of his short career. All of these fights were in Maryland or Ohio. He was only 23 years old when he hung up his gloves, possibly at the urging of an eye doctor.

Bobo won thirty-six of his forty-five fights and twenty-four of the thirty-six by knockouts -- not a bad percentage at all. No one did more during the early part of the Second World War to keep boxing viable in Pittsburgh.

In retirement, he tended bar in East Liberty and the Hill District. Later, he worked at the same job in Philadelphia, where he died at 45 after complaining of a headache and then collapsing.

Another hard hitter with a wartime following in Pittsburgh was Juste Fontaine, a pint-sized dynamiter. Originally from Milwaukee, he came here to be managed by Fritzie Zivic. He won his first thirteen fights for Zivic, usually by the knockout route. Fontaine put everything he had into every punch. In just a little over a year he was appearing in ten-rounders at Forbes Field.

Pittsburgh never had seen a little guy with such power -- until Pittsburgh saw Dorsey Lay of Philadelphia on January 28, 1946. Lay could hit just as hard as Fontaine, and he won a ten-round decision. Not long afterward, Fontaine returned to Milwaukee for a match with his old hometown's biggest gate attraction, Doll Rafferty, and lost by a seventh-round knockout.

Here were three lightweights of comparable ability who could throw a punch and take one. Before they were through, Fontaine had three fights with Lay and four with Rafferty. Andy DePaul, a future Western Pennsylvania boxing commissioner, saw most of those fights as a kid, and he said that if television had existed back then, the Sweet Science would now be illegal. When Fontaine boxed either Lay or Rafferty they wiped the floor with each other.

"Down, up, down, up -- it was unbelievable," DePaul said. He recalled that during one fight, Frtizie Zivic gave smelling salts to Fontaine -- "which is against the rules" -- and revived him on another occasion by sticking his head into the water bucket.

Fontaine won two of his three fights with Lay. They were all at Duquesne Gardens. In the third fight, Fontaine was a knockout winner, but Lay hung around until the tenth and last round. Fontaine's first return bout with Rafferty was a draw. His only win over Rafferty was in the only fight between them in Pittsburgh. They met at Zivic Arena -- or Hickey Park, the Millvale location Zivic owned for a time and temporarily renamed -- and Fontaine got the decision. By the tenth and last round he had punched himself out but miraculously stayed on his feet. Their fourth fight, like the first two, took place in Milwaukee, and Rafferty won in ten rounds for a 2-1-1 edge in the series.

A trait Fontaine shared with his manager was a willingness to fight anybody anywhere. In the gym one day he was hammering a young preliminary boy from Washington, Pennsylvania, Sammy Angott's hometown, while Angott, the still-active former lightweight champion, looked on in a state of agitation. Wrathfully, he accused Fontaine of hitting low. They argued about it, and almost at once the argument became heated.

It was Fontaine, the story goes, who suggested a way to settle their dispute. Without delay, Angott took him up on it. He borrowed a cup and a pair of boxing shoes and got into the ring with Fontaine. The first punch Fontaine threw was a good six inches below the belt. Angott returned the favor, and they were fouling each other with such viciousness from then on that Joe Luvara, the man in charge of the gym, jumped between them and declared a cease-fire.

Fontaine had long arms, wide shoulders, and a plume of brown hair that gave him the look of a cockatoo. He drove a fancy white convertible with his name on the door in red paint. During some back-and-forth over a fender bender on Butler Street in Lawrenceville one day, a truck driver addressed him by a name that was not his and that Fontaine didn't like. In the next moment they were duking it out.

The average street fighter has no idea how overmatched he can be if he is foolish enough to take on a pro. Fontaine was about 5 feet 5 or 6. In condition, he weighed between 135 and 140 pounds. The truck driver, who towered over him and must have weighed in the vicinity of 200, never had a chance. Fontaine threw a short-left hook to the midsection that "went in up to the wrist," as a witness described it, and the truck driver collapsed like a punctured balloon. It was Fontaine's quickest knockout.

Skilled boxers survive all their street fights, if any, unharmed. It's the punishment they take in the ring that does them in, and the battering's Fontaine took from Rafferty and Lay were severe. After his second fight with Rafferty, he started losing as often as he won. In Philadelphia, Ike Williams, the National Boxing Association's lightweight champion, knocked him out in four rounds. In New York, at St. Nicholas Arena, Terry Young knocked him down three times in the first round, automatically ending the fight. Other defeats followed. "If there's anything more pathetic than a washed-up fighter, it's a washed-up fighter who doesn't know he's washed up," wrote Carl Hughes in the Pittsburgh Press after Fontaine dropped an eight-round decision to Dave Marsh of Akron, Ohio, at the Aragon Ballroom on May 15, 1950 -- the fourth time in a row he had been on the losing end.

The Pennsylvania State Athletic Commission enlightened Fontaine on the question of whether or not he was washed up by taking away his license. After one last fight, a knockout win over Bill Dowling in Miami, he went back to Milwaukee and opened a bar, and Pittsburgh forgot about the two-fisted little crowd pleaser until his name turned up in a headline once more -- a headline over an obituary.

CHAPTER 17

RUSTY

On a spring afternoon in 1948, Jack McGinley, matchmaker for the Rooney-McGinley Boxing Club, welcomed two unscheduled visitors to his office in the Fort Pitt Hotel. One was Charley Burley, a Pittsburgh middleweight highly esteemed by McGinley and many others. Introducing his companion, a stranger, Burley said, "Jack, this guy's from San Diego, and he can fight. His name is Rusty Payne."

McGinley sized Rusty Payne up: Slope-shouldered. Long arms. About 5 feet 11. Between 180 and 185 pounds. Mocha-colored, like Burley. Slight tinge of red in his hair. A sort of devil-may-care look.

Rusty Payne wanted work. On McGinley's desk was a copy of the Ring Record Book. It told him that, by a substantial margin, Payne had won more fights than he had lost. Added to Charley Burley's endorsement, that was enough. McGinley said, "Rusty, nobody knows you around here. How would you feel about a semi-final at Hickey Park? We've had some good shows out there."

Payne shook his head. "I'm a main-bout fighter," he said.

McGinley said, "Well, look -- every once in a while we'll run a show with three eights. Would you be interested in that?"

Payne thought it over. A co-feature, it seemed to him, was different. A co-feature was not a preliminary.

He agreed to an eight-rounder with a heavyweight from the Hill district, Lin Brosier. And Charley Burley, it turned out, had overstated nothing. Brosier was a competent journeyman but simply no match for Payne, who punched him all over the ring and won in three rounds by a knockout.

A day or two later McGinley took a phone call from Charley Jones, in Louisville. Jones managed Sammy Angott, the former world lightweight champion, among others. He said, "Jack, I've got a fighter named Sid Peaks who's a cinch to be heavyweight champion. Absolutely no question. If you use him now, you can use him when he's champ."

With what Payne did to Brosier fresh in his mind, McGinley said, "Charley, there's a guy in town from San Diego. I don't know how good he is. He's tough. He can punch."

Jones said, "Jack, I don't care if he can punch. This guy of mine can beat anybody in the world."

McGinley made the match for the following week, and Jones brought his fighter to Pittsburgh. At the sight of him, McGinley's mouth fell open. Sid Peaks was so massive he could barely get through the door. Reflecting on the contrast between this man's size and Payne's, McGinley felt a surge of apprehension. Peaks, in addition to being large, had won twenty-nine fights in a row, and only one of those fights had gone the distance.

But to Rusty Payne, it couldn't have mattered less. At the appointed hour, he climbed through the ropes at Hickey Park without a worry in the world. The first time he hit Peaks with a right, McGinley thought the ring was coming down. Only it wasn't the ring; it was Peaks, landing heavily. Twice more in the first round, Payne had Peaks on the floor. The referee was counting him out when the bell rang. In round two, Payne finished the job.

Charley Jones, as McGinley remembered it, was "heart-broken." He said, "Jack, we've got to have a rematch." McGinley was more than willing, but meanwhile, for batting practice, Payne went to work on Erv Sarlin, "the Human Rock of Gibraltar." Carl Hughes of the Pittsburgh Press likened Sarlin to "a turtle with grappling hooks." He was indestructible -- never off his feet in more than sixty fights, including two with the leading heavyweight contender, Ezzard Charles. Payne couldn't knock him out, or knock him down, but he cracked one of Sarlin's ribs. At the bell for the start of the seventh round, Sarlin remained in his corner.

From then on, Payne was a man about town, a celebrity -- recognized wherever he went. Unlike his sponsor, Charley Burley, a skilled but careful counter-puncher, he could generate excitement. The return bout with Peaks, too important for Hickey Park, was at Forbes Field. Payne liked to hang around the ticket office in the Fort Pitt Hotel, checking on the advance sales, and one day, McGinley recalled, "this lady came in. She said, 'Where can I buy tickets? I'm a big Rusty Payne fan.' Rusty was standing there, by the counter. He pulled out a roll of bills and said, 'Give her two ringsides . . . on me.'" Payne knew the value of good public relations.

He had a manager in Pittsburgh -- Burley's manager, Al Slutsky -- and a manager in San Diego, a man named Travis Hatfield. Unannounced, Hatfield turned up to see the rematch with Peaks -- and to collect one thousand dollars Payne owed him. He was dapper, like Payne, and they were still on good terms. Payne turned over the thousand and Hatfield watched him demolish Peaks once again.

It took a little longer -- four rounds. As in their first fight, Peaks was on the canvas in the round preceding the knockout. As in their first fight, he was saved by the bell. Forever afterward, Charley Jones stopped referring to Peaks as his future champion. And Jake Mintz, who managed Ezzard Charles, a sure-enough future champion, discouraged all talk of a Charles-Payne match. "I would not allow Charles to fight Payne except for big money -- *real* big money," he said.

Edging nearer to the big money himself, Payne took on the most dangerous puncher in the heavyweight division just then, Curtis Sheppard, the Hatchet Man, and got off the floor to knock him out. In the fifth round, Hatchet Man's right made connections, and the count had reached seven, Payne said after the fight, before his head cleared. "I never knew anyone could hit that hard," he added. There were no quotes from Sheppard about the left hook by Payne that put him away in the ninth.

Payne now had won five straight fights in Pittsburgh, four by knockouts and one by a TKO. He was riding high. For his next opponent, McGinley selected Johnny Flynn, right name Kowalczyk, from Rochester, New York. Flynn was not a behemoth, like Peaks, but he was bigger than Sheppard. He could box a little -- Payne couldn't box at all -- and he could hit fairly hard with his right. Yet, as slow as he was, he figured to be easy for Payne. As it happened, he was anything but, winning a ten-round split decision at Duquesne Gardens on the strength of a knockdown in the sixth.

There were stories that Payne had been "misbehaving." What "misbehaving" meant seemed open to various interpretations. In any event, it left him precious little time for training. New York City's Madison Square Garden booked an encore between Payne and Sheppard -- their first fight had been in Pittsburgh --, and the result was a disappointment: "a dull ten-rounder," in the words of the United Press report, witnessed by an apathetic crowd of 1,300. Despite the embarrassment of being knocked through the ropes and onto the ring apron for a nine-count, Payne won a clear-cut decision. Sheppard, the United Press man wrote, was washed up.

So was Payne, it turned out. His rise had been sudden; his descent was just as swift. In a ten-rounder at Duquesne Gardens, Jimmy Bivins kept him at bay with moves he never had seen. Payne lost the fight and lost stature.

Auditioning in Rochester for a return match with Flynn, he knocked out Ted Lowry -- it was over in less than a round -- but Flynn, the home-town boy, had his number. When they met again, it was more of the same. Flynn out boxed Payne and outslugged him. Back in Pittsburgh, Payne lost to Johnny Shkor, a Boston heavyweight in the Flynn mold. Gone for good was the Payne who had pole-axed the giant Sid Peaks. "The only trouble with the Rusty Payne fable," wrote Carl Hughes, "was the absence of a happy ending."

Time to go home, Payne decided. Farewell, Centre Avenue. Farewell, Wylie Avenue. Word filtered back from San Diego that he had lost two fights to a no-name, Al Spaulding. In the second one, Spaulding knocked him out. Up in Portland, he decisioned Joe Kahut. The heavyweight they were talking about in Pittsburgh now was Bob Baker, who had just knocked out Johnny Flynn. A Baker-Payne match, although not the attraction it might have been, seemed at any rate justifiable to McGinley. Whether or not the fable was over, Payne deserved one more chance, and for Baker it would be a rite of passage.

When they met at the Gardens on April 24, 1950, Payne had Charley Burley in his corner. "Bob and weave," Burley told him. "Sidestep." But evasive tactics were not in Payne's repertory. Down in the first round, and down again in the second, he was counted out in the fourth. "He goes in there with his head up -- it's a target," complained Burley, unable to comprehend such a witless approach.

Payne, analyzing the knockout, said, "I feinted, like Charley wanted me to do, but I over-feinted my guard. I didn't know I was holding my right so low, and Baker came in with that big left hook."

Pittsburgh never saw Payne again. Up and down the Pacific Coast, he continued to over-feint his guard and lose fights, and then in a California seaport called Eureka he won the last two he ever had. Baker, meanwhile, was putting together loose ends. Sid Peaks came back to town, and Baker knocked him out in five rounds.

If one fable had ended, another was taking shape.

Harry Bobo, "The Peabody Paralyzer", became a top contender for Joe Louis' title in the 1940s. He was regarded highly enough to be considered "duration champion" by Ohio and Maryland while Louis was in the Army during WW II. (photo courtesy of Douglas Cavanaugh)

"Jolting" Juste Fontaine was brought to Pittsburgh by Fritzie Zivic, who was the young fighter's hero. Juste liked to be high profile and was known for his flashy ways (he drove a convertible with his name painted in red on the door). This raised eyebrows in blue-collar Pittsburgh, but Fontaine backed up his bravado by scoring 17 stoppages in 26 wins in his adopted hometown. (photo courtesy of the Fontaine family)

Power-punching Rusty Payne was brought to Pittsburgh by Charley Burley and had a brief but spectacular run, stopping Curtis Sheppard and Erv Sarlin (among others) in impressive fashion. But ultimately his lack of dedication in training cost him when Burley left him and soon after he began losing more than he won. (photo courtesy of Douglas Cavanaugh)

Bob Baker, perhaps the most skilled heavyweight Pittsburgh ever produced, was a top contender in the 1950s. Like Rusty Payne a decade earlier, he just didn't have the motivation to train like he should and so never reached his true potential. (Photo from the author's collection)

Charley "Zivic" Affif was another fine fighter managed by the ubiquitous Fritzie Zivic. He showed enough promise that Zivic arranged for his pro debut, after which the grateful Affif began calling himself "Young Charley Zivic." The name was a way to honor Fritzie, but also to hide his prizefighting ambitions from his mother, who abhorred the sport. As his career progressed he went back to his given name. (photo courtesy of Mark Affif)

Tommy Yarosz (right), talented younger brother of Teddy, and his colorful manager Bunny Buntag (left). (photo courtesy of the Yarosz family)

Wilf Greaves came along during the 1950s, when boxing in Pittsburgh was in its death throes. Fighting under the management of Jake Mintz, he did well against many of the top fighters of his era but couldn't quite topple the elite. (Photo from the author's collection)

Enjoying a beer with *Pittsburgh Post-Gazette* writer Brian O'Neill (left) is Roy McHugh (right). Working at the *Pittsburgh Press* for the better part of five decades Roy is one of the greatest sports writers that has ever graced the city of Pittsburgh. McHugh also co-authored a book with Art Rooney Jr. called *Ruanaidh: The Story of Art Rooney and his Clan*. (Photo courtesy of Kathy Rooney)

Roy McHugh (left) with another iconic Pittsburgh figure Phil Coyne (right). Phil was an usher for 81-years at Forbes Field, Three Rivers Stadium and PNC Park until he retired at 99-years old in 2018. (Photo courtesy of Kathy Rooney)

Donora slugger Lee Sala had a left hook that was among the most lethal in the middleweight division. He never received a title shot, but he remained one of the most exciting 160-pound men of his era (photo courtesy of the Sala Family)

Teddy Yarosz was a smooth boxing Polish lad from Monaca via the Northside. He went 59-0 before suffering his first loss and went on to become middleweight champion during a tough era. He engaged in a controversial and bitterly contested three bout series with Billy Conn. (Photo courtesy of the Yarosz family)

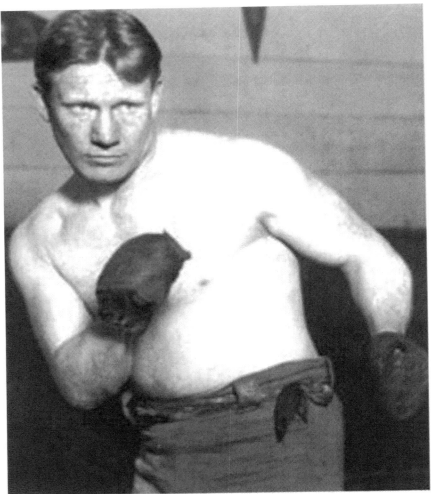

Northsider Frank Moran, "The Pittsburgh Dentist", twice fought for the heavyweight crown versus Jack Johnson and Jess Willard, respectively. After his career was over he moved to Hollywood and had a successful run as an actor in motion pictures. (Photo courtesy of Douglas Cavanaugh)

Middleweight Champion Harry Greb is considered by many to be the greatest prizefighter the game has ever seen. He was a top contender in three divisions at once and spent many years chasing the champions there who were reluctant to fight him, including heavyweight king Jack Dempsey. (Photo courtesy of JJ Johnston)

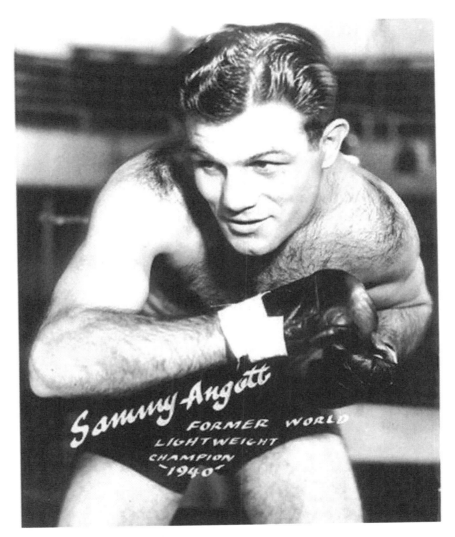

Known as "The Clutch", Sammy Angott was detested by many purists for his mauling, disruptive style. But he earned everyone's begrudging respect by beating such greats as Willie Pep, Ike Williams and Bob Montgomery and becoming lightweight champion during one of the toughest stretches the division had ever seen. (Photo courtesy of Dee Angott)

As it was with Wee Willie Davies years earlier, Charley Burley was simply too good for his own good. The Hill District boxer beat future world champions from welterweight to light-heavyweight, including Fritzie Zivic, Billy Soose and Archie Moore, but still was unable to secure a title shot in any division. The main character in the movie "Fences" was based on Burley, who lived across the street from playwright August Wilson. (Photo courtesy of Douglas Cavanaugh)

Flyweight Wee Willie Davies was twice denied opportunities he'd earned in boxing. As an amateur he was disallowed a slot on the 1924 Olympic squad due to his Welsh citizenship. Later on as a professional he beat several world champions but could never coax any of them to fight him with the title on the line. (Photo courtesy of the Davies family)

Jack McClelland was the Steel City's first ranking contender of the 20th Century. He gave Featherweight Champion Abe Attell such a bad beating in their non-title bout that the Attell camp steered clear of ever fighting him again. (Photo courtesy of Douglas Cavanaugh)

Pictured above is the famed Table O' Micks that assembled at Atria's Restaurant in Pittsburgh. Seated left to right is Art Rooney Jr., Douglas Cavanaugh, Tim Conn, the son of legendary world light-heavyweight champion Billy Conn, and the iconic Pittsburgh sports writer Roy McHugh. (Photo courtesy of Douglas Cavanaugh)

CHAPTER 18
A NIGHT TO REMEMBER

It began as a feint -- "a feint to the body," said Jersey Joe Walcott. Walcott knew as well as anyone did that Ezzard Charles, the heavyweight champion of the world, protected himself from punches downstairs with perhaps too much zeal. "He was dropping his hand to block my left hook when I lifted it to his chin," Walcott said.

It was neatly done. Charles fell flat on his face and lay motionless. At the count of five he struggled to push himself up. From a crouching position, gloves and knees on the floor, he lurched to his feet. The count was at nine. He stood there wavering, took a single step backward, and collapsed. Nothing else that ever happened in a Pittsburgh prize ring compares with that moment as theater.

Kept under cover until the seventh round, Walcott's left hook was a bolt from the blue. It made him, at 37, the heavyweight division's oldest champion up to then. With his oddly spry way of moving around, Walcott had the look of a foxy grandpa. He was six feet tall, the same height as Charles, and weighed 195 pounds. His torso, A. J. Liebling once wrote, was cylindrical, with a smaller cylinder of a head rising directly out of it. Actually, Walcott's head was more like a sphere. The cylindrical bronze torso, supporting a square set of shoulders, made the creases in his face look incongruous. Except for some fuzz on top, he was bald -- this at a time when razor-induced baldness had not yet become a fashion statement. Balancing Walcott's physical condition, admittedly first-rate, against his age and his record, which gave them pause, boxing men had agreed that the 6-to-1 odds in favor of Charles were just about right. Not even the matchmaker, Jack McGinley, offered a dissenting word. "I thought that Charles was a sure thing," McGinley said.

To purists, the fight seemed unnecessary. Twice Charles had shown, in performances so lackluster that nobody wanted another encore, his ability to outbox Walcott. But fighters have to fight -- it's what they do. Jake Mintz and Tom Tannas, the Western Pennsylvanians who managed Charles, had committed him to a title defense in Pittsburgh as a favor to a friend, Al Abrams. Sports editor of the Pittsburgh Post-Gazette, Abrams raised money for the newspaper's charities through his Dapper Dan Club, and the Dapper

Dans had a deal with the Rooney-McGinley Boxing Club, nominally headed by Art Rooney, Jack McGinley's brother-in-law, and Barney McGinley, his father, to share in the net proceeds of one fight show a year.

The Dapper Dans' cut was ten percent. It figured that for a heavyweight title fight -- Pittsburgh's first since John L. Sullivan dispatched a sacrificial goat named Frank Herald at a skating rink in Allegheny City in 1886, or maybe since Jack Johnson and Tony Ross boxed a no-decision six-rounder at Duquesne Gardens in 1909 (Ross could have become champion by flattening Johnson) -- ten percent would be a windfall. An additional slice, fifty percent of what was left after the fighters were paid, would go to the International Boxing Club, known unaffectionately as Octopus, Incorporated. The reason for the IBC's participation was its contract with Charles, which called for exclusive rights to his services. Without the IBC, there would not be a fight. The selection of an opponent was up to Jack McGinley. He had a date, July 18, 1951, and a venue, Forbes Field, but no challenger.

The difficulty was that there weren't any challengers worthy of the name. Other than Rex Layne, who was training for a fight with the still untested Rocky Marciano, Charles had disposed of them all -- or, rather, both. In March, he had beaten Walcott for the second time. In May, he had beaten Joey Maxim, the light-heavyweight champion, for the fourth time. McGinley had two choices: Walcott again or Maxim again. He preferred Walcott, who at least would have a puncher's chance.

Born Arnold Raymond Cream (do you see why he changed his name?) in Merchantsville, New Jersey, Walcott had been boxing intermittently for twenty-one years. Six different times he had interrupted his career to work in the Camden, New Jersey, shipyards, or to work on a garbage truck; six different times he'd decided to give the ring another try. Such pedestrian heavyweights as Abe Simon and Al Ettore had knocked him out. So had Tiger Jack Fox, a light-heavyweight with a paralyzing punch. He had lost to Rex Layne. In heavyweight championship fights, he had lost to Joe Louis twice, or so the record book said. Louis himself knew that Walcott had beaten him the first time. Walcott's tricky little shuffle, copied years later by Muhammad Ali, had distracted Louis, and when Louis tried to attack, looking desperate, Walcott would dig in and punch. In the first and fourth rounds, he knocked Louis down with hard rights. Thinking he was too far ahead to lose; he spent the last third of the fight backing up. He still had the better of what exchanges there were, but the two judges, outvoting the referee, made a gift of the decision to Louis.

Early in their return bout, Louis went down again, for no count, only to recover and win by a knockout. The time had now come to retire, Louis felt. Truman Gibson, his attorney, devised a plan whereby Louis would abdicate as titleholder, sign the leading contenders to exclusive contracts, and sell the right to promote an elimination tournament to James D. Norris and Arthur Wertz, sports-minded multimillionaires from Chicago. Norris, the more active partner, owned the Chicago Stadium and the Detroit Olympia. He owned the hockey teams that played their home games in those arenas. He owned the Hollywood Ice Revue. He owned a horse-racing stable,. And he owned enough stock in Madison Square Garden to have a voice in its operations. Norris and Wertz paid $150,000 to Louis and $150,000 to lease the Garden and created a new promotional organization -- one to be reckoned with. They called it the International Boxing Club.

As it happened, there was no elimination tournament. Louis -- named the IBC's "boxing director" at a salary of $15,000 a year -- picked Walcott and Charles to fight for his vacated title. They met on June 22, 1949, in Norris's Chicago Stadium, and Charles won a fifteen-round decision. The National Boxing Association recognized him as champion; the New York State Athletic Commission did not, suspending judgment for more than a year.

Cool-headed and workmanlike, a superb technician, Charles entirely lacked flair, but he was satiny smooth. Because he boxed so mechanically, and had little or no stage presence, the public and the press underrated him. For one thing, he was not a natural heavyweight. He had been at his best, the critics all agreed, when he weighed between 170 and 175 pounds. He now weighed 185.

Charles and his original managers, Charley Dyer and Max Elkus, were from Cincinnati. Before Charles was 21, he had beaten Teddy Yarosz and Charley Burley. The fight with Burley introduced him to Pittsburgh. In the main event at Forbes Field that night, Fritzie Zivic was at the top of his form, winning by a tenth-round technical knockout from Lew Jenkins, but Charles and Burley, the Post-Gazette declared, "stole the show." Al Abrams called it "one of the best and hardest fights ever seen here."

In the strictest sense, Charles was still a high-school student. His class did not graduate until the following day. But he had beaten a fighter no champion would risk taking on. One month later, before a record crowd of 4,000 at Hickey Park in Millvale, Charles won from Burley again. So respectful of Charles that he fought with self-preservation as his goal, Burley "fell into clinches, rarely used his right, and seldom let go with a hard punch," Abrams wrote.

Jake Mintz, at the time, was making matches for the Rooney-McGinley Club, and he booked Charles as often as he could after that, always against a reputable opponent. And Charles beat them all. He won a ten-round decision from Maxim, who was not yet the light-heavyweight champion, and outpointed him again in Cleveland, Maxim's hometown. Cleveland had two light-heavyweights who were even better than Maxim, and Charles fought them both -- biting off more than he could chew. He lost to Jimmy Bivins on points and to Lloyd Marshall by an eighth-round knockout.

Drafted into the Army before his fight with Marshall -- the Second World War was under way -- Charles hadn't properly trained. As a soldier, he won the Inter-Allied light-heavyweight championship, and when the war came to an end he was ready for Marshall and Bivins. In 1946, 1947, and 1948, he had two fights with Marshall, knocking him out both times, and three with Bivins, knocking him out once and winning a pair of decisions.

He was beating other good fighters as well -- Archie Moore, to name one. As referee Ernie Sesto scored it, Charles won every round of their fight at Forbes Field. They boxed in Cincinnati, and again Charles won. He was now the best light-heavyweight in the world, but still unappreciated.

To make any money in the 1940s, a fighter with black skin needed exceptional ability, which Charles had, personal magnetism, which Charles did not have, and, more than anything else, the right connections, which Dyer and Elkus didn't have. Approaching Jake Mintz, a wily insider, they offered him fifteen percent "off the top" to join them in managing Charles. It wasn't necessary for Mintz to think twice.

He knew he could put Charles in Madison Square Garden, and on June 25, 1947, that is what he did. Outweighed by twenty pounds, Charles lost a split decision there to Elmer (Violent) Ray. The consensus of the working press was that Charles had won. The judge who was outvoted gave him eight of the ten rounds, and when the referee lifted Ray's hand the crowd booed. Even so, there was no easy way to call it a triumphant debut for Charles in New York.

Mintz persevered, taking all the fights he could get. In Cleveland, matched for the third time with Moore, Charles knocked him out. He got a rematch with Ray in Chicago and won by a kayo in the ninth. In Buffalo, he won for the second time from a Pittsburgh fighter, Erv Sarlin, "the Human Rock of Gibraltar." At last on December 10, 1948, Madison Square Garden opened its doors to him again -- and the result was another fiasco.

The party of the second part, a liberated coal miner from eastern Pennsylvania named Joe Baksi, had clubbed his way to the top of the heavyweight rankings. Joe Louis, who had not yet gone public with his decision to retire, made a tentative promise. Whether Charles beat Baksi or Baksi beat Charles, the winner would get a title shot. There was one stipulation: he must win both "impressively and spectacularly."

With his usual competence, Charles gave Baksi such a thorough trouncing that in the eleventh round, bleeding from several cuts, the graduate of the coal mines stopped fighting. He turned to the referee and said that he'd had enough. So Charles was the winner; he was not, however, an impressive or spectacular winner, failing to meet Louis's benchmarks. Outweighed by an even greater margin than in his fights with Ray, he appeared to lack the punch it would take "to campaign successfully among the big boys," wrote Carl Hughes in the Pittsburgh Press. There was irony here of the bitterest kind. Just ten months earlier, in Chicago, Sam Baroudi, a middling light-heavyweight from Akron, Ohio, had died of a brain hemorrhage after losing to Charles by a knockout. The accounts of the affair were painful to read. In the tenth and last round, Baroudi had gone down from "three savage rights to the head." He never regained consciousness. "Charles was not taken into custody," the United Press story noted, but "a technical charge of manslaughter was filed."

There were no grounds for prosecution, of course, and soon Charles was fighting again in Chicago. From the receipts for his return bout there with Ray, Baroudi's family received ten thousand dollars. The whole unfortunate occurrence affected Charles so deeply, it was said, that he purposely stopped trying for knockouts from then on and contented himself without boxing his opponents. A plausible theory. But Charles knocked out Ray with a left-right-left combination that put him flat on his back.

If the knockouts were coming less frequently now, it doesn't follow that Charles was pulling his punches. With Jake Mintz fully in charge, and looking for big bucks, he was giving away poundage to the heavyweights he fought. Charley Dyer and Max Elkus, convinced that managing Charles was not the road to riches, were by this time out of the picture. They departed almost unnoticed after Mintz began to clamor for more than fifteen percent of Charles's earnings. Dyer went first. Perhaps feeling isolated, Elkus then sold his majority interest in the fighter to Tannas, a Westmoreland County political operator, for sixty thousand dollars.

Tannas lived in Arnold, where in name at least he was city clerk. His more private sources of income were not generally known, but documents made public in the 1990s identified him as "a top-echelon figure" in the racketeering empire run by the Mannarino brothers, Kelly and Sam, of New Kensington. In any case, Tannas and Mintz complemented each other -- the big, soft-spoken partner, easy-going and unobtrusive, calming and restraining the small, excitable, terrier-like front man.

Mintz had boxed some as a flyweight -- avoiding few punches, to judge by the appearance of his nose. Art Rooney's brother Dan, a Franciscan missionary in China during the 1930s, told of going into a village and being stared at by two men who were getting their first look at an Occidental. In a Chinese dialect the priest understood, one of them said to the other, "My God, isn't he ugly?" Father Dan could not allow it to pass. Addressing the men in their own tongue, he said, "You should see Jake Mintz."

It never bothered Mintz to be the object of anyone's humor. When Al Abrams nicknamed him "Malaprop" and started quoting Jake's syntactical errors, actual or invented by others, Mintz went along with the gag. For banquet speeches, he developed a routine of his own. "I thought I had golf stones," he would say, discussing his health, "but they couldn't find any. Then they took an autograph of my heart. It finally turned out I had ulster's."

Jack McGinley respected Mintz as "a top boxing guy who knew what he was doing." Having been a promoter himself, putting on fights at Forbes Field, Duquesne Gardens, Hickey Park, Motor Square Garden, Moose Temple, and the North Side Grotto, Mintz was familiar with all sides of the business. Pittsburgh back then was overstocked with promoters, few of whom lasted very long. Art Rooney and Barney McGinley were the first to develop an organization. Mintz and all the others except Apples Meyers, whose Meyers Bowl in Braddock flourished for only one year, promoted out of their hats.

Barney McGinley, a saloon keeper and horse-room operator from Braddock, met up with Art Rooney in the 1930s. They became partners in the fight game, and McGinley made an investment in Rooney's unprofitable football team, the Pittsburgh Steelers. At some point, Bert Bell, later the commissioner of the National Football League, also had a piece of the team and shared an office with Mintz after Rooney and McGinley hired him to be the matchmaker for their boxing club. Bell's voice was so loud, and he gave so little rest to it, that when Mintz had to make a telephone call he would crawl under the desk they both used.

The other McGinley, Barney's son Jack, was a student at Pitt. Graduating, he went into the war-time Navy and became the engineering officer on an LST -- landing ship/tank -- with the rank of lieutenant junior grade. Before dawn on the morning of June 6, 1944, his LST was carrying 216 men in half a dozen amphibious landing-craft vehicles across the English Channel to Omaha Beach. In addition, they had a load of "ducks" -- floatable tanks -- also with troops in them. Seven miles offshore was as close as they could get. "It was too jammed up. We had to let the men out," McGinley recalled. Whether their passengers made it to the beach they never knew.

The LST returned to England and boarded more troops on the night of June 8th. In the middle of the channel, headed for Normandy again, they took a hit from a German torpedo boat. Then another. The LST sank. It was 3 a.m.

"God only knows how many people we lost. Hundreds," McGinley guessed. "I was told the casualties were terrible." He was tossed about in the water for the next three hours. "We had life belts," he explained, "and six of us held onto one of those little rubber doughnuts. As we were leaving the ship, one fellow said, 'We'd better take this along.'" It saved their lives. Around daybreak, a British destroyer picked them up.

McGinley came out of the Navy a full lieutenant with two citations for heroism. Back in Pittsburgh, and married to Art Rooney's sister Marie, he went to work in the family's sports conglomerate, doing whatever had to be done. His most important job was to learn the boxing business.

"I had a knack for it," he said. "I studied it. I knew what a good match was. I had a knack for telling who could beat who. I could tell in advance, within fifteen hundred dollars, what the gate receipts would be."

After Jake Mintz turned to managing, McGinley took over the matchmaking. In effect, he became the Rooney-McGinley Club's promoter. His father and his brother-in-law, busy with the football team, no longer had time for boxing.

McGinley brought character and integrity to the sport. To say that this made him unique would be wrong. Contrary to popular belief, there were people of good reputation among the leeches, hoodlums, and thieves. But even by comparison with the best of them, McGinley stood out. Andy DePaul, a fighter who became the state athletic commissioner for Western Pennsylvania, described him once, in words that many others had used, as "the nicest man I ever met in boxing."

McGinley's first big promotion, in September of 1948, was a match at Forbes Field between two home-grown middleweights, Charley Affif and Lee Sala. He promoted fights at Duquesne Gardens involving Bob Baker, Pittsburgh's best-looking heavyweight prospect. But Charles, who had boxed more often in Pittsburgh than many Pittsburgh fighters, and who now had a Pittsburgh manager, was working for out-of-town promoters.

In Cincinnati, he decisioned Maxim for the third time to qualify for the Louis-sanctioned title fight with Walcott, the one in Chicago. It was not an interesting fight. By boxing defensively, Walcott forced Charles to do all the leading. The only excitement came when Mintz, upstaging his new champion before a national television audience, fainted dead away at the announcement that Charles had won.

Mintz now moved aggressively to cash in on the title, never mind that challengers happened to be scarce. For a match in New York, the International Boxing Club settled on Gus Lesnevich, who had just lost his light-heavyweight championship to the Englishman Freddie Mills. Charles put him away in seven rounds. In San Francisco, unexpectedly, home-town product Pat Valentino. a relentless body puncher held his own for seven rounds before Charles knocked him out in the eighth with a sudden left-right combination. In Buffalo, it took fourteen rounds for Charles to dispose of Freddie Beshore.

Joe Louis had just completed a seemingly endless barnstorming tour -- forty-four exhibition bouts spanning eighteen months. His motivation was money, or the absence of it. He needed money to pay his debts and back taxes, money to finance his lifestyle. But there was never enough.

As Barney Nagler tells it in his biography of Louis, "Brown Bomber," the 36-year-old champion emeritus went to Jim Norris. "I guess I have to fight again," he said. Norris was pleased, according to Nagler. He knew that Charles was not a champion the public had ever accepted. He also knew that Charles could beat Louis, and that beating Louis would authenticate him. Norris summoned Mintz and Tannas to his office in New York and laid out the terms for a fight at Yankee Stadium. Charles's split, he said, would be twenty percent, Louis's thirty-five percent.

Mintz let out a yelp. "Why? Why? Why?" He jumped to his feet and paced back and forth.

Tannas, the voice of reason, said quietly, "I don't think it's fair, Jim."

"Well, that's the way it has to be," Norris answered.

And that's the way it was.

Blinded to the obvious fact that Louis had become an old man, the sporting crowd made him a 2-to-1 favorite. One of the few dissenters other than Norris -- and Norris kept his opinion to himself -- was Carl Hughes. From New York, he filed a story to the Pittsburgh Press predicting that Charles would win. The paper's editor, W. W. Forster, saw the headline across the top of the page and just missed having a seizure. Not altogether in jest, he sent Hughes a telegram: "If you're wrong, don't come back."

Hughes wasn't wrong. Overweight and undertrained, Louis could do nothing with Charles, who beat him to the punch all night. Out of pity combined with respect, Charles saw to it that Louis went the distance, fifteen rounds. Afterward, the once great champion shed tears.

With television and radio money, Charles and his managers had $102,000 to split. Then, for much more modest purses, Mintz kept Charles busy knocking over stiffs until the IBC matched him with Walcott again. This was the fight at Norris's Detroit Olympia. Charles clearly won, knocking Walcott down in the ninth round, but at the end of the fifteenth the crowd booed the decision.

For a heavyweight title fight, the crowd was a small one -- 13,800. Increasingly in boxing, financial success or failure would henceforth depend on television. For this fight, television paid the IBC $25,000. For the one between Charles and Maxim in Chicago two months later, the take was four times as large -- and though the crowd fell short of 8,000, Charles more than doubled his purse, which came to $62,000.

He had an easy time winning, too, which removed any doubt that his opponent at Forbes Field would be Walcott. In Detroit, Walcott had actually out finished Charles, who spent the last five rounds protecting a puffed-up left ear.

For their Pittsburgh fight, Walcott chose as his training quarters the Rainbow Gardens, an amusement park in the McKeesport suburb of White Oak. At once he began to talk big. "One thing I know for sure, they won't need judges," he said to Carl Hughes. "The only guy who'll have any work to do is the referee. He'll be counting Charles out, and I mean that from my heart." Charles, training in the hills near Ligonier, was characteristically bland.. "I'll do my best," he said. "If I can knock Walcott out, I will, of course." Cautiously, he added, "But I'm making no promises."

As fight day approached, Walcott grew more expansive. He spoke of Rainbow Gardens and the surrounding environment in superlatives. Nowhere in memory had he ever been treated so well. He vowed that after winning the title he would stop at every house he had passed while doing roadwork and "thank all the people for their kind words and good wishes."

A God-fearing, long-time married man, the father of six children, Walcott personified what have come to be known as family values, and the public's good wishes were genuine. Any such warmth of feeling for Charles, whose domestic life evoked little interest, was undetectable. The sportswriters, however, with clear-eyed realism, unanimously picked him to win.

Carl Hughes tacked on a disclaimer: "Although Walcott's only hope is to get lucky, no one underestimates the power of his right hand." If the right hand did not find its target, Charles would win by a knockout, becoming once more "the ripping, slashing tiger of his youth" (he had just observed his thirtieth birthday).

Pittsburgh Press sports editor Chet Smith shadow-boxed with the issue until the very last paragraph of his column and then predicted "a fight almost sure to go the distance, with no new titleholder to be introduced at the finish." Having reached this conclusion, Smith added, he was now free to concentrate on learning to spell the name of Walcott's manager, Felix Bocchicchio.

A slight, distrustful, acidulous fellow, Bocchicchio played an unacknowledged role in the selection of a referee. Ernie Sesto, a good friend of Al Abrams, assumed that the job would be his. The three state boxing commissioners -- John Holahan, George Jones, and Ox DeGrosa -- assumed no such thing. As a friend of Al Abrams, Sesto might have passed muster. But he was also a friend of Jake Mintz, which made him unacceptable to Bocchicchio. Late on the afternoon of the fight, the commissioners chose Buck McTiernan to referee. Sesto, relegated to working the preliminary matches, openly grieved about it for weeks.

When the fighters entered the ring with their coteries, it was Mintz, not Bocchicchio, who started howling. Only one judge, Red Robinson, was from Pittsburgh. Mintz rushed over to where the commissioners were seated.

"We will not fight this fight!" he shouted. "We will not fight this fight unless all the officials are Pittsburghers! This is a black market" -- the malapropism, for a change, was surely unintentional -- "against our local officials!" The commissioners told Mintz that no changes would be made.

"Shivering with rage," as Chet Smith reported it, "Mintz ran around the ring haranguing the occupants of the press rows. Charles," Smith wrote, "seemed to cringe." Ten minutes passed, with the irate Mintz almost out of control and television recording the whole farcical scene. Finally Ox DeGrosa, the biggest of the commissioners, a havoc-wreaking tackle in his football days at Villanova, gave Mintz an order: "Get the hell out of the ring!" Two policemen appeared. They hustled Mintz beyond reach of the cameras, and, with no further ado, the fight got under way.

Walcott, who'd been reading the Bible in his dressing room, said that he prayed as he waited for the bell and prayed before the start of each subsequent round. The first was the only round he lost, but it was Walcott's own doing, not the Lord's. For vague strategic reasons, he had failed to throw a punch.

From then on, he outmaneuvered Charles. Going into the seventh round, Walcott was well ahead. His right had opened a cut below Charles's left eye. Still, nothing much seemed to be happening, and the knockout came unexpectedly. With one left hook, the title passed to Walcott.

The last time Charles had lost -- and on a questionable decision, at that -- was in 1947 to Elmer Ray. In the four years since then, he had won twenty-four fights in a row. It had been eight years and four months since anyone had knocked him out. Walcott's left hook, wrote Smith, "could well go down as the most famous single punch in the history of the ring.." In any event, Smith continued, "this was a fight they'll be talking about for years to come." Walcott, whose boast that he would win by a knockout had sounded like mere bravado, explained why it wasn't: he had learned in their second fight that he could beat Charles with the hook.

In McKeesport the next day, Walcott paid a visit to the mayor and publicly thanked "all the wonderful people who were so good to me while I was training." He did not take his gratitude door-to-door.

The fight did well at the box office. A crowd of 28,000 paid $245,000. Television brought in an additional $100,000, so that the total receipts exceeded those for the first Charles-Walcott fight in Chicago. Charles's purse was $101,000 and change, Walcott's $85,000 and change. With the Dapper Dans' share subtracted, $52,000 was left for the Rooney-McGinley Club to divide fifty-fifty with the IBC.

Before the end of the year, Charles was back in Pittsburgh, fighting again at Forbes Field. On October 10th he knocked out Rex Layne, who a short time before had been knocked out by Rocky Marciano. "I think I can hit a little," Charles said afterward, veering dangerously close to self-praise. The crowd was so small -- 6,300 -- that only the television money -- $25,000 -- kept the Rooney-McGinley Club out of the red. Again the IBC took a fifty percent cut.

Charles had two more fights in December, both on the West Coast. Over a span of nine days he won another decision from Maxim, in San Francisco, and knocked out Joe Kahut in Portland. The decks were now clear for a fourth fight with Walcott, to be held the following June at Municipal Stadium in Philadelphia.

At his training camp in New Jersey, Walcott gave the reporters nothing but platitudes. He could not be goaded into predicting another knockout. As before, people who thought they knew the fight game put their money on Charles. They had learned just enough from the fight in Pittsburgh to make him a 2-to-1 favorite instead of a 6-to-1 favorite.

Pontificating for the Pittsburgh Press, I picked Charles myself. Having had no fights since the previous July, exhibition matches aside, Walcott didn't figure to be sharp, and he was not. At the built-up weight of 191½ pounds, neither was Charles. Walcott outsmarted and sometimes outfought him. He fended Charles off with his jab, which was really nothing more than a push, and kept the now dreaded hook in reserve as a threat. Using only his right hand to punch with, he won a debatable but unanimous fifteen-round decision.

In his next fight, also in Philadelphia, Walcott lost the title. Rocky Marciano knocked him out in the thirteenth round with a short, straight right to the jaw that was every bit as sudden and explosive as the left hook delivered by Walcott in Pittsburgh.

Eight months later, Marciano won their rematch with the first punch he landed in the first round, an uppercut few people saw. It put Walcott down, and he sat where he had landed, peacefully at rest in a corner of the ring, until the count reached ten. Only then did he get up. When the referee signaled a knockout, the crowd in Chicago Stadium began to boo. Walcott, combative now for the first time all night, stamped his feet and pounded his gloves together as evidence of a desire to continue. But the fight -- and his career -- was over.

Charles, showing stolid determination, had two more chances to win back the title, losing both times to Marciano in Yankee Stadium. The first fight went fifteen rounds. Charles took an early lead, but Marciano's aimless-seeming, nerve-deadening punches wore him down -- and left his head the size and shape of a pumpkin. While he was fresh, Charles could outbox Marciano, and he proved it again in their return bout. After seven rounds, it appeared that the fight would have to be stopped. In close, with the effect of a sharp knife, Charles's elbow had ripped open Marciano's nose. The blood that poured out was a vivid red. With his nose literally split down the middle, the only way Marciano could possibly keep his title was by knocking Charles out. So he knocked Charles out in the next round, the eighth.

In the two years between his fourth fight with Walcott and his first with Marciano, Charles had lost to Rex Layne, once a punching bag for him; to Nino Valdes, a Cuban with the silhouette of a whale; and to Harold Johnson, an efficient but unremarkable light-heavyweight. After the two fights with Marciano, his decline accelerated. He was losing routinely to no-names and has-beens. Late in 1956 he retired.

Jake Mintz died in 1957. In 1958, Charles resumed fighting. After five straight defeats in places like Boise, Idaho; Juarez, Mexico; and Oklahoma City, he quit for good. He died in 1975 of Lou Gehrig's Disease -- amyotrophic lateral sclerosis. He was 54.

Walcott lived to be 80. His fame as an ex-champion landed him several jobs -- sheriff of Camden County, New Jersey, chairman of the New Jersey State Athletic Commission, director of special projects for the New Jersey State Department of Community Affairs. "Special projects" involved work with handicapped and retarded children.

Jack McGinley stopped promoting in 1953. He did so regretfully, because, as he said, "I enjoyed the fighters, I enjoyed the managers." Co-owner, with Fritz Wilson, of the Miller beer franchise in Pittsburgh, he was doing well financially and understood what many did not -- that it was "all over." Television, by giving away the product, had destroyed boxing's customer base. By the end of the 1950s there were no small fight clubs developing new fighters for the networks to devour. For the networks, this was no problem; without missing a beat, they turned to other forms of entertainment. But the fight clubs never came back.

McGinley's epitaph for boxing was: "Television killed it." Actually, network television killed it and cable television revived it. Held in the gambling casinos of Las Vegas and Atlantic City and in one or two places where boxing never really died -- Los Angeles, for example -- most fights today are on ESPN (usually with some championship nobody ever heard of at stake) or on pay per view (the major attractions, such as they are). The fighters who make it big are raking in money. But spectacles like the one that drew 28,000 people to Forbes Field on the night of July 18, 1951, when Jersey Joe Walcott won the only heavyweight championship there was, knocking out Ezzard Charles with a left hook from nowhere, belong to the unreclaimable past.

CHAPTER 19

BUNNYS BOYS

Bunny Buntag was an optimist and a visionary. "I can see it now," he would crow, sitting across a desk from the Pittsburgh Sun-Telegraph's sports editor, Harry Keck. "Art Swiden the heavyweight champion. Tommy Yarosz the light-heavyweight champion. Lee Sala the middleweight champion." Buntag was talking about the fighters he managed, and no one could say that he was talking through his hat, invariably a high-crowned fedora which he seldom removed. All three of his fighters had ability. All three were prospects. All three, in the end, disappointed him.

Fight managers today are peripheral characters, their numbers, their importance, and their influence sadly diminished. In Buntag's time, encompassing more than half of the twentieth century, the manager was always at the forefront. He did the thinking for his fighters; he did the public relations. Managers tended to be colorful and imaginative. Some were better known than the fighters whose destinies they controlled.

That is no longer the case. At the upper levels, managers as such do not exist. Fighters who make the big money have promoters, not managers. When the prison system disgorged Mike Tyson, the first thing he said was, "Don King will be my promoter." Floyd Mayweather's stature reached the point that he was able to promote some of his own fights. Ordinary champions need a trainer, a business agent, an accountant, and a lawyer, but that is all. Maybe one of these factotums will be called the manager, but traditional full-service managers belong to an earlier pugilistic age.

Around Pittsburgh, anyway, Peter J. Buntag was the last of the tribe. Stately, loquacious, adept at the soft con, he worked at his trade from 1914 until the mid-1960s. His knowledge of fights and fighters was encyclopedic. Going back to Frank Klaus, the middleweight champion who succeeded Stanley Ketchel, he had seen all the good ones. At the Park Athletic Club in Braddock, where Klaus trained, Buntag was a part of his retinue -- the hanger-on, the go-fer, the towel swinger. He spent his youth in that gym, and he boxed just enough to make an astute career decision, arrived at early in life: he would manage fighters, not be one.

His model was George Engel, who managed Klaus and, for a time, Harry Greb. Rifts between Greb and his regular manager, Red Mason, were periodic occurrences; during one of them Greb turned to Engel until he patched things up with Mason. Engel wore derbies and smoked cigars. Engel *looked* like a manager. Mason looked like W. C. Fields. He had a Fieldsian paunch and a bulbous Fieldsian nose, its ruddiness a match for his hair. Mason was notorious for his unhygienic habits in the corner. He would take a deep swig from the water bottle and spray the whole mouthful onto his fighter's face. If a fighter he managed was down near the end of a round, and in even the slightest danger of being counted out, Mason would grab the water bottle and pound on the timekeeper's bell. Buntag, except in moments of extreme agitation, was as dignified as a U.S. senator.

Jimmy Dime, a contemporary of Engel and Mason, came to this country in the 1880s from Ireland and was boxing in small New York towns at the age of 24. His birth name wasn't Dime, it was Fox -- James Fox. He adopted his alias after winning a foot race for a prize of ten cents. As Jimmy Dime, he boxed until 1899, winning an ersatz title, the "lightweight championship of America," by knocking out Billy Frazier, who'd been previously knocked out by the undefeated world champion, Jack McAuliffe. Dime had a few fights in New Castle and settled down there after hanging up the gloves. A dapper-looking fellow, 5 feet 5 ½ inches tall, he made a smooth transition into managing and training.

His first fighter of any renown was an Italian immigrant named Tony Ross. At Duquesne Gardens in 1909, Ross went the distance, six rounds, in a no-decision bout with the recently crowned heavyweight champion, Jack Johnson. The fight was one-sided, but afterward Johnson praised Ross for his "toughness" and "willingness to take on black fighters." Dime, as it happened, was Duquesne Gardens' matchmaker at the time. By refereeing the fight himself, he reduced the promotion's overhead.

. Presumably Ross could have taken Johnson's title by knocking him out; the chances of that were minuscule, but Ross could hold his own with any of the other heavyweights except the two black contenders even Johnson avoided after winning the championship, Sam Langford and Joe Jeannette. He lost to Langford by a knockout and twice to Jeannette by knockouts.

Ross was a White Hope who made a habit of winning from rival White Hopes, among them Frank Moran. In one of his last fights before facing Johnson, his opponent was Marvin Hart, who had been the semi-official champion during part of the inter-regnum after Jim Jeffries retired. It was

Jeffries himself who designated Hart as his successor on the strength of Hart's knockout win over Jack Root. Defending this hand-me-down title, Hart lost it to Tommy Burns, who lost it to Johnson, whose subsequent knockout of a Jeffries dragged away from his peaceful bucolic existence unhinged white America but removed any doubt as to Johnson's authenticity. Marvin Hart and Tommy Burns had been pretenders; beating Jeffries put Johnson in the direct line of descent.

The Hart-Ross fight was in New Orleans. Ross took a beating for twelve rounds but knocked Hart down in the thirteenth for a nine-count and then knocked him down again. With Hart on his hands and knees, Ross went wild with excitement and threw a right-hand punch that landed on Hart's back like a blow from a hammer. Properly, the referee called it a foul and declared Hart the winner.

Jimmy Dime and Red Mason had unusually large stables of better-than-average fighters. Dime's included, along with Ross, George and Joe Chip, Patsy Brannigan, and Tom McMahon, an import from Illinois. McMahon learned to box as a sparring partner for one of George Chip's forerunners as middleweight champion, Billy Papke, When Dime took him over in 1910 he was still a preliminary fighter. The manager put him in with George Chip, who was also a comparative novice at the time, and Chip won a six-round newspaper decision. It was a good way for McMahon to get his feet wet.

By 1914, he was fighting light-heavyweight and heavyweight contenders. One night in Youngstown, he won a twelve-round newspaper decision from the gargantuan Jess Willard, who was two years away from knocking out Johnson for the heavyweight championship. Sportswriters fabricated a nickname for McMahon -- the Pittsburgh Bearcat. In four tries he could never beat Battling Levinsky, a light-heavyweight champion, but won from Jack Dillon, the champion before Levinsky, and boxed a draw with Dillon besides losing to him once. A knockout loss to Sam Langford was his only such defeat until he was too far past his prime to be fighting at all.

Bunny Buntag never managed a champion or, for that matter, a near-champion unless it was Chalky Wright, a wanderer from California who won the featherweight title after Buntag turned him over to Henry Armstrong's manager, Eddie Mead. The best of his own fighters, Buntag always said, was Buck McTiernan, a middleweight from Swissvale. "Let me tell you something," Buntag would begin, and then elaborate on the thesis that

McTiernan was the equal of Sugar Ray Robinson as a stylist. "A picture fighter," Buntag would say, aglow with an almost paternal affection. "And he could take you out with either hand. McTiernan never made a bad fight."

If McTiernan never made a bad fight, then why, it was natural to ask, did he lose so many? McTiernan could beat fighters who could beat Jimmy Belmont, but Belmont beat McTiernan every time they fought, knocking him out twice and winning a decision. In the 1930s, McTiernan boxed five world middleweight and welterweight champions and lost to four of them. The fifth, Joe Dundee, although knocked down by McTiernan, scuffled his way to a draw.

What all of this added up to was something a bit short of the perfection Buntag described, but there were two Buck McTiernans, it seemed -- the McTiernan who lost big fights and the McTiernan who might have been. An illness, rheumatic fever, had robbed the likable picture fighter of his stamina. "Retire," a doctor advised him. For much too long, he wouldn't listen. His moment came at last, but in an unanticipated way.. On the night of July 18, 1951, when the heavyweight championship passed from Ezzard Charles to Jersey Joe Walcott before the largest crowd ever to see a fight at Forbes Field, Buck McTiernan, a picture referee with his high cheekbones, florid complexion, and snow-white hair, smoothly and efficiently ran the show.

Buntag's confidence in McTiernan did not at times serve the fighter's welfare.. When in 1930 Madison Square Garden proposed a match for McTiernan with a Spaniard named Ignatius Ara, Buntag was elated. Madison Square Garden! Those were magical words. But then his friend Bobby Massick, a boxing man who had scouted Ara, said, "Bunny, don't let McTiernan fight that guy."

"Why not?" Buntag demanded.

"He'll get knocked out."

Massick's prophesy came true -- in the eighth round. A crowd of just four thousand, one of the smallest ever at the Garden, turned out to see a card headlined by Vince Dundee and Ben Jeby, future champions. McTiernan versus Ara was the semi-final.

Buntag never doubted that any of his fighters could take a punch. A heavyweight he managed, George Panka, had a top-ten ranking when Buntag threw him in with Two-Ton Tony Galento, who, at 5 feet 9, appeared to consist entirely of stomach. Although he was present that night at Motor

Square Garden, Buntag did not see the fight. At the opening bell, he shook hands with Panka, turned, and started down the steps from the ring apron. Panka was still facing the crowd. Confident and relaxed, he waved to some friends. Galento, meanwhile, had come rolling out of his corner like a beer barrel gone berserk. As Panka wheeled around, ready at last to get on with the night's work, he took a thunderous left hook to the jaw and was roadkill when Buntag looked up.

In search from then on of another heavyweight, he found one at last, fifteen years after Panka's fall from the heights, in Art Swiden, a tall, dark, rakish-looking steelworker with curly black hair. By the age of 19, he had an 18-3 record with an excellent knockout ratio. Sportswriters, aware that he worked at the Edgar Thomson slab mill, passed over the fact that his hometown was West Mifflin and called him the Braddock Bomber.

The name seemed to fit. "Arthur," Buntag told him, having accepted a match in Chicago with the dynamic Bob Satterfield, "you hit like Dempsey." Satterfield hit like Satterfield, and, with one punch, an overhand right, he knocked Swiden out in the first round.

Lee Sala, from Donora, was a left-hook specialist with somber good looks who knocked out thirty-five of his first fifty-three opponents, decisioned seventeen others, and lost only once -- to a guy who fought out of a shell. Sala's fifty-fourth opponent was Joey DeJohn of Syracuse, perhaps the hardest-hitting middleweight around, but a fighter with a weakness: no defense. Sala, Buntag reasoned, would polish him off quickly.

On the contrary, Sala had to fight for his life. So did DeJohn. Nate Liff, who worked in Sala's corner that night in DeJohn's hometown, vividly recalled their ordeal. "If I ever felt sorry for two fighters," he said, "it was DeJohn and Sala. I lost track of how many knockdowns there were. I know that Sala was up and down like an elevator. The referee came to his corner after the fifth round and said, 'Lee, I'm gonna stop it.' Sala said, 'Let me try one more round.' He went out for the sixth and hit DeJohn with a left hook that broke DeJohn's ribs. Then he brought the left up and broke DeJohn's jaw. Then he knocked him out with a right. It was like winning the lottery -- a thousand-to-one shot."

Together, both fighters were carted off to the hospital, where Liff said to Sala, "Lee, I'd rather see you lose than win like this." Sala's answer, Liff said, was, "Nate, it's never going to happen again."

Sala won fourteen of his next fifteen fights, with eleven knockouts, and then he was back in Syracuse, matched again with DeJohn in a ball-park fight that drew 22,000 cash customers. "In the second round," Liff said, "Sala took a punch to the shoulder and went down for a count of nine. The punch that knocked him out, though -- a right to the jaw -- was legitimate."

Sala had good bloodlines. His father and an uncle had been professional boxers. Until Buntag got hold of him, he boxed out of Tampa. In Pittsburgh, he sparred with Art Swiden, who said of Sala's left hook that it could "lift you right off your feet." So it could, but Sala rationed it. He fought covered up, with his right glove protecting the left side of his face and his left arm protecting his midriff. An opponent like DeJohn could force him to trade punches; his preference, though, was to pace himself, waiting to throw the left hook.

One of Sala's few moments of unrestrained ferocity was in a fight with Charley Affif on September 15, 1948, at Forbes Field. They were friends and rivals and sparring partners and not unevenly matched. In fact, their sparring sessions at the Pittsburgh Lyceum had strengthened Affif's belief that he could beat Sala.

Affif was tough and resolute, a left-hooker like Sala but without Sala's firepower, which he fatally underestimated. In the second round, Sala moved Affif into a corner and landed a stunning left hook. The ropes kept Affif from going down, but he was helpless, and Sala bombarded him with lefts and rights until he sagged to the floor. The fight was over.

"I'm sorry it had to be Chinkie," Sala told reporters, using Affif's nickname, "but he'd have done it to me if he could. It was business, and we both got a payday."

Others along with Buntag were predicting now that in due time Sala would be the middleweight champion, and New York was ready to see what he could do. Showcased at St. Nicholas Arena, Sala won as expected from Reuben Jones, but the critics were not enthralled. His performance had been lackluster, and New York proceeded to forget about him.

Plodders like Tony DiMiccio, a crouching, weaving fat boy from upstate New York, brought out the worst in Sala. It was DiMiccio who gave him his first defeat, after forty-eight consecutive wins. He had lost to Sala before and would do so again but outpointed him on the night of their fight in Buffalo. Beating DiMiccio types did nothing for Sala's reputation and not very much for his bank account, but Buntag didn't see it that way. The match that could have made both the fighter and his manager some money -- a Forbes Field blockbuster with Tommy Yarosz, Sala's former stablemate -- never came off. Buntag didn't want it.

The reasons for this were difficult to fathom. A year or two earlier, Yarosz had parted with Buntag to fight for a better-known New York manager, Ray Arcel. The colorless younger brother of Teddy Yarosz, middleweight champion in the mid-1930s, Tommy Yarosz was a tall, blond, smooth-as-butter light-heavyweight from Monaca who finished his career with an 82-9-1 record. Over a stretch of seven years, he was undefeated in fifty-five fights.. He had a quick, accurate jab, but no punch. His instinct was to fight backing up.

Arcel persuaded him to be more aggressive, and a welcome transformation began. In Madison Square Garden, the new Yarosz lost an unpopular decision, booed by the crowd, to Jake LaMotta. The best he could do with Charley Affif in Pittsburgh was a draw, but he was winning fights, too -- from Chuck Hunter and Sylvester Perkins, middleweights with solid credentials, and from Floyd Morris, a former national Golden Gloves middleweight champion from the Hill district who packed a wallop. Halfway through their ten-rounder at Heidelberg Arena, Yarosz took a right to the chin that dropped him to one knee momentarily. Explaining his recklessness -- no one had ever knocked him off his feet -- he said, "If all I had done was box, it wouldn't have been much of a fight."

Ray Arcel's advice was sinking in. When Yarosz decisioned the Australian aborigine Dave Sands in London, he made the cover of Ring magazine. With that, his career reached its zenith. Increasingly, he found it hard to get work. For a fight with Sala, Arcel would have accepted twenty-two and a half percent of the gate. Buntag, although satisfied with the twenty-seven and a half percent offered to Sala, haggled endlessly overweight-making. His final demand, that Yarosz would have to fight at 162 pounds, was a deal breaker. It had been years since Yarosz weighed 162. Smaller men like Sands, Hunter, Perkins, and Morris had been willing to fight him at any weight, for while Yarosz might outbox them, and did, that is all he would do. There was nothing to fear from Yarosz except the grim possibility of a bloody nose. Buntag, adamant, insisted on 162 pounds or no fight, and the promoter, Jack McGinley, stopped negotiating.

Having protected Sala from Yarosz's left jab, Buntag cheerfully exposed him, for less money, to Joey DeJohn's heavy artillery. This was the fight Sala won at great cost, by getting off the floor six times, and it took something out of him. He continued to box for another four years, but never again beat an opponent of any great stature. After DeJohn knocked him out in their rematch, he lost by a knockout to a future middleweight champion, Bobo Olson, in San Francisco. Sala went down in the second round, putting up little resistance. His last fight -- with Willie Troy, a contender -- was on national television, and he lost in the fifth round after staggering Troy but making no discernible effort to finish him.

So Buntag was left with only Swiden, a changed fighter himself as a result of his knockout loss to Satterfield. "From that day on," Swiden told me, "I forgot about hitting like Dempsey and concentrated on boxing like Tunney." He boxed like Tunney with several modifications of his own. Tunney avoided leads by slipping them, ducking them, stepping inside, or pulling away. In a scholarly essay for the 1929 edition of the Encyclopedia Britannica, he explained that "this gives a boxer the free use of his two hands for hitting, a great improvement over the older style of using one or both arms to parry, which effectively warded off the blows, but by doing so ,prevented the use of the hands to counter." Swiden, when he had to, could slip, duck, step inside, and pull away with the best of them, but he chose rather to ward off blows in the old-fashioned style, using his powerful steelworker's arms to block them. Entire rounds went by in which countering seemed to be the last thing on his mind.

Swiden boxed like Tunney (in his own way) and bent the Marquess of Queensberry rules (also in his own way) like Fritzie Zivic and Harry Greb. His bag of tricks was, if anything, more diversified than theirs. Stronger than most heavyweights, he twisted and turned his opponents, stepped on their feet, and picked off their punches with an open glove as he slouched against the ropes. His instructor in these techniques was Liff, an old bantamweight. Liff had taught Swiden how to push on the other fighter's shoulder and keep him from "getting off," how to hook the other fighter by the back of the neck and pull him right into a punch.

It was not the kind of artistry that went over big with the fans, but in one town, at least -- Charlotte, North Carolina -- Swiden became a celebrity of sorts. Working out in Charlotte for a fight with home-town hero Wayban

(Tugboat) Thomas, he sparred much longer than he had planned on doing because "fighters and past fighters," a local columnist wrote, "hungered to see why no one could penetrate the enticingly cool defensive barricade."

Among those who failed to penetrate it was Tugboat Thomas in the fight itself, which Swiden easily won. Back home in Pittsburgh, enticingly cool defensive barricades failed to entice. Even before the Satterfield fight, the public had soured on Swiden. His first big main event was with Jackie Cranford, a morning glory from Washington, D.C., at Duquesne Gardens. The advice he received from Buntag, Swiden said, was: "Keep that left hand on him. Choke him. Cut off his wind." But choking was Fritzie Zivic's specialty, and Swiden did not yet have Zivic's finesse. Still the Braddock Bomber, he knocked Cranford down in the fourth round, but lost on a foul in the ninth for choking and hitting low.

When he lost at the Gardens to Pedro Bradley, a turtle-like blob of a fighter whose face he never saw except between rounds, Swiden was finished as a home-town attraction. For the next eight years, from 1951 to 1959, he boxed exclusively on the road.

Even in the gym he was ostracized. Billy Conn, officially retired but preparing for an exhibition match somewhere, wanted nothing more to do with Swiden after two rounds of sparring. "The hell with this," Conn told him. "You hold me. You twist me. You turn me. What good does it do?" Rocky Marciano, training for his first fight with Jersey Joe Walcott, worked three rounds with Swiden and failed to land a punch. Having seen all he wanted to, Marciano's manager, Al Weill, sent Swiden home with an airplane ticket and a hundred-dollar bill. Marciano's farewell was a lecture. As repeated by Swiden in a dead-on imitation of a Massachusetts twang, it went like this:

"Aht, you brainless jackass, look at all those bums who couldn't lay a glove on you makin' big money. Get in shape and staht usin' the talent you were born with."

But Swiden was not disposed to get in shape. There were far more interesting things to do. "I had ladies of the evening," he confessed. Unremorseful and unrehabilitated, he boxed somebody in Bayonne, New Jersey. At the end of the fifth round, the promoter, Willie Gilzenberg, ran down the aisle to Swiden's corner, shouting, "Hey, *Sweden*! Do something! Throw a punch!" An even better idea occurred to him. "Get knocked out!"

His pockets empty, Swiden went to work for Hymie Schwartz, who had a Chevrolet dealership on Baum Boulevard in East Liberty and managed fighters on the side. Billy Conn was Hymie's business partner. For the two or three fighters in their stable, they rigged up a gym on the second floor of the dealership, where one afternoon a manager appeared with an unknown heavyweight from St. Louis named Sonny Liston. In town for a main event at the Gardens, the visitor wanted to spar. Swiden, although he had not had a fight in two years, was tempted by an offer of twenty dollars for two rounds. Just to survive them, he had to use his full repertory of tricks. He twisted and turned Liston, stepped on his feet, smothered his punches with a barricade of arms. Afterward, Swiden said, "Toughest double sawbuck I ever made, but he hasn't hit me yet. Anyway, not on the chin."

Swiden had stood up to this behemoth and survived, which led him to re-examine his priorities. He decided to give boxing another try -- not in Pittsburgh but out on the West Coast. A manager-trainer named Mickey Davies took him in hand, preaching, as Marciano had, the benefits of getting in shape. This time Swiden was receptive, and Davies booked a fight for him in Dallas with Buddy Turman, a Texas heavyweight billed as "the next Jack Dempsey." "I was lean as a greyhound, hard as a board," Swiden recalled. "I had the guy down in the second round, and I boxed his ears off."

Swiden credited Davies with raising him from the dead, but he still had a contract with Buntag, and Buntag resumed calling the shots. Back on the road, Swiden boxed the ears off Oscar Pharo in Birmingham, Tugboat Thomas again in Charlotte, and Bert Whitehurst in Ottawa, Ontario.

"He's a fighter with every move in the book, every block," Buntag explained to sportswriters who were getting their first look at Swiden. "He knows how to jab. He knows when to throw the right" -- which was seldom. As an exhibition of restraint, Swiden's use of the right could not be improved on. As entertainment, it lacked something.

In Las Vegas, he used his left hook to jack-knife Zora Folley, the top-ranked heavyweight contender, putting him down for what looked like a ten-count until Folley's alert manager, Bill Swift, bounded into the ring screaming, "Foul!" Instantly, Buntag, too, was in the ring, and going after Swift. A dozen state troopers followed on his heels and an indeterminate number of spectators joined the melee. Swiden, eager to help restore the peace, delivered a swift kick to Swift but could not shut him up.

Swiftian argument persuaded the referee to declare a fifteen-minute rest period for Folley. When the fight resumed, it went the distance, ten rounds, and Folley, the 6-to-1 favorite, got the decision, which Buntag hotly disputed.

In Reno, Swiden lost a decision to a home-town fighter, Howard King, that even the crowd thought was unfair. King had just boxed a draw with Archie Moore, the forever young light-heavyweight champion, but Swiden made him look bad. (Swiden could make anyone look bad without looking good himself.) A ruckus at the weigh-in, when King's manager, Charley Schultz, raised the issue of "dirty fighting" and then traded punches with Buntag, may or may not have influenced the referee, who repeatedly warned Swiden for low blows and took away a round he had won.

The Swiden-Buntag partnership ended soon afterward. With boxing more than ever in decline, Buntag tried his luck at the siding business and got into trouble. Charged with misrepresentation of some kind, and convicted, he spent a few months in jail. Swiden, under the management of his one-time boss at the Chevrolet dealership, Hymie Schwartz, kept fighting, and there was work for him suddenly in the second-floor auditorium of a McKeesport building called the Palisades. His eight-year exile was over. The promoter well knew that he was taking a gamble, but it worked. Swiden sold the place out, an achievement somewhat less impressive than selling out Yankee Stadium, or even Hickey Park.

For his opponent, Ollie Wilson, a babe in the woods from Hartford, Connecticut, the experience was a nightmare. After losing nine of the ten rounds, Wilson sat with an ice bag pressed to his face and complained about Swiden's deceitfulness.

"He kept talkin' to me," Wilson told a reporter. "He'd say, 'Come on, throw the right hand.' Then he'd say, 'If you don't do it, I will. Watch out, now, here comes the right.' And that's just what he'd throw. I'd be lookin' for him to throw the left hook and he threw the right hand every time."

It was Swiden's nature, perhaps, to mislead the gullible. Half Syrian and half Hungarian, he encouraged a belief that he was Jewish by wearing, in his early fights, a Star of David on his trunks. In other ways, too, he was not at all trustworthy.

"He does so many funny things," Bert Whitehurst said after losing a return bout to Swiden at the Palisades. Although Whitehurst must have known what he was letting himself in for, his post-fight remarks, like Wilson's, were full of grievance. "Boxing is supposed to be an art, and he makes a joke of it," Whitehurst pouted. "Did you see him stepping on my feet? It gets worse every time we fight."

Swiden's trick of catching a punch with his open glove and holding it like a captured bird was what irritated Whitehurst the most. He protested to the referee -- Buck McTiernan -- and McTiernan told him, "You do the same thing." Scandalized, Whitehurst answered, "I cannot resort to dirty tactics." A graduate student at the City College of New York, he had a cultivated way of expressing himself.

Actually, there is nothing in the rules against using a glove to catch punches. Hymie Schwartz, setting everybody straight, said, "It's legal. It don't look like it, but it is."

Swiden's next -- and last -- opponent, Wayne Bethea, complained of other transgressions. He was being held, the New Yorker said after their Palisades ten-rounder, he was being backhanded, and roughed up with Swiden's glove laces. And of course, his feet were being stepped on.

The referee, Ernie Sesto, listened to Bethea with calm indifference. Swiden himself was more responsive. He talked to Bethea ("Here comes the right, champ"), winked at him, stared at him -- and landed enough punches to win every round, knocking Bethea down once for an eight-count.

In his own unique way, he never had looked better. Hymie Schwartz made hopeful noises about a fight in Miami with Liston, but Liston's handlers were not fools. Building Sonny Boy up for a title shot, they needed Swiden about as much as a house fly needs flypaper. Weeks and then months went by. Abandoning the ring for good, Swiden went to work as the manager of a jazz club, the Encore, in Shadyside. Buntag, meanwhile, could not resist taking a curtain call.

A fat and feckless heavyweight named Mert Brownfield, cannon fodder for rising young prospects, unexpectedly asked Buntag to manage him. Just to show that, at 69, he had not lost his touch, the wily old spinmeister consented. He would do it, he said, for one fight. Boxing was still in his blood. "I've always liked fights more than anything," he said. "Fights is my lingo."

He found a trainer for Brownfield, a benign disciplinarian called Cherry Red. When Brownfield was in halfway decent shape, Buntag notified

Freddie Lux, promoter pro-tem at the Palisades. Lux had a show coming up and said he could use Brownfield on the undercard.

"I don't manage preliminary fighters," Buntag coldly informed him. Ten minutes later, he had shown Lux the wisdom of putting Brownfield in the main event with Irish Jimmy McClain, beaten only once as a pro.

At the weigh-in, Buntag removed a corncob pipe from his mouth and said to Brownfield, "Now, I'm gonna tell you something. You can be a ten-dollar fighter or a twenty-five-hundred-dollar fighter. You're as big as that other guy and you know who he is. He's no one. Nobody. Just go out and throw punches."

Neither a ten-dollar fighter nor a twenty-five-hundred-dollar fighter but a one-hundred-and-fifty-dollar fighter, for that was the amount of his purse, Brownfield went out and threw punches. From a chair at the far end of the half-empty hall, Buntag watched him knock McClain down in the first round and immediately get knocked down himself. Unperturbed, Buntag said, "That fellow McClain will not go the distance."

McClain went as far as the eighth round, in which Brownfield's left hook put him down again. The back of McClain's head took the impact of the fall, and he was out for five minutes.

In the dressing room, Buntag greeted Brownfield effusively, shouting, "Jack Dempsey! Jack Dempsey!' Pigmentation-wise, Brownfield resembled Joe Louis, rather than Jack Dempsey, but in other respects he was similar to neither. Buntag, though, could not have been happier, fights being his lingo. Long, long after the fans and the boxers and the officials had left the building, he was showing Cherry Red how the great Charley Burley dealt with counter-punchers.

CHAPTER 20
BY THE NUMBERS

If there's a pugilistic equivalent of perfect pitch, Bob Baker had it. The techniques of boxing came to him easily. His teachers, Frank Goosby and Lou Ledbetter, thought of Baker as a heavyweight champion in the making.

They had noticed him one day at the Centre Avenue YMCA in the Hill district, lifting weights. The Second World War had ended and he was home from the Navy. Ledbetter managed preliminary fighters; Goosby's job was to train them. In answer to a question, Baker said he never had boxed. Talked into it by Ledbetter, he put on the gloves with an experienced amateur heavyweight, and even though he was clearly overmatched, Ledbetter and Goosby liked his style. He stood up straight and punched in a short arc, with surprising quickness. He was 6 feet 1, or a little taller, and weighed about 200 pounds.

Goosby, an old middleweight who never quite reached the top, knew as much about boxing as anyone did but lacked tutorial skills. Ledbetter interpreted for him, getting his ideas across. The text came from Goosby, the exposition from Ledbetter.

They started Baker out as an amateur, and he lost only two fights -- one to a steelworker from Homestead named "Art something," as he recalled, and the other to Coley Wallace for the 1948 national Golden Gloves championship. In an earlier round of the tournament, Wallace had beaten a short, clumsy, roundhouse swinger from Brockton, Massachusetts. It was no big deal, just a paragraph or two in the New York newspapers, but Rocky Marciano, as the ring announcers called him, "Rocco Marchegiano" being too much of a mouthful for them, never would lose another fight. Again in 1949, Wallace and Baker boxed for the national title, and this time it was Baker who won. Not long afterward, he turned professional.

Right from the beginning, there were those who spoke of him as "another Joe Louis." Physically, the resemblance was strong, except that Louis had a softer, rounder face. Even Baker's manner -- the dignified impassivity -- reminded people of Louis. After losing to Baker twice -- by a technical knockout and then a decision (he was down nine times in their second fight) -- Omelio Agramonte, who had lasted twenty-eight rounds in four fights with Louis, two of them exhibitions, said that Louis hit harder but that Baker's hands were faster. Never mind that when Agramonte boxed him, Louis was past his prime; up to that time there never had been a heavyweight whose hand speed compared with Louis's. "Baker's punches don't hurt you, but they jolt you," said Rusty Payne, having sampled enough of them in a four-round knockout loss to be something of an authority on the subject.

While remaining deeply involved, Ledbetter had turned over the management of Baker to a man named Dusty Better. (The explanation, which sounds like a pun, was that Better's connections were better than Ledbetter's.) Better now echoed Ledbetter and Goosby in assuring Baker, "You can be champion of the world." Rusty Payne told him, "You're going places." He did go places, in a manner of speaking, but not to the places envisioned for him.

One problem was that his hands, in addition to being fast, were small and fragile. They were unsatisfactory percussive instruments. He kept breaking them . . . and having operations . . . and breaking them again. In the dressing room after his second fight with Agramonte, he held out his hands for reporters to inspect. Each one looked like the upper half of a melon cut in two.

The surgeons were no help. "They tried everything," Baker recalled. "They scraped the bone. I don't know what all they did to these hands. The next time I fought, I'd bust 'em up again."

Something else kept Baker from realizing his potential. He hated to train - - hated to train and liked to eat. Given those two factors, he hardly ever fought at his best weight, 208 pounds. For the rematch with Agramonte, he was 225. "Who can beat him if he ever gets in shape?" asked Carl Hughes in the Pittsburgh Press, and then he answered his own question: "No one."

"I gave my trainers a lot of headaches," Baker confessed. "Lou would get mad. Goosby wouldn't."

The third reason Baker fell short, at least by the standards set for him, was a certain absence of purpose. "To be a champion," he said, looking back on his career, "you have to have determination. You have to have desire." It was only too apparent that Baker had neither. "Boxing to me was just a sport, just a game," he said. "I enjoyed myself. I went along for the ride. As far as being champion of the world, it didn't mean a thing."

Because he took no pleasure in beating guys up, patrons of the art felt cheated by Baker. He climbed through the ropes as though reporting for work. Ledbetter, coaching from the ring apron, would call out, "Number three," the signal for a left hook to the body and a right to the head, and Baker would respond like a cook at a greasy spoon filling an order. There were other numbers for other combinations of punches. "We had a code," Baker said. "Lou was a good observer. He could pick a guy apart real well."

Doing it by the numbers, Baker was undefeated for two and a half years. Until his hands began to deteriorate and his weight became a drag, almost all of his fights ended in knockouts.

Later, when inferior opponents went the distance with Baker, he was jeered. At no time, however, did anyone ever question his gameness. Sid Peaks, thought of in those days as gargantuan, dropped him twice with thunderous rights. Baker got up to win the fight by a knockout. In their return bout, although he took some direct hits, Baker won the decision with something to spare. Also, he fractured both hands. There were no knockdowns.

Baker's twentieth fight was his New York debut. At St. Nicholas Arena, he was unimpressive in beating Elkins Brothers. The New York boxing writers, having expected to see the next Joe Louis, were disappointed, but Ray Arcel counseled patience. The highly esteemed trainer and manager said that Baker was "still a great prospect."

When Baker stopped Agramonte, cutting his left eye, the referee and both judges had the Cuban ahead. In their second fight, overpowered, Agramonte was up and down like a yo-yo. Joe Louis had floored him only once.

Baker's next two fights were with Dale Hall in Pittsburgh and Billy Gilliam in Providence, and he won them by knockouts, his sixteenth and seventeenth. Only seven of his fights had gone the distance. From then on, and he boxed for another eight years, he won only three more by knockouts.

Every time he fought he was damaging his hands. "Oh, how they ached. I was hurting myself more than the other guy," he said ruefully. There was only one thing to do. "I quit being a puncher and became a boxer."

In his twenty-fifth fight, he out boxed Jimmy Bivins, an achievement he was gracious enough to minimize. Bivins, he acknowledged, had seen his best days. The Bivins fight was on November 5, 1951. On November 13th, in Cincinnati, Kid Riviera held Baker to a draw. It was the first time Baker hadn't won. Which hardly seemed to matter. Aside from Ezzard Charles, who had lost the heavyweight title to Jersey Joe Walcott but could not be denied a rematch, Baker was now the top-rated contender.

Clarence Henry was No. 3. They met at Madison Square Garden ten nights after the Baker-Riviera fight, and Henry knocked Baker out in the eighth round. Jack McGinley, who'd been promoting Baker's fights in Pittsburgh, was there. "Baker's a better fighter than Henry, but his hands are gone," McGinley said.

After that, it was never the same for Baker. In 1952 he had only three fights, all with Billy Gilliam, winning the first two and losing the third. The fights were not exciting, just close. Early in 1953 a Brooklyn promoter matched them yet again, and Baker won.

He was living the good life, getting by on his talent. He won from Cesar Brion and from Nino Valdes. For the Valdes fight, in Huntington, West Virginia, Baker's announced weight was 227 pounds. His actual weight -- "Do you want the God's truth?" he said to me once -- was 285. "I damn near died after the fight," Baker said. "I went in the shower and laid on the floor and let the cold water come down on me."

Six weeks later, in Chicago, Baker had an easier time of it. Bob Satterfield knocked him out in one round. "He caught me with a left hook right in the gut," Baker said. Baker's gut had become a target no one could miss.

Only Satterfield and Henry ever knocked Baker out. A referee in Miami Beach stopped his fight with Archie Moore, the 40-year-old light-heavyweight champion, because of a cut. Baker that night weighed 250 pounds. He had trained just three days for the opponent he considered the best he ever fought.

After losing to Moore, Baker slimmed down and won thirteen fights in a row between May 1954 and the end of the next year. He won from Coley Wallace twice, from Rex Layne three times, and from Nino Valdes when Valdes was the No. 1 contender. Most of these fights were out of town -- sometimes in Cleveland, sometimes in New York, sometimes in West Jordan, Utah (Rex Layne country). Then in Madison Square Garden on February 3, 1956, he lost to the freakish Hurricane Jackson, who exasperated his opponents by tapping and slapping and taking their best punches and in the end just wearing them out.

The following September, at Forbes Field, Ben Anolik promoted a Baker-Jackson return match for the Dapper Dan Club. Baker's purse was to be the biggest of his career, $33,000. Certain he couldn't lose, he bet the entire amount -- "every nickel of it" -- on himself. It was not a well-advised move. He did lose, ploddingly, by a decision that might have gone the other way, When Baker got home that night, he said to his wife, "Where's the bottle at? I blew all the money."

His subsequent fights were unimportant ones. Baker was now a trial horse, an unthreatening opponent for fighters in search of credibility. Dusty Better had sold his contract to a business-man type, Sid Reichbaum. Examining the fighter's hands, a doctor asked Reichbaum, "How much money do you have in this guy?" "Four thousand dollars." "Get rid of him," said the doctor, a man who believed in going straight to the point.

Instead, Reichbaum kept Baker on tour, extracting full value from a depreciating asset. In London, Baker outpointed an Englishman, Dick Richardson. In Porthcaul, Wales, Richardson outpointed Baker. In Juarez, Baker lost to a Mexican, Alfredo Zuany. In Toronto, he won from George Chuvalo, a Canadian.

A Texan, Roy Harris, whose quaintly named hometown, Cut 'n Shoot, had made him saleable goods, was being groomed for a shot at Floyd Patterson's heavyweight championship. Baker went down to Houston and floored Harris five times in the first integrated fight in Texas since Jack Johnson and Joe Choynski defied the Jim Crow laws around the turn of the century, but the officials gave Harris the decision. When Harris boxed Patterson, he was still on his feet at the start of the twelfth round. Patterson then knocked him out.

In Charlotte, North Carolina, Baker knocked out Tugboat Thomas and wondered if the fight would be his last. "I thought I was going to get lynched," he said. "A woman jumped into the ring, screaming and hollering that 'niggers' weren't allowed to beat a white man in North Carolina." Not even waiting to pick up his paycheck, Baker made a hurried departure.

The way things turned out, Baker's last fight was in McKeesport, where he lost a ten-round decision at the Palisades to a California import, Frankie Daniels. on October 20, 1959. As in Charlotte, he left the arena empty-handed. IRS agents attached his purse of $335.06 for back taxes. "That's it," Baker said. "That's the killer. I've had enough." He was 33 years old.

In retirement, Baker stopped making even a minimal effort to keep his weight under control. "I ballooned to 315 pounds," he told me. "I was eating everything, eating like a horse." His son, Robert, Jr., came back from

Vietnam, looked at him, and laughed. "Mama," he said, "you've got a year-round Santa Claus in the house."

The words stung. In the next twelve months, Baker lost exactly one hundred pounds.

Refereeing a Golden Gloves tournament at the Hyatt House in 1979, he was down to 205. He carried himself with uncommon authority, separating the fighters by voice. "All right, gentlemen, clean break," he would say, and never once did the words go unheeded. His pepper-and-salt beard was short and neatly trimmed. It seemed to lend him an air of distinction. He'd been refereeing around Pittsburgh for ten years or so, meanwhile working as a maintenance foreman for the Pennsylvania Department of Transportation. At ringside, waiting for his turn to officiate, he reminisced. He said:

"I went into boxing with no cash balance and came out with no cash balance. But I'm happy. I've got my health. I've got my faculties. Dusty Better and them, they begged me. They said, 'You can win the title.' I wasn't that eager to win the title. My ambition was just to be a good human being and get along with people."

He was and he did. On that, there was general agreement. In the profession Baker chose -- or perhaps allowed others to choose on his behalf -- being a good human being and getting along with people are not the prime requisites for success. Yet who is to say that Bob Baker's priorities were wrong? Who is to say that he wasted his opportunities?

CHAPTER 21

BULLDOG

When they buried Ossie Harris on May 25, 1968, Fritzie Zivic was a pallbearer, a final manifestation of the bond that existed between them. If Fritzie had a favorite opponent, it was Ossie Harris.

They boxed four times, Fritzie winning the first three fights and Harris the fourth, by a split decision. "It's a funny thing for me to say," Fritzie later admitted, "but I'm kind of glad I lost. Even then, I was kind of glad. It made him so happy. He came across the ring and kissed me on the cheek and said, 'Fritzie, I'd rather beat you than win the title.'"

Harry Pittler, who managed Harris, named him Bulldog because he looked like one, but Ossie was the gentlest of fighters outside the ring. "I'd see him around," Zivic said, "and he'd never fail to ask about Charley, my little boy, and Helen, my wife."

Ossie wasn't easy to fight. Explaining why, Zivic said, "He seemed to be all head and shoulders. He was short and he had a big head and he must have had a sixteen-inch neck. You couldn't choke him. He'd sort of bob and weave and get close to you, and the only place you could hit him was on the forehead just over his eyes."

Ossie had three hundred amateur fights before he turned pro. Until Harry Pittler took him over, the managers back then wanted nothing to do with him. "He smoked," Pittler said, leaving it at that, "and he looked like a kid who would be more trouble than he was worth."

His third pro fight was a ten-round main event. Ossie won and became, in Harry Pittler's words, "the best club fighter Pittsburgh ever had." His training habits remained the same as before -- deplorable.

On a Fourth of July at the Soho Recreation Center, Ossie was matched with a middleweight out of Harrisburg, Jess Moraney. The preliminaries had started when Ossie arrived at the arena, limp from a night of revelry. In the dressing room, he caught up on his sleep. Pittler, meanwhile, taped Ossie's hands and put on his gloves and shoes without disturbing him. As the semi-final ended, Ossie awoke feeling refreshed. He walked down the aisle to the ring and gave Moraney a good drubbing.

Ossie boxed four world champions -- Zivic, Ray Robinson, Tony Zale, and Jake LaMotta -- but never with a title at stake. "On the strength of fighting guys like that," Pittler said, "he had a name, and I could get him work. He lost to Sugar Ray Robinson in Toledo, and before the fight was over I had a fight for him with Cecil Hudson in Washington."

"Aintcha gonna give me a rest?" Ossie once demanded of Pittler.

"Only way I can keep you in shape," Pittler told him.

There were occupational hazards. In 1946, Ossie's pursuit of a livelihood took him to Philadelphia, where for nine rounds he was having his own way with an undefeated light-heavyweight named Billy Fox. Before the tenth and last round, a man in a tight coat paid a visit to Ossie's corner and made some remarks about a stretcher. The man's coat, Ossie noticed, was bulging a little in the right-hand pocket.

"In those days," Pittler said, "things were different. You had the mob. If you wanted to stay healthy and keep getting fights, you co-operated."

Co-operating, Ossie lost by a knockout in the tenth. A rematch followed in Pittsburgh. Ossie again lost by a knockout in the tenth. He took the count of ten with a smile on his face, a few puzzled ringsiders observed.

It was one of his last good paydays. Ossie never made a lot of money, and all that he did make he spent. Trainer Jack Godfrey, knowing, he said, that he wouldn't be paid for it, got Harris ready for his fourth fight with Zivic. "And here's what makes me like Fritzie Zivic," Godfrey recalled. "After the fight, he came to our dressing room and handed me four ten-dollar bills."

Such was the effect on Zivic of losing to Ossie Harris. Giving forty bucks to Ossie's trainer was Fritzie's way of saying, "My pleasure."

CHAPTER 22

CHARLEY WITH AN E-Y

It may have started on the night a preliminary fighter closed Charley Affif's left eye. Affif never knew for sure. A long time later, on an airplane bound for the Pacific Coast, he was playing cards. Every few minutes his hand would go up to his eye.

"What's wrong?" he was asked.

"Nothing. I got in late last night."

One of the other card players looked at him closely. "Hey, that's a cataract," he said.

It was worse -- the beginning of a detached retina. Eventually a doctor told Charley that the left eye would have to come out. Affif was 42, a smiling, popular, battle-scarred liquor salesman who worked the best places in town. He put off the operation for months. His doctor then told him, "Better to be blind in one eye than two." Affif agreed to the surgery.

The new eye was brown, like the right eye. "It moves like the right eye, too," Affif informed all his friends. He liked to joke about his physical handicaps. Describing himself, he would say, "One kidney, one eye, an arm and a half -- and I'll live to be 189."

In his own mind, he was never overmatched against anyone -- not even Father Time.

He broke his arm when he was eight years old, jumping from a second-story window. It seemed unimportant -- a part of growing up on the Lower Hill, in Basin Alley. All that worried him was the sound of his first name -- Walter -- and the fact that his sister, younger than he, was three or four inches taller. On confirmation day, he picked the name Charles, "because Charley, with e-y at the end of it, sounded tough." And he went to a doctor for growing pills, unaware that they did not exist.

Without any help from medical science, Charley Affif got to be 5 feet 9 and a 140-pound quarterback at Fifth Avenue High School. He could pass pretty well with a plate in his right arm, but the coach of the Diulus sandlot team moved him to fullback. After every game the arm would puff up. There were two more broken bones in it now. The Marines turned him down in 1944 when the recruiting sergeant said, "Touch your right hand to your shoulder," and Charley couldn't even come close.

He went to work in a mill producing steel for the war, but decided it wasn't for him. As he estimated later, he had eighteen jobs in the next twelve months. When the 1946 football season ended, Charley and his teammates were left with eighteen dollars apiece after splitting up the gate receipts for the year, and Charley lost his share in a crap game. "I didn't have two pennies to rub together," he said.

But Fritzie Zivic needed sparring partners just then, and he was paying ten dollars a round. For Charley, it was steady employment. And Fritzie said to him, "I like your left hook."

"What's a left hook?" Charley asked. Over the next eight years, it earned him a living.

He lost his first fight by a TKO in the first round. Charley didn't believe in doing roadwork. Zivic, his manager now, would say, "Did you run today?" and Charley would lie. He'd say yes. He was ready to quit, but his friends started whispering, "Who'd ever figure Charley to be yellow?"

"I was never anywhere near that color," Charley answered. A few weeks later he knocked out a guy who had knocked out the guy who had TKO'd him in one round.

At first Charley boxed as Kid Zivic. After he and Fritzie split, he used his own name, which was Lebanese in origin. It got to be fairly well known. His thirteenth fight -- with Sammy Adragna -- was a main event, and he won. "That made me," Charley always said. "And you know who told me how to beat him? Ossie Harris. Adragna fought inside, and Ossie Harris told me, 'Punch up. When Sammy stops punching, punch up.'"

In just a few years, Affif reached the middleweight top ten, and he did it with one hand. To use his right at all, he had to move in and hook. Boxing Sonny Horne one night, he broke his right thumb, and three months later, in Madison Square Garden with Herbie Kronowitz, he broke it again. Going the last eight rounds with a broken thumb, he won the decision. Afterward, a surgeon removed a bone from his hand.

The highest rated fighter Charley ever beat was Lavern Roach, a Texan. He drew with Tommy Yarosz and drew with O'Neill Bell, who had beaten Yarosz. Lee Sala blitzed Charley, knocking him out early. In the ninth round of a fight at Duquesne Gardens, Charley was winning from Laurent Dauthille, the number one middleweight title contender, when the Frenchman put him down. Unhurt, he scrambled to his feet. But just as Ernie Sesto, the referee, finished the mandatory eight count, Dauthille moved in, and with Sesto inadvertently giving him cover, landed a vicious overhand right that Charley never saw. Sesto could have counted to a hundred.

To the press, Dauthille said, "I knew I had to knock him out to win. I was behind on points. Nobody needed to tell me that."

In 1953, Charley was getting ready for a fight with Bobby Dykes in Miami when he suddenly felt a virus coming on. Only it wasn't a virus. And Charley never fought Bobby Dykes -- or, from then on, anyone else. Back in Pittsburgh, his doctor took a look at an X-ray and spotted a dead kidney. It had been dead, the doctor said, since 1944 -- the result of a football injury, not a boxing injury.

"But, Doc," Charley said, "how did I get through fifty-eight fights with a dead kidney?"

The doctor said, "I'll know when I operate." Later, he told Charley that the muscles in his back were so thick they protected him like armor.

One kidney. One eye. An arm and a half. But Charley Affif said he'd live to be 189. He died well short of 189 -- 130 years short, to be exact -- of a heart attack. It was the first time in any way that Charley Affif's ticker ever failed him.

CHAPTER 23

MOM, POP AND WILF

Inside many wrestlers, there's a boxer trying to get out. More often than not, that boxer should stay put. The two disciplines have little in common.

Wilf Greaves was a wrestler who wanted to reinvent himself and did. He had a sturdy physique and a full supply of will power and that was all. His actions in the ring were not instinctive. He was just a wild swinger, the critics said. He couldn't move fast, they said, He took too many punches, they said. But opponents who should have beaten him easily, and they included five world champions, struggled to beat him at all. He won a couple of titles himself -- obscure ones, it is true. He boxed in Madison Square Garden, on top. Not once, but twice, he put the deified Ray Robinson on the floor.

In Canada, where he was born and grew up, he wrestled as an amateur, yearning all the while to be a prizefighter. He made the switch at an early age, attracting the attention of Pittsburgh's Jake Mintz when Mintz took his worn-out former heavyweight champion, Ezzard Charles, to Edmonton, Alberta, Wilf's hometown, for a fight with Vern Escoe in April of 1955. Sometime afterward, Mintz told reporters back home that all he had heard in Edmonton was talk about Greaves. In retrospect, that seems astonishing, for the record book tells us that Greaves did not have his first professional fight until four months and two days after Mintz's return to Pittsburgh.

It may be that Mintz had the gift of prophecy. He described Greaves to his newspaper friends as "the British Empire middleweight champion." The day would come when Greaves really did hold that title, but at the time Mintz spoke it had not yet arrived. Clearly, Mintz was making a sales pitch, and making it to an audience of one -- himself. Ezzard Charles, pushing 34. had been boxing since the age of 16. In Edmonton, he knocked out Vern Escoe, but time was running out on Charles, and, by extension, on Mintz, for there was nobody else of any market value in his stable. By the end of the year he had Greaves.

To imagine him as a father figure was difficult, but that is what Mintz became to the fair-haired young immigrant. Childless, Jake and his wife, Julia, lived in Squirrel Hill, and they took Greaves in as a member of the family, treating him like a son. He called Jake "Pop" and he called Julia

"Mom." He was 20 years old, clean-cut and ingratiating, with the look of an innocent abroad.

Almost alone, Mintz saw the makings of a top-ten fighter in Greaves. More objective observers, after watching him go through his paces, scoffed at such an idea. Mintz turned a deaf ear to the negativity. For his previous manager, starting late in the summer of 1955, Greaves had been active on the American side of the Canadian border in large northeastern cities like Cleveland, Syracuse, and even New York, boxing four-rounders and six-rounders. He had a record of two wins, two losses, and one draw. Mintz now propelled him through the rest of his brief apprenticeship.

He started off with three fights in Pittsburgh -- preliminaries -- and then made the jump to main events. There were two ten-rounders in Winnipeg (home territory) and Greaves won them both. Next, he decisioned the fairly well-known Al Andrews in ten rounds at Duquesne Gardens and won by a seventh-round technical knockout over the not quite as well-known Jimmy Sanders in Steubenville. His winning streak stood at eight in a row when Mintz threw him in against Ralph (Tiger) Jones, a familiar figure on national television. Greaves lost the decision in their Washington, D. C. fight, but he was now a plausible opponent, Mintz thought, for the brand-new middleweight champion, Gene Fullmer, who had taken the title from Robinson.

That fight was in Madison Square Garden. As a sort of welcome-home party, Salt Lake City, where Fullmer more or less hailed from, now sought an opponent for him who would not spoil the fun, and Greaves fit the profile. Just as a precaution, however, his match with Fullmer would be an over-the-weight, non-title bout. Showing his usual toughness, Greaves went the distance, ten rounds, but, predictably enough, he lost..

Less than two months later, once again making it to the final bell, he lost in Chicago to Spider Webb, a well-thought-of contender. At this stage of his development, whether Greaves won or lost was inconsequential, Mintz thought, for he was holding up well. He wasn't getting hurt. And promoters were beginning to see that he could give the customers their money's worth.

Mintz always knew how to move a fighter. So that the wins and losses would not look unbalanced, he took Greaves out of the lions' den now and then, as when in Edmonton one night he polished off Arley Seifer in seven rounds. Seifer could be counted on to do his very best, but back in

Pittsburgh, where he lived on the North Side, he was strictly a preliminary fighter -- the opponent Mintz had selected, in fact, for Greaves' successful debut under his management.

On a bright July day in 1957, two years and three months after first setting eyes on Greaves, Mintz suddenly died of a heart attack. A fight was coming up for Greaves with Reybon Stubbs at Forbes Field. The previous February, Greaves had knocked out Johnny Eubanks in two rounds at Duquesne Gardens, so the expectation was that Stubbs would not be an impediment for him. In a ballyhooed meeting between Stubbs and Eubanks at the Gardens, they had put the crowd to sleep with a friendly sparring match. Stubbs and Eubanks were flashier than Greaves, and better boxers, but not as strong, being welterweights. That Eubanks got the decision over Stubbs only made him the preferred opponent for Greaves. Now it was Stubbs's turn, but Greaves asked the promoter, Ben Anolik, to call off the fight as a mark of respect for Mintz.

Rudderless and adrift, he stopped training. What could he do and where could he go? Julia -- his "Mom" -- had a plucky solution. She would take over Greaves's management, making history. Never before had the Pennsylvania Athletic Commission granted a manager's license to a woman, reporters were told.

Under Julia's uncertain direction, Greaves had five fights, winning two and losing three. Bobby Gordon, a Charleroi-based newcomer from Akron, Ohio, out boxed and outslugged him over ten rounds in Jeannette. Joey Giardello, inching forward on his long, hard slog to the middleweight championship, out boxed and outfoxed him in Denver. A short time afterward, sensing, perhaps, that she was not in the right business, Julia sold Wilf's contract to Tony Ross, Jr. of Detroit for "between three thousand and four thousand dollars."

Ross was born in Carnegie, and he had boxed around Pittsburgh as a teen-age welterweight in 1942 and 1943. World War II was in progress, and Ross enlisted. In the Battle of the Bulge, he lost a leg. Returning to civilian life with a prosthetic, he boxed exhibitions. His trainer was his father, Tony Ross, Sr., a Pittsburgh lightweight in the 1920s who fought such headliners as Cuddy DeMarco, Billy Petrolle, and Jack Bernstein. These two Rosses were not related to the Tony Ross from New Castle who boxed Jack Johnson at Duquesne Gardens in 1908.

Greaves signed a five-year contract with Tony Ross, Jr. and joined a stable headed by Duke Harris, a middleweight he had beaten in Detroit while Julia Mintz was his manager. The referee called the fight a draw, but Ross, Jr. shared the opinion of the judge who awarded all ten rounds to Greaves. "It was Greaves all the way," Ross, Jr. said. Greaves himself, "very confident" that he was ready to move up the ladder, announced, "If I can't make it now, the boxing game isn't cut out for me."

In truth, the boxing game wasn't cut out for him. His principal assets, determination and stamina, were not quite enough to take him where fighters who've made it end up.

Matched with no-names in Detroit and its Canadian cross-river neighbor, Windsor, he won thirteen fights in a row for Ross, Jr. His fourth-round knockout of Cobey McCluskey in Windsor gave him the Canadian middleweight championship. Then came a return match with Fullmer, who had lost his world title to its previous holder, Robinson -- lost it stunningly and precipitously when Robinson knocked him out with one punch.

Since then, in a stretch of twenty-one months before his do-over with Greaves in Madison Square Garden, he had won all eight of his fights. Fullmer and Greaves fought exactly the same way, constantly pressing forward, and they were evenly matched. But though Greaves could overpower a welterweight like Eubanks and overpower certain middleweights, he was up against an immoveable object in Fullmer, who backed up for nobody. Greaves took it down to the wire in this second meeting between them only to lose by a majority decision (two votes for Fullmer, one for a draw).

Erratically, Greaves now embarked on a series of ups and downs, or, rather, of downs and ups and then more downs. He lost his next two fights, won the four after that, concluding with a decision over Tiger Jones, and then in Madison Square Garden again he succumbed in four rounds to the explosive left-hooker from Argentina, Eduardo Lausse. It was the first time Greaves had been stopped. Two months later, in St. Paul, a stick-and-move artist, Del Flanagan, had him floundering most of the night and he blew the decision.

The date was May 17, 1960. On June 22nd, he won the fight that, in retrospect, stood out above the thirty-five others in which he came out on top. Before a partisan gathering in Edmonton, he pounded out a fifteen-round split decision over Dick Tiger, the British Empire middleweight champion from Nigeria who was destined to be the middleweight champion of the world and then the light-heavyweight champion.

Greaves, as it turned out, kept the British Empire title only until his first defense, a return match with Tiger. In Edmonton again, he lost by a TKO when the referee stopped the fight in the ninth round.

More ups and downs were to follow. He took a salutary three-month rest and then won an encore with Obdulio Nunez, who had unexpectedly beaten him between his two fights with Tiger. Both fights with Nunez were close. Backsliding again, he lost in succession to television favorite Chico Vejar, to Giardello a second time, and to Juan Carlos Rivero. Giardello and Rivero were TKO winners. Lausse, it appeared, and maybe even Tiger, had taken some of the iron out of Greaves.

This time for therapy he made a second visit to Mormon country and knocked out the forgettable Willie Ross in Ogden, near Salt Lake City. He then lost honorably to Jimmy Ellis in Louisville. Ellis had lately moved up from preliminary bouts to main events, but the war in Vietnam would elevate him to greater heights -- a piece of the vacated heavyweight title after Muhammad Ali was sent into exile for turning down a chance to shoulder arms and perhaps get shot at by strangers with whom he did not have the semblance of a quarrel.

Failing to beat Ellis, then, although Greaves couldn't know it, was not a disgrace. In any case, only one month later, on September 25, 1961, in Detroit, he was boxing Ray Robinson. By a split decision, the aging virtuoso scraped out a win, but it wasn't easy. Two seconds before the end of the eighth round, Greaves ripped a left hook to the body and Robinson went down. He was helped to his corner, protesting that the punch had been low. Referee Lew Handler disagreed. In the ninth and tenth rounds, according to a United Press International dispatch, Greaves looked "hesitant" and "reluctant." Just by holding his own for those last six minutes, Robinson protected an early lead.

Arrangements were promptly made for a return match in Pittsburgh on December 8th, and Greaves was quick to promise a different result. "I have never been so sure of winning a fight in my life," he said. He was sure for the following reason: "I know I beat Ray in Detroit and I know if my corner hadn't told me to slow down in the last two rounds I'd have knocked him out."

Tellingly, Greaves had again changed managers. A man named C. W. Smith had purchased his contract from Tony Ross, Jr. A title bout with Fullmer, champion again after knocking out Carmen Basilio, was in the offing, Smith suggested, if Greaves got by Robinson. And Greaves not only believed he could get by Robinson but that the title would then be his for the taking. "Fullmer," he said, disregarding the outcome of their two previous fights, "is one fellow I know I can beat."

One fellow he could not beat was old man Robinson. Witnessed by a crowd of nine thousand, their fight at the Civic Arena was even for seven rounds. In the second round, Greaves had put Robinson down again, dropping him to one knee with a right to the head. Robinson took the mandatory eight count, and later Greaves said, "I thought he was playing possum. I became too careful." (Note that he was blaming himself, not his corner.) "I gave the fight away."

Maybe he did and maybe he didn't. Whatever the reality, Sugar Ray found the range with a lightning-bolt left hook that knocked Greaves flat in round eight. He was up before the count of ten, just making it, and Robinson pounced, slamming home a right. Greaves went down again and stayed down.

He continued to fight for another six years. His last good showing, perhaps, was in a split decision loss to Joey Giardello nine months before Giardello at last became the middleweight champion by winning from Dick Tiger. Over in Milan, an Italian, Sandro Mazzinghi, knocked Greaves out. In Canada, he had three fights with Blair Richardson for the dominion middleweight title but won only the first.

In 1967, he retired, and with no need for apologies. Working against the grain, he had made himself the fighter he was -- not by any standard a truly exceptional fighter, but certainly the best he could be.

CHAPTER 24

THE DREAMER

Boxing, for Don Elbaum, was a drug, an obsession, a necessity. He was nine years old when he saw his first fight. "Holy cow!" he remembers saying to himself, dazzled by the scene.

In the center of the auditorium, under a bright cone of light, stood the ring, an elevated, roped-off, canvas-floored square. Boxers appeared, climbed between the top two strands of the ropes, did their thing, and made way for the next pair. Elbaum was transfixed. The good fights excited him; the bad fights held his attention. Then came the main event, and he saw that what had gone on before was just a foretaste of the drama to come. The voice of the ring announcer -- "In this corner, weighing . . . " -- took on resonance. Something important, Elbaum sensed, was about to occur. The main-event fighters, waiting for the bell, and even the referee, watchful and unobtrusive, impressed him as nothing else ever had. He looked at the upturned faces in the crowd and felt suspense, expectation, uncertainty. From that moment on, he knew what he wanted to do.

Elbaum was like Gatsby -- a hopeless romantic. He started boxing in the amateurs at the age of 14. His father, who owned a hearing-aid business in Erie, did not disapprove but hoped that the boy would go to college, which he did, you could almost say. Penn State had a boxing team and a scholarship for him. He spent a week on the campus, deliberating, and then turned the scholarship down.

His next offer came from the U.S. Army, and it wasn't negotiable. Elbaum went off to Korea, thirsting for battle. The shooting was over, yes, but there were boxing tournaments to enter, tournaments for the troops. "I carried this dream," he used to say. "I was going to be a champion. Nothing could stop me."

The fact is that Elbaum at one time *looked* like a champion, and the champion he looked like was Barney Ross. In his prime, Ross had pale skin, black hair, narrow eyes, and a flattened nose. So did Elbaum. They were roughly the same size and build. There the similarity ended. "In a period of nine days," Elbaum confessed, "I boxed three of the best welterweights in my outfit and lost to all three. Suddenly it hit me -- I didn't have it."

The realization stunned him. Uncharacteristically, he was "down in the mouth," but not for long. With one little suggestion, a Korean acquaintance, a boxing promoter, lifted him out of despondency. "The day after my last thumping, this Korean guy came to me and said, 'Don, why don't you and I get together? Let's put on some shows. You get the American fighters and I'll get the Korean fighters. We'll pack 'em in.'"

And pack 'em in they did. "We ran five shows," Elbaum said, "and our smallest crowd was ten thousand. I put myself on every card. I never overmatched myself. And I paid myself very well. The Korean guy took care of the box office, and he was robbing me right and left, but I still came out of it with ten thousand dollars."

Back in the States, a civilian once more, he used the ten thousand as venture capital. He promoted. He fought on his own cards, picking his own opponents. He managed other fighters -- "advised" them, rather; there were boxing commission rules to finesse. He promoted in places like Erie and Youngstown and Steubenville; like Wheeling, West Virginia; like Zanesville, Ohio, and Painesville, Ohio, not to forget Mingo Junction, Ohio -- anywhere the policy of officialdom was live and let live.

Small-time boxing was never a pot of gold for Elbaum. His promotions drew meager crowds. Subsidies of $250 to $350 a show from Madison Square Garden kept him going. On the side, he made matches for the forty or so boxers he advised.

"I do it openly," he said at the time to sportswriters. "If I book a fight for one of my guys, I take ten percent. If they fight on my own show, I take nothing." Boxing commissions looked the other way. In Western Pennsylvania, the commissioner was Paul Sullivan. "I sat down with him," Elbaum said. "I told him, 'Mr. Sullivan, I'm moving Johnny Bizzarro'" -- Johnny Bizzarro was the jewel of Elbaum's stable -- "'and I also promote.' It was like he understood."

Sullivan did understand. He understood that the fight game around Pittsburgh was in its death throes and that scufflers like Elbaum were boxing's life-support system.

One of Elbaum's uncles, an editor at a publishing firm, offered him fifty thousand dollars to find a more reputable occupation. Elbaum wasn't tempted. To placate his father, he gave the hearing-aid business a shot.

Recalling what that was like, he said, "It drove me nuts." Six months later, he was back in the fight game.

Where else could you meet such interesting people? A 33-year-old Philadelphia sports reporter named Jack McKinney had the notion that although he knew a great deal about boxing, having sparred in the gym with Sonny Liston, there was still a tremendous gap in his resume. To be the very best boxing writer he was capable of being, he must take part in an actual fight.

Elbaum arranged one. Anything for a friend. On a Painesville show, the four-round opener matched McKinney, not identified as a journalist, with Alvin Green, a middleweight from Cleveland hand-picked by Elbaum for his lack of ferocity. As fight time approached, Elbaum began to worry. No newspaperman, he thought, belonged in the ring with even the least accomplished professional fighter, but the power of the press astonished him.

"McKinney came out swinging like you wouldn't believe," Elbaum said. "The first time he nailed Green, *boom*! The guy went down. McKinney stood over him, yelling, 'Get up, you yellow bum, or I'll kill you!' The guy got up. McKinney knocked him down again." Elbaum, refereeing, was afraid of what McKinney might do if Green decided to quit. As fast as he could get out the words, Elbaum counted to ten.

In Johnstown, Elbaum had Sugar Ray Robinson and Willie Pep on the same card, fighting stiffs. Both were old men, but there never had been an attraction like it, not in Johnstown, anyway. The only drawback was that Elbaum had scheduled the show for a Friday night in October. There were eighteen high school football games within a radius of fifty miles that night, and almost nobody came to see Robinson and Pep.

Elbaum was more successful with his memorable four-rounder between Johnny Howard and Bobby Spencer in Warren, Ohio. Johnny Howard's record was no victories and thirteen defeats; Bobby Spencer's record was no victories and nine defeats. They were the two losingest fighters in America.

Interest built up.

"It became more important than the main event," said Elbaum in a moment of fond reminiscence. "I got the two guys to agree that the loser would retire from the ring. They went in there and stood toe to toe -- the greatest fight you ever saw." The only decision possible was a draw.

And so neither fighter retired. Howard, in fact, saved a later promotion for Elbaum in Youngstown. Johnny Bizzarro was in the main event, and his opponent backed out at the last minute. Elbaum asked Howard to substitute. Bizzarro, who was moving up in the lightweight rankings, groused that it would make him a laughingstock to beat someone famous for never having won a fight. As resourceful as ever, Elbaum came up with a quick solution. He changed Howard's name to Johnny Milton.

That night at the arena, the Youngstown boxing commissioner made an unexpected visit to the dressing room. He was waving a piece of paper.

"Hey, Elbaum," he said. "Milton forgot to sign his contract."

"Johnny Milton!" Elbaum shouted, looking directly at Howard. "Johnny Milton, you didn't sign your contract. Johnny Milton . . ."

After what seemed to Elbaum like eons, Howard caught on. He took the piece of paper and, spelling out the letters as he wrote, put down "Johnny." Elbaum held his breath. Proceeding, Howard wrote: "M -- I -- L -- " and abruptly stopped.

"Hey, Don," he said, "what comes after the L?"

Elbaum had the answer. He always did.

Elbaum first laid eyes on Johnny Bizzarro, a hungry-looking kid with a mop of curly black hair, in a Golden Gloves tournament in Erie. Joe Luvara, Bizzarro's trainer, gave the newspapers a story about an Italian "war orphan." The actual facts were not as colorful. Bizzarro was born in Italy, all right, but to American citizens who were caught there at the start of World War II and detained. After Italy and its ally Germany surrendered, they returned to the United States, very much alive, with their family.

Bizzarro's "manager of record" was Mike Brady, a foreman in an Erie wheelchair factory. Joe Polino, a trainer from Philadelphia who had worked with Sonny Liston, taught Bizzarro two things -- how to take advantage of his natural speed by moving in and out and how to uppercut. The learning process was a slow one. Elbaum made Bizzarro's matches and kept him away from hard punchers. Bizzarro had twenty-eight four- and six-rounders before his first main event. He polished his technique against tough Pittsburgh club fighters like Tony Cristy and Freddy Martinovich.

Eventually he was ready for a lightweight title fight with the champion, Carlos Ortiz. In the planning for this one, Elbaum revealed a breadth of imagination unequalled since Tex Rickard made a sex symbol of Georges Carpentier, the Orchid Man, thus inducing women to attend his fights.

The Bizzarro-Ortiz match, Elbaum announced, would be a black-tie affair at the Holiday House, near Monroeville, and it would be in a pink tent on the parking lot. Tickets were to be sold "by invitation only" and limited to 750. In reality, there would be 1,000 tickets on sale, but a number like 750, Elbaum believed, was psychologically preferable. "It makes the promotion seem more exclusive," he explained. The tickets were to be priced at $125 each.

Elbaum's partner in the enterprise was Tim Tormey, a self-described "creator of events." Among the previous events Tormey had created was the appearance of the Beatles at the Civic Arena. Not surprisingly, they sold the place out.

To what extent Tormey influenced Elbaum's thinking is guesswork, but the evening at the Holiday House was to start with a cocktail party "hosted by former world champions." After cocktails, dinner; after dinner, the fight, preceded by one preliminary bout and followed by "a gala stage show starring Tony Martin [a popular singer of the day] and many other celebrities." For those who had not had their money's worth, the "former world champions" would then host a "victory party," regardless of whether Ortiz or Bizzarro turned out to be the guest of honor.

None of these things except the fight itself, scheduled for fifteen rounds, came to pass. It would be impossible, the promoters' attorneys had promised, for the Pennsylvania Liquor Control Board to deny their application for a license. So what happened? The Pennsylvania Liquor Control Board denied their application for a license. "Flatly," said Tormey, breaking the news to the press. And the reason? "They didn't give us a reason, except . . . " He turned to Elbaum for help. "Do you know how they phrased it, Don?" Elbaum did. "'Not in the best interest of the general public.'" Minus the gala stage show, the promotion was moved to the Civic Arena. Top ticket price: twenty dollars. If there was a victory party, the attendees did not include Bizzarro.

Until the seventh or eighth round, he more than held his own against Ortiz. He bobbed in and out, tapping and slapping, piling up a lead on points. Ortiz, shoulders hunched, padded after him. The Puerto Rican's left jab was harder than Bizzarro's overhand right, but speed, for a while, neutralized strength. Ortiz kept chasing Bizzarro and catching him and getting hit.

In Bizzarro's corner, Joe Luvara cautioned him not to become careless. "Don't even think of trading punches." Bizzarro, full of confidence now, went right ahead and traded punches -- and began to absorb heavy punishment. In the twelfth round the referee stopped the fight. Bizzarro had been down and was reeling all over the ring.

Elbaum and Tormey needed a $65,000 gate to break even. The box-office net was only $25,000. Tormey, the partnership's money man, took the hit. More certain than ever that there's no business like show business, he returned to the creation of musical events.

Elbaum went back to work on the creation of a light-heavyweight contender. His male, pugilistic version of Eliza Doolittle was Jack Rodgers, a shoe salesman and part-time photographer's model from Uniontown. Rodgers had blue eyes, black hair, a straight nose, perfect teeth, and no scar tissue. He was maybe 5 feet 11 with a sculpted physique. "He's beautiful," Elbaum told Philadelphia sportswriter George Kiseda. "The girls go wild over him. You've never seen anything like it. Every time he fights they jam the arena. They leave notes on his car with their telephone numbers."

If the girls who went wild over Rodgers were jamming any arenas, the Palisades in McKeesport, where Elbaum had been showcasing his fighter, wasn't one of them. And yet most of what Elbaum had said contained a basis of truth. Boxing writers took to calling Rodgers "the best-looking light-heavyweight since Billy Conn -- outside the ring."

Inside the ring . . . well, to say that Rodgers was no Billy Conn understates it. Rodgers couldn't box and he couldn't hit hard. He walked right into his opponents, persistently throwing left hooks and showing a cavalier disregard for his profile. That he remained photogenic was a mystery.

It may not have been a mystery to Elbaum, a fanatical believer in "the lost art of building guys up." "There is nothing wrong," he would say, "with taking a fighter and giving him stiffs -- bums. By that, I don't mean guys who lay down. I've never, ever talked to an opponent of Jack's and told him I wanted him to lose."

What he told Johnny Otto, billed for his Palisades appearance with Rodgers as the light-heavyweight champion of New England, was: "Johnny, if you knock Rodgers out -- and it's the only way I think you can beat him --

the return match will be fantastic." Otto didn't knock Rodgers out or prevent him from going through with a modeling appointment scheduled for the day after the fight, depending on whether or not his face was unmarked. There would be no modeling and no $100 fee if he came out of the fight with a cut or a black eye. There was never any danger. Otto, in losing by a technical knockout after ninety-seven seconds of the first round, failed to land a single punch, and Rodgers posed for the photographer. There was no further discussion of a return match.

Taking these baby steps, Elbaum continued to insist, would eventually get Rodgers into the big money. "I feel a fighter needs three or four fights just to learn how to climb into the ring," Elbaum explained. "I feel the worst thing that happens in boxing is the way managers rush their fighters and ruin them. The only way a fighter can learn is, first, by going in with ordinary guys. If he can't beat ordinary guys, he's in trouble."

Rodgers, by this time, was very good at climbing into the ring. After winning from Johnny Otto and other assorted ordinary guys -- or stiffs, as Elbaum sometimes absent-mindedly referred to them -- he was still undefeated with a 17-0 record. Ring magazine ranked him ninth in the world and Elbaum received an offer of $2,500 for a fight with Bob Foster in Washington, D.C.

Alarmed, he said, "Nothing doing." Bob Foster, as it happened, was the hardest-hitting light-heavyweight in captivity. He was to prove it not long afterward by knocking out Dick Tiger for the championship. Elbaum hung up the phone on Washington, D. C. and dialed Ring magazine's number. "I realize this may sound weird," he said to Nat Fleischer, the editor, "but would you please drop Jack from your ratings? We're getting offers to fight guys like Bob Foster, and Jack isn't ready for them yet. He needs a little more schooling." Nat Fleischer thanked Elbaum, and Rodgers disappeared from the ratings.

He continued to beat "ordinary guys." But he was 28 years old, and Elbaum decided it was now or never. He signed a name opponent for Rodgers -- Joey Giardello, former middleweight champion, attempting, at 36, to make a comeback. They were to meet on May 22, 1967, at the Civic Arena, but first there would be a tune-up fight for Rodgers with Ray Vega, from "somewhere in Arkansas."

"He's a catcher, but, like, tough," said Elbaum, describing Vega to the press. "It would take a heavyweight to knock him out with one shot." Rodgers, who was not a heavyweight, knocked him out quickly with either one shot or two. Opinions differed. Elbaum said, "I didn't want this. It doesn't get Rodgers ready for Giardello."

Truly concerned, he engaged Johnny Morris, Pittsburgh's top middleweight, to be a sparring partner for Rodgers. Morris had boxed Giardello when Giardello was a contender and had given a good account of himself. Reporting on his workouts with Rodgers, he told a sportswriter (me): "If Giardello still has a heartbeat, Rodgers will lose his first fight. I boxed with him twice. I wasn't allowed to throw no right hands or left hooks. I hit him with a jab and they said I was jabbing too hard. All he knows how to do is come right to you. If you jab, he's right there to catch it. He doesn't know how to back up. He doesn't know how to circle a man. And he can't punch at all."

Such comments did nothing for the ticket sale.

It was the 121st fight for Giardello and the 22nd for Rodgers. Giardello looked old, fat, and slow. He made it interesting: he out boxed Rodgers and took his best punches. But the younger, stronger fighter clearly won, although Giardello complained about the decision.

"I want a rematch," he said, and he got one. Six months later in Philadelphia, his hometown, they met again, and Giardello reversed the outcome. It would be his last fight.

Rodgers boxed one more time. Elbaum, continuing to dream, had another former champion lined up for him, a former heavyweight champion, no less -- Sonny Liston. Three years had passed since the second of Liston's two knockout defeats at the hands of Muhammad Ali, but he was still an intimidating figure. The huge disparity between Liston's size and Rodgers' size didn't bother Elbaum in the least. He planned to capitalize on it, "building the whole thing around Billy Conn and Joe Louis, with Rodgers as Billy Conn."

It was not a role to which Rodgers aspired, but Elbaum assured him that he could win, saying, "Jack, you're too fast for Liston. After five or six rounds, he'll be out of gas and you'll stop him. Meanwhile," Elbaum added, "I'm getting you a fight that will make you look good." It was with Mert Brownfield -- "a real mountain," Elbaum allowed, but also a stiff. Rodgers already had beaten him. Their previous fight was six rounds, and Elbaum did not believe that Brownfield could go ten.

Brownfield didn't have to go ten. He trained as though preparing for a title bout, unloaded on Rodgers early, and knocked him out. Since Rodgers was a photographer's model, not an artist's model, no one had seen him on canvas before. Plans for a fight with Liston were shelved -- the last good break that Rodgers was ever to get.

Finished with boxing, he opened a bar and grill in Uniontown. One day a year or two afterward, Rodgers got into an argument there with a man who was using a letter opener to clean his fingernails. Suddenly the argument became violent, and Rodgers ended up in a hospital with the letter opener stuck in his rib cage. Two days later, he checked himself out against the wishes of the physician who was treating him. Between the hospital and home, Rodgers died in his car.

Elbaum by then was promoting in Cleveland, having given up on Western Pennsylvania after six of his last nine shows at the Palisades -- a squat, rectangular, three-story riverfront dance hall, shrouded night and day in the sulphurous exhalations of a steel mill -- had lost money. The promotion that sent him packing drew $884 at the box office. The official paid attendance was 198.

In Cleveland one day, a friend called Elbaum and said, "Don, I'm with a fella named Don King. This black hospital in town is going under, and Don wants to keep it open. We'd like to talk to you." The next voice Elbaum heard was King's. "Don Elbaum!" King shouted into the telephone. "Mah man! I can do a benefit show with Muhammad Ali, but I know I can't do it without Don Elbaum, because Don Elbaum *is* boxing in Cleveland. How much do you charge?"

Elbaum told him five thousand dollars. "In two minutes," Elbaum recalled, "King had me down to fifteen hundred." Elbaum had heard of King, an important numbers writer with a gravity-defying Afro that made it look as though invisible hands were pulling him upward by the hair. He was just out of prison for manslaughter, having killed a fellow hustler in a street fight.

The man, King explained to the judge, owed him six hundred dollars.

"I sat down with King," Elbaum told me, "and was mesmerized by the guy. We put on the show for the hospital -- Muhammad Ali boxing four opponents over ten rounds. It did ninety thousand dollars at the gate. I said to him, 'Don, you're incredible. You're what boxing needs -- a black promoter.'

"So you could say I started King out. All told, we put on three shows. I was very high on him. Then I started to see what he was like. First of all, the hospital thing bothered me. All the hospital got out of it was fifteen hundred dollars. Ali boxed for just his expenses, but I came across a receipt from him for ten thousand dollars. I believed that the receipt was a phony, that the money had gone to King."

His motive self-protection, Elbaum "walked away." The next time he saw King was on television. Dealing with a company called Video Techniques, Elbaum had obtained the rights in Ohio to the closed-circuit telecast of the Joe Frazier-George Foreman heavyweight title fight. The government of Jamaica was putting it on with a man named Alex Valdez as the promoter. "Watching the screen, I see Frazier, the champion, go into the ring, and who's with him but Don King," Elbaum said. "Three rounds later, George Foreman is now the champion, and who's leaving the ring with him? Don King."

That was in January of 1973. In October of the following year, King was promoting the ten million-dollar Foreman-Ali fight in Zaire -- the "Rumble in the Jungle." For a long time afterward, King owned the heavyweight title. On an infinitely more grandiose scale than Elbaum ever dreamed of, he united the incompatible functions of managing and promoting.

Leaving Cleveland eventually, Elbaum promoted in Toronto, Atlantic City, and New York. With an associate, "a big produce guy," he managed Simon Brown, the International Boxing Federation's welterweight champion. "Don King stole him from me," Elbaum said. "I had a $900,000 fight lined up with Buddy McGirt. King put $75,000 cash into Simon Brown's pocket, and all of a sudden we get a letter from Brown saying he wasn't with us anymore. We took him to court and got $250,000."

One day in 1989, when he was living in Atlantic City, Elbaum had callers -- "two guys from the criminal division of the IRS. It was unreal," Elbaum said. "They claimed I hadn't reported five million dollars in income for the years 1982, 1983, and 1984." The accusation had something to do with checks made out to Elbaum's partner, the big produce guy, and deposited in Elbaum's bank account, with Elbaum's permission. At his trial, Jack

Newfield and Pete Hamill, New York newspaper columnists, were character witnesses. Police officers, FBI men, and politicians wrote letters to the judge on his behalf. None of this kept him from going to Allenwood, a minimum-security prison.

Sports Illustrated quoted Elbaum as saying, "I like it at Allenwood. All of my friends are here." Elbaum swore that the quote was a fabrication. Allenwood, he said, was "no country club." Sentenced to six months, he served only four and a half.

And then, as a sort of vagabond promoter, he resumed his career. For years he staged fights wherever opportunity led him, and it not only led him from coast to coast in the United States, but to Canada, Sweden, Ireland, France, Italy, Jamaica, the Dominican Republic, and Puerto Rico. His permanent base for a while was Philadelphia, where he served as house matchmaker at the Blue Horizon until it closed. In 2011, the year the Pennsylvania Boxing Hall of Fame inducted him, along with five fighters, some deceased, and a manager, also deceased, he was "still going strong." His most recent accomplishment, according to a biographical sketch provided by the Hall, was getting a cruiserweight title fight in Germany for Ron Nakash of Israel. Whether Nakash won or lost was not revealed.

The last time I spoke with Elbaum, back in 1999 or 2000, he was saying that the Sweet Science had seen its best days. Fighters, he explained, were rushed too fast because of the money being generated by pay-per-view telecasts. And there were too many weight divisions, resulting in too many title fights. "They have strawweight, mini-flyweight, and flyweight divisions. Ridiculous. There should be no junior divisions and no super divisions."

Still, he was positive that boxing would never completely die out. The reason, he suggested, is that human nature doesn't change -- life is survival of the fittest. "As long as you have two people standing up," he told me, his faith in Darwinian principles rock-solid, "you'll always have boxing. It's the most basic form of competition."

CHAPTER 25
UNHAPPY WARRIOR

Johnny Morris had trouble with managers. He chastised and walked out on his first manager, Fats Wingo, for successfully predicting the outcome of a fight, the return match in 1958 between Morris and Bobby Gordon. In their first fight, Gordon had decisioned Morris. In the return match, just as Wingo foretold, Gordon knocked Morris out.

After parting company with Wingo, Morris said indignantly, "Fats was my manager and he was telling me I was going to lose." Morris could only look upon this as an unacceptable lack of faith in his ability.

Morris was from East Liberty. He and his older brother, Floyd, had been outstanding Golden Gloves boxers. A husband and father, he worked as a stock clerk at Kaufmann's department store. Morris had to work at a 9-to-5 job because his earnings in the ring were insignificant. With fighters who constantly change managers, and Morris changed managers the way Elizabeth Taylor changed husbands, that is often the case.

His managers after Wingo were all from out of town and they were all like the one from New York, of whom Morris said wearily, "He promised to keep me busy. I'm still waiting. I call him up, and they say, 'He's not here.'"

Off and on, with results no less disappointing, Morris undertook to manage himself. It was never easy. On the principle of nothing to gain, everything to lose, fighters with reputations avoided him, and Morris himself was not a box-office attraction. He lacked the dynamism it takes to be a popular favorite.

Lean and muscular, a natural middleweight, he boxed well and hit hard. In the gym, Morris sparred with Bob Baker, who outweighed him by seventy-five pounds. "Wanna know something?" Baker said. "I'll tell you the truth. Morris hits as hard as a heavyweight."

Gee Bee Thomas ran the East Liberty Gym, and he believed in having seasoned fighters spar with beginners. "That way, nobody gets hurt," he explained. "If you put two beginners in with each other, they flail away. A seasoned fighter will act like a control mechanism. But Johnny Morris . . . " Gee Bee shook his head. "It's hard to get Johnny to hold back. I had a fighter named Willie Parker, and I let him spar with Johnny one time. Johnny was lifting him right off his feet. I said, 'That's enough, Willie, that's enough." He said, 'Don't worry, Gee Bee, I'm not getting hit.' I said, 'If you get hit any more, you'll be dead.'"

Even as Gee Bee spoke, Morris was boxing with another of his amateur hopefuls. Gee Bee had his back to the ring. He said, "If that kid up there happens to hit Johnny, I don't know . . . He could wind up on the floor." There was a thud, and somebody said, "That's where he is now." Gee Bee turned around to see Morris, all apologies, helping the kid to his feet.

In his first five years as a pro, Morris beat everybody he fought except Gordon. Like Morris, Gordon had complaints about all of his managers. Among them were Sammy Angott, the former lightweight champion, and his partner, a man named Vincent Risko. Their arguments with Gordon were so incessant that at last they sold his contract to Dr. Charles Rosenbloom, a physician and surgeon from Charleroi. Physicians and surgeons are supposed to have more than a layman's knowledge about the effect on the brain of punches to the head, but for Rosenbloom there were other considerations.

"It's a matter of prestige and achievement," he said. "It's a matter of getting this kid" -- Gordon -- "to the top."

Gordon moved his family from Akron, Ohio, to Charleroi and won six fights in a row under Rosenbloom's direction, including the first one with Morris, an eight-rounder at the Palisades in McKeesport. Rangier than Morris, Gordon seemed to intimidate him. Actually, Morris was eager for their return bout. "He forced me to take it," said Wingo. "I knew that Gordon was too good for him, but he begged me. And look what happened."

What happened was that Gordon took Morris out in the ninth round. What happened a year later was that Gordon hit the skids, losing his Pennsylvania middleweight title to Jimmy Beecham of Philadelphia, who subsequently lost it to Morris, out boxed in twelve rounds at the Palisades.

Concluding that prestige and achievement were not realizable goals, Dr. Rosenbloom gave up on Gordon after a dispute between the fighter and his trainer and a series of lackadaisical performances. (When Gordon explained a loss to Willie Dockery, a broken-down middleweight from Brooklyn, by pointing out that Dockery had been "a moving target," Rosenbloom said icily, "What did you expect him to do -- stand there and let you nail him?")

As for Morris, he continued to beat second-level opponents, including two on a foray to London, of all places. At the same time, he was pestering Teddy Brenner, the matchmaker at Madison Square Garden, for a television fight. Helpfully, Morris even named the opponents he'd be glad to accept. Gene Fullmer, the National Boxing Association's reigning middleweight champion, was one. Paul Pender, the New York commission's champion, and Carmen Basilio, a former champion, made the list too. But when Morris did get a fight in New York, it was an eight-round semi-final at St. Nicholas Arena with Paul Diaz, neither a champion, a former champion, nor a future champion.

Morris outpointed Diaz, and his reward was a main event at St. Nick's. He lost a decision to Billy Pickett, and there was nothing shameful about it, for Pickett had a 19-1 record, but United Press International kissed off the fight as "dull." Booing Pickett as well as Morris, the crowd seemed to agree.

So Morris had to lower his sights. In Louisville, he lost a six-rounder to Jimmy Ellis. Although Ellis would one day be the holder of the World Boxing Association's heavyweight title, it was only his third fight as a pro. In his first fight, he had knocked out Arley Seifer, a welterweight from Pittsburgh's North Side, and in his fourth fight he decisioned Wilf Greaves, Canadian by birth, Pittsburgher (for a spell) by adoption.

When Greaves lost to Sugar Ray Robinson at the newly opened Civic Arena, Morris was on the undercard, winning a ten-rounder from the South American Lino Rendon. His fights from then on were few and far between.

In 1962, somebody named Cliff Murkey knocked him out in Chicago, and he lost to Joey Giardello in Baltimore. That fight was close enough for Morris to claim he'd been robbed. Ten months dragged by, and then all of a sudden there was work for Morris in Pittsburgh. He knocked out Jimmy Beecham, retaining his state middleweight title on the Pittsburgh Symphony Orchestra's barge in the Allegheny River off Point State Park. After that, he surprised the fight game's insiders by winning a ten-round decision from George Benton at the Civic Arena. Benton for several years had been "the uncrowned champion" (a phrase that has disappeared from the lexicon; boxing today is so saturated with champions there could be no such thing as an uncrowned one). If only in Philadelphia, where he lived, Benton at the time was thought to be the world's best middleweight.

Beating him turned out to be a bad career move for Morris. "Worst thing I could've done," he reflected. More than ever, it had made him an undesirable opponent for name fighters. What was almost as upsetting, recognition continued to elude him. Benton, after winning from Giardello, had been ranked No. 4. Ring magazine now dropped him completely out of the top ten. "But did they give me a rating?" Morris asked bitterly. "No. I beat the guy, and they dismissed it as a fluke."

He wracked his brain for an explanation. "Maybe it's my personality," he suggested at last. "If you don't walk around looking ugly and mean, nobody thinks you can fight."

When Teddy Brenner came to town for the Civic Arena match between welterweight champion Emile Griffith and Rubin (Hurricane) Carter, a middleweight from New Jersey who walked around looking ugly and mean, Morris accosted Brenner at the weigh-in and offered to fight Carter at Madison Square Garden with the proviso that he would give back his purse unless he won by a knockout inside of three rounds.

Brenner turned away without answering.

Hurricane Carter could fight, or at any rate punch. Inside of one round, he made a tottering wreck of Griffith. A left to the body, a right to the chin, and a left hook high on the forehead knocked him out, after which Griffith went back to fighting welterweights (he was still champion) and Carter began to clamor for a shot at the middleweight title, the uncontested property now of Giardello. Morris, out in the cold as usual, signed to fight Benton again, this time in Philadelphia for his first decent purse, three thousand dollars.

The decision, a split one, went to Morris -- or so it appeared for a good long while after Pete Tomaso, the referee, lifted Morris's hand. There had been two votes for Morris, including Tomaso's, and one for Benton. As Larry Merchant put it in the Philadelphia Daily News, Morris was ahead in the early returns.

But like Tom Dewey's lead over Harry Truman in the 1948 presidential election, Morris's failed to hold up. He had left the ring and gone to his dressing room while Joe Polino, Benton's brainiest corner man, was demanding a recount. Polino never studied at MIT, but he knew how to add. If Tomaso did, he was having an off night. Polino took the trouble to audit Tomaso's scorecard, and he saw that the totals were wrong. At Polino's insistence, a member of the Pennsylvania State Athletic Commission corrected them, making Benton the winner.

"That's a good joke on me," Tomaso chuckled.

Morris, for his part, was not amused. He could only assert, truthfully, "Even Benton's friends thought I won." Larry Merchant thought so, too, observing that never in Benton's fourteen years as a pro had he looked "more futile and frustrated."

Benton's idolaters, their illusions destroyed, stopped calling him "Champ." The irony was that he now held the worthless state middleweight title. Morris himself kept fantasizing about the ultimate title, Giardello's.

Picking up a copy of Ring magazine one day, he turned to the middleweight rankings. "Dick Tiger, Rubin Carter, Joey Archer . . . They say Tiger and Carter are the toughest. I'll fight them first. Dick Tiger, he'd be cake, because of his style. Tiger just walks in. He wants you to stand still. If you know how to box, Tiger and Carter would be easy. Archer would be easier yet. You could box him to death and then punch. Florentino Fernandez is rated fifth. He's nothing."

Luis Guitterez wasn't much, either, after Morris knocked him out in one round. The fight was in Philadelphia, where Morris's newest manager, Sam Weinberg, had some influence. Philadelphia took a liking to Morris. Welcomed back, though, for a match with Luis Rodriguez, who had been welterweight champion between the first and second of his three title bouts with Emile Griffith, he blew the opportunity, failing to get past the second round.

The knockout defeat was discouraging at first, but Morris came to regard it as a blessing in disguise. "You know what?" he said to Weinberg. "I bet I've got a chance to fight Carter now." Morris understood how boxing men think. He sensed that Carter, having lost to Giardello for the title and then to Rodriguez, no longer could pick his spots. He'd be willing to fight anyone, even Morris. And that was the way it turned out. Promoter Ben Anolik made the match for January 18, 1966, at the Civic Arena.

Carter was an ex-con. Long before other young males adopted the fashion, he shaved his head. He wore a Fu Manchu beard that gave him a sinister look, and his scowl said, "Beware. Keep your distance."

His manager, Pat Amato, was the warden at the Hudson County Jail in Jersey City, which strengthened their rapport. More often than not since the age of 12, Carter had been serving time: five years in the reformatory for stealing polo shirts; four and a half years in the penitentiary for beating up three men in the street. Carter's own father, "a church deacon who believed in punishment," according to Amato, had learned of the polo-shirt theft and reported it to the police. "Venting his emotions," Carter took up boxing in prison.

"It was an outlet for him," said Amato. "He was getting even with people in the ring. He knew if he punched anybody outside the ring he'd go to jail. He's changed now -- he hasn't got that chip on his shoulder anymore, but when the bell rings he's a different person, a ferocious person."

His ferocity did not frighten Morris. It made him careful, however. Round after round, Morris jabbed and retreated. Round after round, Carter plunged after him, missing badly with left hooks and wild rights. When Carter trapped Morris and forced him to trade, Morris would beat him to the punch. Billy Conn, watching from ringside, caught the eye of a sportswriter, pointed to Morris, and mouthed the word: "Easy."

Morris backpedaled all night, keeping Carter at arm's length with his jab. In the ninth round, brimming over with confidence, he executed a little dance step and said to Carter, "Come on, let's work." Carter rushed Morris into a corner and knocked him down with a right to the jaw. "Boy, was I surprised," Morris said later. But he bounced to his feet and took a mandatory eight count. Carter was too exhausted to catch up with him again, and, insultingly, Morris won the tenth round. He also won the fight, on a split decision.

Carter was an ungracious loser. "How you gonna fight when you're the only one fighting?" he demanded. There was worse luck ahead: a court-ordered deduction of $2,100 from his purse for an unpaid debt. And soon he would find himself back behind bars.

In 1967 Carter and a friend, John Artis, were charged with shooting and killing two men in a Paterson, New Jersey, saloon. On the testimony of two petty criminals, they were sentenced to life imprisonment. In 1974 the two witnesses recanted, but the judge who had heard the case did not believe them. Two years after that, when new evidence turned up, the New Jersey Supreme Court granted Carter and Artis a new trial, and they were reconvicted.

Their plight attracted widespread attention. Muhammad Ali, Bob Dylan, and other celebrities campaigned on their behalf, raising money to finance appeals. Finally, in 1981 a parole board gave Artis his freedom. Carter remained in prison until 1985, when a federal judge ruled that prosecutors had denied him his civil rights in both the 1967 and 1976 trials.

Morris, by 1968, was the last main-event fighter in Pittsburgh, a distinction akin to being the only good dog-sled racer in New Guinea. He found that winning from Carter was like winning from Benton. Nothing came of it. He boxed only three more times, against nondescript opponents. In fights spread out over twenty-two months, he won from Jesse Smith in Philadelphia, lost to Curtis Bruce there (inactivity was taking its toll), and lost to Davey Russell in McKeesport.

At 29, Morris was finished. At a somewhat more advanced age, boxing in Pittsburgh also was finished -- at least for the time being. Together, they had died on the vine.

PART FOUR
Miscellany

HARRY GREB VS GENE TUNNEY I
162 POUNDS   1922   174 POUNDS

Heavyweight champion Gene Tunney only lost one fight in his illustrious career, to the legendary Pittsburgh champion Harry Greb in a violent, bloody battle in 1922. (Photo courtesy of Douglas Cavanaugh)

Twilight Time

After World War II, boxing in Pittsburgh entered a period of steady decline, but even then there were tales to be told.

CHAPTER 26

IN MEMORIAM: GENE TUNNEY

While Gene Tunney was on the seat of his pants during the seventh round of his second fight with Jack Dempsey, five people listening to the radio broadcast died of heart attacks. In the 1920s, Tunney could excite the public but not without help.

Of his eighty-three fights, he lost only one -- to Harry Greb. There are those who contend that he lost at least two fights to Greb, or maybe three. He was remarkably handsome, a pair of cauliflower ears notwithstanding. Before and after retiring from the ring, he strove to improve his mind, and succeeded. He married into high society, became the chairman of a profitable corporation, and associated mainly with the intellectual and financial upper crust. None of this made him a folk hero, for his personality did not appeal to the masses. When he died at the age of 81, his obituaries were somewhat perfunctory.

"Perfunctory," by the way, is a word that Gene Tunney might have savored. Economical in the ring, the master of a classically simple boxing style, he was lavish with syllables. Explaining why it would not be possible for Dempsey to beat him, Tunney said, "He has lost that flaming impetuosity."

Dempsey had to ask what it meant.

Tunney's grammar, like his form in delivering a punch, was always correct. "May the better man win," he said to Dempsey when they met for the ritual handshake before the start of the fight in which Tunney won the heavyweight championship. Dempsey's mumbled reply -- "Yeah, yeah" -- betrayed irritation.

Not that Tunney minded. Vulgarians, he had learned, would always show irritation. But Tunney was a man who knew when to say, "I shall" and did so at every opportunity.

"I have been ridiculed as a poseur and damned as a snob," he wrote -- perhaps with secret satisfaction. Tunney had friends like Thornton Wilder, H. G.. Wells, and George Bernard Shaw. There were scandalous rumors that they often discussed Shakespeare. Asked to lecture at Yale on "Troilus and Cressida," he told the fascinated students that the Trojan warrior Ajax reminded him of Jack Sharkey -- "a braggart of gigantic dimensions" who could not win the big one. The fight mob, of course, snickered at this, but Tunney was undismayed. "The phenomenon of the ringster who is interested in literature," he observed, "arouses incredulity, scorn, suspicion, and a singular amount of hostility."

He returned the hostility of certain sportswriters, Damon Runyon and Ring Lardner among them. He was fond of the benign Grantland Rice. "I don't care for what you might call the rougher and readier ones," Tunney said.

Kap Monahan of the Pittsburgh Press did not write sports -- he was a drama critic -- but apparently Tunney considered him rough and ready. They did not get on well when Monahan interviewed Tunney about a film he had made called "The Fighting Marine" -- based, supposedly, on his own life. "He was very short with me," Monahan recalled.

Obnoxiously, Monahan pestered Tunney into giving his honest opinion of "The Fighting Marine." "It's a lousy picture and I'm a lousy actor," Tunney snapped. For Monahan, this was a reportorial coup. Tunney had grown up as a stevedore's son in New York, but seldom for publication did he revert so nearly to the language of the docks.

With someone like Max Beerbohm, the author, artist, art critic, ironist, and sophisticate, he was more at ease. They met for the only time at Bernard Shaw's flat in London. "A charming man, a delightful man," Beerbohm told an interviewer. "Not at all what you would have expected. He took me by the arm and led me to the window, which looked out over the river, and compelled my attention to the beauties of the sunset." Tongue in cheek, Beerbohm continued, "I felt I could not reach his level. I could not match his appreciation." When the journalist and historian William Shirer met Tunney, he was lectured "at great length," he wrote, on "marine painting" and modern literature.

Tunney left boxing as the undefeated champion. For his second fight with Dempsey, witnessed at Soldier Field in Chicago by the largest crowd in the history of boxing, 120,000, he earned the unimaginable sum of $990,000. He married an heiress, Mary Josephine Rowland Lauder, called Polly, whose father was a nephew of Andrew Carnegie. Polly and Gene had a son, John Varick Tunney, who won election in the 1970s to the United States Senate. Tunney himself went into the distillery business and added another million to his fortune. During World War II he directed the Navy's physical fitness program. He was fanatical about fitness, but selectively so. A Madison

Square Garden publicist named John Condon, who also served in the war-time Navy, told me that Tunney once harangued him on the dangers of cigarettes while downing a mixed alcoholic drink.

Before the 1920s there had been no big money and not an excessive amount of interest in sports. Then along came Dempsey, Babe Ruth, Red Grange, Bobby Jones, and Bill Tilden, and suddenly America was sports crazy. Tunney never had the magnetism of these others.

But his first fight with Dempsey in 1926 in Philadelphia was the starting point of Dempsey's immense popularity. The crowd preferred the champion, earlier disdained as a World War I draft dodger, to Tunney, the clean-cut ex-Marine. Dempsey fought instinctively, always pressing forward, and Tunney with cold calculation. "If you held out a thousand-dollar bill," said Tommy Loughran, the light-heavyweight champion, "Tunney wouldn't reach for it."

Tunney reached when the reaching was good. As Mel Heimer wrote in his book "The Long Count," one of the first things Tunney noticed about Dempsey was that he "took an extra hitch" for leverage whenever he threw a left hook. The next time he tried it, Heimer continues, Tunney stepped in with a hard, straight right and won the fight then and there, although it lasted ten rounds.

The knockdown in the seventh round of the second fight a year later put Tunney on the canvas for fourteen seconds. Granted a stay of execution when Dempsey failed to go to a neutral corner, he got to his feet and won another decision. The so-called long count is one of boxing's most memorable occurrences. Few still recall that in the next round, the eighth, it was Tunney who had Dempsey on the floor, dropping him briefly to one knee.

And even in the seventh round after Tunney got up, he landed what Dempsey said was "the hardest blow I ever received -- a straight right under the heart." His words are in Heimer's book. "It was not a question in my mind of being knocked out," Dempsey said. "I thought I was going to die."

CHAPTER 27

AL QUAILL

Rugged Brookline middleweight Al Quaill was a good and entertaining performer. But he had trouble achieving what his talent merited while fighting in a city that featured such huge stars as Billy Conn, Teddy Yarosz and Billy Soose (photo courtesy of Susan Quaill-Kirk)

During one of those amateur boxing tournaments that were commonplace in Western Pennsylvania way back when, Al Quaill, who ran a gym on the South Side, was working in a middleweight's corner. Halfway through the second round, the kid stopped defending himself. He turned his back on his opponent and signaled to the referee that he'd had enough. Quaill looked embarrassed and sick.

He could not understand a fighter who just simply gave up.

In 1938, at Hickey Park in Millvale, Oscar Rankins hit Quaill so hard that the punch fractured his sternum. When the bell rang to start the next round, the fifth, Quaill was unable to raise his hands. His trainer had to do it for him and repeat this routine at the start of every subsequent round. Quaill fought on, and the decision was a draw.

Quaill had the conviction that no one could beat him. Early in his career, he saw Frankie Battaglia, one of the top-rated middleweight contenders, lose to Babe Risko. "I can lick that Battaglia," Quaill told his manager, Chappy Goldstein. He kept repeating this, over and over, until Goldstein believed it too. So in his thirteenth professional fight, Quaill's opponent was Frankie Battaglia.

Years later, he said that his scouting of Battaglia had been faulty. A mobster named Frankie Carbo was a powerful influence in boxing at the time, and when Carbo took an interest in any given fight the performance of the fighters was apt to be unpredictable. Quaill always had an idea that Carbo took an interest in the Battaglia-Risko fight.

At any rate, the Battaglia who confronted him at Motor Square Garden was not the same Battaglia who had lost to Risko. Quaill remembered nothing distinctly after the first time Battaglia knocked him down. "Everything went black," he said.

At one point, momentarily, the lights came back on. He looked across the ring and noticed something odd. Battaglia seemed to be taking a break. He was down on one knee, with his head bowed. "Why, that louse," Quaill said to himself, unaware that he had just floored Battaglia. "He's been beating me to a pulp, and now he's resting."

Battaglia got up at the count of eight, and in the sixth round he knocked Quaill through the ropes and out of the ring. With the help of a spectator, Quaill climbed back in. The spectator was his brother Tom. "What a favor he did me," Quaill said. "He pushed me back in there, and Battaglia knocked me out cold."

Solidly put together, Quaill had the build of a football lineman, which, at South Hills High School, he had been. He took up boxing when his coach recommended a strenuous summertime activity. No form of athletic competition is as elemental as fist fighting, and Quaill liked it better than football.

Quaill had fifty fights all told, winning forty, with two draws. He won from a middleweight champion, Solly Krieger, while Krieger was on the way up, but lost to three others -- Ken Overlin, Teddy Yarosz, and Billy Soose -- and quit the ring young, at 25. He was losing the sight of one eye, and though boxing commission doctors hadn't noticed anything wrong, his plans for the future did not include total blindness.

As a city policeman for thirty years, he cheerfully risked life and limb. In 1946, off duty, he was driving past the site of a Teamsters election when suddenly it turned into a shoot-'em-up. Quaill stopped his car, ran into the crowd unarmed, and took a .32-caliber revolver from a man who had pumped five slugs into five of his fellow union members.

At the YMHA in Oakland one night, Quaill had his stable of amateur boxers working out. In the same part of the gym were half a dozen or so wrestlers. One in particular caught his eye. He was more than the other wrestlers could handle, and they were members, Quaill learned, of the University of Pittsburgh team.

As soon as he had a chance, he asked the young Hercules if he ever had tried boxing. The kid said he hadn't -- he was strictly a wrestler. After a certain amount of urging, he consented to spar with Quaill's only heavyweight and was having no trouble with him. Then the boxer threw a punch with unexpected force behind it. Countering, the wrestler grabbed him and took him down with a hold that dislocated his shoulder.

Quaill was impressed. This fellow, he said to himself, is another Jim Jeffries -- big, powerful, quick as a cat. "What's your name?" Quaill wanted to know. "Bruno Sammartino." He had come to this country at the age of 14 from Italy and had graduated from Schenley High School. His command of English, Quaill noticed, was excellent. "Why do you wanna wrestle?" he asked. The money, he went on, was in boxing.

Bruno Sammartino listened to Quaill's sales talk and agreed to take lessons at his gym. To start with, they worked on fundamentals, but soon a difficulty came up. Sparring partners of the requisite size and experience were hard to come by in Pittsburgh. Seeing no other alternative, Quaill sent his protégé to New York City, where he could make faster progress. The well-known Whitey Bimstein would be his trainer. The equally well-known Vic Marsillo would help.

Sammartino was in good hands, Quaill thought, and then one day Marsillo instructed his novice to put on the gloves with a black guy who'd been boxing in prison. Everybody called the black guy "Sonny" -- a name that did not seem to fit. Large and expressionless and the opposite of cuddly, in no way did he resemble anybody's cute baby brother.

Sammartino boxed five rounds with Sonny. "And all I did," he said, looking back on the experience a long time afterward, "was be a punching bag. The only thing I had to brag about," he added, "I was in there five rounds with Sonny Liston and he never put me down."

In due time, Sonny Liston became the heavyweight champion of the world. Sammartino stopped thinking about the pot of gold at the end of the boxing rainbow and rededicated himself to wrestling. In explanation, he said, "It was not the beating I took from Liston that bothered me, it was just that I had no love for boxing. My love was on the mat. I loved wrestling."

And for him, as he soon discovered, wrestling was where the money turned out to be. In a surprisingly short time, Bruno Sammartino was the biggest gate attraction wrestling ever had known -- always triumphant (or almost always) while selling out Madison Square Garden and other arenas and taking home cash by the carload.

Al Quaill, in the meantime, abandoned any notion of managing a professional fighter, one who could make it to the top. He was happy from then on to work with amateurs. Simply knowing how to box has a value of its own, he believed. What it does is develop self-confidence. And self-confidence enables one to act in a crisis.

Quaill was certain of that. He continued to teach boxing until he died, and he continued to believe that he had strengthened the fiber of the young men he taught. It may be that he was right. Who knows? But whatever the mixture is that results in an Al Quaill can probably not be acquired. The qualities he possessed had to come from within.

CHAPTER 28

NONCOMBATANTS

The McBride Act of 1923 regulates boxing and wrestling in Pennsylvania. It divides the state into three geographical areas with a commissioner from each, chosen through patronage. They tend to be friends or friends of friends of politicians. Sometimes they know a little or even a lot about boxing and/or wrestling. Sometimes they don't.

A commissioner back in the 1930s, Harvey Boyle, was the sports editor of the Pittsburgh Post-Gazette. In times gone by, retired football players were considered uniquely qualified. Ox DeGrosa (Villanova tackle), Harp Vaughan (an early Steeler quarterback), Chuck Bednarik (Philadelphia Eagles linebacker and center), and Jimmy Crowley (one of Notre Dame's mythical Four Horsemen) all served as commissioners in the 1950s and '60s.

For nine years starting in 1955, the Western Pennsylvania commissioner was Paul G.. Sullivan, a sportswriter, lawyer, and tennis player. His extensive vocabulary and general erudition impressed and often mystified boxing men. A newspaper colleague of Sullivan's once asked if there was anyone else who had seen Harry Greb fight and had read, in its entire twenty volumes, Thomas Aquinas's Summa Theologica.

Small and wiry, with a shock of red hair, he brought a peppery disposition to the fight game. When David L. Lawrence, a distant relative, offered to put him on the commission, he at first demurred. It happened like this; Sullivan recalled later on:

"My phone rang one Saturday morning and a voice said, 'This is Dave Lawrence. Can you come over to my office? I want to talk to you.' Lawrence and my father were first half-cousins. I'd never met him until I was in my thirties. I went down to the City-County Building -- he was mayor then, not yet governor, but the boss, the most influential Democrat in the state and maybe the country -- and he said, 'Look, will you take the athletic commissionership? We have to have somebody by Monday.'"

Lawrence had just learned that his original choice for the job -- Billy Conn -- was unacceptable to Governor George Leader. State Senator Joe Barr, a political henchman of Lawrence who in time would succeed him as mayor, suggested Sullivan. "He's a lawyer and he's in sports," Barr pointed out.

Sullivan stalled, reminding Lawrence that the commissioner whose place he would take, John Holahan, was "a Duquesne man," like himself. Both had strong ties to the university. "Well, Holahan's out," Lawrence said with finality. Sullivan, who covered hockey and tennis for the Pittsburgh Sun-Telegraph, then asked if Lawrence had considered Harry Keck, the paper's sports editor. Lawrence dismissed Keck with a shake of his head. "We couldn't take that," he said. Keck had a reputation for inflexibility.

Unable to think of another good way to turn Lawrence down, Sullivan gave in. As they parted company, Lawrence said to him, "There are two things against you in this job. You're the second Irish name on a three-man commission" -- Jimmy Crowley was serving at the time -- "and you're related to me."

That observation, it seemed to Sullivan, summarized Lawrence's political philosophy, which was: "One, spread it around, and, two, avoid a situation that looks like nepotism." As first half-cousins once removed, Lawrence and Sullivan were little more than acquaintances, but Lawrence must have known what to expect. "The next day in my own paper," Sullivan recalled, "a page-one story said I was Lawrence's nephew."

Sullivan turned out to be a hands-on commissioner. At the Enright Theater in East Liberty one night, Jersey Joe Walcott was working in the corner of a heavyweight named Garvin Sawyer. With the old champion calling out instructions, a violation of a rule that was seldom enforced, Sawyer had started out well. He was holding his own against the more experienced Bob Satterfield until Sullivan -- no respecter of celebrity seconds -- ordered Walcott to shut up. Although the fight went the distance, ten rounds, Sawyer lost.

Another time, at the Palisades in McKeesport, Sullivan refused to let a substitute box Jackie Matesic, a popular welterweight from Lawrenceville whose original opponent was a no-show for some reason. During the first preliminary bout, the fans who had come to see Matesic started heckling Sullivan. When two of the biggest loudmouths yelled, "Give us our money back!" Sullivan escorted them to the box office, saw that they got their refunds, and made certain they left the building. There were no further complaints from Matesic fans.

With rare exceptions, Sullivan always went by the book. He invoked a widely-ignored rule that prohibited amateurs 18 and under from boxing opponents 19 and older, a rule that made it difficult for promoters to fill cards. Amateur Athletic Union officials felt that by using their own infallible judgment they could always prevent mismatches. Sullivan, refusing to be budged, insisted on conformance with the law.

` On one occasion his zeal to protect an inexperienced professional heavyweight perhaps did the fighter no good. North Side heavyweight Emil Brtko, possessor of a modest winning streak, appeared to be ready for main events -- at least his manager, Jake Mintz, thought so -- and Sullivan approved a ten-rounder at Duquesne Gardens between Brtko and Charley Powell, a former professional football player from the West Coast. When Powell in the meantime was an unexpected knockout loser to somebody else, Sullivan approved a match between Brtko and Johnny Summerlin of Detroit, and then Summerlin lost unexpectedly. While Mintz and the promoter were wondering what to do next, Sullivan received orders to report for Naval Reserve duty in Washington, D. C.

"Well," he said, "I picked up the paper one night and read that Bob Satterfield had been signed to fight Brtko. Did you ever look at Satterfield's record? It was KO, KO, KO, KO, KO by, KO. He had a glass chin, but he was dynamite." Brtko, matched with opponents who were no more advanced than himself, had been chopping them down with a ponderous left hook. He was big, strong, slow, awkward. As the English writer Hugh McIlvanney remarked about somebody else -- a big, strong, slow, awkward European fighter -- he had the build of a Greek statue but fewer moves. "I thought if I let Brtko fight Satterfield, he'd get killed," Sullivan said.

He called his office in Pittsburgh the next morning and dictated a press release forbidding the match. "Forty-five minutes later, Jake Mintz was on the phone. I couldn't get him off. He argued for an hour. I was destroying Brtko's career. Finally, I said that I had to go to lunch, and darned if he didn't call back. I told him there was no possibility of changing my mind, and at last he came up with another opponent, somebody from St. Louis with a record about the same as Brtko's." Sullivan okayed the match.

"And that was how I protected Brtko from Satterfield and delivered him up to Sonny Liston," he said.

Brtko, of course, lost -- knocked out in the fifth round.

At meetings of the National Boxing Association, Sullivan argued tirelessly for stronger regulations. He felt that Madison Square Garden had too much to say about who fought for titles and who did not. A bit reluctantly, Abe Greene, the NBA's president, allowed him to set up a ranking committee. The new rules Sullivan wrote specified that when somebody won a championship he could fight one time for a payday; after that, he had to defend his title against the NBA's top contender or lose it by forfeit.

All went well until 1962, when the NBA tried to do an about-face. Pennsylvania had suspended the aforementioned Sonny Liston, by this time No. 1 in the rankings, for a brush with the police in Philadelphia. Two cops patrolling Fairmount Park late at night had spotted him in a parked car, talking with a woman in another parked car. When the cops approached to investigate, Liston drove away. Absurdly, he was charged with resisting arrest. In Sullivan's view, Liston had been guilty of nothing more serious than an indiscretion, but rather than disagree with his fellow commissioners, Jimmy Crowley and Al Klein, he concurred in their vote to suspend.

Liston was in bad odor with the commission because three Philadelphia racket guys -- Pep Barone, Blinky Palermo, and John Vitale -- owned his contract. Under pressure, he severed himself from them and acquired an "interim" manager the commission had approved, George Katz by name. Meanwhile, a Catholic priest from Colorado, a Father Murphy, had taken a paternal interest in Liston. With Murphy acting as his unofficial probation officer, he lived and trained in Denver for eight months -- learning, while he was there, to write his name -- and the commission reinstated him.

Back on the side of the angels, he knocked out a heavyweight from Germany, Albert Westphal, in one round. He had not lost a fight in eight years, but when the NBA met in Chicago the executive committee proposed to let the champion, Floyd Patterson, defend his title against the No. 2 contender. Irate, Sullivan got up and said, "If you go through with this, I'm calling a press conference tomorrow morning and I'm telling the newspapers that you don't have the guts to do what your own rules call for." The specter of bad publicity, Sullivan knew, was terrifying to the NBA. "I had no idea how to go about calling a press conference in Chicago," he admitted, "but these guys on the executive committee didn't realize that. So they turned it around and said that Patterson would have to fight Liston."

There remained the question of Patterson's compliance. It was clear that his manager, Cus D'Amato, wanted nothing to do with Liston. Sullivan, invoking the NBA's rather dubious clout, prepared a statement declaring that

Patterson must fight Liston or be stripped of his title. Patterson did fight Liston, in Chicago that same year, and lost his title in the ring by a first-round knockout.

Very few state commissioners have had any actual boxing experience. The exceptions include Andrew DePaolo -- Andy (Kid) DePaul in his fighting days. A liquor salesman, DePaul joined the commission in 1989, when boxing in at least the western half of the state was all but extinct. His own career had begun in the twilight years after World War II. He won the Pittsburgh and national Golden Gloves lightweight titles and caught the eye of Joe Vella, who managed the light-heavyweight champion, Gus Lesnevich. Vella signed DePaul to a contract and took him to Cliffside, New Jersey, to live and train.

DePaul, Lesnevich, and Rocky Graziano, the middleweight champion, worked out together at a fight camp near Cliffside. "I boxed a thousand rounds with Lesnevich and a thousand rounds with Graziano, and they didn't try to kill me," DePaul remembered. Graziano's crude style could make a left-jab artist look good, and DePaul had a nifty left jab. He was not a hard puncher, but he put Graziano down once, with a right to the heart. Graziano made no attempt to avenge himself. "He was a gentleman," DePaul said.

Maturing, DePaul had become a welterweight. After his fourth pro fight, at Sunnyside Gardens in New York, a sportswriter likened him to "the original Packey McFarland," and the headline over his story referred to DePaul as Packey McFarland's "ghost." Active in the early part of the twentieth century, McFarland was a welterweight-sized lightweight from Chicago who lost only once in 113 fights.

The first fight Packey McFarland's ghost lost was in Bergen, New Jersey, to somebody named, if you took his word for it, Billy Wade. With DePaul and "Wade" in the ring, waiting for the bell, Al Weill, Rocky Marciano's manager, said to Vella, "Do you know who you're fighting?" "Sure," answered Vella. "He's a local kid."

"Local kid? That's Holly Mims," Weill told him. Mims, one of the world's best middleweights, had adopted an alias in order to get work. Even Sugar Ray Robinson was ducking him. Interested only in a payday, he "did just enough," DePaul recalled, to win their fight, an eight-rounder.

Not long afterward, Vella matched DePaul with a raw young beginner from upstate New York, but the New York commission ruled that the kid was "not a suitable opponent" for the ghost of Packey McFarland, so DePaul never did fight Carmen Basilio, future welterweight and middleweight champion.

DePaul's top purse was $3,600 for a six-rounder "underneath" the night that Graziano was knocked out by Tony Zale in the third fight between them for the middleweight title. Returning to Pittsburgh, DePaul moved up to ten-rounders. At 155 pounds, he was something of a misfit -- a little too heavy to be a welterweight and a little too light to be a middleweight. Of his first twenty-nine fights, he won twenty-seven on boxing ability, but his handlers were telling him that boxers did not appeal to the public. Unwisely, DePaul changed his style. "I tried to be a puncher," he said. When he tried to be a puncher in fights with full-grown middleweights like Charley Affif and Floyd Morris, they outmuscled him. Morris, who was almost a light-heavyweight and could be a puncher without even trying, knocked him down a couple of times..

What he needed, Vella decided, was a job that would build up his physique. Accordingly, DePaul went to work on a construction crew. Cutting down trees with a power saw, he mangled an index finger, which kept him out of action for a year. The Army then drafted him -- the Korean War was winding down -- and he spent a few months in Japan. Demobilized, he had three more fights. He won two, lost one, and retired with a 31-8-3 record.

Whether commissioners who have boxed are more insightful than commissioners who have not is debatable. Marion Klingensmith was a commissioner who had boxed. He was also a commissioner who had served in the State Legislature. In 1968 he ran for re-election. Richard Nixon was making his second try for the presidency that year, and Klingensmith declared himself to be a Nixon supporter. However, when Raymond Shafer, Pennsylvania's Republican governor, came out for Nelson Rockefeller, Klingensmith changed horses, explaining with great eloquence that Shafer was the boss. Rockefeller lost out to Nixon at the Republican convention and Klingensmith lost out in the November election to a Democrat. Two months later, Shafer appointed him to the state athletic commission. The commissioner who lost his job, one-time Steeler quarterback Harp Vaughan, had alienated Shafer by remaining loyal to Nixon.

Politics aside, Klingensmith seemed to be a logical choice. His knowledge of boxing was an asset, but commissioners have to supervise wrestling, too, and he did not understand a few basic truths about wrestling.

A wrestling show he attended just a day or two after taking office was the first he had seen since his boyhood in Brownsville, and he could scarcely believe his eyes. The viciousness and brutality of the star performer, a certain Killer Kowalski, astounded him.

"He was choking the other guy, and kicking, too," Klingensmith said. "He took the sole off the other guy's shoe -- that's a thirty-dollar piece of leather -- and rubbed it in his face. The bell was ringing, and he paid no attention. He paid no attention to the referee." So Klingensmith jumped into the ring, got an impromptu half-Nelson on Kowalski, and dragged him away from his victim.

Justifying this act to an unsympathetic audience in the studio of Pittsburgh television station WPXI, where wrestling matches in those days were usually held, Klingensmith announced, "It's not the American way of life to use unfair tactics."

That first year as commissioner was a learning experience for him. He learned a few things about wrestling and he learned a few things about the American way of life.

Two weeks after the choking and kicking and footwear-destroying incident, Klingensmith suspended the region's most picturesque referee, Izzy Moidel, for allowing Kowalski to bash someone's head against a ring post. The suspension was not well received. Wrestling fans regarded Moidel as an indispensable part of the entertainment. His popularity equaled, or in many cases exceeded, that of the wrestlers themselves.

"The reaction I got, Slugger," Klingensmith told a reporter, using his mode of address for everybody he knew, except possibly his wife, "was: 'Aren't you aware these fellas are playing?' I answered, 'No. When a man can get hurt, it's not play.'"

Resolutely, Klingensmith monitored the next big show at the Civic Arena. He stationed himself near the ring and kept a close eye on the proceedings. When a tag match ended, and the wrestlers ignored the bell, he ordered a mass disqualification. Following the tag match, Killer Kowalski wrestled Batman. "And all they did, Slugger," Klingensmitth said, "was kick, kick,

kick." To the growing aggravation of the crowd, he disqualified both contestants,

Then Bruno Sammartino, the world champion, went to the mat with Waldo von Erich. "And, Slugger," Klingensmith continued, "that's the only thing they did -- kick one another. The referee warned them three times, and Sammartino just pushed him away. The third time, the referee stopped the fight. And I agreed with him."

Nobody else did. "Slugger," said Klingensmith, "they booed and booed and booed." Klingensmith was a large, well-set up man, with a politician's stately bearing and a shiny bald head that made him easy to identify, and the spectators were now giving him their undivided attention. "It's a good thing they didn't have Coca-Cola bottles, Slugger," he said. "They threw paper cups, they threw ice, they threw popcorn boxes and programs. It looked like the Democratic convention." He meant the riotous convention in Chicago the previous year, when opposition to the war in Vietnam was at its height.

As the assault on Klingensmith intensified, police came to the ringside and offered him an escort to a safer part of the building. With the gameness he had shown as a mid-level middleweight twenty years earlier, he refused to leave his post. "I wanted to see the midgets wrestle," he said.

But minute by minute the crowd's ugliness grew, and Lou Barry, the ring announcer, was getting nervous. "Commissioner, I think you'd better go while the going is good," he suggested. Choosing not to wait for the midgets after all, Klingensmith took cover in the dressing room.

Subsequently, after a long, earnest discussion with Bruno Sammartino, he began to see that the American way of life was perhaps more elastic than he had realized. In the next few days, letters and phone calls further broadened his outlook. One call was from Frank Wildman, the athletic commission's chairman.

"Slugger, what are you trying to do up there?" Wildman asked. "I hear you got yourself in some trouble the other night."

"Trouble?" said Klingensmith. "I almost got lynched."

"Well, if I were you," Wildman advised him, "I'd be less severe with those wrestlers."

"But I thought you wanted the rules and regulations followed," Klingensmith protested.

"Nah," Wildman said. "Not in wrestling. They don't hurt one another and the crowd enjoys it and the state gets tax money out of it."

"Don't hurt one another?" Klingensmith was incredulous, but in general he acknowledged the soundness of Wildman's argument. "Slugger," he said to a reporter soon afterward, "I've got to regroup my thinking. I'm not going to be as strong an enforcer from now on."

He remained dead set against kicking -- "excessive kicking. It degrades an athlete as far as I'm concerned. A man could lose an eye or fracture his back. I might let a couple of harmless kicks go by, but nothing excessive."

In the same new spirit of tolerance, he ended the suspension of Izzy Moidel.

With boxers, he was still uncompromising. They were ordered to "shave off excessive facial hair and appear neatly dressed at the weigh-ins."

He said, "I hate to see a man, especially a prizefighter -- anyone portraying a sportsman -- who doesn't look clean." Klingensmith himself -- well barbered, well-scrubbed, and hairless on top -- resembled the Mr. Clean of the television commercials. "I'm going to stick to the rules in boxing," he promised, "but people don't expect it in wrestling. I didn't know that."

With the help of Bruno Sammartino, Frank Wildman, and a worked-up crowd in the Civic Arena, he was undergoing a cultural transformation. He had the capacity, as they say, to grow in office.

CHAPTER 29
GYMS

Until they tore the place down in the urban renewal phase of the city's first Renaissance, all the good fighters in town -- all the good white fighters -- trained at the Pittsburgh Lyceum.

The original Lyceum, a public lecture hall in Athens, was a gathering place for philosophers, rather than pugs. Aristotle hung out there. Pittsburgh's Lyceum was an adjunct of Epiphany Church in the Lower Hill district. It had been a neighborhood landmark since the start of the twentieth century, when the church's pastor, the Rev. Lawrence O'Connell, borrowed fifty thousand dollars to build a three-story red brick recreation center.

There was a dance hall in the Lyceum, and a swimming pool and a theater and a basketball court, but no lecture hall. In the 1940s and 1950s, Joe Luvara presided over the health club, on the third floor, and the gym, on the second floor. The gym was a single small room, containing a "puncher's ring," as the fighters called it: fifteen feet by fifteen feet. "That was what made Billy Conn a great boxer," Luvara would say. "When he was still just a kid -- 17, 18 years old -- he'd be in there with the tough guys, and he had to move. He said it was like going to college."

Out-of-town fighters trained at the Lyceum for their Pittsburgh appearances. If the fight coming up was a big one, the ring would be moved to the basketball court and spectators were charged twenty-five cents to watch the sparring sessions. Out-of-town fighters with black skin had to train somewhere else, apartheid being the order of the day.

The Rev. Eugene Harkins supervised the Lyceum from 1925 to 1944. "The Lower Hill then," Joe Luvara recalled, "was Italians, Syrians, and Jews. Right around the Lyceum, that's where the Italians were. They had Italian grocery stores with loops of garlic hanging from the ceiling. You'd buy the baccala, the dried codfish, for three cents a pound. Take it home and let it soak, and you'd eat for a week.

"In those days a lot of people had houses without bathtubs. For five dollars a year, they could join the Lyceum and take a shower. A towel and a bar of soap cost a nickel. The Lyceum kept the people clean.

"Upstairs, we had steam cabinets and two other cabinets with light bulbs in them, maybe fifty bulbs. You'd get in there and stick your head out and we'd turn the lights on. That was your dry heat. Then you'd take a shower and have a rub.

"It was fifty cents a rub, and the Lyceum got the money. Fritzie Zivic's manager, Luke Carney, thought fifty cents was too much. He'd tell Fritzie, 'A good fighter don't need a rub and a bad fighter don't deserve one.' My pay was fifteen dollars a week plus tips, and Father Harkins knew how many rubs I would get from a bottle of rubbing alcohol. So, what I'd do, I'd mix a little water in. I'd get an extra rub out of each bottle."

Father Harkins was fastidious and tough. "In the summertime," Luvara said, "he wore a straw hat. He looked like a real dude, but he ran the Lyceum with an iron hand. They had a library, and you weren't allowed to talk. If he heard any noise, he'd walk in there and say, 'Look -- that's enough.' He wouldn't stand for any spitting in the gym, and if you sneezed, you'd better cover your face with a handkerchief.

"I remember one-time Billy Conn was eating an orange. He threw the peels on the stairway, and Father Harkins made him pick them all up. This was after Conn won the title. He was light-heavyweight champion of the world. People in those days had a lot of respect for the collar.

"Troublemakers were barred from the gym for life. If you swore, you were barred for life. Father Harkins didn't tolerate rowdyism. Important citizens belonged to the Lyceum -- businessmen who went there to exercise. To be a member of the health club cost ten dollars a year, to use the gym and the basketball court, five dollars a year."

Joe Luvara's job included maintenance. The Lyceum wasn't like Stillman's Gym in New York, which Luvara said was the crummiest he'd ever been in. Lou Stillman, the owner, never had the windows washed. He never opened one, either, except when Gene Tunney came in to box. Tunney insisted on fresh air. The trainers and managers smoked cigars and threw the butts on the floor. After buying sandwiches at the lunch counter, they'd throw what they didn't eat on the floor.

At the Lyceum, Izzy Moidel, a boxer and trainer himself, and later a celebrated wrestling referee, helped Luvara with the mop bucket. "Izzy used to mop for a roast beef and a bottle of pop," Luvara said. "Whenever Izzy was hungry, the floor got mopped."

By comparison with other gyms, the Lyceum was palatial. In Luvara's opinion, all a gym needed was a ring, one speed bag, one heavy bag, a rubbing table, and a shower. A full-length mirror for shadow boxing was desirable, but not necessary. There should be posters on the wall, advertisements for long-forgotten fights. There should be photographs of boxers, famous or barely known. There should be an aroma composed, in roughly equal parts, of wintergreen, rubbing alcohol, resin, and sweat.

As for the sounds of a gym, the author George Plimpton sorted them out carefully on a visit to Stillman's:

"The *slap-slap* of the ropes being skipped, the thud of leather into the big heavy bags that squeaked from their chains as they swung, the rattle of the speed bags, the muffled scrape of gym shoes on the canvas of the rings (there were two rings), the snuffle of the fighters breathing out through their noses, and, every three minutes, the sharp clang of the ring bell."

In the 1950s you could see, hear, and smell all these things at the classically squalid East Liberty Gym, accessible by climbing a dark, narrow flight of stairs to the cavernous third floor of a loft building. Gee Bee Thomas was the boxing instructor. Lou Caponi, a labor-union organizer, paid the rent, one hundred dollars a month. Everybody who went through the door, fighters not excepted, dropped twenty-five cents into a dish on a table. Sometimes a sneak thief would scoop up the change and make off with it.

Caponi, a squat, bald man with a prominent nose, wore thick, round, horn-rimmed glasses that gave him an owlish look. He managed a few preliminary fighters and staked them to room and board. When a fighter of his was on the undercard somewhere, Caponi bought a ticket like everyone else.

"Why do you fool around with this stuff?" a reporter once asked him.

"Insanity, maybe," he said.

Charley Daniels ran a gym on a shoestring. It was in the basement of a social club in the Upper Hill. There was no ring. There wasn't even a mat. The boxers who trained there had to spar on the bare wooden floor. The room was fifteen feet by twelve feet. "We had some padding on the wall, but I took it down," Daniels said. "When two guys are boxing and get close to the wall, I'd holler, 'Be careful!'" The ceiling was so low that fighters over six feet tall usually didn't try to skip rope.

Daniels wasn't complaining. "We've got light, heat, and hot water," he said, "and the guy who owns the building doesn't charge me any rent. Jack

Rodgers trained in my gym and beat Joey Giardello. Then I took him to Philadelphia for the rematch and put him in a regular gym and he lost."

Daniels had a stable of amateur fighters but refused to manage pros, although he trained them. "To manage pros," he explained, "you need money, man. It's bad enough to have amateurs, always asking for quarters. Pro fighters ask you for dollars." Daniels ended up as director of boxing in the state penitentiary system.

By the 1990s, one of the few places where fighters could work out was Jack's Uptown Gym, a cluttered back room on the otherwise empty ground floor of a dilapidated building on Fifth Avenue. Jack Godfrey, the man in charge, came to Pittsburgh from Georgia during the black migration of the 1930s. "All the colored people came up from the South and got off the train at Freedom Road as soon as they saw smoke," he said.

Godfrey was a boxer who had only one fight. He was 6 feet 6 and weighed 270 pounds. "I got knocked down three times in the first round," he said. "I went back to the dressing room and asked a guy, 'Do you want a pair of boxing shoes?' I asked another guy, 'Do you want a pair of gloves?' That was the end of my ring career."

He took up managing. "They'd call me from Cleveland or somewhere. 'We want three fighters -- two middleweights and a welterweight.'

"I'd say, 'How do you want them?'

"'Three to go, one to stay.'

"This was the Depression, before the war. Nobody had no money. I'd get a kid out of the pool parlor. I'd say, 'You know you gotta go in the third, don't you?' He'd say, 'Jack, I'm going to the top.' I'd say, 'No. You're not going to the top.'

"Back in those days, to give you an idea of what black fighters went through, the guy who owned the Washington Redskins -- George Preston Marshall -- had a fighter named Honey Boy Jones. He was good. Marshall had him fighting Billy Conn here, and he knocked Billy Conn down in the third or fourth round. When the fight was over, Billy Conn got the nod, and George Preston Marshall said to Jones, 'You son of a bitch, why did you hit that boy?'"

One day when Godfrey was "loafing in front of a pool parlor called Rosie's, right next to the police station on the Hill, a cop took him back to the cell block. "There behind bars," he recalled, "was a black guy built like a

Greek Adonis." The black guy turned out to be Curtis Sheppard, a heavyweight who had moved to the Hill from parts unknown and whose nickname -- "Hatchet Man" -- derived from the way he could punch. The Hatchet Man had been locked up, Godfrey said, for making unwanted advances to a lady.

"Jack," the cop asked, "can you do something with him?"

Godfrey said he thought it was possible.

"Take him out the back door," the cop said.

Sheppard's manager at the time, a Pittsburgh jeweler named Eddie Kapphan, described him as "the hardest puncher the ring has ever produced." His top weight as a fighter was 185 pounds or thereabouts. Kapphan also managed Harry Bobo, who weighed about 210. One day when they were sparring in the Centre Avenue Gym, according to Kapphan, Sheppard hit Bobo so hard that he was "blacked out for four hours." Old-time managers like Eddie Kapphan were gifted in the art of exaggeration, but that's what the man said to the Pittsburgh Courier.

Anyway, Godfrey got in touch with Kapphan after escorting Sheppard "out the back door" of the police station on the Hill. Kapphan called a promoter in Baltimore and booked a fight for Sheppard with Lee Q. Murray. Godfrey went along to work in the Hatchet Man's corner. "And this is what things were like then," he said. "Curtis Sheppard's pre-fight meal was a ham sandwich And Eddie Kapphan ate half of it."

The way things are today, with pay per view, the fighters on top make enough money to wipe out famine everywhere in the world, and the ones who train at places like Jack's Uptown Gym are still half-a-sandwich guys, or the modern equivalent.

CHAPTER 30

WHY?

Bravery of any sort never disgraced the human race. I don't care how pointless it is

-- *Jimmy Cannon*

On a trip through Spain, the novelist and travel writer Paul Theroux reluctantly watched a bullfight. Then another bullfight. Then a third -- and a fourth. "What perversity in the Spanish character demanded this sickening spectacle?" he was moved to ask.

What perversity in Paul Theroux's character, a Spaniard might ask, kept him from swearing off bullfights after the first one? There is no understandable answer to a question like that. What perversity tolerates boxing, which can also be a sickening spectacle?

Ernest Hemingway, who wrote the primer on bullfighting, "Death in the Afternoon," had a "feeling of elation" after watching a good *corrida.* Prizefighting elated him, too, although he never comes right out and says so. "Fifty Grand" is his best-known boxing story. Clothed in Hemingway's most stripped down just-the-facts-ma'am prose, it's a eulogy to gameness.

Paul Theroux maintains that in the bullfighting chapters of Hemingway's first novel, "The Sun Also Rises," the blood and the physical cruelty get lost. "Fifty Grand" contains some of prizefighting's ruthlessness -- the protagonist's deliberate low blows are basic to the plot -- but the tone is celebratory.

A. J. Liebling ignored the blood and the cruelty altogether. His widely admired non-fiction pieces about boxing "enthrall but do not excite," the critic J. C. Bonebrake has noted. "The flow is poetic, gurgling." To the annoyance of Joyce Carol Oates, the author of a book that deals with the moral ambiguity of boxing, Liebling glosses over and sanitizes.

She dislikes most of all his relentless "jokiness." The difficulty for him and for the magazine that printed his stories, The New Yorker, "must have been how to sell a blood sport like boxing to a genteel, affluent readership to whom the idea of men fighting for their lives would have been deeply offensive, how to suggest boxing's drama while skirting boxing's tragedy," she writes, ever mindful of tragedy.

Liebling, for his part, seemed to regard boxing as a harmless intellectual exercise. His pleasure was in analyzing styles, in figuring out the strategic and tactical problems two fighters might create for each other, and in trying to envision "their rival patterns of ratiocination." Liebling attended fights to see how correct his judgment had been.

Most people, including Joyce Carol Oates, have no such clear notion of why they attend fights. The psychologists offer theories that are not necessarily on the mark. Jimmy Cannon wrote that the fight racket disgusted him but gave him his greatest kicks. Indoctrinated, like Joyce Carol Oates, by a father who thought of boxing as family entertainment, he saw his first fight as a child. "My old man took me to the amateurs when I was very small." After years of writing sports, he confessed, "I still get sweaty and jumpy when fighters come into the ring for the big one."

So does Joyce Carol Oates, but that is not the way she expresses it. Not remotely the way. "To go from an ordinary preliminary match to a Fight of the Century -- those between Joe Louis and Billy Conn, Muhammad Ali and Joe Frazier, most recently Marvin Hagler and Tommy Hearns -- " she wrote in 1985, "is to go from listening or half listening to a guitar being idly plucked to hearing Bach's 'Well-Tempered Clavier' being perfectly played. Do you see what I mean?"

The English novelist Arnold Bennett, waiting for Georges Carpentier and Joe Beckett to answer the bell, got sweaty and jumpy from a mixture of anticipation and parsimony. "The sublime moment approached. You had a unique sensation. You admitted to yourself that it was well worth ten guineas . . ."

Afterward, Bennett repaired to his club, sipped "an aged Courvoisier brandy," and calmly played devil's advocate. "Was it a moral show?" he asked himself, and answered, "It was -- as moral as an inter-university rugger match. Was it an aesthetic show? It was. Did it uplift? It did. Did it degrade? It did not. Was it offensive? No. Ought the noble art to continue? It ought. I was deeply interested."

The American Medical Association, also deeply interested, believes that the noble art ought not to continue. It has thought so, the record shows, since 1984, when it passed a resolution to that effect. Men of letters -- the Bennett's, the Liebling's, and countless others -- commonly make excuses for boxing, which seems to fascinate them; even Plato extolled it as fine preparation for war. Joyce Carol Oates, a woman of letters, is both attracted to the noble art and repelled by it. People ask her, she writes, "How can you enjoy so brutal a sport?" She explains that she doesn't "enjoy" boxing, that in any case it isn't always brutal, and, finally, that she doesn't think of it as a "sport." She thinks of it as "an art form -- America's tragic theater." She writes about the fight racket in such metaphysical terms that a critic named Robert W. Smith, thoroughly nonplussed, began his review of her book "On Boxing" with the sentence, "What Joyce Carol Oates doesn't know about boxing would fill a volume -- namely this volume." Not true. Joyce Carol Oates brings an original and worthwhile perspective to boxing.

A. J. Liebling, in a preface to his story collection, "The Sweet Science," establishes his credentials by saying that well into middle age he "boxed for fun" (although not to keep in trim, never an obsession with Liebling). Ernest Hemingway's idea of fun was to put on the gloves with friends or acquaintances and try to knock their heads off. He wasn't very good at it, by the way. He badgered Hugh Casey, a pitcher for the old Brooklyn Dodgers, into a sparring match one night when both had been drinking, and Casey took him apart. Hemingway won fights in his mind. Whenever he wrote a book, he was slugging it out with Tolstoy for the heavyweight championship of the literary world -- and prevailing.

Lord Byron tested himself in actual competition with a bare-knuckle champion, Gentleman John Jackson, who undoubtedly pulled his punches. He was "Gentleman" John, after all. Jack Dempsey pulled his punches for nobody. If Paul Gallico, the first of the participatory journalists, expected Dempsey to take it easy when they sparred wearing sixteen-ounce gloves, he could not have been more mistaken. Gallico's intention was to write about the experience in his newspaper column. As it happened, there was not much to tell. "What's the matter, kid?" Dempsey asked him just before they squared off. "Don't your editor like you no more?" A few seconds later, Gallico was flat on his back, knocked cold.

Gallico in time became a novelist, which may or may not be proof that he suffered no brain damage. That brain damage to some extent afflicts every old boxer is hard to deny. With many, it results in pugilistica dementia -- steady, irreversible mental deterioration, ordinarily not apparent until late in life. Often the fighter's family objects to the diagnosis. When old boxers die in a neurological ward it is customary to read that they suffered from

Alzheimer's Disease. Also in denial, A. J. Liebling simply blew off the whole idea that prizefighting entails any risk. "If a boxer ever went as batty as Nijinski," he wrote, "all the wowsers in the world would be screaming, 'Punch-drunk.' Well, who punched Nijinski?"

Not even a ballerina, to the best of anyone's knowledge, but a more pertinent question might be: How many ballet dancers ever died on the stage? For boxers, death is an occupational hazard. Of course, the same can be said of many other activities. Cigarette smoking, for example, takes a higher toll in the long run.

Among football players, the mortality rate starts to spike about twenty or thirty years after retirement. Why so soon? Steroids, probably -- steroids in combination with repeated brain concussions. Tellingly, there are boxers who wouldn't think of playing football: it's too rough for them. Boxers are unaccustomed to being blindsided, unaccustomed to being hit by two or three opponents at once or by somebody twice their size.

Yes, I know -- theoretically, there's a difference of intent between boxing and football. In boxing the ultimate goal is to render one's adversary unconscious. In football, injuries are supposed to be a by-product: what football players are trying to do is advance a ball or keep the opposition from advancing it. Putting a bounty on your opponent's best players -- giving a bonus for a hit that puts the other team's quarterback, let's say, out of commission -- is officially frowned upon in the National Football League, an offense that subjects the perpetrators to fines and suspensions of as long as a year. And yet there are ways within the rules to achieve the same objective. Ask a quarterback who has just been legally "sacked," as the euphemism goes, by a 280-pound human torpedo. Ask a wide receiver shot down in the act of leaping high for a pass. Airborne wide receivers -- and quarterbacks in a pocket full of holes -- are football's sitting ducks.

More so than in boxing, football is a contact sport. Certain coaches like to say it's a collision sport. There are boxers less interested in hitting than in not getting hit. Or there once were, I should say. When football players explain what attracts them to the game, nine out of ten will answer, "The contact." Or, "Hitting people." Football players are coached to seek out contact. They tackle. They block. They crash into one another, helmet first -- and plastic helmets are weapons. It is contact up close and personal. Linemen take hits -- and give them -- on every play. To insist that the object is not to do physical harm begs the question. Physical contact and physical harm are inseparable when the contact is violent, which in football it nearly always is.

Has anybody noticed that prizefighters tend to live a long time if their lifestyle has not exposed them to drugs and street violence, while football players -- since steroids came into the game -- die young? For one thing, prizefighters don't commit suicide the way football players have been doing of late. The football players who die on the practice field from heat exhaustion, heart failure, and "undetermined" causes are another story.

If the fact that boxers generally survive into their dotage suggests that blows to the head are good for you, the analogy is a false one, because football players also take blows to the head. Jim Kelly, the Buffalo Bills' quarterback from the early 1980s to the mid-1990s, told a Los Angeles Times reporter that it is probably impossible to play an entire game without incurring what is known as a grade-one brain concussion -- in layman's language "confusion of thought with no loss of consciousness or memory." Grade-two concussions (no loss of consciousness but confusion with amnesia) and grade-three concussions (loss of consciousness) happen less often but often enough.

` The New York Times, in September of 2008, reported that doctors at Boston University's Center for the Study of Traumatic Encephalopathy had examined the brains of six deceased NFL players (all of whom died in their thirties or forties) and found evidence in five of neurological disease, which the director of the center, Dr. Ann C. McKee, said was "identical to the pugilistica dementia I've seen in boxers in their seventies and eighties." Three of the players -- Mike Webster, Terry Long, and Justin Strzelczyk -- had been Pittsburgh Steelers. The Pittsburgh connection goes even further; as brought to light by Jeanne Marie Laskas in GQ magazine, it was a young Nigerian-born medical examiner in the Allegheny County coroner's office, Dr. Bennet Omalu, who first identified traumatic encephalopathy in a football player, and he did so as the result of the autopsy he performed on Webster. More studies at Boston U. and elsewhere, some of them involving Omalu, have added many names to the list. In 2013 the NFL paid $765 million to settle a lawsuit brought by more than 4,500 retired players claiming brain damage and other football-related injuries

Boxers who've been knocked out do not, with official sanction, fight again for six weeks. Brain-concussed football players are back on the field in seven days, ordinarily. Most of them can't wait to get back. There seems to be little fear among football players of ending up crippled or paralyzed and seemingly no fear at all of brain damage. (Lynn Swann, a former Steeler who's in the Hall of Fame, must have thought about it at any rate. He played the high-risk position of wide receiver and took so many vicious hits -- cheap shots resulting in concussions -- that he quit the game while he was still in his prime. After one such vicious hit, Swann's coach, Chuck Noll, darkly alluded to a "criminal element" in football. The rate at which football players get into trouble with the law may be proof that he was not overstating it.)

For whatever reason, the compulsion to be a fighter is not as easy to explain as the compulsion to be a football player. When there were fewer well-paying professional team sports, boxing was seen as a way to climb out of poverty. There was also the belief, less widely shared today than in an earlier time -- *much* less widely shared -- that fighters were special people. "Shake the hand that shook the hand of John L. Sullivan," men used to say when the heavyweight champion was at least as well known as the president of the United States and almost always more greatly admired.

One thing fighters and football players have in common: they disregard the warning on the label. Brain damage? Why worry? Facetiously -- or maybe not -- George Foreman, a two-time heavyweight champion, once said that "anybody going into boxing has brain damage already."

If they are able to think about it at all, most brain-damaged or nerve-damaged fighters regret nothing. Muhammad Ali paid a price, the price of being Muhammad Ali, and no doubt he would do it again. If the object was just to get rich, Ali succeeded. In the bargain, he ended up famous and beloved. If he never had laced on a boxing glove, how far -- despite his charm, good looks, creativity, wit, and bravura-- would his lack of education and 78 I.Q. have taken him? Boxing allowed him to rise in the world, spreading his wings, and it took away some of his faculties. For Ali, the exchange was not a bad one.

Boxing's true sad cases are the displaced persons -- the stiffs, the ham-and-eggers, the palookas. "What are they doing here?" asked Joyce Carol Oates, watching two of them stumble through a Madison Square Garden four-rounder, hooted at by the crowd. What they were doing there was attempting to define themselves, attempting to be something they were not. The really baffling question is: Why?

Historically, boxing in the United States has been an escape hatch from low-paying, hard manual labor for the sons of immigrants. The immigrant waves overlapped but were roughly sequential. First came the Germans and the Irish, then the Jews, then the Italians, then the Slavs, and so on. As each ethnic group joined the mainstream, there continued to be an unchanging source of supply -- the perennial black underclass, augmented since the 1930s by the northward flow of Hispanics.

For some, their fists are their fortune. More than a few others come to grief, battered and broken. It is fair to ask what they are doing there, and it's fair to ask what the spectators are doing there. George Bellows, in "Stag at Sharkey's," painted fight fans as bloodthirsty cretins. His fighters are just as grotesque, charging at each other like bighorn sheep in the rutting season. Bellows exaggerates absurdly, but in the sense that fight fans prefer brawlers to craftsmen, he had it right. Bellows was aware of human nature. Why is football so popular? Because the fans like the contact, the hitting. They like it even more than the players do. And what is it that excites the people who go to hockey games? The body checking and of course the fights, which the powers that be in hockey not only condone but encourage.

In boxing, the craftsmen -- the artists -- are almost extinct. Mike Gibbons, the St. Paul Phantom, used to stand on a handkerchief and let a sparring partner throw punches which he would slip, block, or duck. He couldn't be squarely hit. Connecting with the chin of Teddy Yarosz, middleweight champion in the 1930s, was almost impossible. But now the sideways stance favored by Yarosz and other defense-minded practitioners has fallen into general disuse. Fighters today square off, toe to toe. "You hit me and I'll hit you." To take evasive action carries a stigma. In the old days a boxer of inferior natural gifts could prevail over a stronger, quicker opponent by making the right moves. You don't see much of that anymore. Punch-outs are what is wanted on pay per view.

Boxing mirrors society, and society today is in some respects debased. Has there been another time in which fights between women were tolerated? Or those anything-goes "ultimate fighting" abominations -- free-for-alls in a cage? Joyce Carol Oates, in case you haven't had enough of her, wrote that boxing as opposed to undisciplined slugging can be "a highly complex and refined skill belonging solely to civilization." Don't laugh. Who invented boxing? The civilized ancient Greeks, and they handed it down to the civilized but savage ancient Romans. There was no boxing at all in the Dark Ages -- no boxing anywhere until after the Renaissance. In the seventeenth century came the English revival.

Which spread to America, where such molders of opinion as the New York Herald could perceive some "good consequences." As the newspaper noted in 1837, boxing promoted fair play. "Three or four people do not fall upon and beat a single individual" (as in football today and less structured forms of violence). In boxing, observed the Herald, "the single man struck down by his opponent is permitted to rise again and put himself, as it were, in something like a state of equilibrium, and if he chooses to cry, 'Hold, enough!' no bowie knife enters his vitals." It would seem that life in the 1830s, thanks to the noble art, was becoming more humane. As an outlet for hostility and aggression, boxing appeared to be a step forward.

For two hundred years, the English and later the Americans fought with bare knuckles. They fought to a finish, hour after hour. There was lots of blood. "Claret," the boxing writers called it. Sometimes a fighter died of exhaustion, but brain damage was rare. A punch to the head -- a hard punch to the head -- could result in a broken hand. So, prudently, bare-knuckle fighters resorted to cuffing, slashing, gouging, mauling, and bear-hugging.

The Marquess of Queensberry rules, introducing gloves, three-minute rounds, and the ten count, eliminated much of the gore but also made boxing more lethal. Wrapped in a few ounces of tape and padded leather, the fist was a more dangerous percussive instrument. Although prize-fighting wasn't as messy as in the old days, the after-effects could be worse. And yet, compared with the Roman cestus -- a blackjack conveniently lashed onto the hand -- the boxing glove is benign. Cosmetically, we have come a long way.

PART FIVE
Exotica

Billy Soose may have been the greatest amateur fighter in history, amassing an imposing record of 170-6, plus three Golden Gloves titles and the US Amateur Crown. As a pro he became middleweight champion but retired eight months later, former heavyweight champion Gene Tunney personally recruiting him into the Navy in the aftermath of the Japanese bombing of Pearl Harbor. (Photo courtesy of Douglas Cavanaugh)

CHAPTER 31
THE SINGULAR SENEGALESE

1

Stefan Lorant was the original Zelig. He knew the kind of people that other people only read about. In his time, which covered all but a few years of the twentieth century, for he was 96 when he died in 1998, Lorant knew everybody everywhere, or so it seemed.

Better than he might have wished, Lorant knew Adolf Hitler. In Munich in the late 1920s and early 1930s, Lorant was the editor of a magazine called *Munchner Illustrierte* (circulation 750,000) and Hitler was the editor of a magazine called *Beobachter Illustrierte* (circulation 10,000). "I met him once, in a beer garden," Lorant recalled. "We were sitting with other journalists, and Hitler did all the talking. He talked about the same things over and over. He talked about the Versailles Treaty. He talked about the unfairness of blaming Germany for the First World War. He talked about the steep reparations Germany had been forced to pay. I thought to myself, 'What a bore,' and went to another table."

The day after Hitler took power, the Gestapo came looking for Lorant. As an "enemy of the Third Reich," he spent the next six months in jail. Lorant was Hungarian, and he knew the right people in Hungary -- government officials who still had some influence with Hitler. Against all odds, Hitler listened to them and set Lorant free.

It behooved him, he decided, to get out of Germany as fast as he could. Proficient in English, he made his way to London and did well there. By 1938 he was editing Picture Post, a magazine with a circulation of one and a half million. He had written a book, "I Was Hitler's Prisoner," and he knew almost everybody important, Winston Churchill included. When the Second World War started and Churchill became prime minister, he sent for Lorant. "I can't be modest about this," Lorant used to say. "He told me I must go to America. He felt that sooner or later America would be in the war. 'Find out what Americans are thinking,' he said. 'Write about it for your magazine.'"

To Lorant, the United States had been "Al Capone, Cecil B. DeMille, marathon dancing, goldfish eating, and flagpole sitting." A seven-week tour of the country expanded his point of view. Divorced from his first wife, a Russian ballet dancer, he made up his mind to come and live here. In Great

Britain, he was Churchill's information collector but also a registered alien. He moved to this country in 1940, when Britain was at war with Germany, applied for citizenship, and settled down eventually in the Berkshire Hills of Massachusetts.

In London, Lorant had known H. G. Wells, George Bernard Shaw, and Aneurin Bevan. He knew the U.S. ambassador, Joseph Kennedy. He knew Sigmund Freud. For purposes of research, Freud had questioned him about Adolf Hitler's sexual orientation, and Lorant was able to confirm that Hitler liked women. Lorant liked women himself. Among the women he liked and knew and went out with in Munich was Geli Raubal -- Hitler's niece. He was never willing to speculate on the reason for Geli's suicide, attributed by some to the nature of her relationship with Hitler.

In the United States, he met, married, and eventually parted with a Harvard graduate student forty years his junior. In his sixties, although he never had been to college, he became a Harvard graduate student himself. He knew Henry Steele Commager, Sinclair Lewis, the two Arthur Schlesinger's, Leonard Bernstein, and Norman Rockwell. He knew the department-store impresario Edgar J. Kaufmann, who had read the "pictorial" histories that were now Lorant's specialty and urged him to write a book about Pittsburgh. Lorant almost laughed in his face, but Kaufmann was unrelenting. He badgered Lorant into a three-day exploratory trip on which the reluctant visitor discovered to his surprise that Pittsburgh was "a microcosm of America." With no further prodding, Lorant wrote the book -- put it together, actually, utilizing the work of contributors. A labor of ten years, it was published in 1964 and periodically updated into the 1990s. "Pittsburgh, the Story of an American City," was its durable author's most durable production.

Lorant of course came to know the architects of Pittsburgh's first Renaissance, David L. Lawrence and Richard King Mellon. In other parts of the country, his circle of acquaintances was a wide one. He knew certain legendary movie actresses, having been a director and cameraman in the Berlin of the 1920s. (He liked to talk about the time a good-looking but overweight fraulein came to him for a screen test. The poor thing, he could see, had no talent. He advised her to go home, find a husband, and raise children. That was how he met Marlene Dietrich, who disregarded his counsel but accepted him as a friend. For the rest of her life, which was almost as long as his, they kept in touch.) He knew the sexiest film goddess of them all, Marilyn Monroe. She had read, or said she had read, a book by Lorant, a pictorial biography of Lincoln. And he knew Greta Garbo. In New York, where she lived after the Hollywood years, they would go to the movies together, Garbo wearing dark glasses, a phantom-of-the-opera cloak, and a black hat with the brim pulled down over her eyes. She hated to be stared at, she complained to Lorant, hated to be asked for an autograph. "Dah-ling," he assured her, "take off your disguise and no one will recognize you."

He knew a young Massachusetts congressman named John Fitzgerald Kennedy, the son of his old London acquaintance, but only by repute until Kennedy dropped in on him one day, unannounced, and said without preamble, "What was Mr. Lincoln doing in a theater on Good Friday?" Lorant said, "Maybe he wasn't a Catholic." Kennedy then explained the purpose of his call. He was running for the Senate and wanted a few choice Lincoln quotations to use in his campaign speeches. Lorant served them up cafeteria style. If Lincoln had been a contemporary, Lorant would have known him.

He knew Henry R. Luce, the publisher, and as a matter of course his wife, Clare Boothe Luce -- editor, playwright, congresswoman, and diplomat. At selecting and cropping pictures to tell a story, Lorant was acknowledged to be a genius, "the godfather of photojournalism," and Henry Luce consulted him on the layout for the first issue of Life.

As a musician, which he started out to be, Lorant was something a bit less than a genius, but otherwise he may not have made the acquaintance, if he did make the acquaintance, of Franz Kafka. It either happened or did not happen when he was 20 years old, an unemployed violinist looking for a job in a small Czech town on the German border. Thinking back on it years later, he had an uncanny feeling that the stranger who told him a fiddler could find work playing background music for silent films at the movie theater just down the street must have been Kafka. So quite possibly he knew the author of "Metamorphosis," however briefly. Unless the stranger was somebody else.

There's a question about that -- a pretty big one. But for certain Lorant knew Battling Siki, as vivid a personality, not to put too fine a point on it, as any or all of the above.

2

Between September 24, 1922, when he knocked out Georges Carpentier in Paris, and March 17, 1923, Battling Siki was light-heavyweight champion of the world. His fight with Carpentier, in those days still the idol of France, is remembered by connoisseurs of the bizarre. Siki, a round-faced, unsophisticated black man from the French West African colony of Senegal, had beaten a lot of nobodies in places like Algiers, Rotterdam, Marseilles, and Barcelona. Together with an impressive physique, his record, dubious as it was, made him an acceptable-looking title contender. And yet the fight with Carpentier had an odor of fishiness about it. Right up to the moment they entered the ring at an outdoor arena called, for some reason, the Buffalo Velodrome, there were rumors of a fix.

Carpentier's manager, Francois Descamps, was the kingpin of boxing in France, a man who controlled things. He had assembled around Carpentier a hard-working stable of lesser lights. Referees, judges, and sportswriters belonged to him, too, people said. One year before, in 1921, he had pulled off his greatest managerial coup by steering Carpentier into the successfully marketed Battle of the Century with heavyweight champion Jack Dempsey.

The Battle of the Century filled a huge wooden bowl that was built for the occasion by promoter Tex Rickard on an empty tract of land near Jersey City, and the gate receipts were far in excess of the hoped-for, unprecedented sum of a million dollars. Dempsey, as expected, demolished Carpentier, who weighed no more than 170 pounds, but without doing harm to the handsome and graceful Frenchman's reputation. Carpentier had a fast right hand, which he landed effectively midway through the second round -- landed it three times in a row, staggering Dempsey. This one demonstration of brilliance, this heart-stopping burst of incandescence, gave rise to the myth that Dempsey was on the brink of defeat. In reality more surprised than hurt, he shook off the blows and returned to the job of punishing Carpentier. In another two rounds the fight was over.

When the knuckles he had broken on Dempsey's chin were mended, Carpentier got ready for Siki by knocking out a couple of English fighters in London. Knocking out Brits was nothing unusual for Carpentier. Far from resenting him for it, English boxing fans were enthralled. In the hero-worshipping press, he was Gorgeous Georges, the Orchid Man. Novelist Arnold Bennett, recording his thoughts in the minutes before the bell rang for

Carpentier's fight with Joe Beckett, wrote that "nobody could have taken him for a boxer. He might have been a barrister, a poet, a musician, a Foreign Office attaché, a fellow of All Souls, but not a boxer. He had an air of intellectual or artistic distinction." The Prince of Wales, later Edward VIII, invited Carpentier to St. James Palace for tea. George Bernard Shaw had predicted with foolish confidence that he would overcome Dempsey. When the opposite happened, David Lloyd George, the prime minister, cabled to the loser, "I admire you more than ever."

The French, although proud of Carpentier, were by nature more blasé than the English, and they had idolized the gorgeous one for too many years. A professional since the age of 14, he had been the champion of France in every weight division, but he was now 27 and clearly on the wane. Without any doubt, he could handle the likes of Siki, and yet . . . Descamps was not a manager of the kind who took chances. And what would the unskilled African have to lose, after all, by doing business? As fight day approached, the fix rumors multiplied.

Siki and Carpentier had one thing in common: distinguished World War records. Carpentier was a decorated reconnaissance pilot, Siki a rifleman in the French Army's 8th Colonial Infantry Regiment who had won the ultimate decoration, the Croix de Guerre, for capturing nine Germans, herding them into a shell hole, and exploding a few hand grenades in their midst. On top of that, he had won the Medaille Militaire for bravery under fire.

He had not yet acquired a nickname. That was to come later, in America, where sportswriters called him the Singular Senegalese. They called him other things, too -- "child of nature," for example, and "jungle man" -- that were racist in tone and exaggerated his lack of refinement. The story was that a Frenchwoman, an actress on tour in West Africa, had taken a fancy to Siki when he was not yet into his teens. She put him to work as her "pageboy" and gave him a new name, Louis Phal, from which the sportswriters drew ribald conclusions. Siki's ring name, coined by an imaginative promoter, was equally synthetic. It sounded "African," the promoter believed.

Nobody ever had fought like Siki, whose acrobatic leaping and lunging bewildered his opponents and entertained the customers. In or out of the ring, he was playful, impulsive, exuberant, emotional. He boasted that he trained on wine. Away from the gym, he preferred absinthe.

Even by Siki's standards, his fight with Carpentier was a strange one. It took place in the afternoon before the largest boxing crowd in European history, fifty-five thousand. Shortly after the opening bell, Siki went down on one knee for no apparent reason. The referee, a man named Henri Bernstein, ordered him to get up.

For the first two rounds, Siki threw very few punches and did not come close to landing one. Carpentier pursued him, but Siki was a tantalizing prey . . . jumping around, hopping up and down. At the start of the third round, the scenario was the same -- Siki retreating and Carpentier chasing him, flailing away. Twice after taking light blows, Siki dropped to one knee. Another time, without being hit at all, he went into a full squat, resting for a moment on his haunches.

At last when Carpentier actually did knock him down, unleashing the famous right, he stayed on one knee for a count of seven. Then he bounded to his feet and attacked. Unbelievably, Carpentier himself went down, for a count of four. From then on, Siki hammered him. Often they were head to head, floundering, hanging onto each other. Once when Carpentier swung and missed, he sprawled on all fours. When Siki, pulling out of a clinch, fell over backwards, Carpentier helped him get up. Showing no gratitude, Siki continued to batter the champion.

In the sixth round, finally, an avalanche of punches sent Carpentier spiraling to the canvas, one leg entangled with one of Siki's. He was clearly out cold, his other leg caught in the middle strand of the ropes, but two attendants climbed into the ring and carried him to his corner before the referee's count reached ten.

Bernstein then disqualified Siki for "tripping" Carpentier. The fifty-five thousand spectators erupted. Regardless of their affection for the Orchid Man, they wanted justice. Wrote Edwin L. James in the New York Times: "A mighty roar went up. Women screamed, men shouted." The men, hundreds of them anyway, stormed the ring. Gendarmes surrounded Bernstein to protect him from bodily harm. In the confusion, Descamps made his escape. Descamps, you might say, decamped.

The crowd, still furious, refused to disperse, and three alarmed officials from the French Federation of Boxing went into a huddle. Forty-five minutes later, reversing the referee, they declared Battling Siki the winner. Notified of this in his dressing room, he burst into tears. It was his usual way of relieving stress, or of showing happiness.

Rumors of a fix became rumors of a fix gone wrong. Rapidly the word spread that Carpentier had been the victim of a double-cross. The new champion, meanwhile, was enjoying his renown. He strolled the Champs Elysees with a monkey perched on his shoulder and a lion cub trailing him on a leash. He drank astonishing quantities of absinthe and even larger amounts of champagne. His only appearance in a ring was as a second for a fighter he knew. When the other man knocked his friend out, Siki rushed across the ring and assaulted the winning fighter's manager. The Boxing Federation promptly suspended him, and British officials rescinded their approval of a Siki-Beckett match, depriving him of a chance to beat Carpentier's time-of-knockout record against Beckett, thirty seconds.

Disconsolate, Siki appealed to the Senegalese representative in the French Chamber of Deputies. To this official, he confessed that there indeed had been an understanding with Francois Descamps. In the first round and again in the third, he was to take a short count as confirmation that the deal was on. In the fourth, he was to go down and stay down. But out of "pride and loyalty to the public" he had changed his mind.

The Senegalese deputy could do nothing for Siki through the government. He called a press conference, however, at which Siki repeated his story. It was an obvious case, the deputy told the reporters, of society exploiting a simple, uneducated immigrant. At these words, wrote John Lardner in a 1949 New Yorker piece, Siki wept. The Boxing Federation, unmoved, voted to continue his suspension.

Shortly afterward, it took up the question of whether his fight with Carpentier had been on the level. At a public hearing, Siki's manager, a small-timer named Heller's, denied any knowledge of a fix attempt. So did Descamps. So did Carpentier, fully recovered from his fight injuries. In the final moments of the sixth round, he had sprained an ankle. Only Bernstein, the referee, backed up Siki. "In the fourth round," he testified, "I heard Carpentier say, 'Will you lie down? Get down!'" On January 16, 1923, almost four months after the fight, the Boxing Federation declared Carpentier and Descamps innocent of all charges.

3

At the height of Siki's celebrity, a film crew from Germany made a movie in Paris that was based on his life, with Siki himself in the leading role. Stefan Lorant, 21 at the time, was the cameraman.

"The movie was called 'Dunkle Gassen' -- 'Dark Streets' or 'Dark Lanes.' I prefer 'Dark Streets.' It sounds better in English that way," Lorant reminisced.

"Siki was no actor," he said, "but we were pals. In the morning, he would come to the studio and kiss me on both cheeks -- that was his greeting. He was interested in the camera. I told him, 'I will make you beautiful so all the girls will love you.'"

Siki did have a girl who loved him -- "his wife," Lorant said. "She was a lovely Dutch woman, very blond, slim, as tall as Siki. I don't know if they were married or just living together. Anyway, this girl was his business manager. She spoke German. I don't remember whether Siki spoke German. His language was French, but he could speak a little English. The three of us conversed in a mishmash of languages -- English, French, German.

"Siki was like a child, a sweetie pie. He always needed love. One day he was warming up for his fight scene. He had the bag there, the punching bag. They put it up, and *bim, bim, bim* -- he hit it for my amusement. Fantastic. Siki could make music with a punching bag.

"Another time, he was lying on the floor in his boxing trunks. He said, 'Jump on my stomach.' I said, 'What do you mean? I will hurt you.' I was the same size as Siki -- 175 pounds, 5 feet 11. He said, 'Do it.' I got up on a table and I did it. I jumped. It was like coming down on a rock.

"We had this lamp in the studio. You weren't supposed to look at it. We did, and we both got conjunctivitis. So he came to me like a child and he put his head on my shoulder and he cried like a little baby. I said, 'Now, look -- it will go away.' And a woman came with cold compresses. Always he needed love. He put his head on my shoulder and he cried because it hurt, poor guy. The tears were coming, and we telephoned for a doctor, and the doctor put some drops in our eyes. Those ghastly lamps, I shouldn't have looked at them. But I did, and Siki did, too."

It might appear that, for a prizefighter, Siki's threshold of pain was surprisingly low, but there are other, contradictory clues. Late in his career, being pummeled by Paul Berlenbach, a light-heavyweight with a heavyweight's punch, Siki just laughed. He appeared to be having the time of his life. Westbrook Pegler wrote: "The more Paul slugged him, the more he seemed to enjoy the joke." At any rate, although Siki told the press that he could not allow Carpentier to beat him because of pride, the reason he gave Lorant was different, and at odds with his behavior in the Berlenbach fight: Carpentier, he said, had broken a promise not to hit hard.

It was Lorant who brought up the subject of the knockout, asking Siki, "How did it happen?"

And Siki said, "Oh, that son of a bitch!" He was talking about Carpentier. "My manager said I would get good money -- good money for going down. I said, 'OK, but I don't want to be hurt.' He said, 'You won't be.' Then in the ring we played around, and Carpentier hit me. And I said, 'You don't supposed to do that.' I was so mad. I said to myself, 'I won't let this bastard do this to me.' I started hitting, and the next thing I saw, he was on the floor, knocked out. And my manager said, 'My God, what have you done?' And I said, 'He hit me.'"

Lorant was in Paris while the Boxing Federation investigated. "The sportswriters knew the whole story, but I don't think they wrote it," he said. "At that time, journalism was a profession of decent people. If somebody did something wrong -- cheated on his wife, say -- they didn't put it in the paper. Nowadays, they put everything in. There was much better contact between sportswriters and athletes then."

Undoubtedly. For better or for worse. At any rate. the press, if not the public, accepted the investigating committee's report uncritically. "The fallen idol" -- Carpentier-- "can hold his head high again," wrote the Paris correspondent of the New York Times, leaving it for the reader to decide just how high that would be, given the thoroughness of Carpentier's defeat. Farther down in the story, the Times man strove for perspective. "Whatever the actual truth is," he asserted, "the fight was an inglorious affair."

Re-examining the evidence after twenty-five years, John Lardner concluded that the actual truth was just as Siki had told it. "My own opinion," he wrote, "is that being champion constituted Siki's chief sin in the eyes of the Federation." Even today, the films of the fight are extraordinarily clear, and they bear out Siki's contention that he dropped to one knee in the first and third rounds voluntarily. "A 'sign of good faith' -- a preliminary fall or lapse of some other kind -- is a standard device in the plotting of sports frameups," Lardner wrote. "Besides," he went on, "Siki's tale confirmed the rumors that were current before and after the fight; it was in keeping with the character of Descamps and of Continental boxing methods in 1922, and it is believed by every European and American I know who was familiar in any degree with the time, the place, and the actors."

Of Siki's two explanations for not taking a dive, the more plausible is the one he gave to Lorant -- that he double-crossed Carpentier because Carpentier double-crossed him first, by going back on a pledge to pull his punches. Getting hit is an occupational hazard in boxing, but getting hit for the sake of appearances, to make a fake fight look authentic, probably seemed unnecessary to Siki, and Carpentier had to pay for overdoing things. Siki's talk of honor, pride, and so forth comes across as just that -- talk. Referee Bernstein, in his testimony, recalled hearing Siki say to Carpentier, "Don't hit so hard. What is the use to hit so hard when it is all settled?" As Westbrook Pegler observed some time later, Siki tried desperately to understand civilization but never quite got the idea.

Ultimately, his naivete cost him the championship. Still under suspension in France and estranged from his manager, he agreed to defend the title against an Irishman, Mike McTigue, on St. Patrick's Day, 1923, in Dublin. The locale, the date, and the nationality of his opponent meant nothing to Siki, nor did the fact that a Sinn Fein insurrection was going on. Siki's only hope was to win by a knockout, and McTigue dispelled any chance of that. In a fog of cigar smoke, he backpedaled shamelessly for the entire twenty rounds, pausing once or twice to stick his left in Siki's face. The decision in McTigue's favor, announced over the sound of Irish rebels firing on British troops outside the arena, surprised no one. Neither then nor afterward, at least for the record, did Siki claim he'd been robbed, but it was one more example of his failure to comprehend the ways of the world.

4

"Dunkle Gassen" opened at movie theaters in Germany the following August. The reviews were not good. Siki's loss of the championship couldn't have helped at the box office, but Stefan Lorant believed that the film made some money. Its entire cost, he explained, was no more than a few thousand dollars.

The Federation had lifted Siki's suspension, and he boxed once in Paris, winning by a knockout from an opponent of no consequence, before an American manager named Bob Levy brought him to the United States. His first fight on these shores, at Madison Square Garden in New York, was with the very competent Kid Norfolk, who trounced him. After that, the only fights he won were with second- and third-raters. In Lorraine, Ohio, one night, after eight dreary rounds with Mike Conroy, he announced, "I quit," walked over to Conroy's corner, kissed him on both cheeks, and left the ring.

Still popular because of his crowd-pleasing style, he earned, by one account, more than one hundred thousand dollars during his two years in America, the last two years of his life. He spent and tipped lavishly and dressed like an English lord: white tie and tails at night; silk hat, frock coat, and striped pants in the daytime. He wore spats, a red Ascot tie, and a monocle, and he carried a gold-headed cane. When he was drunk he would rough up cab drivers, bartenders, and even policemen, getting himself into trouble. Eventually the New York State Athletic Commission suspended him. At the hearing, Siki wept.

He was now unwelcome back in France, and he was indisputably married -- to a woman from Memphis, Tennessee, Lillian Werner. The "lovely Dutch girl" of his movie-making days turned out to have been a common-law wife. She lived in a suburb of Paris with the child she had named Battling Siki, Jr. "Could I have a better wedding certificate?" she asked.

Siki's suspension prompted the Immigration and Naturalization Service to threaten him with deportation. Instead of moderating his behavior, he continued to hang out in speakeasies, drinking and brawling. On December 16, 1925, the New York World ran a story that began: "Just before dawn yesterday, a policeman found a powerful black man dead in the gutter of West 41st Street near Ninth Avenue with two bullet holes in his back." West 41st Street near Ninth Avenue was in a part of New York called Hell's Kitchen. The Singular Senegalese had come to an end that was hardly singular for the neighborhood in which he caroused.

He left an estate valued at six hundred dollars to his American widow. In March 1926, police arrested a 19-year-old hoodlum and charged him with Siki's murder. He was indicted, held in the Tombs for seven months, and then released. The only evidence against him, an overheard telephone conversation, was too insubstantial to warrant his prosecution.

Stefan Lorant, who knew Siki, thought of him in personal terms. He was an unforgettable eccentric: good-humored, lovable -- a "sweetie pie." The ironists of his day regarded him as more of a case study. He was the uprooted primitive, confused by the rules of a higher social order. To Siki, it must have seemed that the rules were double-edged. He learned this painfully, from various instructors.

They were the people who hung medals on Siki for killing German soldiers and telephoned the police when he impulsively used his fists in a bar-room altercation. Who offered him money to take part in a crooked fight and ran him out of town for turning it into an honest one. Who winked at Prohibition but not at public intoxication. Life made more sense in his native Senegal, where it was reasonable to expect that you could get to the final chapter without being shot in the back.

CHAPTER 32
ATHLETE OF THE CENTURY

(ED Note: Roy McHugh speaks of Muhammad Ali in the present tense as the chapter was written years before Ali passed away in 2016.)

1

On the afternoon of November 29, 1961, in room 806 of the Sheraton-Seelbach Hotel in Louisville, Kentucky, Cassius Marcellus Clay, Jr. -- he was not yet Muhammad Ali -- came rolling out from under the bed, jumped to his feet, and, with an energetic display of shadow boxing, introduced himself to me.

Unforgettable first impressions were his specialty.

I had driven over from Evansville, Indiana, for the fight at Freedom Hall that night between Clay and Willi Besmanoff, a German-Jewish heavyweight of no great distinction. Public interest in Clay was on the rise. Still a newly-minted professional, not quite 20 years old, he had won all nine of his previous fights, living up to the promise he had shown as light-heavyweight gold medalist at the 1960 Olympic games in Rome. His repartee, I had read, was as quick as his left jab, the quickest in Rome, and I'd been wanting to write about him for my paper, the Evansville Sunday Courier and Press.

On the house phone in the hotel lobby I called his trainer, Angelo Dundee, an old friend (Angelo was everybody's old friend). "Come on up, Cassius is here," he said right away. "You can get acquainted."

Perfect. But two surprises awaited me when I reached the eighth floor: Angelo's customary breeziness was absent and he appeared to be alone in the room. He *was* alone, he told me, looking glum. He said that Cassius had left abruptly, by way of the stairs, in order to avoid being interviewed. "He's shy, you know," Angelo explained, his voice full of bogus sincerity. "Newspapermen scare him to death." As I stood there wondering what the game was, out from under the bed popped Clay.

Muhammad Ali, "Athlete of the Century," venerated folk hero, igniter of the Olympic flame at the 1996 games in Atlanta, is a demi-god now, his place in the mythology secure, but a demi-god punished for the gift that sustained bim. He suffers from what the doctors called Parkinson's Syndrome, almost surely the result of the battering he took in the ring. When last he appeared in public, he shuffled. His face was puffy. His hands shook.

And there was one last irony, the bitterest of all: his affliction had left him mute. In Atlanta, where the head of the International Olympic Committee draped a special gold medal around his neck, a replacement for the medal Ali won in Rome and impulsively tossed into the Ohio River (he said) after returning to segregated Louisville, he could only manage to whisper.

For ability plus charisma, no other boxer ever equaled Ali, but it was not for his physical prowess alone that GQ magazine, jumping the gun a little, named him Athlete of the Century in 1998. His stand against the war in Vietnam, or, more precisely, the "intellectual courage" it demanded, placed him with Babe Ruth, Joe Louis, Jackie Robinson, and Michael Jordan as one of those rare athletes, and the greatest of them, for he "towered above the competition," who "actually forced a seismic shift in society." He "transcended his sport, transcended all sports," and became, in the process, "the first truly global athlete." All this according to GQ.

My vision failed me, I admit, on that long-ago afternoon in Louisville. Little did I suspect that an intellectually courageous, world-wide, transcendent seismic force -- in the larval stage, of course -- was rolling out from under the bed. Instead, there materialized a smooth-cheeked adolescent prankster. He had reached his full height, 6 feet 2 ½ inches, and would weigh, for the fight with Besmanoff, 193 pounds. "Interviewing" him turned out to be effortless. You did not ask questions for fear of interrupting the flow. He had the clear, resonant baritone of a revival-tent spellbinder, and the words poured out as though memorized. There were no halting sentences to be pushed along a phrase at a time with that overworked little verbal engine "yuh know."

He talked, for the most part, of his plan to win the heavyweight championship -- held, at the time, by Floyd Patterson, but certain to become the property of Sonny Liston, everyone thought, if ever the twain should meet. When they did meet, Liston demolished Patterson, taking care of the job in less than two minutes. A scowling ex-con with a police record as long as his knockout record, Liston appeared to radiate an almost visible hostility. Combined with his size and strength, the effect was so intimidating to weak-willed opponents like Patterson that they entered the ring feeling doomed. Cassius Clay took a look at this ogre and saw personified the chance of a lifetime. "Way they buildin' Liston up," he pointed out to me that day in his hotel room, "whoever whups him gonna be a hero, man." And fate, Cassius was certain, intended him for the role.

It would be my job, meanwhile, to notify the three hundred thousand or so readers of the Evansville Sunday Courier and Press. "He who tooteth not his own horn," goes a saying attributed to Damon Runyon, "the same shall remain untooted." Cassius believed that implicitly; he believed with equal fervor in the importance of soliciting help. "I got a writer here from True magazine," he informed me, referring, I knew, to Myron Cope, in those days a freelance journalist whose destiny as the voice that would launch the Terrible Towel had not at this early date become manifest even to himself. Almost at once, as though in answer to a summons, came a knock at the door. Angelo Dundee pulled it open, and there, full of purpose, stood Cope.

With him were two companions -- Odessa Clay, the horn tooter's mother, a stately, dignified woman, and Rudolph Clay, his solemn-looking, taciturn younger brother. Cassius, barely giving these newcomers a glance, proceeded with his monologue. Nothing, it seemed, could distract him. In rapid-fire order, he expounded at great length on the flashiness of his footwork; he dismissed with a few words the allegation of certain sportswriters that one thing he lacked was a punch; he scoffed at the notion of Liston's invincibility. Cope, having taken a chair, scribbled away. We both did, while Cassius talked on. He talked and talked and talked, until Angelo, peering through the curtained window, directed our attention to a darkening sky.

"Time to go, time to go," he announced, and Cassius, enlisting Cope and me in an entourage he would lead, called out happily, "Come on! I'll take you to the fight in my pink Cadillac!"

2

Second-hand, but indubitably pink, the Cadillac was a fringe benefit, made possible by the contract Clay had signed with eleven Louisville businessmen. "They're his board of directors," Angelo had told me. "Five of the eleven are millionaires and three more will be millionaires when their daddies die." Millionaires back then were rare birds, looked upon and spoken of with something akin to awe. "They mean well for this boy. They gave him ten thousand dollars to sign the contract and they guarantee him three hundred and thirty dollars a month. He gets thirty percent of his purses on top of the guarantee. They put fifteen percent of what's left into government bonds and fifteen percent into a trust fund." In 1961, when no one could have imagined the value of a property like Clay, that was lavish.

Five of us -- all except Angelo, who had peeled off to travel by other means -- piled into the Cadillac. Rudolph, ordered to drive, drove, with Odessa beside him and Cassius ensconced between his out-of-town visitors in back, the better to communicate. Still thinking long-term -- he had not mentioned Besmanoff even once -- he laid out his time-table.

He must win the heavyweight championship, he stressed, no later than thirty-six days before his twenty-second birthday, which would fall on January 24, 1964. The deadline, it seemed, could not be extended by a tick of the clock past midnight on that date because Patterson, Cassius reminded us, had won the title thirty-*five* days before his twenty-second birthday, thereby becoming the youngest heavyweight champion ever. "He made history," Cassius declared. It was necessary, therefore, to break Patterson's record. "And when I do it -- when I win the title . . . "

He pounded a fist into his palm. "Boom! *Double* history!"

Outside Freedom Hall was the proof that such goals were attainable -- a huge electric signboard advertising: CASSIUS CLAY vs. WILLI BESMANOFF. "Mama," said Cassius excitedly, leaning forward, "remember when I tell you I wanna see my name up there? Well, now look!" As inspired as Keats must have been at the sight of a Grecian urn, he burst into poetry.

"Yeah, yeah, look at the lights,
"All the people come here whenever Cassius fights. "

We tumbled out of the car. "Move closer, like you're my bodyguards," he instructed Cope and me, looming over us. Side by side, if not shoulder to shoulder, we navigated the parking lot, two tugboats escorting an ocean liner.

No trace of nervousness was visible in Clay. Seated on a table in the dressing room, he massaged his gleaming chest with Vaseline. "This is when I'm gladdest to be alive, wearin' these nice white trunks and these pretty white shoes," he said dreamily. The trunks and the shoes reminded him of how handsome he was. "I'm gonna stay good lookin'," he promised. "I don't ever wanna get my face smashed up."

His face was stern and businesslike as he danced down the aisle to the ring. Beetle-browed Besmanoff, shorter than Cassius, and stockier, waited impatiently, glowering. An experienced journeyman who prided himself on giving promoters and customers their money's worth, Besmanoff carried a grudge into the fight. He knew that Cassius had called him an "unrated bum" on a television show the night before. Trash talk, back then, was uncommon. Although not the inventor of that juvenile art form -- Two Ton Tony Galento was calling his opponents bums in the 1930s -- Cassius created the fad, which would soon infest basketball and football. And now it was time to back up his words.

Nothing could have been easier. Cassius set the pattern right from the start. Icily efficient, he peppered the German with jabs and straight rights and banged him with hooks and uppercuts. As round followed round, he landed more often and harder. Besmanoff, swinging hopelessly at an out-of-reach, springy-legged target, pounded the air.

In round six -- there were reasons for this -- Cassius eased up and heard boos. From the rear of the auditorium a foghorn voice thundered: "I thought you were gonna finish it early." Cassius, it was true, had called the round, had said more than once that "Besmanoff must fall," but the round he had called was the seventh, not the sixth, and in the seventh round Besmanoff did fall. To be exact, he fell twice, the second time flat on his back. The referee counted to two and then stopped.

Afterward, unlacing the pretty white shoes, Cassius had thoughts about the nature of fight fans. There was just no pleasing them, whatever their loyalties. "Knock a man out too soon, and they boo. Wait around too long, and they boo just as much." All you could do about it was shrug.

3

Myron Cope's story for True was the first full-length profile of Clay in a national magazine. It won a journalism prize (best sports magazine story of the year) and invigorated a months-old debate over whether or not Clay could fight.

In New York, where reputations were made, he was vaguely perceived as just a blowhard, not that the New York boxing critics had seen him in the flesh. When they did, they were less than overwhelmed. "He throws right-hand leads," a big-name columnist told me. "I know another guy who did that. He's driving a taxi now."

Angelo Dundee admitted that Clay had "defects," which he would overcome. Angelo's pupil, unchastened, referred to his defects as his style. He was rangy and fast and he knew his capabilities. Besides leading on occasion with his right, he carried his hands low and pulled away from punches instead of slipping or blocking them, the approved technique. Fight experts shook their heads. Editors, meanwhile, had discovered that Clay was good copy, and late in the summer of 1962, with an assignment from Sport magazine, I found myself back in Louisville, tracking his every move just as Cope had.

Again, he was more than cooperative. We met at curbside in front of the Sheraton-Seelbach, Cassius behind the wheel of his gorgeous pink Cadillac. "I'm gonna drive you around town and let you see how I am," he said as I got into the car.

How he was less of a secret than on my earlier visit. He had won five more fights, two of them in New York. Out in Los Angeles, he had put away Alejandro Lavorante, a South American, in five rounds. Also, in Los Angeles, Archie Moore had needed ten to dispose of the same opponent, so Los Angeles would be the site of a showdown between Lavorante's conquerors. (It is thought that the two knockouts in so short a time span accounted for the fact that a third fight that year, with the supposedly unthreatening George Ringer, proved to be Lavorante's last. Taken from the arena to a hospital, he died there of a brain hemorrhage.)

Priming himself for Moore, Cassius was resolved to outtalk as well as outfight the old windbag. Moore was the sporting world's supreme elocutionist -- garrulous, inventive, polysyllabic, relentless. But now a fresh new contender with fresh new material had appeared.

Vocabulary and wisdom favored Moore. Clay, by comparison, seemed a whippersnapper whose voice was still changing. In their first long-distance exchange, Moore's experience told. "I am working on a new punch for Clay -- the lip buttoner," he announced. "I got a new punch, too," retorted Cassius, playing catch-up. "I call it the old-age pension punch." The first rhetorical round belonged to Moore, it was clear, but Cassius had become the aggressor.

"Here's how I want you to put this," he said, easing us into traffic. "There's not a heavyweight in the ring as fast as I am, there's not a heavyweight who punches as fast and hard, there's not a heavyweight has the footwork that I do, there's not a heavyweight as smart as I am. I am the boldest fighter in the ring today, the most talked-about fighter -- and know why?" He paused to create suspense. "My big mouth!" He was smiling in a pleased sort of way. Underneath the dashboard, a record player throbbed. Rudolph Clay, alone in the back seat and silent until now, harmonized gently with the lyrics, his voice a soft, sad falsetto.

Cassius pulled into a service station, parked at the car wash, and leaped out. A brush in one hand, a hose in the other, he immediately went to work on the chrome. Rudolph, seizing a whiskbroom, busied himself inside the car. The service-station attendant looked on benignly. "You're pretty good at that job," he said to the hard-working pair. "You're better at that job than I am."

Oblivious to the water stains on his polo shirt, Cassius scrubbed the fenders and hood. The attendant -- deemed capable, apparently, of unskilled labor -- filled the tank. From a distance, a small boy was watching. Cassius beckoned to him.

"Come over here. Know who I am?"

A hesitant "No."

"Who the best boxer in Louisville?"

More hesitation. "Don' know."

"Ever hear of Cassius Clay?"

The boy grinned.

"Well, I am Cassius Clay. Remember that -- hear?"

The education of the young taken care of, Cassius now asked if Sport magazine writers had generous expense accounts. I can take a hint; I paid for the gasoline. Cassius, back behind the wheel, flicked on the ignition and then flicked it off. "Hey, get that," he ordered the attendant, pointing to a speck on the windshield. "Somethin' like that run me crazy."

"Don't go crazy, man," drawled the attendant, removing the speck.

The Cadillac sparkled in the afternoon sun. Past garages, past billboards, past vacant lots, we drove to the San-Se-Re barber shop, which occupied a low wooden building on a corner. Cassius, tiptoeing, glided unseen through a side entrance. With a loud popping noise, a hollow click of tongue against palate, he announced his presence. Two barbers cutting hair, a man and a woman, snipped away, absorbed in their work.

San-Se-Re, a line on the barber shop's window explained, stood for "Sanitation, Service and Relaxation." There were prints by well-known artists on the wall, among them a self-portrait of the one-eared Van Gogh, who never knew where to stop when he was shaving himself with a straight razor, and a juke box played up-to-date jazz. But for Cassius the main attraction was the young female barber.

He addressed her familiarly as "Country Girl." "She's from a real little town," confided Rudolph under his breath. Darker and more angular than Cassius and not as tall, Rudolph seldom spoke unless spoken to, and then with the utmost brevity. Christened Rudolph Arnett, he had changed his middle name -- his older brother's idea -- to Valentino.

While Rudolph sat morosely, Cassius had fun teasing Country Girl. Delilah-like, she offered to cut his hair. Samson-like, he refused. At length Cassius asked, "What time tonight?" Careful not to be in a hurry about it, Country Girl answered, "Nine o'clock."

On the busy expressway, heading for the two-story, seven-room, red brick house that Cassius had bought for his parents, we flew along at eighty miles an hour. Offhandedly, Cassius remarked that he drove to and from Miami Beach, where Angelo supervised his training, because airplanes were unsafe. Still up near eighty, the Cadillac zoomed into an exit.

"Can we make the turn, can we make the turn?" Cassius screeched.

Tires screeching too, we made the turn.

`` The neat little house in the suburbs was furnished in grays and pinks. Cassius Clay, Sr., Odessa Clay, and a relative named Antonio Greathouse were gathered in the kitchen for an early dinner, and Rudolph Clay promptly joined them. Cassius, Jr., after parking me in the living room, made a short reconnaissance trip to the kitchen and came back with the word that "what they eatin'" wasn't "good enough" for company.

Denied food, I had reading material -- his half-filled scrapbook, gigantic in size. I had barely dipped into its contents when Cassius, Sr., emerging from the kitchen, set before me a plate of gingerbread -- baked, he said, by himself, and topped with a mound of whipped cream. The gingerbread could not have been tastier

Cassius. Sr. was a wiry, middle-sized man. Calling my attention to a snow scene on the wall, he identified himself as the artist. For a living, he painted houses. His landscapes and portraits were works of the imagination, he said. "I make 'em all up in my head," he informed me.

Antonio Greathouse took over the conversation. In appearance, he resembled Cassius, Sr. Having been a professional boxer in his youth, he imparted training tips to Cassius, Jr. -- tips such as "Keep your hands active and keep 'em soft. When you go into combat, get 'em tough." There were others, like "chew a big wad of gum on the way to the ring." "That's what Sugar Ray Robinson does," Antonio went on. "It's the reason he can take so much punishment. Gum keeps the mouth damp. They think they got Sugar Ray hurt, and then that ol' man, he just *rain* on 'em."

While Antonio and Cassius, Sr., entertained me, Cassius, Jr., and Rudolph disappeared. They had gone to their rooms to nap. Thirty minutes later, refreshed, the brothers reappeared, ready for the evening.

"Don't drive fast," Mrs. Clay called after us as we left. Antonio Greathouse piped up with: "Fast drivers die young. Not but one fast driver still alive, and that's Eddie Rickenbacker." Cassius, Jr., winked at me. "They know I roll," he said, and we rolled at high speed to the San-Se-Re, where Country Girl still was on duty.

Disregarding Samson's fate, Cassius allowed her to cut his hair, and then we rolled at high speed to Country Girl's rooming house. While she went upstairs to change from her white linen hair-trimmer's smock into something more appropriate for a night on the town, the rest of us sat in the parlor, Cassius chatting with Country Girl's landlady, Rudolph tight-lipped and detached. When Country Girl came back down, a chaperone -- her mother -- was in attendance.

Crowded into the Cadillac, we drove a short distance to Champion Lanes, the neighborhood bowling center. "I'm king here," Cassius announced, quickly adding, "Why do you think they call it Champion Lanes?" In an atmosphere as wholesome as that of a church supper, family groups were clustered around formica-topped tables, and if Cassius was king, Country Girl may have been queen. Greeted joyfully by friends, she accepted an invitation to bowl. "Come and keep score, Mama," she chirped, and they were swept away to the alleys, the ever-subordinate Rudolph trotting along in their wake.

Cassius, free to table hop, remained in the lounge. Like a politician in campaign mode, he worked the room thoroughly -- greeting people, shaking hands . . . kissing babies. "Listen, folks," his body language declared, "I'm running for heavyweight champion and I'd appreciate your vote."

Swiftly, the minutes ticked by. With no hands left to pump, no infants left to nuzzle, Cassius felt a poem coming on. "Ready to write?" he asked. I whipped out my notebook, and he guided me to a table. Speaking deliberately, and watching me put down each word, he said:

"It starts out . . .

"'*They all knew when he stopped in town*

"'*Cassius Clay was the greatest around . . .*'"

He hesitated, reconsidering the meter. "Make that:

"'*Cassius Clay was the greatest* fighter *around . . .* '

"OK . . .

"'*His fights only last a few rounds,*

"'*He even made them look like clowns . . .* '"

There was more in the same vein, with the poet breaking off to ask, "Got that?" several times, or even more often, "Pretty good, ain't it?" Finishing, he intoned:

"'*Some said the greatest was Sugar Ray . . .* '

"Lemme think, now . . . "

Then with unconcealed pride in his spur-of-the-moment creative powers,

"'*But they have yet to see Cassius Clay.* '"

Few are the authors who never plagiarize themselves (it's what I'm doing right now), but I could not help reminding Cassius that those last two lines had been lifted from one of his earlier works. 'Oh, you saw that?' he said, unfazed. "Lotsa people didn't, though. That's still a good way to end it."

Endings, back then, were something you could plan. Thus, our night on the town ended the way Cassius had scripted it. Seeking out Country Girl, he informed her in the voice of a tour guide that our departure from Champion Lanes was imminent. Patiently, we waited while Country Girl, taking her time, continued bowling until the last pin had fallen. Only then did Cassius herd us into the Cadillac for what we all understood to be the evening's grand finale -- a stop at a popular drive-in. Without consultation, he ordered for everybody. We had Big Boy sandwiches, French fries, strawberry milkshakes, and some locally celebrated cheesecake -- Sport magazine's treat and no deviations allowed.

Maybe half an hour later, as we sipped at the dregs of our milkshakes, the carhop handed Cassius a ballpoint pen and a paper napkin. "The girl in that car over there," she said, inclining her head toward the person of whom she spoke, "wants to know if you're Cassius Clay. She wants your autograph."

Cassius looked gratified.

"What are you?" the carhop continued. "A singer, or a boxer, or what?" Cassius glanced at me knowingly. "Are you writin' that down?" he asked.

4

Typically, the rhymester, Cassius had predicted that Moore would fall in four (Mo' in fo'), which Moore did. Then came a dry spell. In the first six months of 1963, he boxed only three times, winning from Charley Powell in Pittsburgh, Doug Jones in New York, and Henry Cooper in London. Against Jones and Cooper, he had not been impressive, but there were no other contenders for the title that now belonged to Liston, Patterson having succumbed again to the fearsome, all-conquering champion in another one-round debacle. While promoters debated the wisdom of sacrificing a novice like Clay to Liston, the novice fretted the summer away in the red brick house in Louisville.

On a torrid July afternoon, I found him at home alone. Bare from the waist up, and wearing neither shoes nor socks, he was stretched out flat on the living-room sofa. Stretched out flat, boxing's wise men all said, was where Liston would leave Cassius if he insisted on an immediate showdown.

Bide your time, was the advice he received. Liston, for a fighter, was old -- older by several years, everyone thought, than his record-book age of 31. Let him wither on the vine. Billy Conn was among the spectators when Cassius belted out Charley Powell, a reformed football player, in three one-sided rounds in a packed Civic Arena the previous January, and afterward Billy cautioned him, "Don't fight Liston for five years."

It may occur to you that Conn, when his opportunity came, had not been a model of prudence. Weighing only 169 pounds, he elected to slug it out with Joe Louis. In any event, Cassius wanted no advice, whatever the source. He had vowed, after all, to be champion no later than thirty-six days before his twenty-second birthday, and time was getting short.

"For three years now," he told me, "I been poppin' off and hollerin' and screamin'. For three years I been callin' the rounds -- Lamar Clark in three, Jimmy Robinson in one, Donnie Fleeman in six, Alex Miteff in six, Willi Besmanoff in seven, George Logan in five, Lavorante in five, Archie Moore in four. For three years I been sayin' I be the youngest champ -- and now I'm predictin' that Liston will fall in eight. I have called him the Big Ugly Bear. I can't stand *him*, he can't stand *me*. And so everything's hot, the right moment is here. It could mean an extra two million at the gate -- youngest champ, Liston in eight -- but if I let this blow past, if I wait another seven, eight months, then it won't be the same thing. A year from now it won't be so big. I won't be the youngest champ, it won't be no record if I win.

"Between now and next year I'd have to have a couple more fights. I might miss a prediction. I might even get cut or somethin' and lose. Put it this way: Say Henry Cooper had whupped me in London, England [Cooper lost by a knockout, but his left hook had put Cassius down]. The fight game would be dead and so would I."

The promoter in Clay was irrepressible. There was something else in his makeup, too, that came to the surface as we talked. By the summer of 1963, no longer in Evansville, I was back with the paper I had left two years earlier, the Pittsburgh Press, but now an Evansville writer named Tom Fox, no stranger to Cassius, was strolling up the sidewalk toward the red brick house, a female friend at his side. She was young, sleek, attractive. Catching sight of them through the screen door, and using a descriptive employed by Cassius himself, I said to him, "Here comes Fox with a fox."

And Cassius panicked. There he was, half naked, with an unknown member of the opposite sex approaching. Only swimmers and strippers perform with fewer clothes on than prizefighters do, but this was apparently different. He jumped off the couch and bounded up the stairs. When he returned, minutes later -- I had meanwhile admitted the two callers -- he was wearing a long-sleeved white dress shirt and white woolen socks. The circumstances, I gathered, did not require shoes.

This extremely odd vein of selective prudery -- the world had not yet learned of his conversion to Islam -- co-existed in Clay with "an enormous interest in girls" (Wilfrid Sheed's phrase). As Muhammad Ali, he married four times and traveled around the country with a harem. He complained that his first wife, Sonji, a non-Muslim girl with a mind of her own, wore skirts that were too short. He kept his second and third wives out of sight in the Islamic tradition while brazenly showing off his "extended family of foxes" (Sheed again).

For the record, his foxes -- and his wives -- were always black. (He married wife No. 4, Yolanda Williams, in 1986, five years after his retirement from the ring. Yolanda Williams, called Lonnie, was from Louisville. Her family and his had been neighbors and friends. When she was still just a child, Cassius had held her on his knee. As improbable as it seems, the groom, 44, and the bride, 29, went off to live on a 400-acre farm in Michigan.)

5

On February 25, 1964, a little too late to be the youngest champ, for he was 22 years old, Cassius took the measure of Sonny Liston, who surrendered in his corner at the start of the seventh round. Reduced to teddy-bear status, Liston claimed a shoulder injury. He did not deceive Cassius. Liston had quit after six, Cassius argued, to sabotage his prediction of a knockout in eight.

Miami Beach was the scene of the fight. Because I missed it, I missed the weigh-in, at which Cassius carried on like a madman, a psychological ploy intended to raise Liston's anxiety level.

Supposedly this was payback. They had met by chance in Las Vegas not long before, and, standing behind Cassius at a craps table, Liston had tapped him on the back. Cassius turned his head and Liston slapped him across the face. "Whu' . . . whudjoo do that for?" Cassius stammered. "Because you're too damn fresh," Liston said, and walked away, believing, as others did, that he had frightened all the brashness out of Clay. Anyway, that was the story.

At the weigh-in, Clay's antics so distracted Liston, the folklorists now have it, that he climbed through the ropes a few hours later with his concentration utterly destroyed. All through the early rounds, Liston padded forward mechanically while Cassius beat a nervous retreat, jabbing as he went and punching in flurries. Cassius was leading on points when Liston, frustrated and spent, took the easy way out.

Nothing could have kept me from the once-postponed return match, held fifteen months later in the small industrial town of Lewiston, Maine, the only place on earth that would tolerate it. Cassius by then was Muhammad Ali, having declared himself, the day after winning the title, a Black Muslim. As such, he was demonized automatically in the eyes of white America. Liston, for his part, had behaved in suspect fashion by giving up so abjectly in their first fight. Mindful of his shadowy past, skeptics said it looked like a fix.

In Miami Beach, Liston had been a 7-1 favorite. At Lewiston the odds were 6-5, Liston again favored. That Clay/Ali had won the first fight meant surprisingly little. Clay/Ali's ability seemed fraudulent to the public because fighting and talking are unrelated arts. Jack Dempsey allowed his manager, the verbally gifted Doc Kearns, to do the talking. Joe Louis spoke in monosyllables or epigrams ("He can run but he can't hide"). Liston, in public, only grumbled or growled.

For another thing, Clay/Ali's looks were deceiving. In the imagination of fight fans, Liston would always be a massive, indestructible brute, whereas Ali -- only Howard Cosell was using his new name at the time, but let's update this -- gave an impression of youthful callowness. In truth, Ali was the bigger man, an inch and a fraction taller than Liston and his equal in sheer bulk now at 210 pounds.

The Lewiston fight, attended by fewer than 2,500 cash customers, took place in an ice-skating rink. After executing dance steps for the first half-minute, Ali knocked Liston down with a right-hand chop to the head. What followed was comic opera.

Ali did not go to a neutral corner, but stood over Liston, screaming at him to get up. Jersey Joe Walcott, the referee, pulled Ali away, but then lost his head and neglected to pick up the count. He was still a few seconds behind the timekeeper, whose count had reached ten with something to spare, when Liston finally lurched to his feet.

Walcott, thoroughly confused, allowed the fight to resume. Unable for some reason to make the bell work, the timekeeper was pounding on the ring apron. At his side, Nat Fleischer, the patriarchal boxing historian, led a chorus of voices clamoring for Walcott's attention. They shouted that the fight was over, Walcott belatedly took their word for it, and Ali had his unwanted knockout, a *denouement* in keeping with the scene, the characters, and the cries of "Fake! Fake! Fake!" from the crowd.

Over the next year or two, Ali was at his best as a fighter. Larry Merchant wrote in the New York Post that Ali's combination of size and speed had never been seen in a heavyweight before. There was nobody else in his class; he toyed with or destroyed every challenger. Meanwhile, his act was wearing thin.

The playful high spirits had acquired a show-business gloss. With repetition, the monkeyshines of his youth -- the prattle, the self-praise, the self-parody, the shopworn disparagement of his rivals -- no longer amused. Then an unexpected mean streak came to the fore.

It wasn't satisfying enough to pin an "Uncle Tom" label on Ernie Terrell, who refused to call him Ali. Such audacity required that Terrell be humiliated in cat-and-mouse fashion. "What's my name?" Ali demanded at the end of each round while winning an easy decision over Terrell. It wasn't satisfying enough to taunt Floyd Patterson ("the Rabbit," Ali called him, plucking another nickname from the animal kingdom). Patterson despised the Black Muslims, a/k/a the Nation of Islam, and had to be ruthlessly shown up in the ring, his punishment prolonged for eleven rounds;

The meanness was something new in Ali, as hard to accept as his Black Muslim persona. To the behavior police, he declared unrepentantly, "I don't have to be what you want me to be."

If most white Americans were never exactly sure what they wanted him to be, it was not a Black Muslim, they knew. In the end, it hardly mattered. The Age of Aquarius was dawning.

At first when he announced, "I don't have nothin' against them Viet Congs" and refused induction into the Army, the reaction was disbelief, followed by outrage. A federal court imposed a $10,000 fine and sentenced him to five years in jail for draft evasion. Boxing commissions took away his license and his title. Newspaper writers excoriated him. Promoters and managers -- men who never had spoken out against mobster control of boxing in the 1930s, 1940s, and 1950s -- denounced Ali in the most scathing terms. "I'm almost ashamed of him," Joe Louis said.

Ali had refused induction on religious grounds. The prevailing theory was that the Black Muslims were using him for their own nefarious purposes. True -- up to a point. But religious zealotry is a self-inflicted condition. Ali was his own man. He knew what he was doing, and he never regretted it. No one could have forced him to act against his own best interests, or what he thought of as his own best interests.

For another thing, Ali used others as much as others used him. When he dismissed his first attorney, the young black woman from Louisville who drew up the contract with his original backers, the millionaires and future millionaires, there was not the faintest tinge of regret. "I don't need her anymore," he said, and that was that. It happened to them all -- his first boxing coach, a Louisville policeman; the millionaires and future millionaires; the discarded wives; Malcolm X, his Nation of Islam mentor; various servitors and sycophants and hangers-on. But not, despite numerous squabbles, to Bundini Brown, originator of the floats-like-a-butterfly, stings-like-a-bee commercial. Again and again they parted company, but always

Ali forgot and forgave, and he stood at Bundini's bedside when Bundini lay dying, paralyzed from a fall and speechless.

Severing ties, though, was never much of a problem for Ali. He could be warm-hearted and charming or cold and aloof, as he chose. Ferdie Pacheco, the doctor in his retinue, described him to me once as "a narcissist, in love with his body, incapable of deep interpersonal relationships." When the punches Ali once evaded with ease started finding their mark, Pacheco urged him to quit. He refused. So Pacheco quit, He jumped off the bandwagon. Angelo Dundee, who knew how to cajole Ali, how to indulge him and defer to him and still maintain a certain influence -- who had pushed him off his stool in the first Liston fight with Ali half-blinded by cut medication adhering to Liston's gloves and saying no, he couldn't go on -- Angelo Dundee stuck it out to the end.

Ali was a soft touch for moochers and people down on their luck, but he was never an easy man to manipulate. Nation of Islam doctrine seemed perfectly reasonable to Ali. He swallowed it whole, spaceship stories and all (Elijah Muhammad, the Black Muslims' ayatollah, preached to the faithful that a giant Islamic spaceship would save them from Armageddon). If the Muslims ended up with an exorbitant share of Ali's ring earnings, no sheep ever went more compliantly to be sheared.

While the government dithered over putting him in jail and finally backed off when his view of the war began to look logical to all but the intransigent, he accepted invitations to speak. At the height of the controversy, transparently attempting to strengthen Ali's pacifist credentials, Elijah Muhammad retired him from boxing.

It seemed a shame. Anti-war sentiment was growing and anti-Ali sentiment was receding. Somebody asked about a possible comeback. If there were offers, Ali said, he'd consider them. Wrong answer. Elijah slapped him firmly on the wrist. For the sin of potential disobedience, he could not, until further notice, be called by his Muslim name.

Ali played the part of the prodigal son. For a speech at Duquesne University in the fall of 1969, he wore the full Black Muslim uniform -- dark blue suit, white shirt, conservative tie -- and he was openly contrite. "I'm goin' all out to be a hundred percent Muslim, a follower of our leader," he said. "I've cut myself off from sports, now and in the future." Even at the time, it was not persuasive.

He had come to evangelize, but also to entertain. Entertaining was second nature to Ali. Righteous and raffish, foolish and wise, serious and droll, dignified and frivolous, somber and full of fun, he gave a scintillating performance.

With his first words, he established a mood of levity. "White people, you are my enemy!" he cried, delivering the line with such great good humor and friendliness that the enemy laughed and applauded. The bronze-skinned great-grandson of an Irishman named Grady, Ali was perpetually conscious of race, but without coming across as a firebrand.

In the sing-song voice he used on such occasions, he said to the Duquesne crowd, "We are taught as children to love white and hate black. Everything good is white. Everything bad is black." He was reeling off a set piece, truth in the guise of humor. "On December the twenty-fourth every year, when little black kids look at Santa Claus, they see a big fat white man. When they go to school they learn that Mary had a little lamb whose fleece was white as snow. Angel food cake is white and devil's food cake is black. Go to the store and get two dips of ice cream, chocolate and vanilla. I'll bet you a thousand dollars they put the chocolate on the bottom every time."

He had the fifteen hundred students, all but a few of them white, eating the ice cream out of his hand. They whooped at his next punch line: "Even in black Africa, the king of the jungle is white -- Tarzan." They whooped even louder when he threw back his head, cupped his hands to his mouth, and gave a passable imitation of the Tarzan yell.

Before the echo died down he was lecturing again. 'Onliest way we can be equal is through separation," he said. "Our singin' is different, our eatin' is different, our trash talk is different, our nature is different." Impishly, he offered a compromise. "I'll integrate with you. I'll come to your school and give a speech. I'll ride on a jet with you, 'cause we ain't got planes of our own. But I'm not gonna visit your house and wink at your sister."

The applause -- and the laughter -- let him know that if this was Black Muslim doctrine, nobody thought of it as menacing.

6

Exile restored Ali to his countrymen's good graces. The children of the sixties, rebels against authority, saw him as one of their own. The children of the sixties were the style-setters for the decade that followed. Their attitudes toward political and social issues -- the war, civil rights, long hair, clothes, sex -- came to be the attitudes of the majority. Ali was a beneficiary of this. The peace activists made him a symbol of resistance, and though he hadn't set out to be a symbol of anything, he was happy to oblige. As a matter of course, the intelligentsia took up for him. Litterateurs and deep thinkers hastened his transition from outcast to martyr to icon,

He was having a great time. His humor and love of play-acting resurfaced. The almost hysterical stridency of his last few months as champion was gone. There were die-hards, of course, who continued to regard him as Benedict Arnold.

When Ali got permission to fight again -- a federal judge ordered his reinstatement -- he signed for a tune-up bout with Jerry Quarry to be held on October 26, 1970, in Atlanta, whereupon Lester Maddox, the stay-at-home warrior who was governor of Georgia, declared October 26th a day of mourning in the state.

Then the old animosity between Ali and Joe Louis flared up. Louis still called Ali "Clay" and said that Rocky Marciano could have beaten him. Overlooking no chance to publicize Ali's comeback, the Atlanta promoters arranged a press conference by telephone hookup, with Ali at the fight scene, Louis in Denver, where he was undergoing treatment for drug addiction, and sportswriters in half a dozen other locations.

Although the sportswriters knew that Louis would be on the line, Ali, unaccountably, did not. Right off the bat, a sportswriter mentioned that Louis, speaking from experience, had questioned whether Ali could be in fighting condition after three and a half years away from the ring. Did Ali have a comment?

"Well, Joe Louis was no dancin' master," Ali began. "I'm sure if he stayed out as long as I have, slow as he was, he'd be way off form. It's hard for Joe to predict on me. I'm so much faster and quicker than Joe was. It's hard to imagine."

He was letting himself go. "Joe Louis, Jack Dempsey, Gene Tunney, Rocky Marciano, they could never lay off the way I have and get ready for a fight in six weeks. When you have all these people much older than I am in age, people like Joe Louis and Nat Fleischer predictin' I'll lose, it means I'm not only gonna beat my opponent, I'm gonna beat *them* too . . . "

At this point, Denver broke in.

"Be careful. I'm listening to you."

There was silence for a moment, and then Ali spoke again.

"Uh . . . Who's this talkin'?"

"Joe Louis."

"Joe Louis? Uh . . . what were you sayin', Joe?"

"I said be careful how you talk about me. I'm listening to you."

Another pause.

"Well, when I get in the ring," Ali continued lamely, "I'll just do my best, and then you can jive all you want."

Ali's best was too much for Quarry, whose handlers stopped the fight at the end of the third round. Quarry had not been down, but he was bleeding from several cuts.

Ali looked as agile as ever. Despite physical changes -- the shoulders were thicker, the chest deeper, the waist more convex, the long legs not as trim -- his fighting weight had increased by only two or three pounds. But, having taken the first step, he was strangely subdued, not wholly pleased with himself, and two months later in Madison Square Garden he struggled against the Argentine Oscar Bonavena, who lasted until the fifteenth round.

Although Ali knocked him out, which nobody else had ever done, his performance was not well received. Somehow the orchestration was off. Ali was not fast, not dazzling. At no time did he appear to be dominating Bonavena. He allowed himself to be hit. But he revealed -- who'd have thought it? -- the ability to end a fight with one punch. In the fifteenth round there were three knockdowns, but the first knockdown, the result of a single left hook, had finished Bonavena. When he staggered to his feet, all resistance had left him. He was ready for the kill.

Bonavena was built like a side of Argentine beef. Knocking him down was more than Joe Frazier could do in twenty-five rounds, and Frazier himself had been on the floor twice. Even so, Frazier, the champion now, was much the better fighter of the two, and in his meeting with Ali at Madison Square Garden on March 8, 1971, another "Battle of the Century," he kept his title. For the first time since turning professional, Ali was a loser, knocked down in the final round when the decision could have gone to either man.

Although agreement was general that the fight had been a great one, I didn't see it that way. An exciting fight, yes, but not until the end. Ali came on strong then, and Frazier -- who disliked both Ali and Ali's name for him, "the Gorilla" -- was equal to the test. In the middle rounds, saving themselves, they had slapped and tapped, patty-caked and goaded each other -- "fooling more than fighting," as Angelo Dundee described it. A vocal minority in Madison Square Garden was disgruntled enough at one point to boo. I thought that Cus D'Amato, boxing teacher to champions, gave the most sensible critique. He called it "a hell of a fight to watch" -- the dramatic fifteenth round was responsible for that -- but "artistically second-rate." Ali, it seemed to me, still looked rusty and Frazier looked over trained.

From then on, Ali had his moments. He decisioned Frazier in twelve after Frazier had lost the title to George Foreman. He won back the championship with an eighth-round knockout of Foreman in Zaire (the Rumble in the Jungle, name supplied by Promoter Don King and reiterated ad nauseum by Ali). Then came the Thrilla in Manila (Ali gets all the credit for that one). Four hard years after their first fight, he disposed of Frazier for good. When the fourteenth round ended, Frazier was through. He did not have the strength to go on. Neither, it seemed apparent, could Ali have gone on, but Frazier and his corner hadn't noticed.

Ali was 33, no longer the deadly mixture of butterfly and bee. Punches that once fell short of the pulled-back head were connecting now, and the butterfly/bee had become a tortoise. Instead of avoiding punches, he invited them. To cope with Foreman in Zaire, he introduced the rope-a-dope (Ali had a name, invented or borrowed, for everything). With his back against the ropes, he fought, or, rather, did not fight, from a carapace of arms and gloves, letting the younger, heavier, undefeated Foreman, acting the part of the dope, hammer away to no purpose. By the eighth round, when Ali opened up, Foreman had punched himself out.

In almost every fight, Ali proved his toughness and courage -- unnecessarily, some people thought. The whole world, it seemed, felt protective toward Ali, including the older, crustier sportswriters, who had earlier disdained him as a blowhard. Ali was shrewd. Even though he may not have read them, he could tell who the influential columnists were. Informed that the Hearst syndicate's star, Jimmy Cannon, had written something critical about him, he singled out Cannon in the media crowd at his training quarters the next day. "Jimmy Cannon," he said with mock severity, "you *bold*! You *baad*!" Cannon did not mind the attention. He chuckled and gave Ali kindlier treatment after that.

The heavyweights of the op-ed page, constituents of Ali since the day he refused induction, were the first to observe signs of slippage. After the Bonavena fight -- which Ali won by a knockout, remember -- Pete Hamill grieved for America. What Ali represented was "the promise of something glittering in a time of grayness and dusk," and we had lost it. Between the first and second Frazier fights, Ken Norton actually did beat Ali, breaking his jaw. He broke a few hearts as well. Garry Wills, for whom Ali was "the last sixties hero," the successor to John F. Kennedy, Martin Luther King, and Malcolm X, all but played taps.

With Ali, as with those others, he wrote, "style mattered more than anything else. And style led him on. He could not afford to look like an equal to his foe. He had to clown, give advantages, fight the other man's fight -- never admitting he might be just a fighter in trouble, even when he was. He would stand and slug with slugger Joe Frazier. He would shrug off a broken jaw. He would never live down from his legend."

As a matter of fact, he resurrected his legend, first in Zaire (Norman Mailer wrote a book about it) and again in Manila. Joyce Carol Oates perceived Ali-Frazier III and Ali-Frazier I as "boxing's analogues to 'King Lear' -- ordeals of unfathomable human courage and resilience raised to the level of classic tragedy." She tends, of course, to get carried away, but Ali-Frazier III was no ordinary fight. "What you saw tonight," Ali said afterward, "was the next thing to death."

Quite so. He was never to be the same fighter again -- never, perhaps, the same man.

7

He fought for six more years, losing his championship to the worse-than-mediocre Leon Spinks . . . taking it back from Spinks . . . retiring . . . reconsidering. In 1980, at his camp in the Pocono Mountains of eastern Pennsylvania, he was training to fight Larry Holmes, who had beaten Ken Norton for the title Ali had given up. The camp was in a cluster of hemlock and cottonwood trees at the top of a rise: fifteen log cabins and a small white clapboard mosque. The cabins, drab gray with peepholes for windows, seemed built to repel an Indian attack.

One remarkable decorative touch was a line of boulders, evenly spaced along the edge of a gravel road. Painted in white block letters on each was the name of a legendary boxing champion -- Jack Dempsey, Joe Louis,

Rocky Marciano, Archie Moore, Sugar Ray Robinson -- or of somebody close to Ali, such as Bundini Brown, his court jester. The monument to Bundini was modest in size. Jack Johnson's memorial -- Johnson, the first black heavyweight champion, was in some ways a role model for Ali -- appeared to be a large chunk of anthracite.

I watched Ali work in the camp gym one day. Possibly because of a mustache he was whimsically affecting, his round, full face, though unmarked, had lost its boyishness. He was wearing a rubberized silver body shirt and long black warmup pants, which made him look huge. To start with, he shadow-boxed in the ring for several minutes, bouncing heavily. He was wheezing, snorting, grunting, rotating his neck. The floorboards creaked, the ring posts rattled.

Before sparring, he took off his shirt. In four rounds with a middleweight and three with a heavyweight, he was all sound and fury and joviality, content to threaten his opponents ("Watch me, I'm tricky"), set traps for them ("Show me somethin', you ain't got nothin'") and telegraph his jab ("Ol' man go *pop!*"); The small, respectful crowd cheered on cue, but the middleweight's hands were quicker than Ali's.

The boxing was Act One. Act Two was a magic show. On a rubbing table, Ali spread out his paraphernalia. "Looks like a lot of junk, don't it?" he said. "Well, just wait." There were card tricks, coin tricks, rope tricks, handkerchief tricks. It was almost professional. He milked the crowd for applause ("Pretty good? Pretty good?"), and the crowd delivered.

I visited Ali in his dressing room. After a moment or two, he placed me. It had been nineteen years since our night on the town in Louisville. He was not, I could see, in a mood to reminisce. "Do you like this camp?" he said, to change the subject. "Isn't it beautiful?"

At rest on a worn-out sofa, he was drinking grapefruit juice from a glass full of ice cubes, tossing it down and then replenishing the glass. I asked about his weight. "Two hundred and thirty-eight pounds. You can look at the scale."

His speech was a little slurred. I asked about Holmes. "Sittin' duck. You saw me box today? Seven rounds -- and both of those guys are twice as fast as Holmes." He called for more grapefruit juice. Down it went, in a single gulp.

"I got a man squeezes grapefruit every morning -- crushes real grapes. He's a dietitian. Makes juice out of grapefruit, celery, carrots, blackstrap molasses, and stuff." A camp functionary spoke up. "Carrot juice," he asserted, "strengthens the eyes." Another man in the room belittled that idea. "Never knew anyone blind who could see after drinking carrot juice." "No," said Ali thoughtfully, staring at his glass. "Once you're blind . . . "

In the mess hall, at a long wooden table, he sat by himself. grapefruit juice within reach. Maybe two dozen people were standing around in groups. I questioned Mustafa Hassain, a low-keyed, self-possessed Muslim minister from Pittsburgh, and Abdel Kadir, identified to me as Ali's Moroccan "spiritual adviser," about Muslim teaching. "Does Ali live up to it?"

"Yes, he do," said Hassain. "His intentions are good, but his environmental persuasions sometimes vary. Environment forms a person . . . " Hassain went on to explain how, but I lost the thread. We talked about Ali's name, and he gave me the etymology. "Muhammad means 'praiseworthy.' Ali means 'like a ruler.'"

Appropriately, Ali at that moment was holding court. Petitioners approached him one by one, pulling up a chair next to his and pouring out their stories. A short, black-haired woman leaned on one elbow, her face turned to Ali, whose bored gaze was fixed on the opposite wall. She spoke to him earnestly and rapidly; whatever she was selling he didn't want.

A man with a beard succeeded her, and his proposition must have been stupefying. As the man droned on, making his pitch, Ali yawned. He folded his arms on the table and used them as a pillow. He pretended to sleep; gave it up; lifted his head for a long, reviving draught of grapefruit juice. His undisguised apathy said it all: no sale.

There were others. Ali wasn't buying. Somebody brought him a telephone. While he cupped the receiver to his ear, answering now and then in a word or two, a tall, imposing black woman came to the table and held out a bowl of salad for his approval. Regally, he ignored her. The woman was his cook, Lena Shabazz. She turned away, rolled her eyes, and went back to the kitchen.

It was time for me to leave, so I headed for the door. Ali, glancing up from a conversation at the table with Mustafa Hassain, said, "Where are you going? Take a seat. Have some coffee." I thanked him but said it was

getting late. Abdel Kadir came rushing over. "Sit down!" he commanded
me. "Sit down! He wants you to sit down!"

8

Holmes, of course, was not a sittin' duck -- not for a middle-aged
opponent who had lost his hand speed and foot speed. After ten rounds, Ali
could no longer defend himself, and he made no objection when Angelo
Dundee signaled to the referee that the fight was over.

Unbelievably, Ali wasn't willing to retire one last time. Trevor Berbick,
never one of boxing's immortals, punched him around for ten rounds in
December of 1981. This fight, his last, took place on an island in the
Bahamas. Nearly 40 years old, Ali had been boxing since the age of 11.

Retired to the peace and quiet of farm life, he adopted a son. Eight other
children, some fully grown, were scattered far and wide. Financially, he
appeared to be in good shape -- not as rich as he might have been, but
comfortable. His mind was still functioning normally. A missionary, as he
put it, for "tranquility, love, and understanding," he traveled and continued to
make appearances. He prayed. He studied the Koran.

The effect of physical deterioration on Ali was strange. For many years it
enhanced his presence, giving him a sage, magisterial quality. He had what
the highbrows call gravitas. A Mona Lisa half-smile was his only
expression, together with a twinkle in his eye. The twinkle seemed constant,
making him look perpetually amused, but at what? If there's a joke, Ali was
the only one who knew it. Adulation pleased him, that much you could tell,
and he had learned to accept being pitied.

Most living legends erode with time. The fascination with Ali only
seemed to increase. He was called, for a while, "the most recognizable man
in the world." That distinction belongs now to somebody else (hint: he's a
recently elected head of government), but Ali remains loved and admired.
He is more than just an aging celebrity, more than just another great
champion from the dimly remembered past, more than just a museum piece.
If Barack Obama can turn more heads, if the Pyramids, the Eiffel Tower, and
the Statue of Liberty have a pretty good chance of outlasting Ali, he is still, at
least in memory, a human international historical monument.

FINAL NOTES

(ED Note: Roy McHugh also had these additional thoughts on Gene Tunney to include in a final chapter.)

Gene Tunney belongs in the following collection of odds and ends because of his five hard fights with Harry Greb. Tunney boxed in Pittsburgh only once -- at Motor Square Garden in 1922. As I heard the story from a man who had a ringside seat, and who kept a finger on the pulse of the fight game, he was winning as he pleased from Jack Burke, a home-grown heavyweight originally named Berkowski. At the end of the eighth round, the referee, Joe Keeley, made a visit to Tunney's corner and said, "Why don't you put him away?" Tunney said, "Oh, is that what you want here?" So, acting on Keeley's suggestion, he put Burke away in the ninth. Burke and his friends hung out in Market Square, and the next day one of them told him what Keeley had done. The way my informant described it, Burke went looking for Keeley and "beat the hell out of him."

Roy McHugh

The spare elegance of supreme craftsmanship marked Roy McHugh's column writing for the *Pittsburgh Press* in the second half of the 20th century. McHugh was a native of Iowa and graduate of Coe College, where he cultivated a love of both sports and language. McHugh became both sports editor and columnist-at-large during the City of Champions era in Pittsburgh's distinguished sports history. None of the heroes of that era were any more distinguished than the quiet, meticulous columnist who chronicled their triumphs and foibles. He traveled with Muhammad Ali, contributed with distinction to national magazines, and his humanity and insight was indispensable to the dozens of American journalists who have examined the life and death of Roberto Clemente, Art Rooney, Sr., Billy Conn, and many more.

Gene Collier, Sports Columnist, Pittsburgh Post-Gazette

BACK COVER PHOTO:
LEFT TO RIGHT- ART ROONEY JR., DOUGLAS CAVANAUGH, TIM CONN (SON OF BILLY CONN) & THE LEGENDARY ROY MCHUGH

Printed in Great Britain
by Amazon